Northern Territory

a Lonely Planet guide

Hug

Northern Territory

1st edition

Published by
  Lonely Planet Publications
  Head Office: PO Box 617, Hawthorn, Vic 3122, Australia
  Branches: 155 Filbert St, Suite 251, Oakland, CA 94607, USA
                  10 Barley Mow Passage, Chiswick, London W4 4PH, UK
                  71 bis rue du Cardinal Lemoine, 75005 Paris, France

Printed by
  Colorcraft Ltd, Hong Kong

Photographs by
  Hugh Finlay
  Charlotte Hindle
  Ray Stamp
  Northern Territory Tourist Commission

  Front cover: Magpie geese and egrets feeding in Kakadu National Park (David Curl)
  Title page: Thorny devil (David Curl)

Published
  September 1996

National Library of Australia Cataloguing in Publication Data

Finlay, Hugh
  Northern Territory

  1st ed.
  Includes index.
  ISBN 0 86442 389 6.

  1. Northern Territory – Guidebooks. I. Title (Series :
  Lonely Planet Australia guide).

919.4290463

Hugh Finlay

After deciding there must be more to life than a career in civil engineering, Hugh took off around Australia in the mid-70s, working at everything from spray painting to diamond prospecting, before hitting the overland trail. He joined Lonely Planet in 1985 and has written *Jordan & Syria*, coauthored *Morocco, Algeria & Tunisia* and *Kenya*, was the coordinating author of the current edition of *Australia*, and contributed to several other LP guides. Hugh also wrote the feature on Aboriginal Art which appears in both the *Australia* and *Northern Territory* guides. Hugh's most recent project has been updating the *Nepal* guide. When not travelling, Hugh lives in central Victoria with partner, Linda, and daughters Ella and Vera.

From the Author

This book is the product of two extended trips to the Northern Territory. Many people have made valuable contributions along the way, not least in their enthusiastic encouragement, and to all of them many thanks. In particular, thanks to my partner Linda and our daughters, Ella and Vera, who accompanied me for much of the time and helped in many ways; to Alan Withers, for his help and hospitality in both Borroloola and Gurig National Park; to Denis O'Byrne for tips on the Centre; Peter Yates, who put me in touch with a number of interesting people I otherwise would have missed; to the various staff members at the Darwin office of the Northern Territory Tourism Commission; and to my brother, Peter, for his company in the West Macs and along the Old *Ghan* line track. Thanks also to Ian Fox in Darwin for providing the liquid refreshments, and to Nick Bryce for his help on the Tanami.

Some of the material in this book is based on material which was originally written for Lonely Planet's *Outback Australia* book, much of it by Denis O'Byrne.

From the Publisher

This first edition was edited at Lonely Planet, Melbourne, by Chris Wyness. Rowan McKinnon's contribution as a proofreader was invaluable as was the help given by Brigitte Barta and Mary Neighbour. Matt King did a fabulous job getting the maps right, creating new illustrations and doing the layout with the assistance of Lyndell Taylor, Jacqui Saunders, Jenny Jones, Andrew Tudor and Michelle Stamp. David Kemp and Simon Bracken designed a splendid cover.

Warning & Request

Things change – prices go up, schedules change, good places go bad and bad places go bankrupt – nothing stays the same. So if you find things better or worse, recently opened or long since closed, please write and tell us and help make the next edition better.

Your letters will be used to help update future editions and, where possible, important changes will also be included in an Update section in reprints.

We greatly appreciate all information that is sent to us by travellers. Back at Lonely Planet we employ a hard-working readers' letters team to sort through the many letters we receive. The best ones will be rewarded with a free copy of the next edition or another Lonely Planet guide if you prefer. We give away lots of books, but, unfortunately, not every letter/postcard receives one.

Contents

Map Legend

BOUNDARIES

International Boundary
Regional Boundary

ROUTES

Freeway
Highway
Major Road
Unsealed Road, 4WD Track
City Road
City Street
Railway
Underground Railway
Tram
Walking Track
Bicycle Track
Ferry Route
Tropics

AREA FEATURES

Parks
Built-Up Area
Pedestrian Mall
Market
Cemetery
Aboriginal Land
Beach or Desert
Mountain Range

HYDROGRAPHIC FEATURES

Coastline
River, Creek
Intermittent River or Creek
Rapids, Waterfalls
Lake, Intermittent Lake
Canal
Swamp, Salt Lake

SYMBOLS

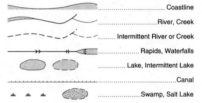

○ CAPITAL		National Capital
◉ Capital		Regional Capital
CITY		Major City
● City		City
● Town		Town
● Village		Village

Embassy, Petrol Station
Airport, Airfield
Swimming Pool, Gardens
Shopping Centre, Zoo
Winery or Vineyard, Picnic Site
One Way Street, Route Number
Stately Home, Monument
Castle, Tomb
Cave, Hut or Chalet
Mountain or Hill, Lookout
Lighthouse, Shipwreck
Pass, Spring
Beach, Surf Beach
Trail Head, Mine
Archaeological Site or Ruins
Cliff or Escarpment, Tunnel
Railway Station

Place to Stay, Place to Eat
Cafe, Pub or Bar
Post Office, Telephone
Tourist Information, Bank
Transport, Parking
Museum, Youth Hostel
Caravan Park, Camping Ground
Church, Cathedral
Mosque, Synagogue
Buddhist Temple, Hindu Temple
Hospital, Police Station

Note: not all symbols displayed above appear in this book

Introduction

The fascinating Northern Territory is the least populated and most barren area of the country with only 1% of the Australian population living in nearly 20% of the country's area, yet it is Australia at its most Australian. This is the picture-book, untamed and sometimes surreal Australia. Even to most Australians, the Territory is still *never never land*, the real outback, and it has a mystique which draws people from around the country, and from around the world.

The heart of Australia – the Red Centre – is not just Uluru (Ayers Rock) bang in the middle of nowhere. There are meteorite craters, eerie canyons, lost valleys of palms, and noisy Alice Springs festivals (where else is there an annual boat regatta on a dry river bed?). The colour red, from which the Red Centre takes its name, is evident as soon as

you arrive – in the soil, in the rocks and in Uluru itself.

At the other end of the Track, the 1500-km strip of bitumen that connects Alice Springs to the north coast, is the tropical Top End which boasts some of the world's most important and spectacular tropical wetlands, foremost among them being those found in Kakadu National Park. The wetlands and escarpments of Kakadu National Park are a treasure house of wildlife and of Aboriginal rock painting.

While the Territory's natural attractions are an obvious draw, there is also a surprising cultural depth. In fact, when it comes to getting a feel for Aboriginal culture, the Territory is by far the best place in the country to do it. The new cultural centres at both Uluru and Kakadu are world class in their

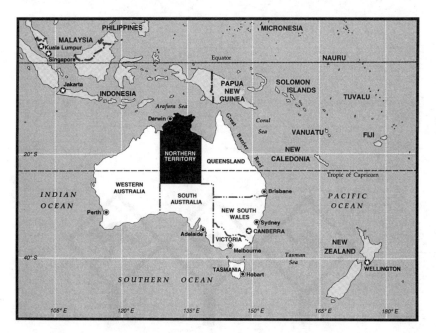

presentation and the various Aboriginal owned-and-operated tourism ventures have become very successful. Darwin, with its Asian food markets and craft fairs, could arguably be called Australia's most cosmopolitan city.

Add to all this some fascinating local history – the struggle of the early European explorers and pioneers and the hardships they endured, WW II and the Japanese air raids over the Top End, or the devastation of Darwin during Cyclone Tracy – and you have the makings of a memorable visit. Few people visit the Northern Territory and come away untouched by the experience – it's that sort of place.

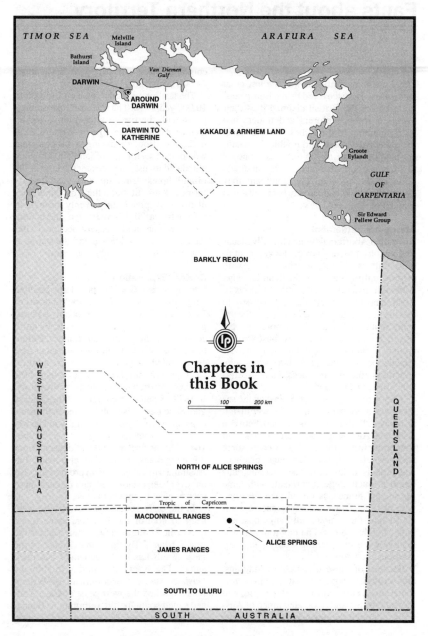

Facts about the Northern Territory

HISTORY

The Australian continent was the last great landmass to be discovered by the Europeans. Long before the British claimed it as their own, European explorers and traders had been dreaming of the riches to be found in the unknown – some said mythical – southern land (*terra australis*) that was supposed to form a counterbalance to the landmass north of the equator. The continent they eventually found had already been inhabited for tens of thousands of years.

Aboriginal Settlement

Australian Aboriginal (which literally means 'indigenous') society has the longest continuous cultural history in the world, with origins dating back to the last Ice age. Although mystery shrouds many aspects of Australian prehistory, it seems almost certain that the first humans came here across the sea from South-East Asia. Heavy-boned people whom archaeologists call Robust arrived around 70,000 years ago, and more slender Gracile people around 50,000 years ago. Gracile people are the ancestors of Australian Aboriginal people.

They arrived during a period when the sea level was more than 50 metres lower than it is today. This created more land between Asia and Australia than there is now, but watercraft were still needed to cross some stretches of open sea. Although much of Australia is today arid, the first migrants found a much wetter continent, with large forests and numerous inland lakes teeming with fish. The fauna included giant marsupials such as three-metre-tall kangaroos, and huge flightless birds. The environment was relatively non-threatening – only a few carnivorous predators existed.

Because of these favourable conditions, archaeologists suggest that within a few thousand years Aboriginal people had moved through and populated much of Australia, although the most central parts of the continent were not occupied until about 24,000 years ago.

The last Ice age came to an end 15,000 to 10,000 years ago. The sea level rose dramatically with the rise in temperature, and an area of Australia the size of Western Australia was flooded during a process that would have seen strips of land 100 km wide inundated in just a few decades. Many of the inland lakes dried up and vast deserts formed. Thus, although the Aboriginal population was spread fairly evenly throughout the continent 20,000 years ago, the coastal areas become more densely occupied after the end of the last Ice age and the stabilisation of the sea level 5000 years ago.

Coastal Exploration

Captain James Cook is popularly credited with Australia's 'discovery', but in terms of European discovery it was probably a Portuguese who first sighted the country's north coast, sometime in the 16th century. Before that it is believed that units of an Asian fleet commanded by Chinese eunuch admiral Cheng Ho (Zheng He) may have visited the northern Australian coast in the 15th century. In 1879 a small, carved figure of the Chinese god, Shao Lao, was found lodged in the roots of a banyan tree at Doctor's Gully in Darwin – it dated from the Ming Dynasty (1368-1644). As the fleet definitely did reach Timor it is quite plausible that they also made it to Australia. However, no firm proof of the visit has ever been established, and no account of such contact is known to exist.

In the early 1600s, the Dutch, who were keen to control the lucrative spice trade, ousted the Portuguese from their bases in the Banda Islands. By then the existence of the great South Land was generally accepted, and the Dutch set out to find it. In 1606 the *Duyfken*, under the command of Willem Jansz, reached the west coast of Cape York and sailed south, before returning to Banda.

It was not until 1623, after Dirk Hartog

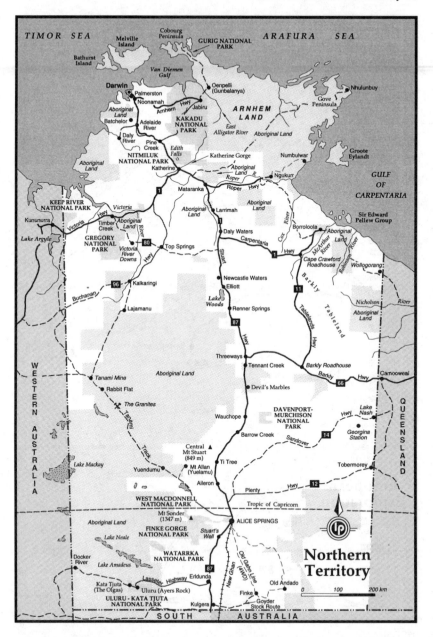

Timor
Sea

Port Essington
Bathurst Island
Mellive Island
Van Dieman
Gulf
East Alligator
River
Crocker Island
Elcho Island
Wessel
Islands

1644

Darwin 1865

1818

Yirrkala Cape Arnhem

Gulf of
Carpentaria

Pine Creek

Daly

River

KATHERINE

Roper Bar

1855-56

1873

Roper
River

Groote Eylandt

1623

Vanderlin Island

Daly Waters

Borroloola

1844-45

1879

1855-56

1644

Elliot

1896

Barkly
Tableland

1877

TENNANT CREEK

1901

1901

Ti Tree

1878

European
Exploration

0   100   200 km

1872

MacDonnell   Ranges

ALICE SPRINGS

1873-74

Kata Tjuta
(Mt Olga)

1873

1904

Uluru
(Ayers Rock)

Finke

1939

1860-62

1855-56

Birdsville

1873

European Exploration	
—··—··—····	Willem van Colster *(Duyfken, 1623)*
············	Abel Tasman *(Limmen, Zeemeeuw & Bracq, 1644)*
—————————	Phillip King *(Mermaid, 1818)*
—··—·—··—	Ludwig Leichhardt *(1844-45)*
------------	Augustus Gregory *(1855-56)*
················	John McDouall Stuart *(1860-62)*
———————	Frederick Litchfield *(1865)*
—·—·—·—·—	William Giles *(1872, 1873-74)*
——— ———	William Gosse *(1873)*
—·——·——·——	Nathaniel Buchanan *(1877, 1896)*
—————————·	Henry Barclay *(1878, 1904)*
———————	Alexander Forrest *(1879)*
———————	David Lindsay *(1883, 1885-86)*
——————	Allan Davidson *(1901)*
··········	Cecil Madigan *(1939)*

had discovered the west coast and several ships had been wrecked on its uncharted coast, that the Dutch decided to explore in more detail. The *Arnhem*, skippered by Willem van Colster, in company with the *Pena*, skippered by Jan Carstensz, repeated the *Duyfken*'s earlier voyage, and then sailed north-west from the foot of the Gulf, making landfall at Groote Eylandt and Cape Arnhem. Both vessels came into contact with Aboriginal people, but they were dismissed as 'indigent and miserable men'.

Further exploratory voyages, fuelled by the hope that the Aboriginal people would have something worth trading, led to the mapping of the northern Arnhem Land coast. The great Dutch navigator, Abel Tasman, sailed the entire north coast from Cape York to beyond the Kimberley in Western Australia, but despite the fact that this voyage was a great feat of navigation, it was deemed a failure as no commercial gain resulted from it, and Tasman's achievements were largely unrecognised.

The Dutch by now had basically lost interest in the continent they called New Holland, although the hoped-for existence of a passage south led to an extended voyage by three Dutch vessels in the early 18th century. They spent three months exploring in the Bathurst Island area, and although they made no startling discoveries, they did have some success at peaceful contact with Aboriginal people.

Other visitors to the northern shores of Australia, from perhaps as early as the mid-17th century, were Macassan traders from the island of Celebes (now Sulawesi). Sailing in their wooden-hulled *praus*, the Macassans came in search of the sea slug known as trepang. These slimy and rather repulsive looking creatures were highly prized by the Chinese as an aphrodisiac, and were found in profusion in the waters off the Australian coast.

Unlike the Europeans, the Macassans had largely peaceful contact with Aboriginal people. They would set up camps for three months at a time, gathering and curing trepang and trading with the Aboriginal people, who found use for dugout canoes, metal items, food, tobacco and glass objects. A number of Macassans fathered children by Aboriginal women, some Aboriginal people made the journey to Macassar, and a few even lived there. The Macassans generally had little impact on the local Aboriginal culture as they were pretty much self-sufficient, and were using a resource not used by the Aboriginal people.

With naval might at its peak, and the colony at Botany Bay now established, the British were keen to fully explore the coast of Australia. In 1801 Matthew Flinders set out on an ambitious mission to chart the entire coastline of Australia. By the time he reached the Gulf, his rotten vessel, the *Investigator*, was in danger of falling apart, and so he was only able to give the northern coast little more than a cursory glance, although many place names along the coast are a reminder of his trip. A couple of years later a French ship, *Le Géographe*, charted some of the western Territory coast, and names such as Joseph Bonaparte Gulf and Perron Islands date from this voyage.

The first person to really chart the waters of the Northern Territory was a remarkable young hydrographer, Phillip King. In four voyages between 1817 and 1821, King charted with great detail the coast, and was the first to discover that Bathurst and Melville islands were in fact islands. The Cobourg Peninsula and the East, South and West Alligator rivers were all named by

King. Such was his accuracy that King's charts form the basis for modern navigational charts of these waters. The decisions on where the future British settlements were to be located were also based largely on King's work.

Although King had noted the existence of Darwin harbour, he did not actually enter it, and this was undertaken by John Wickham, commander of the *Beagle*, and one of his senior officers, John Lort Stokes. Aboard one of the ship's whaling boats, Stokes explored the bay, then named it Port Darwin, after the soon-to-be-famous naturalist who had sailed on the *Beagle*'s voyage to South America. It was on this same voyage to northern Australia that Stokes and Wickham discovered and named the Victoria and Fitzroy rivers to the west.

British Attempts at Settlement

With the commercial success of their colony of Singapore, the British government was persuaded by a merchant William Barns and the mercantile body known as the East India Trade Committee that a similar settlement in northern Australia would also meet with success, as it would be able to cash in on the trepang and spice trades. It was also argued that a British settlement would deter rivals such as the French, Dutch and Americans, and would provide a haven for shipwrecked sailors.

In 1824 the go-ahead was given and a military settlement established on Melville Island. Despite early optimism, Fort Dundas, as named by its founder Captain Gordon Bremer, lasted barely 18 months. Commercially it was a dismal failure as it was nowhere near any of the routes used by trepangers, and isolation, disease and fear of the Aboriginal people compounded the problems.

Undeterred by their initial failure, a second garrison settlement, Fort Wellington, was set up by the British at Raffles Bay on the mainland near Croker Island by Captain James Stirling (who later went on to become one of the founders of the colony in Western Australia). This small settlement also soon

foundered, despite some hopeful reports from the last commandant, Captain Barker, and by 1829 it too had been abandoned.

Back in England the Colonial Office was still keen to settle northern Australia, and in 1838 a third party was equipped and despatched with orders to try again at Port Essington, a site on the Cobourg Peninsula favourably reported on by King some years earlier. Led again by Captain Bremer, a settlement called Victoria was established at Record Point. Before long the 36 marines and a few family members had cleared land and constructed a number of buildings, including a hospital, governor's residence, church and a number of military buildings.

Early hope once again faded, to be replaced by gloom and despair brought on by isolation, disease, death, white ants and a cruel climate. The hoped-for commercial boom had failed to materialise, and within seven years of its establishment no further progress on the settlement was made. For a further four years the settlers battled on, all the while their spirits draining, until finally the decision was taken to abandon what had taken 11 years to establish. Race relations were for the most part pretty good – Aboriginal people helped in the construction of many buildings and, having had contact with Macassan trepangers, were familiar with working on boats. Today the ruins of Victoria lie within the Cobourg National Park. They are still hard to reach, and are a poignant reminder of the tremendous hardships faced by these early settlers.

Inland Exploration

In the early 1840s there was great demand by squatters in New South Wales for cheap Asian labour, and pressure was put on the government to find an overland route to the Port Essington settlement. It was hoped the route would not only provide an easy route in for labourers, but also a route out for exports of horses and cattle.

In 1844 the government refused to fund an expedition, but a Prussian scientist by the name of Ludwig Leichhardt raised the necessary funds by private subscription and set off from Jimbour, an outpost on the Darling Downs in Queensland. The party reached the Gulf of Carpentaria after nine months, and then headed north-west along the coast, on the way discovering and naming a number of major rivers including the McArthur, Roper, Limmen and Wickham.

The party suffered great privations: a number of the horses were drowned in the Roper River and so most of the zoological and botanical specimens had to be abandoned, members were killed in Aboriginal attacks at the Gulf, and food was pretty much limited to bush tucker. They eventually crossed the Arnhem Land escarpment and struggled into Victoria on 17 December 1845, 14 months after setting out from Jimbour. Although Leichhardt became something of a hero, the trip itself was largely a failure as the route was far too difficult for regular use and no new promising grazing areas were discovered.

Another major figure in the exploration of the Top End is Augustus Charles Gregory. In 1854 the Colonial Office in London, in consultation with the Royal Geographical Society, financed the North Australian Expedition whose main brief was to explore east from the Victoria River to the Gulf in the hope of finding new grazing lands for future pastoral development. Gregory was invited to lead the expedition, and another member of the party was the botanist Ferdinand von Mueller (who later designed the botanic gardens in Darwin, Castlemaine and Melbourne).

The party of 18 journeyed up the Victoria River aboard the *Tom Tough*, and set up camp near present-day Timber Creek. Gregory spent six months exploring the Victoria River district, including a thrust down into the Great Sandy Desert. They then headed east, crossing the Daly and Roper rivers, and Gregory named Elsey Creek after the expedition's surgeon.

The eastward route from the Roper River to the Gulf was largely the reverse of Leichhardt's earlier expedition and so both explorers had missed finding the vast Mitchell grass plains of the Barkly Tableland.

Ludwig Leichhardt, scientist and explorer

Gregory eventually arrived in Brisbane after a journey of 15 months. The success of the expedition lay in Gregory's sound judgement, and his favourable reports of the Victoria River district led to the eventual opening up of that area.

During the 1850s the small colony of South Australia began to expand rapidly, and the boundaries of settlement were pushed increasingly further north. Two speculators, James Chambers and William Finke, employed a young Scottish surveyor, John McDouall Stuart, to head north and find new grazing lands. It was the beginning of a quest which would eventually lead Stuart to the north coast of Australia, and a place in the history books as arguably the greatest explorer of the Australian interior.

In March 1858 Stuart's small party of just three men and 13 horses set off, and by mid-April had reached the Finke River and the MacDonnell Ranges, which he named after the South Australian governor. They continued north, reaching Central Mount Sturt (named by Stuart for his former boss, explorer Charles Sturt, and later renamed after Stuart himself), and tried, unsuccessfully, to cross the inhospitable scrub country north-west to the Victoria River. Already weakened by disease and short on supplies, the party eventually turned back after they had a hostile encounter with a group of Warumungu Aboriginal men at a place which Stuart named Attack Creek.

Stuart returned to Adelaide to a hero's welcome and within a matter of weeks was back on the trail north in a government-funded attempt to cross the continent from south to north. With a party of 11 men and 45 horses he returned to Attack Creek and managed to continue for a further 250 km before being forced once again by dwindling rations and hostile country to return south.

Within a month of returning, the dogged Scotsman was heading north again and this time he reached the mangrove-lined shores of the north coast at Point Stuart on 24 July 1862. During the four-month return trip to Adelaide, Stuart's health began to fail rapidly. After a loud but brief welcome back in Adelaide, Stuart soon fell from the public eye, and with his ambition now achieved and his health in tatters he was seemingly a broken man. He returned to England where he died just four years after his famous expedition.

Colonial Expansion

Partly as a result of favourable reports by Gregory and Stuart, there was a push by South Australian governors to annexe the Northern Territory. The Colonial Office was reluctant to spend any more British money on developing the north of Australia, and so in 1863 it agreed to South Australia's claims. This was despite the fact that South Australia was a very young colony with a small population and relatively little money, compared with gold-rich Victoria and the much older New South Wales, which already nominally owned the Northern Territory.

Having gained the Northern Territory,

South Australia's hope was that they would be able to develop it successfully at little cost to the public, as had been the case in their own colony. It was a hope which remained largely unfulfilled, as by Federation in 1901 the Territory had a huge debt and pastoralism, although well established, was hardly booming. The main success was the establishment of a permanent settlement on the north coast of Australia.

In an effort to encourage pioneering pastoralists, half a million acres of cheap land was put on the market in 1864. Ominously, most was taken up by wealthy speculators in London and Adelaide who hoped to turn a fast profit and had no intention of trying to force an existence out of the harsh Territory. Selling the land was the easy bit, the South Australian government then had to turn around and find and survey the 160-acre plots for the new land holders, and establish a new northern coastal settlement and port.

In 1864 the task was given to Boyle Finniss, a surveyor, who had orders to investigate the Adam Bay area at the mouth of the Adelaide River and establish a settlement. The area proved unsuitable as a port as the waters were difficult to navigate and the hinterland was waterlogged in the Wet, but Finniss still went ahead and established a settlement at Escape Cliffs. It wasn't long before Finniss faced censure from his fellow officers and eventually the South Australian government.

Finally, South Australian Surveyor-General George Goyder was sent north in 1869 to have a go at settling and surveying the area, and he headed straight for Port Darwin, having read the 1839 journals of John Lort Stokes who sailed into the harbour in 1839 aboard the *Beagle*. The settlement was officially called Palmerston.

Settlement of the north was slow as the prospective landholders down south proved reluctant to make the move north and settle. Most forfeited their holding and demanded refunds, as it had taken longer than the stipulated five years to survey the plots, mainly due to time wasted trying to establish the settlement at Escape Cliffs.

A saviour was urgently needed and it came in the form of the submarine telegraph cable which was to connect Australia with Britain.

The Overland Telegraph Line

In 1870 the South Australian government won the right to build a telegraph cable overland between Port Augusta and Darwin, where it would connect with a submarine cable connecting Java with India and England. The scheme would for the first time put Australia in direct communication with England. Previously all communication had to travel by sea, so a governor in NSW might wait six months or more for a reply from the Colonial Office in London.

South Australia won the right to have the cable traverse the Territory rather than go from Darwin to Queensland only after serious lobbying, and it only won after somewhat rashly committing itself to finishing the cable in just two years – around 3000 km of cable were to be laid across harsh and largely unpopulated land.

Private contracts were awarded for the construction of the 800-km southern and northern sections, leaving a 1100-km middle section which would be constructed by the South Australian government, under the supervision of Postmaster-General and Superintendent of Telegraphs, Charles (later Sir) Todd.

The southern section, from Port Augusta to near Charlotte Waters was completed ahead of schedule by Ned Bagot. The central section was split into five parts, each under an experienced surveyor, and the names of these men today appear regularly in street names throughout the Territory – McMinn, Mills, Woods, Knuckey and Harvey. John Ross was given the job of scouting and blazing the route. Basically the line roughly followed the route pioneered by Stuart on transcontinental expeditions some years earlier, although Ross had to find a shorter route through the MacDonnell Ranges. Despite massive logistical problems, the southern and central sections were completed on time.

It was on the northern section that the project really ran into problems. The private contractors seriously underestimated the effect the wet season was going to have on their ability to complete the task. In May 1871 the government exercised its right to cancel the contract, despite the fact that good progress had been made considering the difficulties, and the possibility that the contractors could finish the job. By June 1872 the line was complete save for the 350-km section between Daly Waters and Tennant Creek, which was bridged by a pony relay until the lines were physically joined some months later.

While the completing of the line and the opening of the OTL gave a good deal of prestige to South Australia, the state gained little direct benefit. By 1889 the line was largely superseded by another line which came ashore at Broome in Western Australia. What the line did do, however, was open up the country for further exploration and development. In the 1870s Ernest Giles and South Australian surveyor William Gosse both made expeditions west of the line south of Alice Springs, while Peter Warburton toughed it out by camel from Alice Springs across the Great Sandy Desert to the De Grey River near Port Hedland, surviving for much of the way on dried camel meat.

Gold

The next major event in the opening up of the Territory was the discovery of gold in an OTL post hole at Yam Creek, about 160 km south of Darwin. The find spurred on prospectors and it wasn't long before other finds had been made at nearby Pine Creek.

The finds sparked a minor rush, and it was hoped that this would finally be the economic hurry-up that the South Australian government still so desperately needed. Men arrived by ship in Port Darwin and it was there that their problems started. Equipment was expensive, and there was no road south from Southport (southern Darwin) to the goldfields. Those that did make it found that most of the hopeful prospects had been claimed by highly speculative companies from Adelaide. Gold production from the

Pine Creek fields was never high, peaking at £100,000 in 1880 and again in 1890, before dropping away sharply.

While the finds in the Territory were minuscule compared with those in Victoria and Western Australia, they generated activity in an area which was economically very unattractive. In an effort to encourage more people to the area, the South Australian government decided in 1883 to build a railway line from Palmerston (Darwin) to Pine Creek. The line was built by Chinese labourers, who had started coming to the Territory in the 1870s at the instigation of the South Australian premier, the prevailing view at the time being that it would be impossible to really develop the Territory without Asian labour.

By 1888 the European population was outnumbered four to one by Chinese immigrants, who dominated the goldfields. As had happened elsewhere in Australia, the Chinese faced serious obstacles – mainly in the form of racism from Europeans – and many returned home after the gold had petered out. Many, however, stayed on in the Top End and Darwin had a thriving Chinatown right up until the bombing raids of WW II, after which it was not rebuilt.

The Cattle Industry

The increased confidence of the 1870s and '80s in the eastern colonies led to a pastoral boom in the Territory and the foundation of the cattle industry, which for many years was the mainstay of the Territory economy. Cattle were brought in overland from Queensland, initially along the route first pioneered by Leichhardt, to stock the new runs of the north, while those in the Centre were stocked from South Australia along the Telegraph route. Stock routes pioneered by drovers such as Nat Buchanan, Thomas Pearce, Thomas Kilfoyle, Darcy Uhr and the Duracks of the Kimberley soon criss-crossed the Top End.

The Cattle King

More than any other enterprise, it was pastoral activity in general and the cattle industry in particular that led to White settlement in much of inland Australia. Given the vast distances, the often marginal grazing country and the harsh climate, the rearing of cattle was an arduous and risky business. Yet there was no shortage of triers prepared to give it a go, and some went on to make major contributions.

Sir Sidney Kidman was the undisputed cattle king of Australia. He was born in Adelaide in 1857 and ran away from home at the age of 13. He headed north for the 'corner country' of north-western New South Wales where he found work on outback stations. Over the years he became an expert bushman and stockman.

It was in the latter part of the last century that the vast expanses of outback Australia were settled. The infrastructure was virtually nil and getting cattle to markets in good condition was a major problem. Kidman came up with a bold yet superbly simple solution: 'chains' of stations along strategic routes which would allow the gradual movement of stock from the inland to the coastal markets. This in effect split the entire outback into a number of paddocks.

Starting with £400 which he inherited at the age of 21, Kidman traded in cattle and horses, and later in Broken Hill mines, and gradually built up a portfolio of land-holdings which gave him the envisaged 'chains'. Eventually he owned or controlled about 170,000 sq km of land (an area 2½ times the size of Tasmania, or about the size of Washington state in the USA) in chains. One of these chains ran from the Gulf of Carpentaria south through western Queensland and New South Wales to Broken Hill and into South Australia, and another stretched from the Kimberley into the Northern Territory and then down through the Red Centre and into South Australia.

Such was Kidman's stature as a pastoralist that at one time the north-western area of New South Wales was known as 'Kidman's Corner'. His life was portrayed, somewhat romantically, in Ion Idriess' book *The Cattle King*. Kidman was knighted in 1921 and died in 1935. ■

Such was the optimism of the era that many of the new stations were established on marginal or unviable land totally unsuited to pastoralism. The result was that with the economic crash of the 1890s, many stations simply didn't survive, while others changed hands numerous times, usually at a loss each time. Gradually the individual runs were consolidated and became bigger, with large companies such as Goldsborough Mort and the British Vestey Brothers taking up large holdings, but even then they had to struggle against problems such as poor land, distant markets and inadequate road access.

Federation & the Early 20th Century

The strident push for a Commonwealth of Australia by the eastern colonies was never strong in the Territory, although in the referendum of 1898 Territorians still voted overwhelmingly for it. Soon after Federation the South Australian government offered its northern Territory to the Federal government. The great optimism of just a generation ago had turned to a resignation that the Territory was just too tough. Despite efforts to develop it, most projects (and many such as sugar, tobacco and coffee were tried) had failed completely or provided only minimal returns, speculators and investors had lost faith and the Territory remained an economic backwater.

Opposition to the transfer to the Commonwealth came from Adelaide-based investors who held leases in the Territory and from conservative politicians. All were pinning their hopes on the completion of the transcontinental railway line which would link Adelaide with Darwin, and provide easy and rapid access to Asian markets. The transfer finally came in 1911, and it was conditional on the federal government reimbursing the South Australians the £6 million spent on the Port Augusta-Oodnadatta railway, and completing the north-south transcontinental rail link. Unfortunately no time limit was placed on the latter condition, and so even now it remains as oft talked about but no nearer reality than it was then.

The federal government set about trying to find an economic saviour for its new possession. Apparently having learnt little from the South Australians' experience, money was poured into experimental farms in the Top End but virtually everything failed.

In the 1920s, the federal government in its wisdom concluded that the Territory was in fact two different places, and divided it into the separate administrative entities of North Australia and Central Australia, the dividing line between the 20° South parallel of latitude. Based largely on the fear that the populous Asian nations to the north were jealous of this vast and empty land, the three-man commission administrating Northern Australia was given almost a free hand to develop the infrastructure necessary to expand the pastoral industry. Unfortunately a change of government in 1929 forced a rethink of the whole thing and the Territory was returned to its former state and all development plans were shelved.

The 1930s saw yet more forays into commercial ventures, none of them wildly successful. Peanuts became the latest agricultural experiment, but it was only import restrictions protecting the local industry that allowed any of the farmers to make any money at all. Competition from Queensland nuts, combined with the poor Territory soils and marketing problems, meant that only the very biggest producers could actually make a decent profit. A fledgling pearling industry developed from Darwin, but it relied on cheap Asian labour and was severely hampered by competition from Japanese vessels. Other industries, such as the hunting of crocodiles and snakes for their skins, took off but failed to survive the severe depression of the early 1930s.

While the Territory struggled to pay its way, advances in technology and communications meant that it wasn't entirely isolated. The fledgling aviation industry put Darwin on the map as passenger flights, operated by Qantas, had to make an overnight refuelling stop there, and pioneer aviators such as Amy Johnson also landed in Darwin. Other towns, too, started to develop – Tennant Creek became a minor boom town thanks to the mining activity, and Alice Springs now had a rail connection to Adelaide.

During the early years of the 20th century the threat of an Asian invasion was always a consideration in Australian defence thinking. Despite this, little was done to give Darwin any defensive capability at all, and even in the build-up to WW II the Federal government paid scant attention to protecting the north.

20th-Century Exploration

Around the turn of the century, Baldwin Spencer, a biologist, and Francis Gillen, an anthropologist, teamed up to study the Aboriginal people of central Australia and Arnhem Land. The results of their study are still one of the most detailed records of a vanished way of life. Other expeditions to northern Australia and Arnhem Land were led by the British polar explorer G H Wilkins (in 1923) and Donald Mackay (in 1928). Donald Thomson led his first expedition to Arnhem Land in 1935 and his work in northern Australia is still highly regarded by anthropologists and naturalists.

Allan Davidson was the first European to explore the Tanami Desert in any detail. In 1900 he set out looking for gold and found a number of good prospects which led to a minor rush some years later.

In the 1930s, aerial mapping of the Centre began in earnest, financed by Donald Mackay. Surveys were carried out over the Simpson Desert, the only large stretch of the country still to be explored on foot. In 1939, C T Madigan led an expedition that crossed this forbidding landscape from Old Andado to Birdsville; today the untracked route attracts a number of experienced adventurers.

In 1948 the largest scientific expedition ever undertaken in Australia was led by Charles Mountford into Arnhem Land. Financed by the National Geographic Society and the Australian government, it collected over 13,000 fish, 13,500 plant specimens, 850 birds and over 450 animal skins, along with thousands of Aboriginal implements and weapons.

WW II

When Britain declared war on Germany at the outbreak of WW II, Australia did likewise. Australian troops and ships were dispatched to Europe; the only troops stationed in Darwin were there to defend Indonesian islands against a Japanese attack. With the bombing of Pearl Harbor in late 1941 these troops were deployed to Ambon and Singapore, leaving Darwin with a pitifully small defensive force. By early 1942, however, there were some 14,000 Australian and American troops stationed in the Top End, although they had nothing in the way of air or naval support.

Darwin's isolation also proved a nightmare for military planners. Largely spurred on by the demands of the war effort, the road from the southern railhead at Alice Springs to Larrimah was pushed through, and the first military convoy passed along it in early 1941; by October 1943 it was sealed all the way.

With the fall of Singapore to the Japanese in February 1941, the threat to Darwin became increasingly real, although it was underestimated by those in charge in Darwin. The major concession made to those who predicted the worst was that the women and children of the city were evacuated late that year.

At 9.57 am on 19 February 1942 the first bombs fell on Darwin. Nearly 200 Japanese aircraft bombed the harbour and the RAAF base at Larrakeyah, not far from the city centre. At mid-day a second fleet of 54 Betty bombers attacked the city. The loss of life in the raids was heavy, and there was severe damage to the city's buildings. In all, Darwin was attacked 64 times during the war and 243 people lost their lives; it was the only place in Australia to suffer prolonged attacks.

In March 1942 the entire Territory north of Alice Springs was placed under military control, and convoys of men were trucked north, so that by December there were 32,000 men stationed in the Top End. The infrastructure needed to support these convoys was hastily put in place, and many reminders of this era can still be seen along or just off the Stuart Highway between Alice Springs and Darwin.

While the war certainly devastated Darwin, the war effort had produced a number of lasting benefits for the Territory – sealed roads from Darwin to Alice Springs and Queensland, and much improved telephone, power and water facilities among them.

Post-War to the Present

The post-war years in the Territory have seen development which mirrors what has happened in the more populous eastern states, but on a smaller scale and with a time delay. The post-war immigration boom led to high growth in the urban areas of Darwin and Alice Springs, but a shortage of Federal funds for the Territory meant there was little development and the rebuilding of Darwin proceeded at a snail's pace.

One of the main beneficiaries of the war was the pastoral industry, which had the novel experience of having a ready market and high demand for its end product – beef. This demand saw the construction of thousands of km of Commonwealth funded 'beef roads' in the Territory into the late 1960s. This meant that most cattle was now trucked to markets or railheads by road trains, which virtually spelt the doom of the drovers who had played such a vital part in opening up the Northern Territory.

Mining is one of only two industries (the other is tourism) which has really gone ahead since WW II. Copper and gold from Tennant Creek, oil and gas from the Amadeus basin in the Centre, gold from the Tanami, bauxite from Gove, manganese from Groote Eylandt and, most significantly, uranium from Batchelor and more recently Kakadu have all played an important role in the economic development of the Territory.

The big success story of the last 20 years, however, is tourism. At the end of WW II the population of Alice Springs was around 1000; today it has risen to over 20,000, purely on the strength of the tourist industry. For most Australians the outback is where the 'real' Australia lies, and as Uluru lies in the Territory, the Territory has become the major outback destination. The rise in environmental awareness and ecotourism has also led to the huge popularity of Kakadu National Park, and both Uluru and Kakadu each receive close to half a million visitors each year.

The 1970s was a time of great optimism in the Territory, an optimism that was severely tested (although, it seems, undiminished) by the occurrence of the worst natural disaster in Australia's European history. On Christmas Eve in 1974 Cyclone Tracy ripped through Darwin, killing 66 people and destroying 95% of the city's dwellings. Within four years the city had been largely rebuilt and has never looked back since.

Despite its increasing sophistication, the Northern Territory is still frontier country to most Australians, the *never never*, where, it has been said, men are men and women aren't ladies. It's also a place full of surprises – in 1995 the Northern Territory government was the first in the world to legislate on the legalisation of voluntary euthanasia, yet it also steadfastly refused to introduce a methadone program for heroin users, preferring instead to give them a one-way bus ticket south.

GEOGRAPHY

Australia is an island continent whose landscape, much of it uncompromisingly bleak and inhospitable, is the result of gradual changes wrought over millions of years. Although there is still seismic activity in the eastern and western highland areas, Australia is one of the most stable land masses, and for about 100 million years has been free of the mountain-building forces that have given rise to huge mountain ranges elsewhere.

The Northern Territory covers an area of around 1.35 million sq km, about 17% of the Australian landmass, which is roughly equal to the combined areas of Spain, France and Italy in Europe, or the state of Florida in the USA. Although roughly 80% of the Territory is in the tropics – the Tropic of Capricorn cuts across just north of Alice Springs – only the

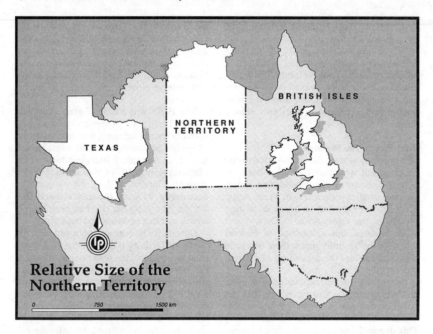

Relative Size of the Northern Territory

0   750   1500 km

northern 25%, known as the Top End, has anything resembling a tropical climate.

The 6200 km coastline is generally flat and backed by swamps, mangroves and mudflats, rising to a plateau no higher than 450 metres. The ruggedly beautiful ochre-red ridges of the MacDonnell Ranges, which reach heights of more than 600 metres, cut an east-west swathe through the Centre either side of Alice Springs. The famous monolith, Uluru (Ayers Rock), 348 metres high, is in the south-western part of the Territory.

The Top End is a distinct region of savannah woodlands and pockets of rainforest. In the north-east, the Arnhem Land plateau rises abruptly from the plain and continues to the coast of the Gulf of Carpentaria. Much of the southern three-quarters of the Territory consists of desert or semi-arid plain.

The main rivers in the north-west are the Victoria and the Daly, which flow into the Timor Sea; east of Darwin the Adelaide,

Mary, South Alligator and East Alligator rivers flow into the Arafura Sea; and further south there's the Roper and McArthur rivers, flowing into the Gulf of Carpentaria. Inland rivers, such as the Finke, the Todd and the Hugh, are dry most of the year. When they do flow, however, their waters often cover a great area before being lost in the wilds of the Simpson Desert.

CLIMATE

The two geographical zones – the Top End and the Centre – also correspond to the two climatic zones. The climate of the Top End is influenced by the tropical monsoons, and so has two distinct seasons – the Wet (November to April) and the Dry (May to October). During the Wet the Top End receives virtually all of its annual rainfall (around 1600 mm), usually in heavy late-afternoon thunderstorms. During the Dry rainfall is minimal and humidity is low, making it an ideal time for a visit. Tempera-

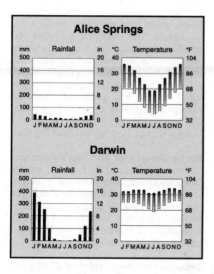

with maximums from 30°C to 34°C and minimums from 19°C to 26°C; rainfall is minimal from May to September, but from December to March there's 250 to 380 mm a month.

FLORA

Despite vast tracts of dry and barren land, much of the Territory is well vegetated. The Top End is a distinct region of savannah woodlands and pockets of rainforest. Many people expect the semi-arid Centre to be barren desert, yet there is a surprising variety of vegetation. Human activities seriously threaten Australian flora but to date most species have survived.

Origins

Australia's distinctive vegetation began to take shape about 55 million years ago when Australia broke from the supercontinent of Gondwanaland, drifting away from Antarctica to warmer climes. At this time, Australia was completely covered by cool-climate rainforest, but due to its geographic isolation and the gradual drying of the continent, rainforests retreated, plants like eucalypts and wattles (acacias) took over and grasslands expanded. Eucalypts and wattles were able to adapt to warmer temperatures, the increased natural occurrence of fire and, later, the use of fire for hunting and other purposes by Aboriginal people.

The arrival of Europeans saw the introduction of new flora, fauna and tools. Rainforests were logged, new crops and pasture grasses spread, hoofed animals such as cows, sheep and goats damaged the soil, and watercourses were altered by dams.

Native Grasses

There are literally hundreds of varieties of native Australian grasses found in a variety of habitats across the country.

Spinifex One of the hardiest and most common desert plants is spinifex, the dense, dome-shaped mass of long, needle-like leaves that you find on sandy soils and rocky areas. There are many species of spinifex but

tures throughout the year remain constant, with daytime maximum/minimum temperatures of around 32/25°C in the Wet and 30/19°C in the Dry.

The Centre has a much drier climate and greater extremes of temperature. In winter daytime temperatures of around 15 to 20° are comfortable, although there are often cold winds. Night-time temperatures are surprisingly low, making camping out a difficult prospect unless you have good gear – at Yulara the mercury often plunges below 0°C at night during winter, catching out many an unwary camper. In summer daytime temperatures are generally far too hot for comfort – an average of around 33° but often much higher – making spring and autumn the ideal times for a visit. Rainfall in the Centre is low all year round.

Alice Springs There are maximums of 30°C and above from October to March; minimums are 10°C and below from May to September. From December to February there's an average of 40 mm of rain per month.

Darwin Temperatures are even year round,

most share an important characteristic: in dry times their leaves roll into tight cylinders to reduce the number of pores exposed to the sun and wind. This keeps water loss through evaporation to a minimum, but even so, most plants will succumb during a really bad drought. Spinifex grasslands are very difficult to walk through – the explorer Ernest Giles called the prickly spinifex 'that abominable vegetable production'. They cover vast areas of central Australia and support some of the world's richest populations of reptiles.

Spinifex leaves have a high resin content, and this resin was used by Aboriginal people to fasten heads to spears and as a general adhesive.

Mitchell Grass Mitchell grass tussocks cover huge areas of arid land in northern Australia, and is the saviour of the cattle industry in the Top End. It has a well-developed root system and is therefore very drought resistant. The grass is usually found on clay soils which develop huge cracks when dry and become quagmires when wet.

Shrubs & Flowers

Callistemons Callistemons, or bottle-brushes (after the brush-like flowers), are native Australian shrubs which are found across the country, including the Northern Territory. They are attractive, hardy and easily grown, making them ideal plants for native gardens. There are about 25 different varieties, which grow from one to 10 metres in height. One of the most common in the Territory is the desert bottlebrush (*C. pauciflorus*), which grows throughout central Australia.

Grevilleas Grevilleas are another major family of shrubs. Of the 250 or so varieties, all but 20 are native to Australia, and around 10 of these are found in the Territory. Like bottlebrushes, they come in a variety of sizes and flower colours, and are popular garden plants. Most grevilleas are small to medium shrubs, such as the honey grevillea (*G. eriostachya*), which has beautiful golden flower spikes, and the holly grevillea (*G. wickhamii*). The rattlepod grevillea (*G. stenobotrya*) is a tall shrub found in sandy country, while the flood and drought resistant beefwood (*G. striata*) is a large tree with very hard wood valued for fencing and building. The resin was traditionally used by Aboriginal people as a glue and medicine. The fern-leaf grevillea (*G. pteridifolia*) is found in the eucalypt forests of the Top End.

Sturt's Desert Pea The Sturt's desert pea (*Clianthus formosus*) is a small, annual flower which flourishes in the sandy country of central Australia, particularly after heavy rain showers soak the ground. The plant is the floral emblem of South Australia, and its distinctive red flowers with black centres make it a popular garden plant.

Saltbush Millions of cattle living in the arid zone owe their survival to dry shrubby plants called saltbush, which get their name from their tolerance to saline conditions. Saltbush – there are 30 species – is extremely widespread and can be dominant over vast areas.

Wildflowers After good spring rains the normally arid inland explodes in a multi coloured carpet of vibrant wildflowers that will take your breath away. The most common of these ephemerals, or short-lived plants, are the numerous species of daisy. Others include docks (which came to Australia in camel-saddle stuffing last century), parakelias, pussy tails and pea flowers.

In a miracle of nature, the seeds of desert ephemerals can lie dormant in the sand for years until exactly the right combination of temperature and moisture comes along to trigger germination. When this happens, life in the desert moves into top gear as the ephemerals hurry to complete their brief life cycles and woody plants likewise burst into bloom. The sandhills, plains and rocky ridges come alive with nectar-eating birds and insects, which adds up to a bumper harvest for predators as well. Everywhere the various forms of wildlife are breeding and rearing their young while food supplies are abundant. For nature lovers this is definitely the best time to tour the inland.

Waterlilies Although the Top End can't match the visual spectacle of the desert in full bloom, it nevertheless has many spectacular wildflowers. One such is the waterlily, which forms floating mats of large, roundish leaves on freshwater lagoons and swamps right across the tropical north. Its root stock is prized as a food by Aboriginal people, who dig it out of the mud and eat it either raw or cooked.

Palms, Ferns & Cycads

Cabbage Palms The most well-known of Australia's 40 palm species are the cabbage palms (*Livistona mariae*) of Palm Valley in the Finke Gorge National Park near Alice Springs. The trees grow up to 30 metres high, and are unique to this area. The growing tip of the tree consists of tender green leaves, and these were a source of bush tucker to Aboriginal people. The mature leaves were also woven into hats by early European inhabitants of the Centre.

MacDonnell Ranges Cycad The unusual MacDonnell Ranges cycad (*Macrozamia macdonnelli*) is one of 18 species in Australia belonging to the ancient cycad family. They are a very slow-growing plant, often seen high up on rocky hillsides and gorges. Seed cones grow at the tip of the short trunk on female plants, while male cones carry the pollen. The seeds are poisonous but were eaten by Aboriginal people after the toxins had been leached out.

Trees

Acacias The Australian species of the acacia genus are commonly known as wattle – and they are common indeed. There are 660 species in Australia, but only about 100 are found in the Territory. They tend to be fast-growing, short-lived and come in many forms, from tall, weeping trees to prickly shrubs. Despite their many differences, all wattles have furry yellow flowers shaped either like a spike or a ball. If you see a plant

with a flower like this you'll know it's a wattle.

Most species flower during late winter and spring. Then the country is ablaze with wattle and the reason for the choice of green and gold as Australia's national colours is obvious. Wattle is Australia's floral emblem.

Mulga The mulga (*A. aneura*) is probably the most widespread of the arid-zone wattles. Although young mulga can look a little like small pines, the adults, which are 10 metres tall at their best, are more of an umbrella shape with a sparse crown of narrow grey leaves. Mulga sometimes forms dense thickets (the explorer John McDouall Stuart complained how the scrub near Alice Springs tore his clothes and pack saddles to bits) but usually is found as open woodland. Mulga leaves are very resistant to water loss, and the tree's shape directs any rain down to the base of the trunk where roots are most dense. With these attributes mulga is a great drought survivor, but being good fodder for stock puts it at risk from overgrazing. The hard wood is excellent for fencing and was preferred by Aboriginal people for making spears and other implements. They also ground the mulga seeds for flour.

Waddy Wood The *Acacia peuce* is another tree with very hard wood which was valued by early settlers for fence posts. This led to them being also completely wiped out. There are three existing stands of waddy, one in the Territory on the western edge of the Simpson Desert near Old Andado station.

Ironwood The ironwood (*A. estrophiolata*) tree, with its rough bark and weeping habit is a graceful inland tree which grows anywhere south of Tennant Creek. Once again, its wood is hard, making it popular for fence posts, and the sugary gum was eaten by Aboriginal people.

Gidgee Also known as the stinking wattle because of the pungent smell given off by the leaves when crushed, the gidgee (*A. cambagei*), with its distinctive silvery grey-green foliage, grows over large areas of central Australia.

Casuarinas Also known as she-oaks, these hardy trees are almost as much a part of the Australian landscape as eucalypts. They grow in a variety of habitats, and are characterised by feather-like 'leaves', which are actually branchlets; the true leaves are small scales at the joints of the branchlets.

Desert Oak Its height, broad shady crown, dark weeping foliage and the sighing music of the wind in its 'leaves' make the desert oak (*Allocasuarina decaisneana*) an inspiring feature of its sand-plain habitat. These magnificent trees are confined to the western arid zone of central Australia and are common around Uluru and Kings Canyon, near Alice Springs. Young desert oaks resemble tall hairy broomsticks; they don't look anything like the adult trees and many people think that they're a different species altogether.

Eucalypts The eucalypt, or gum tree, is ubiquitous in Australia except in the deepest rainforests and the most arid regions. Of the 700 species of the genus eucalyptus, 95% occur naturally in Australia, the rest in Papua New Guinea, the Philippines and Indonesia.

Gum trees vary in form and height from the tall, straight hardwoods such as jarrah, karri, mountain ash and river red gum to the stunted, twisted, shrub-like Mallee gum.

River Red Gum The river red gums (*E. camaldulensis*) are generally confined to watercourses where their roots have access to a reliable water source. Given good conditions they can grow to 40 metres high and may live for 1000 years. This species is fairly easily identified from its habitat and its smooth, often beautifully marked grey, tan and cream bark. River gums are found throughout Australia, and in the outback wherever there is suitable habitat. They have a bad habit of dropping large limbs, so while they may be good shade trees it's certainly not wise to camp under them.

Coolabah The coolabah tree (*E. Microtheca*) was immortalised in Banjo Paterson's poem, *Waltzing Matilda*, and is widespread throughout inland and northern Australia. They are typically gnarled, spreading trees with a rough, dark-brown bark and dull, leathery leaves. Coolabahs can grow to 20 metres high and often provide excellent shade. All eucalypts are hardwoods and this species is said to have the hardest timber of all. It is also very strong and termite-resistant, which made it extremely useful for building fences and stockyards in the days before steel became more readily available.

Ghost Gum The ghost gum (*Corymbia papuana*) is one of the most attractive eucalypts, thanks to its bright green leaves and smooth white bark. They are found throughout central and northern Australia, and were a common subject matter for artists such as Albert Namatjira.

Woollybutt The woollybutt (*E. miniata*, also known as the Darwin woollybutt), dominates the open woodland country of the Top End. This medium-sized tree has rough, dark bark on the main trunk, but smooth-white bark on the upper limbs. This is the tree's in-built fire protection as this thick bark insulates the trunk.

Salmon Gum The distinctive salmon gum (*E. tintinnans*), with its smooth, straight pink trunk and dark green canopy is another beautiful tree found throughout the Top End.

Melaleucas The paperbarks, or *Melaleucas*, are generally easily recognised by the loose, papery bark which hangs in thin sheets around the trunk. This is actually dead bark which stays on the tree, insulating the trunk from extreme temperature and moisture loss. The trees have for centuries been put to many uses by Aboriginal people – drinkable water is obtainable from the trunk, and the bark has been used for things such water carriers, rafts, shelters and food coverings.

Some of the most common varieties found

in the Top End are the long-leaved paper-bark (*M. leucadendron*), the weeping paperbark (*M. leucadentra*) and the broad-leafed paperbark (*M. quinquenervia*), while in the Centre the inland teatree (*M. glomerata*) and the *Melaleuca liniariifolia* are both wide spread in the MacDonnell Ranges.

Boabs The boab (*Adansonia gregorii*) is Australia's most grotesque tree and is only found from the south-western Kimberley to the Northern Territory's Victoria River, where it grows on flood plains and rocky areas. Its huge, grey, swollen trunk topped by a mass of contorted branches make it a fascinating sight, particularly during the dry season when it loses its leaves and becomes 'the tree that God planted upside-down'. Although boabs rarely grow higher than 20 metres, their moisture-storing trunks can be over 25 metres around.

White Cypress Pines The white cypress pine (*Callitris glaucophylla*) is widespread throughout central Australia. Its wood is highly valued as it is termite resistant, while the bark is a good source of tannin, used commercially in the tanning process.

Mangroves Much of the northern coast is dominated by mangrove communities, of which there are over 21 varieties growing in the Territory. These remarkable plants have adapted to life in the water, and usually grow in the tidal zone, where they are an important habitat for many small animals including crabs and fish such as the barramundi. At low tide some species, such as the grey mangrove, have pneumatophores – exposed roots which can actually take in air. There are also the freshwater mangrove (*Barringtonia acutangula*) which is found on the fringes of floodplains which are inundated during the Wet.

Weeds

In the Top End and across tropical Australia, weeds such as mimosa bush are threatening huge areas, while salvinia has begun to choke several waterways.

In central Australia the Finke River has been invaded by athel trees which threaten its entire ecosystem. Introduced weeds can destroy wildlife habitats as well as make pastoral and cropping land unusable.

FAUNA

Australia is blessed with a fascinating mix of native fauna, which ranges from the primitive to the highly evolved – some creatures are unique survivors from a previous age, while others have adapted so acutely to the natural environment that they can survive in areas which other animals would find uninhabitable.

Australian fauna is very distinct, partly because the Australian land mass is one of the most ancient on earth, and also because the sea has kept it isolated from other land masses for more than 50 million years. In this time the continent has suffered no major climatic upheavals, giving its various indigenous creatures an unusually long and uninterrupted period in which to evolve.

Since the European colonisation of Australia, 17 species of mammal have become extinct and at least 30 more are currently endangered. Many introduced non-native animals have been allowed to run wild, causing a great deal of damage to native species and to Australian vegetation.

Marsupials

The major grouping of Australian mammals are the marsupials, mammals which raise their tiny young inside a pouch, or marsupium. Marsupials are largely confined to Australia, and included in this group of around 120 species are some of the country's most distinct and well-known animals – kangaroos, wallabies, koalas, wombats and possums – as well as others less well known, such as the numerous bandicoots and bush mice, the predatory quoll and the now-extinct thylacine (or Tasmanian tiger).

Kangaroo Kangaroos are probably the most instantly recognisable Australian mammal and hardly need a description, although the name is applied to dozens of species.

There are now more kangaroos in Australia than there were when Europeans arrived, a result of the better availability of water and the creation of grasslands for sheep and cattle. Certain species, however, are threatened, as their particular environments are being destroyed or predators such as feral cats and foxes take their toll. About three million kangaroos are culled legally each year but many more are killed for sport or by those farmers who believe the cull is insufficient to protect their paddocks from overgrazing by the animals. Kangaroo meat has been exported for some time but it is only in recent years that it has started to appear on Australian menus.

Red Kangaroo The distinctive red kangaroo (*Macrocarpus rufus*) is among the largest and most widespread of the kangaroos. A fully grown male can be 2.4 metres long and stand two metres high. It's usually only the males which have the reddish tinge; females are often a blue-grey colour. They range over most of arid Australia.

Wallaby Wallabies come in a variety of shapes and sizes. The most commonly seen are the red-necked (*Macropus rufogriseus*), agile (*M. agilis*) and the swamp wallaby (*Wallabia bicolor*), all of which are about 1.7 metres long when fully grown.

The various rock-wallabies are generally small (around one metre long) and are confined to cliffs and rock slopes in various places around the country.

Bandicoots & Bilbies The small, rat-like bandicoots and bilbies have been among the principal victims of the introduced domestic and feral cats.

Bandicoots are largely nocturnal, but can occasionally be seen scampering through the bush. They are largely insect eaters but do also eat some plant material.

The rare bilby (*Macrotis lagotis*) is found mainly in the Northern Territory and major efforts have been made to ensure its survival.

Its rabbit-like ears have recently caused it to be promoted as Australia's own Easter animal: the Easter bilby versus the Easter bunny!

Possum There is an enormous range of possums (or phalangers) in Australia – they seem to have adapted to all sorts of conditions, including those of the city, where you'll often find them in parks. Some large species are found living in suburban roofs and will eat garden plants and food scraps. Possums are also common visitors at camp sites in heavily treed country, and will often help themselves to any food left out.

Probably the most familiar of all possums is the common brushtail (or grey) possum (*Trichosurus vulpecula*), which occurs widely throughout the mainland and Tasmania. If you see a possum splattered on the highway (and unfortunately this is not an uncommon sight), chances are it's a poor old brushtail.

The sugar glider (*Petaurus breviceps*) has membranes between its front and rear legs, which when spread out are used for gliding from the tip of one tree to the base of the next, covering up to 100 metres in one swoop – quite a remarkable sight.

Dasyuroids
Members of the Dasyuroidea family are predatory marsupials, such as quolls, numbats and the Tasmanian devil. The main distinguishing feature of Dasyuroids is a pointy, elongated snout.

Quoll Australia's spotted quolls, or native cats, are about the size of domestic cats and are probably even more efficient killers, but are totally unrelated. Being nocturnal creatures which spend most of their time in trees, they are not often seen.

The native cats include the eastern quoll (*Dasyurus viverrinus*), western quoll (*Dasyurus geoffroii*) and the northern quoll (*Dasyurus hallucatus*).

The spotted-tailed quoll (*Dasyurus maculatus*), also known as the tiger cat, is one of the most ferocious hunters in the Australian bush.

Marine Mammals

Dugong This is a herbivorous aquatic mammal (*Dugong dugon*), often known as the 'sea cow', found along the northern Australian coast. It is found in shallow tropical waters and estuaries where it feeds on seagrasses, supplemented by algae.

Eutherians

Dingo The dingo (*Canis familiaris dingo*), is Australia's native dog and only eutherian (or placental mammal). It's thought to have arrived in Australia around 6000 years ago, and was domesticated by the Aborigines. It differs from the domestic dog in that it howls rather than barks and breeds only once a year (rather than twice), although the two can successfully interbreed.

Dingoes prey mainly on rabbits, rats and mice, although when other food is scarce they sometimes attack livestock (usually unattended calves), and for this reason are considered vermin by many station owners. Efforts to control the number of dingoes have been largely unsuccessful.

Birds

Australia's bird life is as beautiful as it is varied, with over 750 species recorded.

The Royal Australasian Ornithologists Union runs bird observatories in New South Wales, Victoria and Western Australia, which provide accommodation and guides. Contact the RAOU (☎ (03) 9370 1422) at 21 Gladstone St, Moonee Ponds, Victoria 3039.

Emu The only bird larger than the emu (*Dromaius novaehollandiae*) is the African ostrich, also flightless. The emu is a shaggy feathered, often curious bird found right across the country, but only in uninhabited areas. After the female lays her six to 12 large, dark green eggs the male hatches them and raises the young.

Parrots, Rosellas, Lorikeets & Cockatoos

There is an amazing variety of these birds

Sulphur-Crested Cockatoo

throughout Australia. Some, such as the galah, are fairly plain, while others have the most vivid colouring imaginable.

Galah The pink and grey galah (*Cacatua roseicapilla*) is amongst the most common, and is often sighted scratching for seeds on the roadsides. Consequently they often get hit.

Sulphur-Crested Cockatoo This noisy cocky (*Cacatua galerita*), often seen in loud, raucous flocks, is found throughout eastern and northern Australia. It's also the most common variety to be caged as pets.

Rosellas There are a number of species of rosella (*Platycercus*), most of them brilliantly coloured and not at all backward about taking a free feed from humans.

Rainbow Lorikeets The rainbow lorikeets (*Trichoglossus haematodus*) are much more extravagantly colourful than you can ever imagine until you've seen one, with a blue head, orange breast and green body.

Budgerigars Budgies (*Melopsittacus undulatus*), native to Australia, are probably the most widely kept bird in the world. They are widespread over inland Australia but are mainly found towards the Centre. They often fly in flocks of thousands.

Black Cockatoos There are six varieties of the distinctive black cockatoos, the most widespread being the large red-tailed black cockatoo (*Calyptorhynchus magnificus*) and the similar yellow-tailed black cockatoo (*C. funereus*).

Kookaburra A member of the kingfisher family, the noisy kookaburra (*Dacelo novaeguinae*) is heard as much as it is seen – you can't miss its loud, cackling cry. Kookaburras can become quite tame and pay regular visits to friendly households, but only if the food is excellent. It's hard to impress a kookaburra with anything less than top-class steak.

It is common throughout coastal Australia, but particularly in the east and south-west of the country.

Bower Bird The stocky, stout-billed bowerbird, of which there are at least half a dozen varieties, is best known for its unique mating practice. The male builds a bower which he decorates with various coloured objects to attract females. The female is impressed by the male's neatly built bower and attractively displayed treasures, but once they've mated all the hard work is left to her.

The three most common varieties are the great bowerbird (*Chlamydera nuchalis*), the spotted bowerbird (*C. maculata*), and the satin bowerbird (*Ptilonorhynchus violaceus*).

Magpie The black and white magpie (*Gymnorhina tibicen*) is one of the most widespread birds in Australia, being found virtually throughout the country. One of the most distinctive sounds of the Australian bush is the melodious song of the magpie, which is heard at any time of day, but especially at dawn. One of the magpie's less endearing traits is that it swoops at people who approach its nest too closely in spring.

There are five different types of magpie, but they all look much alike to the untrained eye.

Wedge-Tailed Eagle The large wedge-tailed eagle (*Aquila audax*) is Australia's largest bird of prey. It has a wing span of up to two meters, and is easily identified in flight by its distinctive wedge-shaped tail. 'Wedgies' are often seen in outback Australia, either soaring to great heights, or feeding on road-kill carcases.

Jabiru The jabiru (or black-necked stork, *Xenorhynchus asiaticus*) is found throughout northern and eastern Australia, although it is not seen that often. It stands over one metre high, and has an almost iridescent green-black neck, black and white body, and orange legs.

Magpie Goose The magpie (or pied) goose (*Anseranas semipalmata*) is commonly seen in the tropical wetlands of northern Australia – indeed when water becomes scarce towards the end of the Dry season (October) they often gather in huge numbers on the remaining wetlands.

Brolga Another bird commonly seen in wetland areas of northern and, to a lesser extent, eastern Australia, is the tall crane known as the brolga (*Grus rubicundus*). They stand over a metre high, are grey in colour and have a distinctive red head colouring.

Black Swan Commonly seen on stretches of water in the Top End are black swans (*Cygnus atratus*). They are usually seen in quite large numbers, and like to nest on islands in lakes and other water bodies.

Willy Wagtail The distinctive little willy wagtail (*Rhipidura leucophrys*) is one of the few birds to be found right across the range of habitats found in Australia. These small black and white birds get quite cheeky when used to people, and were seen as signs of bad luck in Aboriginal stories.

Gouldian Finch The rare gouldian finch (*Erythrura gouldiae*) is one of Australia's most beautiful native birds. Unfortunately its numbers have been drastically reduced by infestations of the tiny air-sac mite, and it is now threatened with extinction. It is confined to the Top End, in areas such as the Keep River National Park.

Reptiles
Snakes Australian snakes are generally shy and try to avoid confrontations with humans. A few, however, are deadly. The most dangerous are the taipans and tiger snakes, although death adders, copperheads, brown snakes and red-bellied black snakes should also be avoided. Tiger snakes will actually attack.

Crocodiles There are two types of crocodile in Australia: the less aggressive freshwater crocodile (*C. johnstoni*), or 'freshie' as it's known, and the extremely dangerous saltwater crocodile (*Crocodylus porosus*), or 'saltie'.

Freshwater Crocodile Freshies are smaller than salties – anything over four metres should be regarded as a saltie. Freshies are also more finely constructed and have much narrower snouts and smaller teeth. Salties, which can grow to seven metres, will attack and kill humans. Freshies, though unlikely to seek human prey, have been known to bite, and children in particular should be kept away from them.

Saltwater Crocodile Salties are not confined to salt water. They inhabit estuaries, and following floods may be found many km

from the coast. They may even be found in permanent fresh water more than 100 km inland. It is important to be able to tell the difference between the saltie and its less dangerous relative, as both are prolific in northern Australia.

Lizards The frilled lizard (*Chlamydosaurus kingii*) is Australia's most famous lizard, and is commonly seen in bushland in eastern and northern Australia. The frill is a loose flap of skin which normally hangs flat around the neck. When alarmed or threatened, the lizard's frill is raised and the mouth opened to give a more ferocious appearance.

Eastern Blue-Tongued Lizard The large, fat and slow-moving eastern blue-tongued lizard (*Tiliqua scincoides*) is another common Australian lizard. Unfortunately its defence mechanisms of hissing loudly and puffing up its body are little protection against cars; flat blue-tongues are a common sight in the bush.

Goanna Goannas are large and sometimes aggressive lizards which grow up to 1.5 metres long. They'll often be found lurking around picnic or camping areas scrounging for scraps. With their forked tongues and loud hiss they can look quite formidable, and are best left undisturbed as they will stand their ground.

Spiders
Some Australian spiders bite, and it's a good idea to leave any spider well alone.

Redback Spider The redback (*Latrodectus hasselti*) is Australia's most notorious spider – it has a legendary liking for toilet seats – and is widespread in country areas where woodheaps and garden sheds are favourite hangouts. Its bite can easily kill a small child.

White-Tail Spider While this small spider looks harmless enough, some people have extreme reactions to its bite and gangrene can result. It is common in gardens, and is

Saltwater Crocodile

about the size of a dollar coin, with a distinct white spot on its grey-black back.

Wolf Spider Another nasty to look out for is the wolf spider (*Lycosidae* family), which builds a trap-doored hole in the ground. The bite of the wolf spider can cause necrosis.

Introduced Animals

Soon after foxes and rabbits were introduced to Australia for sport in the mid-1800s it became apparent that a dreadful mistake had been made. Both spread far and wide with remarkable speed and it wasn't long before they became pests. Rabbits have had a devastating effect on native plants, particularly in the arid zone, while foxes – and feral cats have chewed great holes in the populations of Australia's smaller marsupials. Feral cats are now found throughout the mainland but rabbits and foxes have yet to successfully invade the tropical north (although in good seasons they push north into the Tanami Desert).

At least 18 introduced mammal species are now feral in Australia and many have become pests. Oddly enough, the dromedary, or one-humped camel, seems to have had the smallest impact even though it's the largest feral animal. Australia's estimated 100,000 wild camels are descended from those released by their owners when the camel trains that supplied the outback for 50 years were replaced by motor vehicles in the 1920s and '30s. Now forming the world's only wild populations of this species (the other 13 million or so in North Africa and the Middle East are domesticated), Australian camels are being exported to the Middle East to improve the local gene pool.

Other introduced animals include the pig, goat, donkey, water buffalo, horse, starling, sparrow, blackbird and cane toad. All are pests, and have multiplied rapidly through lack of natural enemies. The cane toad, native to South America, was introduced into Queensland as a control measure against the cane beetle. Unfortunately it rapidly went feral and is spreading west at the rate of 30 km per year. Colonies are reported west of

Borroloola, and are expected to reach Kakadu by the end of the decade unless a new control measure is found.

NATIONAL PARKS & RESERVES

The Northern Territory has more than 100 national parks and reserves – nonurban protected wilderness areas of environmental or natural importance. As a rule, the parks and reserves are administered by the Parks & Wildlife Commission of the Northern Territory, but known until recently as the Conservation Commission of the Northern Territory (CCNT). The exceptions are Kakadu and Uluru-Kata Tjuta national parks, which come under the domain of the federal national parks body, the Australian Nature Conservation Agency.

Public access is encouraged if safety and conservation regulations are observed. In all parks you're asked to do nothing to damage or alter the natural environment. Approach roads, camping grounds (often with toilets and showers), walking tracks and information centres are often provided for visitors. In most national parks there are restrictions on bringing in pets. Do yourself and Rover a favour and leave him at home.

Some national parks are so isolated, rugged or uninviting that you wouldn't want to do much except look unless you were an experienced, well-prepared bushwalker or climber. Other parks, however, are among Australia's major attractions and two in the Territory – Kakadu and Uluru-Kata Tjuta – have been included on the World Heritage List (a United Nations list of natural or cultural places of world significance that would be an irreplaceable loss to the planet if they were altered).

Other popular parks in the Northern Territory include Litchfield National Park, which is only a few hours from Darwin and has some superb swimming holes and waterfalls; Nitmiluk (Katherine Gorge) National Park, with its series of rugged gorges which are great fun to canoe along; Watarrka National Park, which has as its centrepiece the outrageously picturesque Kings Canyon; and the West MacDonnell National Park, which encompasses some of the most spectacular gorge country in central Australia and offers excellent bushwalking opportunities.

For Parks & Wildlife offices see the Useful Organisations section of the Facts for the Visitor chapter.

GOVERNMENT & POLITICS
Federal Government
Australia is a monarchy, but although Britain's king or queen is also Australia's, Australia is fully autonomous. The British sovereign is represented by the governor-general and the state governors, whose nominations for their posts by the respective governments are ratified by the reigning monarch.

Federal parliament is based in Canberra, the capital of the nation. Like Washington DC in the USA, Canberra is in its own separate area of land, the Australian Capital Territory (ACT), and is not under the rule of one of the states. Geographically, however, the ACT is completely surrounded by New South Wales. The state parliaments are in each state capital.

The Federal government is elected for a maximum of three years but elections can be (and often are) called earlier. Voting in Australian elections is by secret ballot and is compulsory for persons 18 years of age and over. Voting can be somewhat complicated as a preferential system is used whereby each candidate has to be listed in order of preference. This can result, for example, in Senate elections with 50 or more candidates to be ranked!

The Constitution can only be changed by referendum, and only if a majority of voters in at least four states favour it. Since federation in 1901, of the 42 proposals that have been put to referendum, only eight have been approved.

In Federal parliament, the two main political groups are the Australian Labor Party (ALP) and the coalition between the Liberal (conservative) Party and the National Party. These parties also dominate state politics but sometimes the Liberal and National parties are not in coalition. The latter was once

known as the National Country Party since it mainly represents country seats. On 2 March 1996 the Liberals, led by John Howard, and the National Party won the federal election thus bringing to an end 13 years of ALP government.

The only other political party of any real substance is the Australian Democrats, which has largely carried the flag for the ever-growing 'green' movement. Independent politicians with no affiliation to a particular party have also made it into the traditional political structure in recent times. Currently, independents help the Democrats hold the balance of power in the Senate.

The Cabinet, presided over by the Prime Minister, is the government's major policy-making body, and it comprises about half of the full ministry. It's a somewhat secretive body which meets in private (usually in Canberra) and its decisions are ratified by the Executive Council, a formal body presided over by the Governor-General.

Northern Territory Government
Politically the Northern Territory is something of an anomaly in Australia. In 1947 the Chifley government in Canberra created the Northern Territory Legislative Council, a 13-member body (six elected, seven appointed by Canberra) which had the power to do pretty well anything as long as it didn't offend Canberra, which retained the right of veto. One NT parliamentarian commented that it gave Territorians no more rights than 'the inhabitants of Siberian Russia or the inmates of a gaol'.

The elected council members agitated for self-government, but Canberra remained unmoved. In 1958 the size of the council was increased and the MP for the Northern Territory in the House of Representatives in Canberra was finally allowed to vote in the House – but only on matters pertaining to the Territory. It was not until the Whitlam Labor government came to power in Canberra that the Territory got a fully elected Legislative Assembly in 1974, and representation in the Senate in Canberra. Self-government (akin to statehood) came in 1978, although Canberra still has a greater say than it does in the states.

The leader of the Territory's 25-seat parliament is the Chief Minister, whereas in the other states it's the Premier who's in charge. The Territorian Country Liberal Party has been in power since 1974 and holds all but the eight seats held by the ALP. There is no Upper House, although if statehood were granted a senate would be established.

ECONOMY

The Northern Territory economy is dominated by two major industries – tourism and mining – with other primary industry coming a distant third.

Mining & Energy

Mining in the Northern Territory contributes about 20% of gross state product compared with an average of 5% elsewhere in the country.

The major minerals mined in the Territory are: bauxite, with the third-largest bauxite mine in Australia at Gove; gold, with mines in the Pine Creek area, the Tanami Desert and the Tennant Creek area; manganese on Groote Eylandt, one of the world's four major producers of high grade ore; zinc, lead and silver, including one of the world's largest known ore bodies at McArthur River near Borroloola on the Gulf of Carpentaria; and uranium, with 10% of the world's reserves lying in or close to Kakadu National Park.

Oil production is dominated by the offshore fields of Jabiru, Challis/Cassini and Skeea. Gas production is from the Mereenie gas fields west of the MacDonnell Ranges in central Australia.

Tourism

Tourism is one of the Northern Territory's fastest-growing industries. Almost a million people travel to or within the Territory each year, compared with about half that number a decade ago.

Primary Industry

There are over 200 pastoral holdings in the Northern Territory producing cattle for Australian and South-East Asian markets. These vary from small stations of around 200 sq km to huge properties such as Brunette Downs on the Barkly Tableland, which is a shade over 12,000 sq km. Live cattle exports from the Territory are worth around $30 million annually.

Prawn fishing is another important industry, with an annual catch of around 5500 tonnes valued at around $60 million.

POPULATION & PEOPLE

Although the Northern Territory accounts for nearly 20% of the Australian landmass, it has just 1% of the country's population. Around 38,000 of the Territory's 173,500 people are of Aboriginal descent. The non-Aboriginal population is highly cosmopolitan, especially in Darwin where at least 60 different ethnic groups are represented. Darwin also has a significant population of Chinese Australians, descendants of the first non-European immigrants into the Territory last century.

The population of Darwin is around 78,100, while other major centres of population are Alice Springs (22,000), Nhulunbuy (4060), Katherine (9200) and Tennant Creek (3550).

Aboriginal People

When Europeans first settled in Australia, it is believed there were about 300,000 Aboriginal people and around 250 different languages were spoken, many as distinct from each other as English is from Chinese.

In such a society, based on family groups with an egalitarian political structure, a coordinated response to the European colonisers was not possible. Despite the presence of the Aboriginal people, the newly arrived Europeans considered the new continent to be *terra nullius* – a land belonging to no-one. Conveniently, they saw no recognisable system of government, no commerce or permanent settlements and no evidence of land ownership.

Many Aboriginal people were driven from their land by force, and many more succumbed to exotic diseases such as smallpox, measles, venereal disease, influenza, whooping cough, pneumonia and tuberculosis. Others voluntarily left their lands to travel to the fringes of settled areas to obtain new commodities such as steel and cloth, and experience hitherto unknown drugs such as tea, tobacco and alcohol.

The delicate balance between Aboriginal people and nature was broken, as the European invaders cut down forests and introduced numerous feral and domestic animals. Cattle destroyed waterholes and ruined the habitats which had for tens of thousands of years sustained mammals, reptiles and vegetable foods. Many species of plants and animals disappeared altogether.

There was considerable conflict between Aboriginal people and European pastoralists. Aboriginal people occasionally speared cattle or attacked isolated stations and then suffered fierce reprisal raids which left many of them dead. An attack on the Barrow Creek telegraph station in which two whites were killed led to punitive raids in which up to 50 Aboriginal people were killed. A similar attack on a lonely Daly River copper mine in 1884 led to the deaths of three miners and a government reprisal raid during which it is believed many Aboriginal people were killed, although the official report of the incident reported no casualties. Very few Europeans were prosecuted for killing Aboriginal people, although the practice was widespread.

By the early 1900s, legislation designed to segregate and 'protect' Aboriginal people was passed in all states. The legislation imposed restrictions on the Aboriginal people's rights to own property and seek employment, and the Aboriginals Ordinance of 1918 even allowed the state to remove children from Aboriginal mothers if it was suspected that the father was non-Aboriginal. In these cases the parents were considered to have no rights over the children, who were placed in foster homes or childcare institutions.

Many Aboriginal people are still bitter about having been separated from their families and forced to grow up apart from their people. An up-side of the ordinance was that it gave a degree of protection for 'full-blood' Aboriginal people living on reserves, as non-Aboriginal people could enter only with a permit, and mineral exploration was forbidden. Arnhem Land was declared an Aboriginal reserve in 1931.

In these early years of the 20th century, most Territory Aboriginal people were confined to government-allotted reserves or Christian missions. Others lived on cattle stations where they were employed as skilful but poorly paid stockmen or domestic servants, or were living a half-life on the edges of towns, attracted there by food and tobacco, sometimes finding low-paid work, too often acquiring an alcohol habit. Only a few – some of those on reserves and cattle stations, and those in the remote outback – maintained much of their traditional way of life.

White tolerance was still generally low, and punitive raids which saw the deaths of many still occurred – such as at Coniston station north-west of Alice springs in 1928. On this occasion, however, there was enough public outrage, mostly from the urban centres in the eastern states, to prompt a public inquiry. The police were exonerated in this case and another in Arnhem Land in 1934, but the time had finally come when people could no longer kill Aboriginal people and expect to get away with it.

The process of social change for Aboriginal people was accelerated by WW II. After the war 'assimilation' of Aboriginal people became the stated aim of the government. To this end, the rights of Aboriginal people were subjugated even further: the government had control over everything, from where Aboriginal people could live to whom they could marry. Many people were forcibly moved to townships, the idea being that they would adapt to European culture which would in turn aid their economic development. The boys were trained to be stockmen, the women domestic servants, and while many excelled in their field, the policy itself was a dismal failure.

In the 1960s the assimilation policy came under a great deal of scrutiny, and White Australians became increasingly aware of the inequity of the treatment of Aboriginal people. In 1967 non-Aboriginal Australians voted to give Aboriginal people and Torres Strait Islanders the status of citizens, and gave the national government power to legislate for them in all states. The states had to provide them with the same services as were available to other citizens, and the national government set up the Department of Aboriginal Affairs to identify the special needs of Aboriginal people and legislate for them.

The assimilation policy was finally dumped in 1972, to be replaced by the government's policy of self-determination, which for the first time enabled Aboriginal people to participate in decision-making processes by granting them rights to their land.

Although the latest developments give rise to cautious optimism, many Aboriginal people still live in appalling conditions, and alcohol and drug abuse remain a widespread problem, particularly among young and middle-aged men. Aboriginal communities have taken up the challenge to eradicate these problems – many communities are now 'dry', and there are a number of rehabilitation programmes for alcoholics, petrol-sniffers and others with drug problems. Thanks for much of this work goes to Aboriginal women, many of whom have found themselves on the receiving end of domestic violence.

All in all it's been a tough 200 years for Australia's Aboriginal people. One can only be thankful for their resilience, which has enabled them to withstand the pressures placed on their culture, traditions and dignity, and that after so many years of domination they've been able to keep so much of that culture intact.

Aboriginal Land Rights As we have seen, Britain founded the colony of New South Wales on the legal principle of *terra nullius*, a land belonging to no-one, which meant that Australia was legally unoccupied. The set-

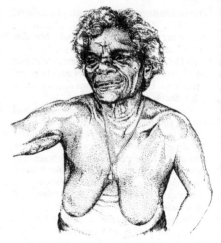

A Tiwi Aboriginal woman from Bathurst Island

tlers could take land from Aboriginal people without signing treaties or providing compensation. The European concept of land ownership was completely foreign to Aboriginal people and their view of the world in which land did not belong to individuals: people belonged to the land, were formed by it and were a part of it like everything else.

After WW II, Australian Aboriginal people became more organised and better educated, and a political movement for land rights developed. In 1962 a bark petition was presented to the federal government by the Yolngu people of Yirrkala, in north-east Arnhem Land, demanding that the government recognise Aboriginal peoples' occupation and ownership of Australia since time immemorial. The petition was ignored, and the Yolngu people took the matter to court, and lost. In the famous Yirrkala Land Case 1971, Australian courts accepted the government's claim that Aboriginal people had no meaningful economic, legal or political relationship to land. The case upheld the principle of *terra nullius*, and the common-law position that Australia was unoccupied in 1788.

Because the Yirrkala Land Case was based on an inaccurate (if not outright racist) assessment of Aboriginal society, the federal government came under increasing pressure to legislate for Aboriginal land rights. In 1976 it eventually passed the Aboriginal Land Rights (Northern Territory) Act, which is often referred to as the Land Rights Act.

Aboriginal Land Rights (NT) Act

The Aboriginal Land Rights (NT) Act of 1976, which operates in the Northern Territory, remains Australia's most powerful and comprehensive land rights legislation. Promises were made to legislate for national land rights, but these were abandoned after opposition from mining companies and state governments. The act established three Aboriginal Land Councils, who are empowered to claim land on behalf of traditional Aboriginal owners.

However, under the act the only land claimable is unalienated Northern Territory land outside town boundaries – land that no-one else owns or leases, usually semi-desert or desert. Thus, when the traditional Anangu owners of Uluru (Ayers Rock) claimed traditional ownership of Uluru and Kata Tjuta (the Olgas), their claim was disallowed because the land was within a national park and thus alienated. It was only by amending two acts of parliament that Uluru-Kata Tjuta National Park was handed back to traditional Anangu owners on the condition that it was immediately leased back to the Australian Nature Conservation Agency (formerly the Australian National Parks & Wildlife Service).

At present almost half of the Northern Territory has either been claimed, or is being claimed, by its traditional Aboriginal owners. The claim process is extremely tedious and can take many years to complete, largely because almost all claims have been opposed by the Territory government. A great many elderly claimants die before the matter is resolved. Claimants are required to prove that under Aboriginal law they are responsible for the sacred sites on the land being claimed.

Once a claim is successful, Aboriginal people have the right to negotiate with mining companies and ultimately accept or reject exploration and mining proposals. This right is strongly opposed by the mining lobby, despite the fact that traditional Aboriginal owners in the Northern Territory only reject about a third of these proposals outright.

Mabo & the Native Title Act

It was only very recently that the non-Aboriginal community, including the federal government, came to grips with the fact that a meaningful conciliation between White Australia and its indigenous population was vital to the psychological well-being of all Australians.

In May 1982, five Torres Strait Islanders led by Eddie Mabo began an action for a declaration of native title over the Queensland Murray Islands. They argued that the legal principle of *terra nullius* had wrongfully usurped their title to land, as for thousands of years Murray Islanders had enjoyed a relationship with the land that included a notion of ownership. In June 1992 the High Court of Australia rejected *terra nullius* and the myth that Australia had been unoccupied. In doing this, it recognised that a principle of native title existed before the arrival of the British.

The High Court's judgment became known as the Mabo decision, one of the most controversial decisions ever handed down by an Australian court. It was ambiguous, as it didn't outline the extent to which native title existed in mainland Australia. It received a hostile reaction from the mining and other industry groups, but was hailed by Aboriginal people and Prime Minister Paul Keating as an opportunity to create a basis of reconciliation between Aboriginal and non-Aboriginal Australians.

To define the principle of native title, the federal parliament passed the Native Title Act in December 1993. Contrary to the cries of protest from the mining industry, the act gives Australian Aboriginal people very few new rights. It limits the application of native title to land which no-one else owns or leases, and to land with which Aboriginal people have continued to have a physical association. The act states that existing ownership or leases extinguish native title, although native title may be revived after mining leases have expired. If land is successfully claimed by Aboriginal people under the act, they will have no veto over developments including mining. Despite (or because of) its complexity, it will no doubt take a number of years and court cases before the implications of the Native Title Act are fully understood.

EDUCATION

Schooling is compulsory in the Territory between the ages of six and 15. There are about 37,000 pupils enrolled in around 170 primary, secondary, area and Aboriginal community schools. In some areas, Aboriginal pupils are taught in both English and their tribal language. The larger towns also have residential colleges for Aboriginal students.

The Northern Territory University in Darwin is the largest provider of tertiary education in the Territory. The University's Institute of Technical & Further Education provides a wide range of trade and technical courses.

ARTS

White Australian Art

In the 1880s a group of young artists developed the first distinctively Australian style of watercolour painting. Working from a permanent bush camp in Melbourne's (then) outer suburb of Box Hill, the painters captured the unique qualities of Australian life and the bush. The work of this group is generally referred to as the Heidelberg School, although the majority of the work was done at Box Hill. In Sydney a contemporary movement worked at Sirius Cove on Sydney Harbour. Both groups were influenced by the French plein-air painters, whose practice of working outdoors to capture the effects of natural light led

directly to Impressionism. The main artists were Tom Roberts, Arthur Streeton, Frederick McCubbin, Louis Abrahams, Charles Conder, Julian Ashton and, later, Walter Withers.

In the 1940s another revolution took place at Heide, the home of John and Sunday Reed in suburban Melbourne. Under their patronage a new generation of young artists redefined the direction of Australian art. Included in this group are some of Australia's most famous contemporary artists, including Sir Sidney Nolan and Arthur Boyd.

More recently the work of painters such as Fred Williams, John Olsen and Brett Whiteley has also made an impression on the international art world. Whiteley, probably Australia's most well-known modern artist, died in 1992.

Literature

Aboriginal Song & Narrative Aboriginal oral traditions are loosely and misleadingly described as 'myths and legends'. Their single uniting factor is the Dreamtime, when the totemic ancestors formed the landscape, fashioned the laws and created the people who would inherit the land. Translated and printed in English, these renderings of the Dreamtime often lose much of their intended impact. Gone are the sounds of sticks, dijeridu and the rhythm of the dancers which accompany each poetic line; the words fail to fuse past and present, and the spirits and forces to which the lines refer lose much of their animation.

At the turn of the century, Catherine Langloh Parker was collecting Aboriginal legends and using her outback experience to interpret them sincerely but synthetically. She compiled *Australian Legendary Tales: Folklore of the Noongah-burrahs* (1902).

Professor Ted Strehlow was one of the first methodical translators, and his *Aranda Traditions* (1947) and *Songs of Central Australia* (1971) are important works. Equally important is the combined effort of Catherine & Ronald Berndt. There are 188 songs in the collection *Djanggawul* (1952), 129 sacred and 47 secular songs in the collection *Kunapipi* (1951), and *The Land of the Rainbow Snake* (1979) focuses on children's stories from western Arnhem Land.

More recently, many Dreamtime stories have appeared in translation, illustrated and published by Aboriginal artists. Some representative collections are *Joe Nangan's Dreaming: Aboriginal Legends of the North-West* (Joe Nangan & Hugh Edwards, 1976); *Milbi: Aboriginal Tales from Queensland's Endeavour River* (Tulo Gordon & J B Haviland, 1980); *Visions of Mowanjum: Aboriginal Writings from the Kimberley* (Kormilda Community College, Darwin; 1980); and *Gularabulu* (Paddy Roe & Stephen Muecke, 1983).

Modern Aboriginal Literature Modern Aboriginal writers have fused the English language with aspects of their traditional culture. The result is often carefully fashioned to expose the injustices they have been subjected to, especially as urban dwellers. The first Aboriginal writer to be published was David Unaipon (*Native Legends*) in 1929.

Aboriginal literature now includes drama, fiction and poetry. The poet Oodgeroo Noonuccal (Kath Walker), one of the most well known of modern Aboriginal writers, was the first Aboriginal woman to have work published (*We Are Going*, 1964). *Paperbark: A collection of Black Australian writings* (1990) presents a great cross-section of modern Aboriginal writers, including dramatist Jack Davis and novelist Mudrooroo Narogin (Colin Johnson). This book has an excellent bibliography of Black Australian writing.

There are a number of modern accounts of Aboriginal life in remote parts of Australia. *Raparapa Kularr Martuwarra: Stories from the Fitzroy River Drovers* (1988) is a Magabala Books production. This company, based in Broome, energetically promotes Aboriginal literature.

Autobiography and biography have become an important branch of Aboriginal literature – look for *Moon and Rainbow* (Dick Roughsey, 1971) and *My Country of the Pelican Dreaming* (Grant Ngabidj, 1981).

The Aboriginal in White Literature Aboriginal people have often been used as characters in White outback literature. Usually the treatment was patronising and somewhat short-sighted. There were exceptions, especially in the subject of interracial sexuality between White men and Aboriginal women.

Rosa Praed, in her short piece *My Australian Girlhood* (1902), drew heavily on her outback experience and her affectionate childhood relationship with Aboriginal people. Jeannie Gunn's *Little Black Princess* was published in 1904, but it was *We of the Never Never* (1908) which brought her renown. Her story of the life and trials on Elsey Station includes an unflattering, patronising depiction of the Aboriginal people on and around the station.

Catherine Martin, in 1923, wrote *The Incredible Journey*. It follows the trail of two Black women, Iliapo and Polde, in search of a little boy who had been kidnapped by a White man. The book describes in careful detail the harsh desert environment they traverse.

Katharine Susannah Prichard contributed a great deal to outback literature in the 1920s. A journey to Turee Station in the cattle country of the Ashburton and Fortescue rivers, in 1926, inspired her lyric tribute to the Aborigine, *Coonardoo* (1929), which delved into the then almost taboo love between an Aboriginal woman and a White station boss. Later, Mary Durack's *Keep Him My Country* (1955) explored the theme of a White station manager's love for an Aboriginal girl, Dalgerie.

Bush Ballads & Yarns The 'bush' was a great source of inspiration for many popular ballads and stories. These were particularly in vogue at the turn of the century but they have an enduring quality.

Adam Lindsay Gordon was the forerunner of this type of literature, having published

Waltzing Matilda

Written in 1895 by the 'bard of the bush', Banjo Patterson, *Waltzing Matilda* is widely regarded as Australia's unofficial national anthem. Most people know it as a catchy but meaningless ditty about a jolly swagman who stole a jumbuck (a sheep) and later drowned himself in a billabong rather than be arrested, but historians have suggested that Patterson actually wrote the tune as a political anthem. The Waltzing Matilda Centenary Festival, held in Winton in 1995, fuelled the controversy over the origins of the song.

The 1890s was a period of social and political upheaval in Queensland. Along with nationalistic calls for the states to amalgamate and form a federation, the decade was dominated by an economic crisis, mass unemployment and a series of shearers' strikes in outback Queensland which led to the formation of the Australian Labor Party, which represented workers' interests.

Patterson visited Winton in 1895, and during a picnic beside the Combo Waterhole he heard stories about the violent 1894 shearers strike on Dagworth Station. During the strike, rebel shearers had burned down seven woolsheds, leading the police to declare martial law and place a reward of £1000 on the head of their leader, Samuel Hofmeister. Rather than face arrest, Hofmeister drowned himself in a billabong.

While there is no direct proof that Patterson was writing allegorically about the shearers' strikes, the song's undeniable anti-authoritarianism and the fact that it was adopted as an anthem by the rebel shearers weigh in heavily in support of the theory. ■

Bush Ballads and Galloping Rhymes in 1870. This collection of ballads included his popular *The Sick Stockrider.*

The two most famous exponents of the ballad style were A B 'Banjo' Paterson and Henry Lawson. Paterson grew up in the bush in the second half of the last century and went on to become one of Australia's most important bush poets. His pseudonym 'The Banjo' was the name of a horse on his family's station. His horse ballads were regarded as some of his best, but he was familiar with all aspects of station life and wrote with great optimism. *Clancy of the Overflow* and *The Man From Snowy River* are both well known, but The Banjo is probably most remembered as the author of Australia's alternative national anthem, *Waltzing Matilda*, in which he celebrates an unnamed swagman, one of the anonymous wanderers of the bush.

Henry Lawson was a contemporary of Paterson, but was much more of a social commentator and political thinker and less of a humorist. Although he wrote a good many poems about the bush – pieces such as *Andy's Gone with Cattle* and *The Roaring Days* are among his best – his greatest legacy are his short stories of life in the bush, which seem remarkably simple yet manage to capture the atmosphere perfectly. Good examples are *A Day on a Selection* (a selection was a tract of crown land for which annual fees were paid) and *The Drover's Wife;* the latter epitomises one of Lawson's 'battlers' who dreams of better things as an escape from the ennui of her isolated circumstances.

There were many other balladists. George Essex Evans penned a lovely tribute to Queensland's women pioneers, *The Women of the West;* Will Ogilvie wrote of the great cattle drives; and Barcroft Boake's *Where the Dead Men Lie* celebrates the people who opened up the country where 'heat-waves dance forever'.

Standing alone among these writers is Barbara Baynton. She is uncompromising in her depiction of the outback as a cruel, brutal environment, and the romantic imagery of the bush is absent in the ferocious depiction of the lot of *Squeaker's Mate* in *Bush Studies* (1902). Squeaker's mate, crippled whilst clearing her selection and powerless to do anything, has to endure the indignity of her husband flaunting his new mistress.

Outback Novelists The author's name if not the content would have encouraged many overseas visitors to read D H Lawrence's *Kangaroo* (1923), which, in places, presents his frightened images of the bush.

Later, Nevil Shute's *A Town Like Alice* (1950) would have been the first outback-based novel that many people read. Other Shute titles with outback themes were *In the Wet* (1953) and *Beyond the Black Stump* (1956).

Perhaps the best local depictor of the outback was the aforementioned Katharine Susannah Prichard. She produced a string of novels with outback themes into which she wove her political thoughts. *Black Opal* (1921) was the study of the fictional opal mining community of Fallen Star Ridge; *Working Bullocks* (1926) examined the political nature of work in the karri forests of Western Australia; and *Moon of Desire* (1941) follows its characters in search of a fabulous pearl from Broome to Singapore. Her controversial trilogy of the Western Australian goldfields was published separately as *The Roaring Nineties* (1946), *Golden Miles* (1948) and *Winged Seeds* (1950).

Xavier Herbert's *Capricornia* (1938) stands as one of the great epics of outback Australia, with its sweeping descriptions of the northern country. His second epic, *Poor Fellow My Country* (1975), is a documentary of the fortunes of a northern station owner. Herbert uses the characters to voice his bitter regret at the failure of reconciliation between the White despoilers of the land and its indigenous people.

One of the great non-fiction pieces is Mary Durack's family chronicle, *Kings in Grass Castles* (1959), which relates the White settlement of the Kimberley ranges. Her sequel was *Sons in the Saddle* (1983).

Australia's Nobel prize-winner, Patrick White, used the outback as the backdrop for a number of his monumental works. The most prominent character in *Voss* (1957) is an explorer, perhaps loosely based on Ludwig Leichhardt; *The Tree of Man* (1955) has all the outback happenings of flood, fire and drought; and the journey of *The Aunt's Story* (1948) begins on an Australian sheep station.

Kenneth Cook's nightmarish novel set in outback New South Wales, *Wake in Fright* (1961), has been made into a film.

Contemporary Novelists Miles Franklin was one of Australia's early feminists and made a decision early in her life to become a writer rather than the traditional wife and mother. Her best-known book, *My Brilliant Career*, was also her first. It was written at the turn of the century when the author was only 20, and brought her both widespread fame and criticism. On her death she endowed an annual award for an Australian novel; today the Miles Franklin Award is the most prestigious in the country.

The works of Patrick White are arguably some of the best to come out of Australia in the last 30 years. He was a prolific writer who won the Miles Franklin Award twice, for *Voss* (1957) and *The Riders in the Chariot* (1961), and the Nobel Prize for *The Eye of the Storm* (1973).

Another contemporary writer of note is Peter Carey, who has won both the Miles Franklin Award for *Bliss* in 1981 and the Booker Prize for *Oscar and Lucinda* in 1988.

Thomas Keneally has won two Miles Franklin Awards and one Booker Prize, and is well-known for his novels, such as *The Chant of Jimmy Blacksmith* (1972), which deal with the suffering of oppressed peoples, in this case Aboriginal people. He also wrote *Schindler's Ark* (1982), upon which the Spielberg film *Schindler's List* was based.

Tim Winton, a young writer from Western Australia, is one of the most exciting writers in Australia today. His works include *Cloudstreet* (1992) and *The Riders* (1994), which was shortlisted for the Booker Prize. *Local Color – Travels in the Other Australia* (1994) is largely a photographic essay by Bill Bachman, but it also includes some fine descriptive prose by Tim Winton.

Thea Astley is far from a household name, yet she is one of the finest writers in the country, and three-times winner of the Miles Franklin Award. Her best books include *The*

Slow Natives (1965), *The Acolyte* (1972) and *It's Raining in Mango* (1987), the last of which is probably Astley's finest work and gives her a chance to express her outrage at the treatment of Aboriginal people.

Elizabeth Jolley is well known as a short-story writer and novelist with a keen eye for the eccentric. *Mr Scobie's Riddle* (1983), *My Father's Moon* (1989) and *Cabin Fever* (1990) are probably her best works.

Cinema

The Australian film industry began as early as 1896, a year after the Lumiere brothers opened the world's first cinema in Paris. Maurice Sestier, one of the Lumieres' photographers, came to Australia and made the first films in the streets of Sydney and at Flemington Race Course during the Melbourne Cup.

Cinema historians regard an Australian film, *Soldiers of the Cross*, as the world's first 'real' movie. It was originally screened at the Melbourne Town Hall in 1901, cost £600 to make and was shown throughout America in 1902.

The next significant Australian film, *The Story of the Kelly Gang*, was screened in 1907, and by 1911 the industry was flourishing. Low-budget films were being made in such quantities that they could be hired out or sold cheaply. Over 250 silent feature films were made before the 1930s when the talkies and Hollywood took over.

In the 1930s, film companies like Cinesound sprang up. Cinesound made 17 feature films between 1931 and 1940, many based on Australian history or literature. *Forty Thousand Horsemen*, directed by Cinesound's great film maker Charles Chauvel, was a highlight of this era of locally made and financed films which ended in 1959, the year of Chauvel's death. Early Australian actors who became famous both at home and overseas include Errol Flynn and Chips Rafferty (born John Goffage).

Before the introduction of government subsidies during 1969 and 1970, the Australian film industry found it difficult to compete with US and British interests. The New Wave era of the 1970s, a renaissance of Australian cinema, produced films like *Picnic at Hanging Rock*, *Sunday Too Far Away*, *Caddie* and *The Devil's Playground*, which appealed to large local and international audiences.

Since the '70s, Australian actors and directors such as Mel Gibson, Nicole Kidman, Judy Davis, Greta Scacchi, Paul Hogan, Bruce Beresford, Peter Weir, Gillian Armstrong and Fred Schepisi have gained international recognition. Films such as *Gallipoli*, *The Year of Living Dangerously*, *Mad Max*, *Malcolm*, *Crocodile Dundee I* and *II*, *Proof*, *Holidays on the River Yarra*, *The Year My Voice Broke*, *Strictly Ballroom* and most recently *Priscilla – Queen of the Desert*, *Muriel's Wedding* and *Babe* have entertained and impressed audiences worldwide.

Music

Popular Music Australia's participation in the flurry of popular music since the 1950s has been a frustrating mix of good, indifferent, lousy, parochial and excellent. However, even the offerings of the most popular acts have done nothing to remove the cultural cringe: the highest praise remains 'it's good enough to have come from the UK/USA'. And it's true that little of the popular music created here has been noticeably different from that coming from overseas.

Which is why the recent success of Aboriginal music, and its merging with rock, is so refreshing. This music really is different. The most obvious name that springs to mind is Yothu Yindi. Their song about the dishonoured White-man's agreement, *Treaty*, perhaps did more than anything else to popularise Aboriginal land-rights claims. The band's lead singer, Mandawuy Yunupingu, was named Australian of the Year in 1993.

Other Aboriginal names include Coloured Stone, Kev Carmody, Archie Roach, Scrap Metal, the Sunrise Band, Christine Anu (from the Torres Strait Islands), and the bands that started it all but no longer exist, No Fixed Address and Warumpi Band.

White country music owes much to Irish heritage and American country influences, often with a liberal sprinkling of dry outback humour. Names to watch out for include Slim Dusty, Ted Egan, John Williamson, Chad Morgan, Lee Kernaghan, Neil Murray, Gondwanaland and Smokey Dawson.

Having written off White popular music, the live-music circuit of Australia really is something to crow about, although the Territory is definitely a backwater when it comes to touring bands.

Folk Music Australian folk music is a derived from a mixture of English, Irish and Scottish roots. Bush bands, playing fast-paced and high-spirited folk music for dancing, can be anything from performers trotting out standards such as *Click Go The Shears* to serious musicians who happen to like a rollicking time.

Fiddles, banjos and tin whistles feature prominently, plus there's the indigenous 'lagerphone', a percussion instrument made from a great many beer-bottle caps nailed to a stick, which is then shaken or banged on the ground. If you have a chance to go to a bush dance or folk festival, don't pass it up.

Architecture

Australia's first European settlers arrived in the country with memories of Georgian grandeur, but the lack of materials and tools meant that most of the early houses were almost caricatures of the real thing. One of the first concessions to the climate, and one which was to become a feature of Australian houses, was the addition of a wide verandah which kept the inner rooms of the house dark and cool.

By the turn of the century, at a time when the separate colonies were combining to form a new nation, a simpler, more 'Australian' architectural style evolved, and this came to be known as Federation style. Built between about 1890 and 1920, Federation houses typically feature red-brick walls, and an orange-tiled roof decorated with terracotta ridging and chimney pots. Also a feature was the rising sun motif on the gable ends, symbolic of the dawn of a new age for Australia.

The Californian bungalow, a solid house style which developed in colonial British India, became the rage in the 1920s and '30s, and its simple and honest style fitted in well with the emerging Australian tendency towards a casual lifestyle.

The variety of climates led to some interesting regional variations. In the 1930s houses were designed specifically for the tropical climate by the Northern Territory Principal Architect, Beni Carr Glynn Burnett. The elevated buildings featured louvres and casement windows, so the ventilation could be adjusted according to the weather conditions at the time. Internal walls were only three-quarter hight and also featured lower louvres to allow for cross-ventilation. The eaves were also left open to aid ventilation. This style has developed into the modern 'troppo' (tropical) style of architecture, which is not only practical, but also takes into account that cyclones are a major feature of the weather up here, a fact that was ignored in the early days and resulted in 95% of Darwin's houses being blown away by Tracy in 1974.

The immigration boom which followed WW II led to today's urban sprawl – cities and towns expanded rapidly, and the 'brick veneer' became the dominant housing medium, and remains so today. On the fringe of any Australian city you'll find acres of new, low cost, brick-veneer suburbs – as far as the eye can see it's a bleak expanse of terracotta roofs and bricks in various shades.

Modern Australian architecture struggles to maintain a distinctive style, with overseas trends dominating large projects. There are some notable exceptions, of course, and in the Territory these are found in Kakadu and Uluru-Kata Tjuta national parks where the federal government has spent large amounts on excellent visitor/cultural centres. Also of interest is the Strehlow Research Centre in Alice Springs, which features a huge rammed-earth wall, at the time of its construction (1990) the largest in the southern hemisphere.

Aboriginal Art

Aboriginal art has undergone a major revival in the last decade or so, with artists throughout the country finding both a means to express and preserve ancient Dreaming values, and a way to share this rich cultural heritage with the wider community.

While the so-called dot paintings of the central deserts are the most readily identifiable and probably most popular form of contemporary Aboriginal art, there's a huge range of material being produced – bark paintings from Arnhem Land, wood carving and silk-screen printing from the Tiwi Islands north of Darwin, batik printing and wood carving from Central Australia and more.

The initial forms of artistic expression were rock carvings, body painting and ground designs, and the earliest engraved designs known to exist date back at least 30,000 years. Art became an integral part of Aboriginal life, a connection between past and present, between the supernatural and the earthly, between people and the land.

All early art was a reflection of the various peoples' ancestral Dreaming – the 'creation' when the earth's physical features were formed by the struggles between powerful supernatural ancestors, such as the Rainbow Serpent, the Lightning Men and the Wandjina. Not only was the physical layout mapped, but codes of behaviour were also laid down, and although these laws have been diluted and adapted in the last 200 years, they still provide the basis for today's Aboriginal people. Ceremonies, rituals and sacred paintings are all based on the Dreaming.

A Dreaming may take a number of different forms – it can be a person, an animal or a physical feature, while others are more general, relating to a region, a group of people, or natural forces such as floods and wind. Thus Australia is covered by a wide network of Dreamings, and any one person may have connections with several.

Western Desert Paintings The current renaissance in Aboriginal painting began in the early 1970s at Papunya ('honey ant place'), at the time a small, depressed community 240 km north-west of Alice Springs, which had grown out of the government's 'assimilation' policy. Here the local children were given the task of painting a traditional-style mural on the school wall. The local elders took interest in the project, and although the public display of traditional images gave rise to much debate amongst the elders, they eventually participated and in fact completed the Honey Ant Dreaming mural. This was the first time that images which were originally confined to rock and body art came to be reproduced in a different environment.

Other murals followed this first one, and before long the desire to paint spread through the community. In the early stages paintings were produced on small boards on the ground or the artist's knee, but this soon gave way to painting on canvas with modern acrylic paints. Canvas was an ideal medium as it could be easily rolled and transported, yet large paintings were possible.

With the growing importance of art both as an economic and a cultural activity, an association was formed to help the artists sell their work. The Papunya Tula company in Alice Springs is still one of the few Aboriginal owned and run galleries in central Australia.

Painting in central Australia has flourished to such a degree that these days it is an important educational source for young kids, as they can learn aspects of religious and ceremonial knowledge. This is especially true now that women are so much a part of the painting movement.

The trademark dot painting style is partly an evolution from 'ground paintings' which formed the centrepiece of traditional dances and songs. These were made from pulped plant material, and the designs were made on the ground using dots of this mush. Dots were also used to outline objects in rock paintings, and to highlight geographical features or vegetation, and over time the use of them has spread to cover the entire canvas.

While the paintings may look random and abstract, they have great significance to the artist and usually depict a Dreaming journey, and so can be seen almost as aerial landscape maps. One feature which appears regularly is the tracks of birds, animals and humans, and these often identify the ancestor. Various items, including people, are often depicted by the imprint they leave in the sand – a simple arc depicts a person, as this is the print left by someone sitting; a coolamon (wooden carrying dish) is shown as an oval shape, a digging-stick by a single line, a camp fire by a circle. The clue to whether a person is male or female is by the objects associated with them – digging sticks and coolamons are always used by women, spears and boomerangs by men. Concentric circles are usually used to depict Dreaming sites, or places where ancestors paused in their journeys.

While these symbols are widely used and are readily identifiable, their context within each individual painting is known only by the artist, or people associated with him or her – either by group or by the Dreaming – and different groups would apply different interpretations to each painting. In this way sacred stories can be publicly portrayed, as the deeper meaning is not evident to any but those with a close association with the image.

The colours used in dot paintings from central Australia may seem overly vivid, and inappropriate to the land or story depicted. However, they are not meant to be true renderings of the landscape, but more as variations in that landscape. The reds, blues and purples which often dominate the outback scenery and became so much a part of Albert Namatjira's painting (see James Ranges chapter), feature prominently.

The Utopia Awely Batik Artists The women of Utopia, 260 km north-east of Alice Springs, have become famous in recent years for their production of batik material. In the mid 1970s, the Anmatyerre and Alyawarre people started to reoccupy their traditional lands around Utopia cattle station, and this was given a formal basis in 1979 when they were granted title to the station. A number of scattered outstations, rather than a central settlement, were set up, and around this time the women were introduced to batik as part of a self-help program.

The artform flourished and Utopia Women's Batik Group was formed in 1978. This group became incorporated and is now called Utopia Awely Batik Utopia Women's Centre Aboriginal Corporation trading as Utopia Silks. The brightly coloured silk batiks are based on the traditional women's body painting designs called awely, and on images of the flora and fauna of bush tucker and bush medicine.

In the late 1980s techniques using acrylic paints on canvas were introduced. Utopian art is now receiving international acclaim.

Other Central Australian Art The making of wooden sculptures for sale dates back to at least early this century; in 1903 a group of Diyari people living on Killalpaninna Lutheran Mission near Lake Eyre in South Australia were encouraged by the pastor to produce sculptures in order to raise funds for the mission.

The momentum for producing crafts for sale was accelerated with the opening up and settlement of the country by Europeans. Demand was slow to increase, but the steady growth of the tourist trade since WW II, and the tourist boom in the 1980s, has seen demand, and production, increase dramatically.

The most widespread crafts seen for sale these days are the wooden carvings with designs scorched into them using hot fencing wire. These range from small figures, such as possums, up to quite large snakes and lizards, although none of them have any Dreaming significance. One of the main outlets for these is the Maruku Arts & Crafts centre at the Uluru National Park rangers' station, where it's possible to see the crafts being made. Although much of the artwork is usually done by women, men are also involved at the Maruku centre. The Mt Ebenezer Roadhouse, on the Lasseter Highway (the main route to Uluru), is another Aboriginal-owned enterprise – and one of the cheapest places for buying sculpted figures.

The Ernabella Presbyterian Mission in northern South Australia was another place where craftwork was encouraged. A 1950 mission report stated that: 'A mission station must have an industry to provide work for and help finance the cost of caring for the natives'. As the mission had been founded on a sheep station, wool crafts were the obvious way to go, and to that end the techniques of spinning, dyeing and weaving of wool were introduced. The Pitjantjatjara ('pigeon-jara') women made woollen articles such as rugs, belts, traditional carry-bags and scarves, using designs incorporating aspects of women's law (*yawilyu*).

With the introduction of batik fabric dyeing in the 1970s, weaving at Ernabella virtually ceased.

Arnhem Land Art Arnhem Land, in the tropical Top End, is possibly the area with the richest artistic heritage. It is thought that rock paintings were being made as much as 40,000 years ago, and some of the rock-art galleries in the huge sandstone Arnhem Land plateau are at least 18,000 years old.

Although Arnhem Land is famous for its rock art, the tradition of bark painting is equally strong. In fact in recent years this portable art form has become very popular, probably because the boom in tourism has led to a high demand for souvenirs. As is the case in many communities throughout the country, producing art works for sale has become a possible form of employment in Arnhem Land, in places where there are generally few opportunities.

The art of Arnhem Land is vastly different to that of the central deserts. Here Dreaming stories are depicted far more literally, with easily recognisable (though often stylised) images of ancestors, animals, and even Macassans – early Indonesian mariners who regularly visited the north coast long before the Europeans arrived on the scene.

Rock Art The Arnhem Land rock-art sites range from hand prints to paintings of animals, people, mythological beings and European ships, constituting one of the world's most important and fascinating rock-art collections. They provide a record of changing environments and Aboriginal lifestyles over the millennia.

In some places they are concentrated in large galleries, with paintings from different eras sometimes superimposed on one another. Some sites are kept secret – not only to protect them from damage, but also because they are private or sacred to the Aboriginal people. Some are even believed to be the residences of dangerous beings, who must not be approached by the ignorant. Two of the finest sites, however, have been opened up to visitors with access roads, walkways and explanatory signs. These are Ubirr and Nourlangie Rock. (Park rangers conduct free art-site tours once or twice a day from May to October.)

From 20,000 or more years ago until 8000 or 10,000 years ago, Arnhem Land was probably a lot drier than today, with the coastline about 300 km further north, as much of the world's water was frozen in the larger polar ice caps. Rock paintings of this era show six main styles succeeding each other through time. Following the earliest hand or grass prints came a 'naturalistic' style, with large outline drawings of people or animals filled in with colour. Stick-like humans are shown hunting in this period. Some of the animals depicted, such as the thylacine (Tasmanian tiger) and the long-beaked echidna, have long been extinct in mainland Australia. Other paintings are thought to show large beasts wiped out worldwide millennia ago.

After the naturalistic style came the 'dynamic', in which motion is often cleverly depicted (a dotted line, for example, may show a spear's path through the air). Most humans shown are males with head-dresses, necklaces, armlets and so on, carrying weapons or dilly bags. Women are usually naked. In this era the first mythological beings appear – with human bodies and animal heads.

The fourth style mainly shows simple, human silhouettes. They were followed by more 'stick figures' usually carrying fighting picks and wearing head adornments and skirts, and finally by the curious 'yam figures' in which people and animals are drawn in the shape of yams (or yams in the shape of people/animals!), with trailing roots and hairs. Yams must have been an important food source at this time, when the climate was probably damp.

With the rising of the oceans about 8000 years ago much of what is now Kakadu National Park was covered with salt marshes. Many fish are depicted in the art of this period, and the so-called 'X-ray' style, showing the bones and internal organs, makes its appearance.

By about 1000 years ago, many of the salt marshes had turned into freshwater swamps and billabongs. The birds and plants which provided new food sources in this landscape appear in the art.

From around 400 years ago, Aboriginal artists also depicted the human newcomers to the region – Macassan fisherpeople from the south Celebes in present-day Indonesia, and later Europeans – and the things they brought, or their transport such as ships or horses.

Bark Paintings While the bark painting tradition is a more recent art form than the rock art, it is still an important part of the cultural heritage of Arnhem Land Aboriginal people. It's difficult to establish when bark was first used, partly because it is perishable and old pieces simply don't exist. European visitors in the early 19th century noted the practice of painting the inside walls of bark shelters.

The bark used is from the stringybark tree (*Eucalyptus tetradonta*), and it is taken off in the Wet season when it is moist and supple. The rough outer layers are removed and the bark is then dried by placing it over a fire and then under weights on the ground to

Above: Ewaninga rock
engravings, south of Alice
Springs; courtesy of the NT
Tourist Commission.

Below: **Pampardu
Jukurrpa** by Clarise
Poulson;
acrylic on linen;
150 x 90cm; 1993;
Warlukurlangu Artists
Association,
Yuendumu, NT;
courtesy of DESART.

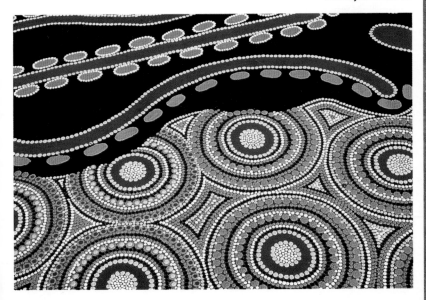

Left: **Bush Tucker and Flowers**, *silk scarf by Rosemary Petyarre; courtesy of Utopia Awely Batik, Utopia Women's Centre Aboriginal Corporation.*

Below: Hand-crafted decorative central Australian carvings made from river red gum root; Maruku Arts & Crafts, Uluru (Ayers Rock), NT; courtesy of DESART.

Kumoken (Freshwater Crocodile) with Mimi Spirits by Djawida, b.c. 1935, Yulkman clan; Kunwinjku language, Kurrudjmuh, western Arnhem Land; earth pigments on bark; 151 x 71cm; 1990; purchased 1990; National Gallery of Victoria.

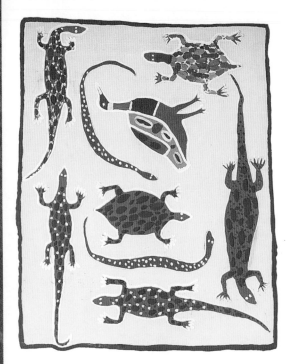

Left: **Some Animals Have Secret Songs** by Amy Johnson Jirwulurr, born about 1953; language group Wagilak; domicile Ngukurr, NT; synthetic polymer paint on cotton duck; 90 x 106cm; 1988; represented by Alcaston House Gallery, Melbourne.

Below: Rock paintings, Nourlangie Rock, Kakadu National Park; courtesy of the NT Tourist Commission.

keep it flat. Drying is complete within about a fortnight, and the bark is then ready for use. Most bark paintings made today have a pair of sticks across the top and bottom of the sheet to keep it flat.

The pigments used in bark paintings are mainly red and yellow (ochres), white (kaolin) and black (charcoal). Because these were the only colours available, their source was an important place. The colour could only be gathered by the traditional owners, and it was then traded with others. Even today it is these natural pigments which are still used, and they give the paintings that superb soft earthy finish. Binding agents were added to the pigments, and traditionally these were items such as birds' egg yolks, wax and plant resins. Recently these have been replaced with synthetic agents such as wood glue. Similarly, the brushes used in the past were obtained from bush materials at hand – twigs, leaf fibres, feathers, human hair and the like – but these, too, have largely been done away with in favour of modern brushes.

One of the main features of Arnhem Land bark paintings is the use of cross-hatching designs. These designs identify the particular clans, and are based on body paintings of the past. The paintings can also be broadly categorised by their regional styles. In the west the tendency is towards naturalistic images and plain backgrounds, while to the east the use of geometric designs is more common.

The art reflects the deeds of ancestral beings and events which occurred during the creation – Dreaming themes. Once again these vary by region. In eastern Arnhem Land the prominent ancestral beings are the Djangkawu, who travelled the land with elaborate dilly bags and digging sticks, which they used to create waterholes each time they stopped; and the Wagilag Sisters, who are associated with snakes and waterholes.

In western Arnhem Land the Rainbow Serpent, Yingarna, is the significant being (according to some clans), but one of her offspring, Ngalyod, and Nawura are also important. The *mimi* spirits are another feature of western Arnhem Land art, both on bark and rock. These mischievous spirits are attributed with having taught the Aboriginal people of the region many things, including hunting, food gathering and painting skills.

Fibre Art Articles made from fibres are a major art form among the women. While the string and pandanus-fibre dilly bags (carry-bags), skirts, mats and nets all have utilitarian purposes, they are still important and many can have ritual uses.

Hollow-Log Coffins Hollowed-out logs were often used for reburial ceremonies in Arnhem Land, and these were highly decorated, often with many of the themes mentioned above. Known as *dupun* in eastern Arnhem Land and *lorrkon* in western Arnhem Land, they too are a major form of artistic expression.

In 1988, a group of Arnhem Land artists made a memorial as their contribution to the movement highlighting injustices against Aboriginals – this was, of course, the year when non-Aboriginal Australians were celebrating 200 years of European settlement. The artists painted 200 log coffins – one for each year of settlement – with traditional clan and Dreaming designs, and these now form a permanent display in the National Gallery in Canberra.

Ngukurr Contemporary Painting Since the late 1980s the artists of Ngukurr ('nook-or'), near Roper Bar in south-eastern Arnhem Land, have been producing works using acrylic paints on canvas. Although ancestral beings still feature prominently, the works are generally much more 'modern' in nature, with free-flowing forms and little formal structure.

Tiwi Island Art Due to their isolation, the Aboriginal people of the Tiwi Islands (Bathurst and Melville islands off the coast of Darwin), have developed art forms – mainly sculpture – not found anywhere else, although there are some similarities with art of Arnhem Land.

The *pukumani* burial rites are one of the main rituals of Tiwi religious life, and it is for these ceremonies that many of the art works are created – bark baskets (*jimwalini*), spears and burial poles (*tutini*). These carved and painted ironwood poles, up to 2.5 metres long, are placed around the grave and represent features of that person's life.

In the last 50 years or so the Tiwi islanders have been producing sculptured animals and birds, many of these being creation ancestors. (The Darwin Museum of Arts & Sciences has an excellent display.) More recently, bark painting and silk-screen printing have become popular, and there are workshops on both islands where these items are produced.

SOCIETY & CONDUCT
Aboriginal Society

Australia's Aboriginal people were tribal, living in extended family groups or clans, with clan members descending from a common ancestral being. Tradition, rituals and laws linked the people of each clan to the land they occupied and each clan had various sites of spiritual significance on their land, places to which their spirits would return when they died. Clan members came together to perform rituals to honour their ancestral spirits and the creators of the Dreaming. These traditional beliefs were the basis of the Aboriginal peoples' ties to the land they live on.

It is the responsibility of the clan, or particular members of it, to correctly maintain and protect the sites so that the ancestral beings are not offended and continue to protect the clan. Traditional punishments for those who neglect these responsibilities can still be severe, as their actions can easily affect the well-being of the whole clan – food and water shortages, natural disasters or mysterious illnesses can all be attributed to disgruntled or offended ancestral beings.

Many Aboriginal communities were semi-nomadic, others sedentary, one of the deciding factors being the availability of food. Where food and water were readily available, the people tended to remain in a limited area. When they did wander, however, it was to visit sacred places to carry out rituals, or to take advantage of seasonal foods available elsewhere. They did not, as is still often believed, roam aimlessly and desperately in the search for food and water.

The traditional role of the men was that of hunter, tool-maker and custodian of male law; the women reared the children, and gathered and prepared food. There was also female law and ritual for which the women would be responsible. Ultimately, the shared effort of men and women ensured the continuation of their social system.

Wisdom and skills obtained over millennia enabled Aboriginal people to use their environment to the maximum. An intimate knowledge of the behaviour of animals and the correct time to harvest the many plants they utilised ensured that food shortages were rare. Like other hunter-gatherer peoples of the world, Aboriginal people were true ecologists.

Although Aboriginal people in northern Australia had been in regular contact with the fishing and farming peoples of Indonesia for at least 1000 years, the cultivation of crops and the domestication of livestock held no appeal. The only major modification of the landscape practised by Aboriginal people was the selective burning of undergrowth in forests and dead grass on the plains. This encouraged new growth, which in turn attracted game animals to the area. It also prevented the build-up of combustible material in the forests, making hunting easier and reducing the possibility of major bush fires. Dingoes were domesticated to assist in the hunt and to guard the camp from intruders.

Similar technology – for example the boomerang and spear – was used throughout the continent, but techniques were adapted to the environment and the species being hunted. In the wetlands of northern Australia, fish traps hundreds of metres long made of bamboo and cord were built to catch fish at the end of the wet season. In the area now known as Victoria, permanent stone weirs many km long were used to trap migrating eels, while in the tablelands of Queensland finely woven nets were used to snare herds of wallabies and kangaroos.

Contrary to the common image, some tribes did build permanent dwellings, varying widely depending on climate, the materials available and likely length of use. In western Victoria the local Aboriginal people built permanent stone dwellings; in the deserts semicircular shelters were made with arched branches covered with native grasses or leaves; and in Tasmania large conical thatch shelters which could house up to 30 people were constructed. Such dwellings were used mainly for sleeping.

The early Australian Aboriginal people were also traders. Trade routes crisscrossed the country, dispersing goods and a variety of produced items along their way. Many of the items traded, such as certain types of stone or shell, were rare and had great ritual significance. Boomerangs and ochre were other important trade items. Along the trading networks which developed, large numbers of people would often meet for 'exchange ceremonies', where not only goods but also songs and dances were passed on.

Aboriginal Beliefs & Ceremonies
Early European settlers and explorers usually dismissed the entire Aboriginal population as 'savages' and 'barbarians', and it was some time before the Aboriginal peoples' deep, spiritual bond with the land, and their relationship to it, was understood by White Australians.

The perceived simplicity of the Aboriginal peoples' technology contrasts with the sophistication of their cultural life. Religion, history, law and art are integrated in complex ceremonies which depict the activities of their ancestral beings, and prescribe codes of behaviour and responsibilities for looking after the land and all living things. The link between the Aboriginal people and the ancestral beings are totems, each person having their own totem, or Dreaming. These totems take many forms, such as caterpillars, snakes, fish and magpies. Songs explain how the landscape contains these powerful creator ancestors who can exert either a benign or a malevolent influence. They tell of the best places and times to hunt, and where to find water in drought years. They can also specify kinship relations and correct marriage partners.

Ceremonies are still performed in many parts of Australia; many of the sacred sites are believed to be dangerous and entry is prohibited under traditional Aboriginal law. These restrictions may seem merely the result of superstition, but in many cases they have a pragmatic origin. For instance, fishing from a certain reef was traditionally prohibited. This restriction was scoffed at by local Europeans until it was discovered that fish from this area had a high incidence of ciguatera, which renders fish poisonous if eaten by humans.

While many Aboriginal people still live in rural areas, those living an urban life remain distinctively Aboriginal – some still speak their indigenous language (or a mix) on a daily basis, and they mix largely with other Aboriginal people. Much of their knowledge of the environment, bush medicine and food ('bush tucker') has been retained, and many traditional rites and ceremonies are being revived.

See the later Religion section for more on Aboriginal beliefs, ceremonies and sacred sites.

Outback Life
Life on remote station properties has been much improved by modern developments such as the Royal Flying Doctor Service, the School of the Air and the expanding national

---

Royal Flying Doctor Service
Established by the Reverend John Flynn with a single aircraft in 1928, the original Flying Doctor has grown into a national organisation, the Royal Flying Doctor Service (RFDS), which provides a comprehensive medical service to all outback residents. Where people once feared sickness and injury, even the most isolated communities are now assured of receiving expert medical assistance within two or three hours instead of weeks.

Almost as important is the social function of the RFDS's HF radio network, which allows anyone without a telephone to send and receive telegrams and to take part in special broadcasts known as galah sessions. Like party lines, these open periods of radio time allow distant neighbours to keep in touch with each other and with events around them in a way the telephone can never rival. ■

telephone network, but many non-Aboriginal communities in the outback are still affected to a greater or lesser degree by the tyranny of distance. Not many city people can imagine living perhaps 500 km from the nearest doctor and supermarket, or having their children sitting down in front of a high-frequency (HF) radio transceiver to go to school.

School of the Air Until recent times, outback children living away from towns either attended boarding school or obtained their education through written correspondence lessons. In 1944, Adelaide Meithke recognised that HF radio transceivers could be used to improve the children's education as well as their social life by giving them direct contact both with trained teachers and their fellow students. Her idea for a classroom of the airwaves, using the RFDS radio facilities, became a reality when Australia's first School of the Air opened in Alice Springs in 1951.

Today there are 14 Schools of the Air (three in the Territory) and most use the RFDS network as their classroom. The major education method is still correspondence lessons – materials and equipment are sent to students, who return set written and audio work by mail – which are supplemented by radio classes lasting 20 to 30 minutes. Students speak to their teachers daily and each has a 10-minute personal session with their teacher once a week. Although face-to-face contact is limited, students and teachers do meet at least once a year on special get-togethers, and teachers visit each of their students on patrols by 4WD vehicle and light aircraft.

With 14 teachers and eight support staff, the Alice Springs School of the Air teaches about 140 children in nine grades, from pre-school to year seven, over a broadcast area of 1.3 million sq km, the furthest student living 1000 km away. In 1992 the school broke new ground once again when it beamed 'live' lessons by satellite to its students.

Shopping Most stations are far from even the most basic facilities such as post offices, libraries and shops, and often neighbours can be 50 km or more apart. Most isolated communities receive mail and newspapers either weekly or fortnightly when the mail plane or mail truck does its rounds. Perishable groceries and minor freight can be sent out with the mail, but a major shopping expedition can mean a round trip of 1000 km or more to the nearest decent shops.

It's not all Bad The outback presents its share of difficulties. Most of these can be attributed to isolation, but as the famous Australian poet A B (Banjo) Paterson wrote in *Clancy of the Overflow*, bush people do 'have pleasures that the townsfolk never know'. One of these is the ready accessibility of wide-open spaces untainted by air pollution, traffic noise and crowds. Another is the sense of self-reliance and independence that's still strong in the outback.

Being forced to make their own entertainment encourages people living hundreds of km apart to get together (usually on the RFDS radio network, although increasingly by telephone) to organise social functions such as horse-race meetings, camp drafts (rodeos) and gymkhanas. This strong sense of community spirit, even when the 'community' may be spread over a vast area, means that even neighbours who don't get on will more than likely assist each other in a crisis. It's these aspects of outback life that help to make the hardships worthwhile.

Dos & Don'ts

Water Most pastoralists are happy for travellers to make use of their water supplies, but they do ask that they be treated with respect. This means washing clothes, dishes and sweaty bodies in a bucket or basin, not in the water supply itself. Always remember that animals and people may have to drink it when you've finished.

Camping right beside watering points is also to be avoided. In the outback the stock is often half wild and will hang back if you're parked or have your tent pitched right where they normally drink. They'll eventually overcome their fear through necessity, which means you'll be covered in dust and develop grey hair as the thirst-crazed mob mills around your camp at midnight. If you must camp in the vicinity, keep at least 200 metres away and stay well off the pads that animals have worn as they come in to drink.

Much the same applies if you drive up to a bore or dam and find the stock having a drink. Stay well back until they've finished, then you can move in for your share. The thing to remember at all times is that this isolated pool or trough might be the only water in a radius of 30 km or more.

Gates The golden rule with any gate is to *leave it as you find it*. You must do this even if a sign by an open gate says to keep it closed – it may have been left open for any number of reasons, such as to let stock through to water. It's fairly common for animals to perish because tourists have closed gates that a pastoralist left open.

Floods Sometimes the outback receives a large part of its annual rainfall in a matter of days. When this happens, unsealed roads and tracks become extremely slippery and boggy. The correct thing to do in this event is either to get out before the rain soaks in or to stay put on high ground until the surface dries out. To do otherwise may see your vehicle gouging great ruts in the road surface, which of course won't endear you to the locals who must live with the mess you've made. Quite apart from that, you'll probably get well and truly stuck in some dreadful place far from anywhere. This is one of the reasons to carry plenty of extra stores on an outback trip. If a road is officially closed because of heavy rain, you can be fined for travelling on it – the norm is $1000 per wheel!

Bushfires Bushfires happen every year in Australia. Don't be the mug who starts one. In hot, dry, windy weather, be extremely careful with any naked flame – no cigarette butts out of car windows, please. On a Total Fire Ban Day (listen to the radio or watch the billboards on country roads), it is forbidden even to use a camping stove in the open. The locals will not be amused if they catch you breaking this particular law; they'll happily dob you in, and the penalties are severe.

If you're unfortunate enough to find yourself driving through a bushfire, stay inside your car and try to park off the road in an open space, away from trees, until the danger's past. Lie on the floor under the dashboard, covering yourself with a wool blanket if possible. The front of the fire should pass quickly, and you will be much safer than if you were out in the open. It is very important to cover up with a wool blanket or wear protective clothing, as it has been proved that heat radiation is the big killer in bushfire situations.

Bushwalkers should take local advice before setting out. On a day of total fire ban, don't go – delay your trip until the weather has changed. Chances are that it will be so unpleasantly hot and windy, you'll be better off anyway in an air-conditioned pub sipping a cool beer.

If you're out in the bush and you see smoke, even at a great distance, take it seriously. Go to the nearest open space, downhill if possible. A forested ridge is the most dangerous place to be. Bushfires move very quickly and change direction with the wind.

Dogs The tourist's best friend is a contentious issue in the outback at the best of times. There's no doubt that the best way to avoid dog-related hassles is not to bring the hound in the first place. If you do have to bring it you will find that many of the best spots in the Territory – such as virtually all the national parks – will be closed to you.

Courtesy These days most outback pastoralists are on the telephone and it's a common courtesy to contact them before you invade their property. Straight-through travel on established roads is not a problem, but if you're thinking of going camping or fishing in some remote spot, the landholder will expect you to ask permission. You'll usually rise in the estimation of the more isolated people if you drop off some very recent newspapers or ask if there's anything they'd like brought out from town. Always remember to take-your-own-everything, as station folk seldom organise their shopping around the needs of ill-prepared visitors.

Cross-Cultural Etiquette Many of the outback's original inhabitants lead lives that are powerfully influenced by ancient traditions, and the average tourist is almost entirely ignorant of Aboriginal social customs. You won't go far wrong if you treat outback Aboriginal people as potential friends. Also, remember that Aboriginal people generally have great senses of humour and love a good laugh.

Most larger communities have a store staffed by White people, and this is the place to go first for information. The store is usually easy to find. If you're not sure, ask someone rather than head off on an unauthorised sightseeing tour that raises dust and could make you unpopular. One sure way to wear out a welcome is to drive around taking photographs without permission.

When speaking with outback Aboriginal people, it's important to remember that English is very much the second language on most remote communities and may not be spoken at all well. Speak distinctly and reasonably slowly, using straightforward English and a normal tone of voice. Don't make the mistake of addressing your audience as you would a slow learner with a hearing problem. See the Language section later in this chapter for more advice on communicating with Aboriginal people.

Alcohol Unfortunately many non-Aboriginal Australians have the idea that Aboriginal people in general drink to excess. This assertion is hypocritical and inaccurate. In actual fact, a smaller percentage of Aboriginal people drink than do non-Aboriginals.

However, Aboriginal people who consume alcohol are more likely than their non-Aboriginal counterparts to drink in public. One reason for this is the fact that

Aboriginal councils have banned the possession and consumption of alcohol on many Aboriginal communities. As a result, many outback Aboriginal people have irregular access to alcohol, and only drink when they go to town. Unfortunately, this is the only time many non-Aboriginal people (and tourists) see them.

Throughout the Territory (and Australia), Aboriginal people are actively involved in the fight against alcoholism. With the assistance of lawyers, they have persuaded some outback hotels and takeaway outlets not to sell alcohol to local Aboriginal people, and signs at such outlets explain that Aboriginal elders ask tourists to not buy alcohol for Aboriginal people. Also, some outlets may refuse to sell you alcohol if you're heading towards an Aboriginal community. Please respect such efforts to combat alcoholism.

RELIGION

A shrinking majority of people in Australia (around 70%) are at least nominally Christian. Most Protestant churches have merged to become the Uniting Church, although the Church of England has remained separate. The Catholic Church is popular (about a third of Christians are Catholics), with the original Irish adherents now joined by the large numbers of Mediterranean immigrants.

Non-Christian minorities abound, the main ones being Buddhist, Jewish and Muslim.

Aboriginal Religion

Traditional Aboriginal cultures either have very little religious component or are nothing but religion, depending on how you look at it. Is a belief system which views every event, no matter how trifling, in a non-material context a religion? The early Christian missionaries certainly didn't think so. For them a belief in a deity was an essential part of a religion, and anything else was mere superstition.

Sacred Sites Aboriginal sacred sites are a perennial topic of discussion. Their presence can lead to headline-grabbing controversy when they stand in the way of developments such as roads, mines and dams. This is because most other Australians still have great difficulty understanding the Aboriginal peoples' deep spiritual bond with the land.

Aboriginal religious beliefs centre on the continuing existence of spirit beings that lived on Earth during the Dreamtime, which occurred before the arrival of humans. These beings created all the features of the natural world and were the ancestors of all living things. They took different forms but behaved as people do, and as they travelled about they left signs to show where they passed.

Despite being supernatural, the ancestors were subject to ageing and eventually they returned to the sleep from which they'd awoken at the dawn of time. Here their spirits remain as eternal forces that breathe life into the newborn and influence natural events. Each ancestor's spiritual energy flows along the path it travelled during the Dreamtime and is strongest at the points where it left physical evidence of its activities, such as a tree, riverbed, hill or claypan. These features are sacred sites.

Every person, animal and plant is believed to have two souls – one mortal and one immortal. The latter is part of a particular ancestral spirit and returns to the sacred sites of that ancestor after death, while the mortal soul simply fades into oblivion. Each person is spiritually bound to the sacred sites that mark the land associated with his or her ancestor. It is the individual's obligation to help care for these sites by performing the necessary rituals and singing the songs that tell of the ancestor's deeds. By doing this, the order created by that ancestor is maintained.

Some of the sacred sites are believed to be dangerous and entry is prohibited under traditional Aboriginal law. These restrictions often have a pragmatic origin. One site in northern Australia was believed to cause sores to break out all over the body of anyone visiting the area. Subsequently, the area was found to have a dangerously high level of radiation from naturally occurring radon gas.

Unfortunately, Aboriginal sacred sites are not like Christian churches, which can be desanctified before the bulldozers move in. Neither can they be bought, sold or transferred. Other Australians find this difficult to accept because they regard land as belonging to the individual, whereas in Aboriginal society the reverse applies. Aboriginal people believe that to destroy or damage a sacred site threatens not only the living but also the spirit inhabitants of the land. It is a distressing and dangerous act, and one that no responsible person would condone.

Throughout much of Australia, when pastoralists were breaking the Aboriginal peoples' subsistence link to the land, and sometimes shooting them, many Aboriginal people sought refuge on missions and became Christians. However, becoming Christians has not, for most Aboriginal people, meant renouncing their traditional religion. Many senior Aboriginal law men are also devout Christians.

LANGUAGE
Australian English
Any visitor from abroad who thinks Australian (that's 'Strine') is simply a weird variant of English/American will soon have a few surprises. For a start many Australians don't even speak Australian – they speak Italian, Lebanese, Vietnamese, Turkish or Greek.

Those who do speak the native tongue are liable to lose you in a strange collection of Australian words. Some have completely different meanings in Australia than they have in English-speaking countries north of the equator; some commonly used words have been shortened almost beyond recognition. Others are derived from Aboriginal languages, or from the slang used by early convict settlers.

There is a slight regional variation in the Australian accent, while the difference between city and country speech is mainly a matter of speed. Some of the most famed Aussie words are hardly heard at all – 'mates' are more common than 'cobbers'.

Lonely Planet publishes *Australia – a language survival kit*, an introduction to both Australian English and Aboriginal languages, and the list that follows may also help:

arvo – afternoon
avagoyermug – traditional rallying call, especially at cricket matches

back o' Bourke – back of beyond, middle of nowhere
bail out – leave
banana bender – resident of Queensland
barbie – barbecue (bbq)
bastard – general form of address which can mean many things, from high praise or respect ('He's the bravest bastard I know') to dire insult ('You rotten bastard!'). Avoid if unsure!
battler – hard trier, struggler
beaut, beauty, bewdie – great, fantastic
big mobs – a large amount, heaps
billabong – water hole in dried up riverbed, more correctly an ox-bow bend cut off in the dry season by receding waters
billy – tin container used to boil tea in the bush
bitumen – surfaced road
black stump – where the 'back o' Bourke' begins
bloke – man
blowies – blow flies
bludger – lazy person, one who won't work
blue (ie 'have a blue') – to have an argument or fight
bonzer – great, ripper
boomer – very big, a particularly large male kangaroo
boomerang – a curved flat wooden instrument used by Aboriginal people for hunting
bottle shop – liquor shop
Buckley's – no chance at all
bull dust – fine and sometimes deep dust on outback roads, also bullshit
burl – have a try (as in 'give it a burl')
bush – country, anywhere away from the city
bushbash – to force your way through pathless bush
bushranger – Australia's equivalent of the outlaws of the American Wild West (some goodies, some baddies)

bush tucker – native foods, usually in the outback

camp oven – large, cast-iron pot with lid, used for cooking on an open fire
cask – wine box (a great Australian invention)
chocka – completely full, from 'chock-a-block'
chook – chicken
chuck a U-ey – do a U-turn
clobber – to hit
come good – turn out all right
counter meal, countery – pub meal
cow cocky – small-scale cattle farmer
crook – ill, badly made, substandard
cut lunch – sandwiches

dag, daggy – dirty lump of wool at back end of a sheep, also an affectionate or mildly abusive term for a socially inept person
daks – trousers
damper – bush loaf made from flour and water and cooked in a camp oven
dead horse – tomato sauce
dijeridu – cylindrical wooden musical instrument traditionally played by Aboriginal men
dill – idiot
dinkum, fair dinkum – honest, genuine
dinky-di – the real thing
dob in – to tell on someone
don't come the raw prawn – don't try and fool me
down south – the rest of Australia
drongo – worthless person
Dry, the – dry season in northern Australia (April to October)
dunny – outdoor lavatory
dunny budgies – blowies

earbash – talk nonstop
esky – large insulated box for keeping beer etc cold

fair crack of the whip! – fair go!
fair go! – give us a break
flog – sell, steal
fossick – hunt for gems or semiprecious stones

from arsehole to breakfast – all over the place
furphy – a rumour or false story

galah – noisy parrot, thus noisy idiot
game – brave (as in 'game as Ned Kelly')
gander – look (as in 'have a gander')
garbo – person who collects your garbage
g'day – good day, traditional Australian greeting
gibber – Aboriginal word for a stone or rock, hence gibber plain or desert
give it away – give up
good on ya – well done
grog – general term for alcoholic drinks

homestead – residence of a station owner or manager
hoon – idiot, hooligan, yahoo
how are ya? – standard greeting, expected answer 'good, thanks, how are *you*?'

icy-pole – frozen lolly water on a stick

jackaroo – young male trainee on a station (farm)
jillaroo – young female trainee on a station
jocks – men's underpants
journo – journalist
jumped-up – arrogant, full of self-importance

knock – criticise, deride
knocker – one who knocks

lair – layabout, ruffian
lairising – acting like a lair
lamington – square of sponge cake covered in chocolate icing and coconut
larrikin – a bit like a lair
lay-by – put a deposit on an article so the shop will hold it for you
lollies – sweets, candy
lurk – a scheme

mate – general term of familiarity, whether you know the person or not
mozzies – mosquitoes

never never – remote country in the outback

no hoper – hopeless case
no worries – she'll be right, that's OK

ocker – an uncultivated or boorish Australian
off-sider – assistant or partner
outback – remote part of the bush, back o' Bourke

paddock – a fenced area of land, usually intended for livestock
pastoralist – large-scale grazier
pavlova – traditional Australian meringue and cream dessert, named after the Russian ballerina Anna Pavlova
perve – to gaze with lust
pinch – steal
piss – beer
piss turn – boozy party, also piss up
pissed – drunk
pissed off – annoyed
piss weak – no good, gutless
plonk – cheap wine
pokies – poker machines
Pom – English person

ratbag – friendly term of abuse
ratshit (R-S) – lousy
rapt – delighted, enraptured
reckon! – you bet!, absolutely!
rego – registration, as in 'car rego'
ridgy-didge – original, genuine
ripper – good (also 'little ripper')
road train – semitrailer-trailer-trailer
root – sexual intercourse
rooted – tired
ropable – very bad-tempered or angry

scrub – bush
sea wasp – deadly box jellyfish
sealed road – surfaced road
session – lengthy period of heavy drinking
sheila – woman
shellacking – comprehensive defeat
she'll be right – no worries
shonky – unreliable
shoot through – leave in a hurry
shout – buy a round of drinks (as in 'it's your shout')
sickie – day off work ill (or malingering)
smoko – tea break

snag – sausage
station – large farm
sticky beak – nosy person
stinger – box jellyfish
stubby – 375-ml bottle of beer
Stubbies – popular brand of mens' work shorts
swag – canvas-covered bed roll used in the outback, also a large amount

tall poppies – achievers (knockers like to cut them down)
tea – evening meal
thongs – flip-flops, an ocker's idea of formal footwear
tinny – 375 ml can of beer; also a small, aluminium fishing dinghy
too right! – absolutely!
Top End – northern part of the Northern Territory
trucky – truck driver
true blue – dinkum
tucker – food
two-pot screamer – person unable to hold their drink
two-up – traditional heads/tails gambling game

uni – university
ute – utility, pick-up truck

wagon – station wagon, estate car
walkabout – lengthy walk away from it all
wallaby track (on the) – to wander from place to place seeking work (archaic)
weatherboard – wooden house
Wet – the rainy season in the north
wharfie – dockworker
whinge – complain, moan
wobbly – disturbing, unpredictable behaviour (as in 'throw a wobbly')
woomera – stick used by Aboriginal people for throwing spears

yahoo – noisy and unruly person
yakka – work (from an Aboriginal language)
yobbo – uncouth, aggressive person
yonks – ages; a long time
youse – plural of you, pronounced 'yooze', only used by the grammatically challenged

Aboriginal Language

At the time of contact there were around 250 separate Australian languages, comprising about 700 dialects. Often three or four adjacent tribes would speak what amounted to dialects of the same language, but another adjacent tribe might speak a completely different language.

It is believed that all the languages evolved from a single language family as the Aboriginal people gradually moved out over the entire continent and split into new groups. There are a number of words that occur right across the continent, such as *jina* (foot) and *mala* (hand), and similarities also exist in the often complex grammatical structures.

Following European contact the number of Aboriginal languages was drastically reduced. At least eight separate languages were spoken in Tasmania alone, but none of these was recorded before the native speakers either died or were killed. Of the original 250 or so languages, only around 30 are today spoken on a regular basis and are taught to children.

Aboriginal Kriol is a new language which has developed since European arrival in Australia. It is spoken across northern Australia and has become the 'native' language of many young Aboriginal people. It contains many English words, but the pronunciation and grammatical usage are along Aboriginal lines, the meaning is often different to what it is in English, and the spelling is phonetic. For example, the English sentence 'He was amazed' becomes 'I bin luk kwesjinmak' in Kriol.

There are a number of generic terms which Aboriginal people use to describe themselves, and these vary according to the region. The most common of these is Koori, used for the people of south-east Australia. Nunga is used to refer to the people of coastal South Australia, Murri for those from the north-east, and Nyoongah is used in the country's south-west.

Lonely Planet's *Australian Phrasebook* gives a detailed account of Aboriginal languages.

Facts for the Visitor

VISAS & EMBASSIES

All visitors to Australia need a visa. Only New Zealand nationals are exempt, and even they receive a 'special category' visa on arrival.

Visa application forms are available from either Australian diplomatic missions overseas or travel agents, and you can apply by mail or in person. There are several different types of visas, depending on the reason for your visit.

Australian Embassies

Australian consular offices overseas include the following:

Canada
Suite 710, 50 O'Connor St, Ottawa (☎ (613) 236 0841; fax 236 4376)
also in Toronto and Vancouver
China
21 Dongzhimenwai Dajie, Sanlitun, Beijing 100600 (☎ (10) 532 2331; fax 532 6959)
also in Guangzhou and Shanghai
Denmark
Kristianagade 21, DK 2100 Copenhagen (☎ 3526 2244; fax 3543 2218)
France
4 Rue Jean Rey, 75724 Paris Cedex 15 Paris (☎ (01) 4059 3300; fax 4059 3310)
Germany
Godesberger Allee 107, 53175 Bonn (☎ (0228) 81 030; fax 810 3130)
also in Frankfurt and Berlin
Greece
37 Dimitriou Soutsou, Ambelokipi, Athens 11521 (☎ (01) 644 7303; fax 646 6595)
Hong Kong
23/F Harbour Centre, 25 Harbour Rd, Wanchai, Hong Kong Island (☎ 2827 8881; fax 2827 6583)
India
Australian Compound, No 1/50-G Shantipath, Chanakyapuri, New Delhi 110021 (☎ (11) 688 8223; fax 688 5199)
also in Bombay
Indonesia
Jalan H R Rasuna Said Kav C 15-16, Jakarta Selatan 12940 (☎ (021) 522 7111; fax 522 7101)

Jalan Prof Moh Yamin 51, Renon, Denpasar, Bali (☎ (0361) 23 5092; fax 23 1990)
Ireland
Fitzwilton House, Wilton Terrace, Dublin 2 (☎ (01) 676 1517; fax 678 5185)
Italy
Via Alessandria 215, Rome 00198 (☎ (06) 852 721; fax 8527 2300)
also in Milan
Japan
2-1-14 Mita, Minato-ku, Tokyo 108 (☎ (03) 5232 4111; fax 5232 4149)
Twin 21 MID Tower, 29th Floor, 2-1-61 Shiromi, Chuo-ku, Osaka 540 (☎ (06) 941 9271; fax 920 4543)
7th Floor, Tsuruta Keyaki Bldg, 1-1-5 Akasaka Chuo-ku, Fukuoka City 810, Kyushu (☎ (092) 734 5055; fax 724 2304)
8th Floor, Ikko Fushimi Bldg, 1-20-10 Nishiki, Naka-ku, Nagoya 460 (☎ (052) 211 0630; fax 211 0632)
also in Sapporo and Sendai
Malaysia
6 Jalan Yap Kwan Seng, Kuala Lumpur 50450 (☎ (03) 242 3122; fax 241 5773)
also in Kuching and Penang
Mauritius
Rogers House, 5 Pres John Kennedy St, Port Louis (☎ 230 1700; fax 208 8878)
Nepal
Bansbari, Kathmandu (☎ (01) 41 3076; fax 41 7533)
Netherlands
Carnegielaan 4, 2517 KH The Hague (☎ (070) 310 8200; fax 310 7863)
New Zealand
72-78 Hobson St, Thorndon, Wellington (☎ (04) 473 6411; fax 498 7118)
Union House, 32-38 Quay St, Auckland 1 (☎ (09) 303 2429; fax 377 0798)
Papua New Guinea
Independence Dve, Waigani NCD, Port Moresby (☎ 325 9333; fax 325 6647)
Philippines
Dona Salustiana Ty Tower, 104 Paseo de Roxas, Makati, Metro Manila (☎ (02) 817 7911; fax 817 3603)
Singapore
25 Napier Rd, Singapore 1025 (☎ 737 9311; fax 733 7134)
South Africa
292 Orient St, Arcadia, Pretoria 0083 (☎ (012) 342 3740; fax 342 4222)
also in Cape Town

Sri Lanka
  3 Cambridge Place, Colombo 7 (☎ (01) 69 8767;
  fax 68 6453)
Sweden
  Sergels Torg 12, Stockholm (☎ (08) 613 2900;
  fax 24 7414)
Switzerland
  29 Alpenstrasse, CH-3006 Berne (☎ (031) 351
  0143; fax 352 1234)
  also in Geneva
Thailand
  37 South Sathorn Rd, Bangkok 10120 (☎ (02)
  287 2680; fax 287 2029)
UK
  Australia House, The Strand, London WC2B
  4LA (☎ (0171) 379 4334; fax 465 8210)
  also in Edinburgh and Manchester
USA
  1601 Massachusetts Ave NW, Washington DC
  20036 (☎ (202) 797 3000; fax 797 3168)
  also in Atlanta, Boston, Chicago, Denver, Honolulu, Houston, Los Angeles, New York and San
  Francisco
Vietnam
  66 Ly Thuong Kiet, Hanoi (☎ (04) 25 2763; fax
  25 9268)
  also in Ho Chi Minh City
Zimbabwe
  4th Floor, Karigamombe Centre, 53 Samora
  Machel Ave, Harare (☎ (04) 75 7774; fax 75
  7770)

Tourist Visas

Tourist visas are issued by Australian consular offices abroad; they are the most common and are generally valid for a stay of either three or six months, and are valid for 12 months. The three-month visas are free; for the six-month visa there is a $35 fee.

The visa is valid for use within 12 months of the date of issue and can be used to enter and leave Australia several times within that 12 months.

When you apply for a visa, you need to present your passport and a passport photo, as well as signing an undertaking that you have an onward or return ticket and 'sufficient funds' – the latter is obviously open to interpretation.

You can also apply for a long-stay visa, which is a multiple-entry, four-year visa which allows for stays of up to six months on each visit. These also cost $35.

Working Visas

Young, single visitors from the UK, Canada, Korea, Holland and Japan may be eligible for a 'working holiday' visa. 'Young' is fairly loosely interpreted as around 18 to 25, although exceptions are made and people up to 30, and young married couples without children, may be given a working holiday visa.

A working holiday visa allows for a stay of up to 12 months, but the emphasis is supposed to be on casual employment rather than a full-time job, so you are only supposed to work for three months. This visa can only be applied for from outside Australia (preferably, but not necessarily, in your country of citizenship), and you can't change from a visitor visa to a working holiday visa.

Conditions attached to a working holiday visa include having sufficient funds for a ticket out, and taking out private medical insurance, and a fee of about $140 is payable when you apply for the visa.

See the section on Working later in this chapter for details of what sort of work is available and where.

Visa Extensions

The maximum stay allowed to visitors in Australia is one year, including extensions.

Visa extensions are made through Department of Immigration & Ethnic Affairs office (40 Cavenagh St, Darwin; ☎ 8946 3100) and, as the process takes some time, it's best to apply about a month before your visa expires. There is an application fee of $135, and even if they turn down your application they can still keep your money! To qualify for an extension you are required to take out private medical insurance to cover the period of the extension, and have a ticket out of the country. Some offices are more strict in enforcing these conditions than others.

If you're trying to stay for longer in Australia the books *Temporary to Permanent Resident in Australia* and *Practical Guide to Obtaining Permanent Residence in Australia*, both published by Longman Cheshire, might be useful.

Foreign Consulates

The following countries have consulates (or honorary consuls) in Darwin. Call first to find out when they are open:

France
    47 Knuckey St, Darwin (☎ 8999 6092)
Germany
    Berrimah Rd, Berrimah (☎ 8984 3770)
Indonesia
    18 Harry Chan Ave, Darwin (☎ 8941 0048)
Japan
    19 Lindsay St, Darwin (☎ 8981 8722)
Portugal
    15 Colsters Cres, Wagaman (☎ 8927 1956)
Sweden
    22 Mitchell St, Darwin (☎ 8981 2971)

CUSTOMS

When entering Australia you can bring most articles in free of duty provided that Customs is satisfied they are for personal use and that you'll be taking them with you when you leave. There's also the usual duty-free per-person quota of one litre of alcohol, 250 cigarettes and dutiable goods up to the value of A$400.

With regard to prohibited goods, there are two areas you need to pay particular attention to. Number one is, of course, dope – Australian Customs have a positive mania about the stuff and can be extremely efficient when it comes to finding it. Unless you want to make first-hand investigations of conditions in Australian jails, don't bring any with you. This particularly applies if you are arriving from South-East Asia or the Indian Subcontinent.

Problem two is animal and plant quarantine. You will be asked to declare all goods of animal or vegetable origin – wooden spoons, straw hats, the lot – and show them to an official. The authorities are naturally keen to prevent weeds, pests or diseases getting into the country as Australia has so far managed to escape many of the agricultural pests and diseases prevalent in other parts of the world. Fresh food is also unpopular, particularly meat, sausages, fruit, vegetables and flowers. There are also restrictions on taking fruit and vegetables between states

(see the aside on Interstate Quarantine in the Getting Around chapter).

Weapons and firearms are either prohibited or require a permit and safety testing. Other restricted goods include products made from protected wildlife species (such as ivory), non-approved telecommunications devices and live animals.

When it is time to leave there are duty-free stores at the international airports and their associated cities. Treat them with healthy suspicion. 'Duty-free' is one of the world's most overworked catch phrases, and it is often just an excuse to sell things at prices you can easily beat by a little shopping around.

MONEY

Currency

Australia's currency is the Australian dollar, which comprises 100 cents. There are coins for 5c, 10c, 20c, 50c, $1 and $2, and notes for $5, $10, $20, $50 and $100. Although the smallest coin in circulation is 5c, prices are still marked in single cents, and then rounded to the nearest 5c when you come to pay.

There are no notable restrictions on importing or exporting currency or travellers' cheques except that you may not take out more than $5000 in cash without prior approval.

Exchange Rates

The Australian dollar fluctuates quite markedly against the US dollar, but it seems to stay pretty much in the 70c to 80c range – a disaster for Australians travelling overseas but a real bonus for inbound visitors.

Canada	C$1	=	A$0.94
France	FF10	=	A$2.54
Germany	DM 1	=	A$0.86
Hong Kong	HK$10	=	A$1.66
Japan	Y100	=	A$1.19
New Zealand	NZ$1	=	A$0.87
United Kingdom	UK£1	=	A$1.96
United States	US$1	=	A$1.28

Changing Money

Changing foreign currency or travellers'

cheques is no problem at almost any bank or licensed moneychanger such as Thomas Cook or American Express.

Travellers' Cheques

There is a variety of ways to carry your money around with you. If your stay is limited then travellers' cheques are the most straightforward and they generally enjoy a better exchange rate than foreign cash in Australia.

American Express, Thomas Cook and other well-known international brands of travellers' cheques are all widely used. A passport will usually be adequate for identification; it would be sensible to carry a Driver's licence, credit cards or other form of identification in case of problems.

Fees for changing foreign-currency travellers' cheques seem to vary from bank to bank and year to year. Currently of the 'big four' (ANZ, Commonwealth, National and Westpac), ANZ and Westpac do not charge any fee, while at the National it's $5 and the Commonwealth $6 per transaction, regardless of the amount or number of cheques.

Buying Australian dollar travellers' cheques is an option worth looking at. These can be exchanged immediately at the bank cashier's window without being converted from a foreign currency and incurring commissions, fees and exchange-rate fluctuations.

Credit Cards

Credit cards are widely accepted and are an alternative to carrying large numbers of travellers' cheques. Visa, MasterCard, Diners Club and American Express are all widely accepted.

Cash advances from credit cards are available over the counter and from many automatic teller machines (ATMs), depending on the card.

If you're planning to rent cars while travelling around the Territory, a credit card makes life much simpler; they're looked upon with much greater favour by rent-a-car agencies than nasty old cash, and many agencies simply won't rent you a vehicle if you don't have a card.

Local Bank Accounts

If you're planning to stay longer than just a month or so, it's worth considering other ways of handling money that give you more flexibility and are more economical.

Most travellers these days opt for an account which includes a cash card, which you can use to access your cash from ATMs found in just about every town. You put your card in the machine, key in your personal identification number (PIN), and then withdraw funds from your account. In all but the most remote town there'll be at least one place where you can withdraw money from a hole in the wall.

ATMs can be used day or night, and it is possible to use the machines of some other banks: Westpac ATMs accept Commonwealth Bank cards and vice versa; National Bank ATMs accept ANZ cards and vice versa. There is a limit on how much you can withdraw from your account. This varies from bank to bank but is usually $400 or $500 per day.

Many businesses, such as service stations, supermarkets and convenience stores, are linked into the EFTPOS system (Electronic Funds Transfer at Point Of Sale), and at places with this facility you can use your bank cash card to pay for services or purchases direct, and sometimes withdraw cash as well. Bank cash cards and credit cards can also be used to make local, STD and international phone calls in special public telephones, found in most towns throughout the country.

Opening an account at an Australian bank is not all that easy, especially for overseas visitors. A points system operates and you need to score a minimum of 100 points before you can have the privilege of letting the bank take your money. Passports, Driver's licences, birth certificates and other 'major' IDs earn you 40 points; minor ones such as credit cards get you 20 points. Just like a game show really! However, if visitors apply to open an account during the first six weeks of their visit, then just showing their passport will suffice.

If you don't have an Australian Tax File Number, interest earned from your funds will be taxed at the rate of 48% and this money goes straight to our old mate, the Deputy Commissioner of Taxation.

Costs

Compared to the USA, Canada and European countries, Australia is cheaper in some ways and more expensive in others. Manufactured goods tend to be more expensive: if they are imported they have all the additional costs of transport and duties, and if they're locally manufactured they suffer from the extra costs entailed in making things in comparatively small quantities. Thus you pay more for clothes, cars and other manufactured items. On the other hand, food is both high in quality and low in cost.

Accommodation is also very reasonably priced. In virtually every town where backpackers are likely to stay there'll be a backpackers' hostel with dorm beds for $10 or less, or a caravan park with on-site vans for around $25 for two people.

The biggest cost in any trip is going to be transport, simply because it's such a vast country. If there's a group of you, buying a second-hand car is probably the most economical way to go.

On average you can expect to spend about $30 per day if you budget fiercely and *always* take the cheapest option; $50 gives you much greater flexibility. Obviously if you stay for longer periods in each place and can take advantage of discounts given on long-term accommodation, or even move into a share-house with other people, this helps to keep your costs to a minimum.

Tipping

Tipping isn't entrenched in the way it is in the USA or Europe. It's only customary to tip in more expensive restaurants and only then if you want to. If the service has been especially good and you decide to leave a tip, 10% of the bill is the usual amount. Taxi Drivers don't expect tips (of course, they won't hurl it back at you if you decide to leave the change).

WHEN TO GO

The Dry season (winter) is generally considered to be the best time to visit the Territory, although this should certainly not deter you from visiting at another time.

Summer in the centre of the country is just too damn hot to do anything much, while in the far north the summer is the Wet season and even though it is usually not as hot as down south, the heat and humidity can make life pretty uncomfortable. To make matters worse, swimming in the sea in the north is not possible due to the 'stingers' (box jellyfish) which frequent the waters at this time. On the other hand, if you want to see the Top End green and free of dust, be treated to some spectacular electrical storms and have the best of the barramundi fishing while all the other tourists are down south, this is the time to do it.

In winter the Top End is dry and warm, but also dusty and brown. In the Centre the fierce summer heat has been replaced by cool sunny days and surprisingly cold nights – overnight temperatures as low as -5°C are not uncommon at Uluru in winter, which is no fun if you're camping! Spring and autumn are good times to be in the Centre, although spring can be marred by plagues of bushflies if there has been any amount of rain. Spring is also the time for wildflowers in the outback and these can be absolutely stunning after rains and are worth going a long way to see.

The other major consideration when travelling in Australia is school holidays. Australian families take to the road (and air) en masse at these times and many places are booked out, prices rise and things generally get a bit crazy. See the Holidays section later in this chapter for more details.

TOURIST OFFICES

There are a number of information sources for visitors to the Northern Territory and, in common with a number of other tourist-conscious Western countries, you can easily drown yourself in brochures and booklets, maps and leaflets.

The Northern Territory Tourism Commission (NTTC) is very active in promoting the Territory both domestically and overseas, with a number of high-profile advertising campaigns. It doesn't maintain tourist offices as such, but does publish very useful *Holiday Guides* to the Centre and the Top End. These guides list accommodation and tour options throughout the Territory, and include prices and booking information. The NTTC also has a Holiday Information Helpline (☎ toll-free 1800 621 336), or you can visit them on the World Wide Web at: www.world.net/travel/australia/ntinfo/nttc.

Local Offices

There are tourist offices, maintained by the local tourism authorities, in Alice Springs, Darwin, Katherine and Tennant Creek.

Alice Springs
    Central Australian Tourism Industry Association (CATIA), corner of Hartley St and Gregory Terrace (☎ 8952 5199; fax 8953 0295)
Darwin
    Darwin Regional Tourism Association Information Centre, 33 Smith St (☎ 81-4300; fax 81-7346)
Katherine
    Katherine Region Tourist Association, Stuart Highway, Katherine (☎ 8972-2650; fax 8972 2969)
Tennant Creek
    Tennant Creek Visitor Centre, Transit Centre, Paterson St (☎ 8962 3388)

Overseas Reps

The Australian Tourist Commission (ATC) is the government body intended to inform potential visitors about the country. There's a very definite split between promotion outside Australia and inside it. The ATC is strictly an external operator; it does minimal promotion within the country and has little contact with visitors to Australia. Within the country, tourist promotion is handled by state or local tourist offices.

While they have nothing specific to the Northern Territory, ATC offices overseas have a useful free magazine-style periodical

booklet called *On the Loose* which details things of interest for backpackers around Australia.

The ATC also recently published *Australia Unplugged*, which is a very good introduction to Australia for young people, giving some information about the country in general and snapshots of the major cities.

The ATC also publishes a number of fact sheets on various topics, such as camping, fishing, disabled travel and national parks and these can be a useful introduction to the subject. It also has a handy map of the country, which is available for a small fee. This literature is intended for distribution overseas only; if you want copies, get them before you come to Australia.

The ATC also maintains a number of Helplines, which independent travellers can ring or fax to get specific information about Australia.

Addresses of the ATC offices for literature requests are:

Hong Kong
    Suite 1501, Central Plaza, 18 Harbour Rd, Wanchai (☎ 2802 7700)
    Helpline: ☎ 2802 7817; fax 2802 8211
Japan
    Australian Business Centre, New Otani Garden Court Bldg 28F, 4-1 Kioi-cho, Chiyoda-ku, Tokyo 102 (☎ (03) 5214 0720)
    Helpline: ☎ (03) 5214 0730; fax 5214 0719
    Twin 21 MID Tower 30F, 2-1-61 Shiromi, Chuo-ku, Osaka 540 (☎ (06) 946 2503)
    Helpline: ☎ (06) 946 2500; fax 946 2473
New Zealand
    Level 13, 44-48 Emily Place, Auckland 1 (☎ (09) 379 9594; fax 307 3117)
    Helpline: ☎ (09) 527 1629; fax 377 9562
Singapore
    Suite 1703, United Square, 101 Thomson Rd, Singapore 1103 (☎ 255 4555)
    Helpline: ☎ 250 6277; fax 253 8431
UK
    Gemini House, 10-18 Putney Hill, London SW15 6AA (☎ (0181) 780 2227; fax 780 1496)
USA
    Suite 1200, 2121 Ave of the Stars, Los Angeles, CA 90067 (☎ (310) 552 1988; fax 552-1215)
    25th floor, 100 Park Ave, New York, NY 10017 (☎ (212) 687 6300; fax 661 3340)
    Helpline: ☎ (708) 296 4900; fax 635 3718

USEFUL ORGANISATIONS
Automobile Associations
The Automobile Association of the Northern Territory (AANT) provides an emergency breakdown service, literature, excellent maps and detailed guides to accommodation and camp sites.

The AANT also has reciprocal arrangements with the various other state motoring organisations in Australia and with similar organisations overseas. So, if you're a member of the National Roads & Motorists Association (NRMA) in New South Wales, you can use AANT services facilities in the Territory. The same applies if you're a member of the AAA in the USA or the RAC or AA in the UK.

The AANT has two offices in the Territory which are located at 79-81 Smith St, Darwin (☎ 8981 3837; fax 8941 2965), and at Gregory Terrace, Alice Springs (☎ 8953 1322)

Emergency Road Service The numbers to ring for breakdown service throughout the Territory are:

Adelaide River ☎ 8976 7046
Alice Springs ☎ 8952 1087
Batchelor ☎ 8976 0196
Darwin ☎ 8941 0611
Elliott ☎ 8969 2018
Katherine ☎ 8972 2733
Tennant Creek ☎ 8962 2468
Yulara (Uluru) ☎ 8956 2188

Parks & Wildlife Commission
The Northern Territory's many parks and reserves are administered by Parks & Wildlife Commission (formerly the Conservation Commission). The exceptions are Kakadu and Uluru-Kata Tjuta national parks, which come under the jurisdiction of the commonwealth national parks body, which is called the Australian Nature Conservation Agency (ANCA).

The facilities provided in the various parks by Parks & Wildlife are among the best in the country. Most parks have at the very least picnic areas and interpretive signs, while those which get heavier use have marked walking trails, camp sites with facilities (sometimes including free gas barbecues) and ranger-guided activities during the tourist season (generally the winter).

Parks & Wildlife also produce informative leaflets on just about every park or reserve under its administration, and these are available from regional Parks & Wildlife offices, or often from the rangers' or park visitor centres on site.

Parks & Wildlife Offices The following regional offices are maintained by Parks & Wildlife:

Alice Springs
   Stuart Highway (☎ 8951 8211; fax 8951 8268)
   At the CATIA office, corner of Hartley St and Gregory Terrace.
Darwin
   PO Box 496, Palmerston (☎ 8999 5511; fax 8999 4558)
   At Darwin Regional Tourism Association Information Centre, 33 Smith St (☎ 8999 3881; fax 8981 0653)
Katherine
   Giles St (☎ 8973 8770; fax 8972 2373)

Australian Nature Conservation Agency
For information on Kakadu and Uluru-Kata Tjuta national parks, contact the ANCA office, MLC Building, 81 Smith St, Darwin, NT 0800 (☎ 8981 5299; fax 8981 3497).

Australian Trust for Conservation Volunteers
This non-political, non-profit group organises practical conservation projects (such as tree planting, track construction and flora and fauna surveys) for volunteers to take part in.

Travellers are welcome and it's an excellent way to get involved with the conservation movement and, at the same time, visit some of the more interesting areas of the country. Past volunteers have found themselves working in places such as Tasmania, Kakadu and Fraser Island.

Most projects are either for a weekend or a week and all food, transport and accommodation is supplied in return for a small contribution to help cover costs. Most travellers who take part in ATCV join a Banksia Package, which lasts six weeks and includes six different projects. The cost is $650, and further weeks can be added for $105.

Contact the head office (☎ (053) 33 1483) at PO Box 423, Ballarat, Vic 3350, or the local office at 4 Burnett Place, Darwin, NT 0800 (☎ 8981 3206).

WWOOF

WWOOF (Willing Workers on Organic Farms) is a relatively new organisation in Australia, although it is well established in other countries. The idea is that you do a few hours work each day on a farm in return for bed and board. Some places have a minimum stay of a couple of days but many will take you for just a night. Some will let you stay for months if they like the look of you, and you can get involved with some interesting large-scale projects.

Becoming a WWOOFer is a great way to meet interesting people and to travel cheaply. There are about 200 WWOOF associates in Australia, although very few of these are in the Territory.

As the name says, the farms are supposed to be organic but that isn't always so. Some places aren't even farms – you might help out at a pottery or do the books at a seed wholesaler. There are even a few commercial farms which exploit WWOOFers as cheap harvest labour, although these are quite rare. Whether they have a farm or just a vegie patch, most participants in the scheme are concerned to some extent with alternative lifestyles.

To join WWOOF send $15 (A$20 from overseas) to WWOOF, W Tree, Gelantipy Rd, Buchan, Vic 3885 (☎ (03) 5155-0218), and they'll send you a membership number and a booklet which lists WWOOF places all over Australia.

National Trust

The National Trust is dedicated to preserving historic buildings. The Trust actually owns a number of buildings throughout the Territory which are open to the public. Many other buildings are 'classified' by the National Trust to ensure their preservation.

The National Trust also produces some excellent literature, including a fine series of small booklets to places such as Newcastle Waters, Katherine and also Myilly Point (Darwin). These guides are available from the National Trust offices and cost $2 each.

In Darwin the National Trust office is in the historic old buildings of Myilly Point, between the city centre and the casino (4 Burnett Place, Myilly Point, Darwin, NT 0820; ☎ 8981 2848).

BUSINESS HOURS & HOLIDAYS
Business Hours

Most shops close at 5 or 5.30 pm weekdays, and either noon or 5 pm on Saturday. There's not much in the way of late-night trading, although a couple of major supermarkets in Alice Springs and Darwin are open 24 hours.

Banks are open from 9.30 am to 4 pm Monday to Thursday, and until 5 pm on Friday.

Of course there are some exceptions to Australia's unremarkable opening hours and all sorts of places stay open late and all weekend – particularly milk bars, convenience stores and roadhouses.

Holidays

The Christmas holiday season is part of the long summer school vacation and the time you are most likely to find accommodation booked out and long queues. There are three other shorter school-holiday periods during the year, falling from early to mid-April, late June to mid-July, and late September to early October.

The following is a list of the main national and local public holidays observed in the Northern Territory.

National Holidays:

New Year's Day
    1 January
Australia Day
    26 January

Easter
> Good Friday and Easter Saturday, Sunday and Monday

Anzac Day
> 25 April

Queen's Birthday
> 2nd Monday in June

Christmas Day
> 25 December

Boxing Day
> 26 December

Northern Territory Holidays:

May Day
> 1 May

Alice Springs Show Day
> 1st Friday in July *

Tennant Creek Show Day
> 2nd Friday in July *

Katherine Show Day
> 3rd Friday in July *

Darwin Show Day
> 4th Friday in July *

Picnic Day
> 1st Monday in August

(* indicates holidays are only observed locally)

CULTURAL EVENTS

Some of the most enjoyable Australian festivals are, naturally, the ones which are most typically Australian – like the outback race meetings, which draw together isolated townsfolk, the tiny communities from the huge stations and more than a few eccentric bush characters.

There are happenings and holidays in the Territory all year round, but particularly during the winter, which is the tourist season.

January
> *Australia Day* – This national holiday, commemorating the arrival of the First Fleet, in 1788, is observed on 26 January.

April
> *Anzac Day* – This is a national public holiday, on 25 April, commemorating the landing of Anzac troops at Gallipoli in 1915. Memorial marches by the returned soldiers of both world wars and the veterans of Korea and Vietnam are held all over the country.
>
> *Central Australian Country Music Festival* – It's not Tamworth, but still a lively three days with acts from all over Australia participating.

May
> *Alice Springs Cup Horse Racing Carnival* – This is three weeks of horse racing, culminating in the Alice Springs Cup.
>
> *Bangtail Muster* – This is Alice Springs' parade and festival honouring outback cattlemen.

June
> *Barunga Wugularr Sports & Cultural Festival* – For the four days over the Queen's Birthday long weekend in June, Barunga, 80 km south-east of Katherine, becomes a gathering place for Aboriginal people from all over the Territory. There are traditional arts and crafts, as well as dancing and athletics competitions.
>
> *Merrepen Arts Festival* – Held in June or July, Nauiya Nambiyu on the banks of the Daly River is the venue for this festival. Several Aboriginal communities from around the district, such as Wadeye, Nauiya and Peppimenarti, display their arts and crafts.

July
> *NT Royal Shows* – These agricultural shows are held in Darwin, Katherine, Tennant Creek and Alice Springs.
>
> *Darwin Cup Carnival* – An eight-day racing festival, highlight of which is the running of the Darwin Cup.
>
> *Darwin to Ambon Yacht Race* – This prestigious yacht race starts in Darwin and boasts an international field.

August
> *Darwin Rodeo* – This rodeo includes international team events between Australia, the USA, Canada and New Zealand.
>
> *Darwin Beer Can Regatta* – These boat races are for boats constructed entirely out of beer cans, of which there are plenty in this heavy drinking city.
>
> *Yuendumu Festival* – Aboriginal people from the central and western desert region meet in Yuendumu, north-west of Alice Springs, over the long weekend in early August. There's a mix of traditional and modern sporting and cultural events.
>
> *Oenpelli Open Day* – Oenpelli is in Arnhem Land, not far from Jabiru in Kakadu National Park. On the first Saturday in August an open day is held where there's a chance to buy local artefacts and watch the sports and dancing events.
>
> *Festival of Darwin* – This mainly outdoor arts and culture festival highlights Darwin's unique position in Australia with its large Asian and Aboriginal populations.
>
> *Australian Safari Race* – A 6000-km Adelaide to Darwin cross-country road rally which attracts an international field of contestants.

October
> *Henley-on-Todd Regatta* – A series of races for leg-powered bottomless boats on the (usually) dry Todd River.

World Solar Car Challenge – An event which sees weird and wonderful solar-powered vehicles sailing down the Stuart Highway from Darwin to Adelaide. It generates a huge amount of interest in the Territory, and attracts contestants from around the world.

POST & TELECOMMUNICATIONS
Postal Rates

Post offices are open from 9 am to 5 pm Monday to Friday, but you can often get stamps from local post offices operated from newsagents.

Letters Australia's postal services are relatively efficient. It costs 45c to send a standard letter or postcard within Australia.

Air-mail letters/postcards cost 75/70c to New Zealand, 85/80c to Singapore and Malaysia, 95/90c to Hong Kong and India, $1.05/95c to the USA and Canada, and $1.20/1.00 to Europe and the UK.

Parcels By sea mail a 1/2/5 kg parcel costs $14.50/18/28.50 to New Zealand and India, $15/19/31 to the USA, Europe or the UK. Each kg over five kg costs $3.50 for New Zealand and India, $4 for the USA, Europe or the UK, with a maximum of 20 kg for all destinations. Air-mail rates are considerably more expensive.

Receiving Mail

All post offices will hold mail for visitors, and Darwin GPO has a very busy poste restante counter.

Telephone
Local Calls Local calls from public phones cost 40c for an unlimited amount of time. You can make local calls from gold or blue phones – often found in shops, hotels, bars, etc – and from payphone booths. Local calls from private phones cost 30c.

STD Calls It's also possible to make long-distance (STD – Subscriber Trunk Dialling) calls from virtually any public phone. Many public phones accept the Telstra Phonecards, which are very convenient. The

cards come in $5, $10, $20 and $50 denominations, and are available from retail outlets such as newsagents and pharmacies which display the Phonecard logo. You keep using the card until the value has been used in calls. Otherwise, have plenty coins handy and be prepared to feed them through at a fair old rate. STD calls are cheaper in off-peak hours – see the front of a local telephone book for the different rates.

Some public phones are set up to take only bank cash cards or credit cards, and these too are convenient, although you need to keep an eye on how much the call is costing as it can quickly mount up. The minimum charge for a call on one of these phones is $1.20.

STD calls are cheaper at night. In ascending order of cost:

Economy – from 6 pm Saturday to 8 am Monday; 10 pm to 8 am every night
Night – from 6 to 10 pm Monday to Friday
Day – from 8 am to 6 pm Monday to Saturday

The STD area code for the Northern Territory is 08.

International Calls From most STD phones you can also make ISD (International Subscriber Dialling) calls. Dialling ISD you can get through to overseas numbers almost as quickly as you can access local numbers and if your call is brief it needn't cost very much.

All you do is dial 0011 for overseas, the country code (44 for Britain, 1 for the USA or Canada, 64 for New Zealand), the city code (71 or 81 for London, 212 for New York, etc), and then the telephone number. Have a Phonecard, credit card or plenty of coins.

It's also possible to make ISD calls with Optus rather than Telstra. The fee structure varies slightly with the two companies, and if you are phoning one country constantly it may be worth comparing the two. This option is only available from private phones in certain areas. Phone Optus (☎ toll-free 1800 500 005) for details on how to access their services.

International calls from Australia are

among the cheapest you'll find anywhere. A Telestra call to the USA or Britain costs $1.35 a minute ($1.03 off peak); New Zealand is $1.09 a minute ($0.72 off peak). Off-peak times, if available, vary depending on the destination – see the back of any White Pages telephone book, or call ☎ 0102 for more details. Sunday is often the cheapest day to ring.

Country Direct is a service which gives travellers in Australia direct access to operators in nearly 50 countries, to make collect or credit card calls. For a full list of the countries hooked into this system, check any local White Pages telephone book. They include: Canada (☎ 1800 881 150), Germany (☎ 1800 881 490), Japan (☎ 1800 881 810), New Zealand (☎ 1800 881 640), the UK (☎ 1800 881 440) and the USA (☎ 1800 881 011).

Toll-Free Calls Many businesses and some government departments operate a toll-free service, so no matter where you are ringing from around the country, it's a free call. These numbers have the prefix 1800 and we've listed them wherever possible throughout the book. Many companies, such as the airlines, have six-digit numbers beginning with 13, and these are charged at the rate of a local call. Often they'll be Australia-wide numbers, but sometimes are applicable only to a specific STD district. Unfortunately there's no way of telling without actually ringing the number.

Mobile Phones Phone numbers with the prefixes 014, 015, 016, 018 or 041 are mobile or car phones. The three mobile operators are the government's Telstra, and the two private companies Optus and Vodaphone. Calls to mobile numbers are charged at special STD rates and can be expensive.

Information Calls Other odd numbers you may come across are numbers starting with 0055 and 190. The 0055 numbers, usually recorded information services and the like, are provided by private companies, and your call is charged in multiples of 25c (40c from

public phones) at a rate selected by the provider (Premium 70c per minute, Value 55c per minute, Budget 35c per minute).

Numbers beginning with 190 are also information services, but they are charged on a fixed fee basis, which can vary from as little as 35c to as much as $30!

Internet If you want to surf the Net, even if it's only to access your e-mail, there's one service provider in Darwin, and with some, such as Pegasus Networks, you can dial from anywhere in the country for the cost of a local call.

Taunet
    (☎ 8941 0699; www.taunet.net.au)
Pegasus Networks
    (☎ toll-free 1800 812 812; www.peg.apc.org)

CompuServe users who want to access the service locally should phone CompuServe (☎ toll-free 1800 025 240) to get the local log-in numbers.

TIME
The Northern Territory is on Central Standard Time, which is plus 9½ hours from GMT/UTC. This is half an hour behind the eastern states, 1½ hours ahead of Western Australia, and the same as South Australia.

Things get slightly screwed up in summer as daylight savings does not apply in the Northern Territory, so from November to March (approximately), the eastern states are 1½ hours ahead of Northern Territory time, and South Australia is one hour ahead.

ELECTRICITY
Voltage is 220-240 V and the plugs are three-pin, but not the same as British three-pin plugs. Users of electric shavers or hairdriers should note that, apart from in top-end hotels, it's difficult to find converters to take either US flat two-pin plugs or the European round two-pin plugs. Adaptors for British plugs can be found in good hardware shops, chemists and travel agents.

WEIGHTS & MEASURES

Australia uses the metric system. Petrol and milk are sold by the litre, apples and potatoes by the kg, distance is measured by the metre or km, and speed limits are displayed in km per hour (km/h).

For those who need help with metric there's a conversion table at the back of this book.

BOOKS & MAPS

In almost any bookshop in the country you'll find a section devoted to Australiana with books on every Australian subject you care to mention. There are a lot of bookshops and some of the better-known ones are mentioned in the various city sections.

At the Wilderness Society shops in each capital city and the Government Printing Offices in Sydney and Melbourne you'll find a good range of wildlife posters, calendars and books.

History

For a good introduction to Australian history, read *A Short History of Australia*, a most accessible and informative general history by Manning Clark, the much-loved Aussie historian, or *The Fatal Shore*, Robert Hughes' best-selling account of the convict era.

Geoffrey Blainey's *The Tyranny of Distance* is an engrossing study of the problems of transport in this harsh continent and how they shaped the pattern of White settlement: transporting produce 100 miles by bullock cart from an inland farm to a port cost more than shipping it from there around the globe to Europe – a handicap that only wool and later gold were profitable enough to overcome.

Finding Australia, by Russel Ward, traces the story of the early days from the first Aboriginal arrivals up to 1821. It's strong on Aboriginal people, women and the full story of foreign exploration, not just Captain Cook's role.

The Exploration of Australia, by Michael Cannon, is coffee-table book in size, presentation and price, but it's a fascinating reference book about the gradual European uncovering of the continent.

The Fatal Impact, by Alan Moorehead, begins with the voyages of James Cook, regarded as one of the greatest and most humane explorers, and tells the tragic story of the European impact on Australia, Tahiti and Antarctica in the years that followed Captain Cook's great voyages of discovery. It details how good intentions and the economic imperatives of the time led to disaster, corruption and annihilation

John Pilger's *A Secret Country* is a vividly written book which deals with Australia's historical roots, its shabby treatment of Aboriginal people and the current political complexion.

Far Country, by Alan Powell, is a very readable history of the Northern Territory. Ernestine Hill's *The Territory* is another worthwhile volume on the history of the Territory.

The Front Door, by Douglas Lockwood, is a history of Darwin from 1869 to 1969. For some good pictures of Darwin during WW II, try *Darwin's Air War*, published by the Historical Society of the Northern Territory.

Women of the Kath-rine, by Pearl Ogden, is a fascinating account of the pioneering women of Katherine. In a similar vein is *Katherine's No Lady*, by Winsome Maff. *Stores & Stories* by Jean Bagshaw delves into the life of a woman running general stores on Aboriginal communities in the 1970s and '80s.

For a taste of Alice Springs early this century, get hold of *Alice on the Line* by Doris Blackwell & Douglas Lockwood. The early days of the Daly River area are recorded in *Spirit of the Daly* by Peter Forrest.

Other books which give an insight into the pioneering days in the outback include *Packhorse & Waterhole* by Gordon Buchanan, son of legendary drover Nat Buchanan who was responsible for opening up large areas of the Northern Territory; *The Big Run*, by Jock Makin, a history of the huge Victoria River Downs cattle station in the Victoria River district; and *The Cattle*

King by Ion Idriess, which details the life of the remarkable Sir Sidney Kidman, the man who set up a chain of stations in the outback early this century.

Aboriginal People

The Australian Aborigines by Kenneth Maddock is a good cultural summary. The award-winning *Triumph of the Nomads*, by Geoffrey Blainey, chronicles the life of Australia's original inhabitants, and convincingly demolishes the myth that Aboriginal people were 'primitive' people trapped on a hostile continent. They were in fact extremely successful in adapting to and overcoming the difficulties presented by the climate and resources (or seeming lack of them) – the book's an excellent read.

For a sympathetic historical account of what's happened to the original Australians since Europeans arrived read *Aboriginal Australians* by Richard Broome. *A Change of Ownership*, by Mildred Kirk, covers similar ground to Broome's book, but does so more concisely, focusing on the land rights movement and its historical background.

The Other Side of the Frontier, by Henry Reynolds, uses historical records to give a vivid account of an Aboriginal view of the arrival and takeover of Australia by Europeans. His *With the White People* identifies the essential Aboriginal contributions to the survival of the early White settlers. *My Place*, Sally Morgan's prize-winning autobiography, traces her discovery of her Aboriginal heritage. *The Fringe Dwellers* by Nene Gare describes just what it's like to be an Aborigine growing up in a White-dominated society.

Don't Take Your Love to Town by Ruby Langford and *My People* by Oodgeroo Noonuccal (Kath Walker) are also recommended reading for people interested in the experiences of Aboriginal people.

Songman, by Allan Baillie, is a fictional account of the life of an adolescent Aboriginal boy growing up in Arnhem Land in the days before White settlement.

Fiction

You don't need to worry about bringing a few good novels from home for your trip to Australia; there's plenty of excellent recent Australian literature including the novels and short stories of writers such as Helen Garner, Elizabeth Jolley, Frank Moorhouse, David Malouf, Thomas Keneally, Peter Carey, Thea Astley and Tim Winton.

There's many Australian classics (these have also been made into films), including *The Getting of Wisdom* by Henry Handel Richardson (the pen name of Ethel Florence Lindesay Richardson), *Picnic at Hanging Rock* by Joan Lindsay and *My Brilliant Career* by Miles Franklin. *For the Term of his Natural Life*, written in 1870 by Marcus Clarke, was one of the first books to be made into a film, in 1926.

The works of Banjo Paterson (*The Man from Snowy River*, for example), Henry Lawson, Frank Hardy, Alan Marshall (*I Can Jump Puddles*) and Albert Facey (*A Fortunate Life*) make interesting reading.

See the Literature section in the Facts about the Country chapter for more on Australia's best known fiction writers.

Travel Accounts

Accounts of travels in Australia include the marvellous *Tracks*, by Robyn Davidson. It's the amazing story of a young woman who set out alone to walk from Alice Springs to the Western Australia coast with her camels – proof that you can do anything if you try hard enough. It almost single-handedly inspired the current Australian interest in camel safaris!

Quite another sort of travel is Tony Horwitz's *One for the Road*, an often hilarious account of a high-speed hitchhiking trip around Australia (Oz through a windscreen). In contrast, *The Ribbon and the Ragged Square*, by Linda Christmas, is an intelligent, sober account of a nine-month investigatory trip round Oz by a *Guardian* journalist from England. There's lots of background and history as well as first-hand reporting and interviews.

The late Bruce Chatwin's book *The*

Songlines tells of his experiences among central Australian Aboriginal people and makes more sense of the Dreamtime, sacred sites, sacred songs and the traditional Aboriginal way of life than 10 learned tomes put together. Along the way it also delves into the origins of humankind and throws in some pithy anecdotes about modern Australia.

The journals of the early European explorers can be fairly hard going but make fascinating reading. The hardships that many of these men (and they were virtually all men) endured is nothing short of amazing. These accounts are usually available in the main libraries. Men such as Sturt, Eyre, Leichhardt, Davidson, King (on the Burke & Wills expedition), Stuart and many others all kept detailed journals.

Sean & David's Long Drive, a hilarious, offbeat road book by young Australian author Sean Condon, is one of the titles in Lonely Planet's new 'Journeys' travel literature series.

Travel Guides

Burnum Burnum's Aboriginal Australia is subtitled 'a traveller's guide'. If you want to explore Australia from the Aboriginal point of view, this large and lavish hardback is the book for you.

For trips into the outback in your own vehicle Lonely Planet's *Outback Australia* is the book to get. The late Brian Sheedy's *Outback on a Budget* includes lots of practical advice. There are a number of other books about vehicle preparation and driving in the outback, including *Explore Australia by Four-Wheel Drive* by Peter & Kim Wherrett.

Australia's Wonderful Wildlife (Australian Women's Weekly) is the shoestringer's equivalent of a coffee-table book – a cheap paperback with lots of great photos of the animals you didn't see, or those that didn't stay still when you pointed your camera at them.

Lonely Planet's *Bushwalking in Australia* describes over 35 walks of different lengths and difficulty in various parts of the country.

Souvenir Books

If you want a souvenir of Australia, such as a photographic record, try one of the numerous coffee-table books like *A Day in the Life of Australia*. There are many other Australian books which make good gifts: children's books with very Australian illustrations like Julie Vivar and Mem Fox's *Possum Magic*, Norman Lindsay's *The Magic Pudding* and *Snugglepot & Cuddlepie* by May Gibbs (one of the first best-selling Australian children's books), or cartoon books by excellent Australian cartoonists such as Michael Leunig or Kaz Cooke.

Maps

There's no shortage of maps available, although many of them are of pretty average quality. For road maps the best are probably those published by the various oil companies – Shell, BP, Mobil, etc, and these are available from service stations. The AANT is another good source of maps, and they are often a lot cheaper than the oil company maps. See earlier in this chapter for addresses. The Department of Land, Planning & Environment also stocks a good range of maps, and has offices in Darwin and Alice Springs.

For bushwalking, off-roading and other activities which require large-scale maps, the topographic sheets put out by the Australian Surveying & Land Information Group (AUSLIG) are the ones to get. Many of the more popular sheets are available over the counter at shops which sell specialist bushwalking gear and outdoor equipment. AUSLIG also has special interest maps showing various types of land use such as population densities or Aboriginal land. For more information, or a catalogue, contact AUSLIG, Department of Administrative Services, Scrivener Bldg, Fern Hill Park, Bruce, ACT 2617 (☎ (06) 201 4201).

MEDIA

Australia has a wide range of media although a few big companies (Rupert Murdoch's News Corporation and Kerry Packer's Consolidated Press being the best known) own an awful lot of what there is to read and watch.

The ownership of media enterprises is closely monitored by the federal government, and foreign ownership of any is limited to 15%. The laws regarding cross-media ownership are also tight, and both laws have led to recent clashes between the government and interested parties, particularly with Canadian Conrad Black's and Australian Kerry Packer's level of ownership of the Fairfax group.

Newspapers & Magazines

There's pretty slim pickings when it comes to local newspapers. The Territory's only daily is the tabloid *NT News*, which is pretty lightweight. In Alice Springs the twice-weekly *Centralian Advocate* provides a bit of local news. There's also the *Australian*, a Murdoch-owned paper and the country's only national daily.

Weekly magazines include an Australian edition of *Time* and a combined edition of the Australian news magazine the *Bulletin* and *Newsweek*. The *Guardian Weekly* is widely available and good for international news.

The Independent is a monthly magazine which explores current social and lifestyle issues in depth, while the *Business Review Weekly* does the same with business matters on a weekly basis.

Good outdoor and adventure magazines include *Wild*, *Rock* and *Outdoor Australia*.

Magazines from the UK and USA are also available, but usually with a delay of a month or so.

Radio & TV

The national advertising-free (so far) TV and radio network is the Australian Broadcasting Corporation (ABC). In most places there are a couple of ABC radio stations and a host of commercial stations, both AM and FM, featuring the whole gamut of radio possibilities, from rock to talkback to 'beautiful music'. Triple J is an ABC youth FM radio station which broadcasts nationally and is an excellent place to hear music (Australian and overseas) which is outside the pop main-stream and to plug in to Australia's youth culture.

Imparja is an Aboriginal owned and run commercial TV station which operates out of Alice Springs and has a 'footprint' which covers one-third of the country (mainly the Northern Territory, South Australia and western NSW). It broadcasts a variety of programs, ranging from soaps to pieces made by and for Aboriginal people.

On the pay TV front Australia is really dragging its feet. Only in 1995 did the first pay TV operation start, and even now it's only available to a fraction of the population, and at relatively high cost. The major players in the industry are still jockeying for position, and until the dust settles pay TV is a bit of a non-starter.

Internet

The World Wide Web is rapidly expanding to become one of the major sources of information on anything you care to name. Although things on the Net change rapidly, some sites which currently contain a range of information on the Northern Territory include:

Guide to Australia
This site, maintained by the Charles Sturt University in NSW, is a mine of information, with links to federal and Northern Territory government departments, weather information, books, maps, etc.
http://www.csu.edu.au/education/australia.html

The Aussie Index
A fairly comprehensive list of Australian companies, educational institutions and government departments which maintain Web sites.
http://www.aussie.com.au/aussie.htm

Australian Government
The federal government has a site, which is predictably unexciting, but it is wide-ranging and a good source for things like visa information.
http://gov.info.au

Taunet
The only service provider in the Territory, with a few links to local sites, and snippets of local info which may be useful.
http://www.taunet.net.au

Northern Territory Tourism Commission
A vaguely interesting site which gives a brief rundown of the Territory.
http://www.world.net/travel/australia/ntinfo/nttc

Lonely Planet
> Our own site is not specific to the Northern Territory (or even Australia) but is still definitely worth a look. Well, we would say that, wouldn't we?
>
> http://www.lonelyplanet.com.au

FILM & PHOTOGRAPHY

Australian film prices are not too far out of line with those of the rest of the Western world. Including developing, 36-exposure Kodachrome 64 or Fujichrome 100 slide film costs around $25, but with a little shopping around you can find it for around $20 – even less if you buy it in quantity.

There are a number of camera shops in Darwin and Alice Springs and standards of camera service are high. Developing standards are also high, with many places offering one-hour developing of print film.

Photography is no problem, but in the outback you have to allow for the exceptional intensity of the light. Best results in the outback regions are obtained early in the morning and late in the afternoon. As the sun gets higher, colours appear washed out. Especially in the summer, allow for temperature extremes and do your best to keep film as cool as possible, particularly after exposure. Other film and camera hazards are dust in the outback and humidity in the Top End.

As in any country, politeness goes a long way when taking photographs; ask before taking pictures of people. Note that many Aboriginal people do not like to have their photographs taken, even from a distance.

HEALTH

Australia is a remarkably healthy country to travel in, considering that such a large portion of it lies in the tropics. Tropical diseases such as malaria and yellow fever are unknown, diseases of insanitation such as cholera and typhoid are unheard of, and even some animal diseases such as rabies and foot-and-mouth disease have yet to be recorded.

So long as you have not visited an infected country in the past 14 days (aircraft refuelling stops do not count) no vaccinations are required for entry. There are, however, a few routine vaccinations that are recommended worldwide whether you are travelling or not, and it's always worth checking whether your tetanus booster is up to date.

Medical care in Australia is first-class and only moderately expensive. A typical visit to the doctor costs around $35. If you have an immediate health problem, phone or visit the casualty section at the nearest public hospital.

Visitors from the UK, New Zealand, Malta, Italy, Sweden and the Netherlands have reciprocal health rights in Australia and can register at any Medicare office. This entitles them to free or heavily subsidised medical treatment at public hospitals and from clinics which 'bulk bill' (ie, the bill for the treatment gets sent direct to Medicare).

Travel Insurance

Ambulance services in Australia are self-funding (ie, they're not free) and can be frightfully expensive, so you'd be wise to take out travel insurance for that reason alone. Make sure the policy specifically includes ambulance, helicopter rescue and a flight home for you and anyone you're travelling with, should your condition warrant it. Also check the fine print: some policies exclude 'dangerous activities' such as scuba diving, motorcycling and even trekking. If such activities are on your agenda, you don't want that policy.

Medical Kit

While facilities in cities and towns are generally of a very high standard, doctors and hospitals are few and far between in the remote areas. If you're heading off the beaten track, at least one person in your party should have a sound knowledge of first-aid treatment, and in any case you'll need a first-aid handbook and a basic medical kit. Some of the items that should be included are:

- Aspirin or paracetamol (acetaminophen in the US) – for pain or fever.
- Antihistamine (such as Benadryl) – useful as a

decongestant for colds and allergies, to ease the itch from insect bites or stings, and to help prevent motion sickness. There are several antihistamines on the market, all with different pros and cons (eg a tendency to cause drowsiness), so it's worth discussing your requirements with a pharmacist or doctor. Antihistamines may cause sedation and interact with alcohol so care should be taken when using them.

- Loperamide (eg Imodium) or Lomotil for diarrhoea; prochlorperazine (eg Stemetil) or metaclopramide (eg Maxalon) for nausea and vomiting. Antidiarrhoea medication should not be given to children under the age of 12.
- Antiseptic such as povidone-iodine (eg Betadine), which comes as a solution, ointment, powder and impregnated swabs – for cuts and grazes.
- Calamine lotion or Stingose spray – to ease irritation from bites or stings.
- Bandages and Band-aids – for minor injuries.
- Scissors, tweezers and a thermometer (note that mercury thermometers are prohibited by airlines).
- Cold and flu tablets and throat lozenges
- Insect repellent, sunscreen, suntan lotion, chap stick and water purification tablets.

Optional items include:

- Antacid indigestion tablets.
- Ear drops.
- Vinegar for jellyfish stings
- Burn cream

Health Precautions

Travellers from the northern hemisphere need to be aware of the intensity of the sun in Australia. Those ultraviolet rays can have you burnt to a crisp even on an overcast day, so if in doubt wear protective cream, a wide-brimmed hat and a long-sleeved shirt with a collar. Australia has a high incidence of skin cancer, a fact directly connected to exposure to the sun. Be careful.

The contraceptive pill is available on prescription only, so a visit to a doctor is necessary. Doctors are listed in the Yellow Pages section of the phone book or you can visit the outpatients section of a public hospital. Condoms are available from chemists, many convenience stores, and vending machines in the public toilets of many hotels and universities.

Basic Rules

Everyday Health Normal body temperature is 98.6° F or 37° C; more than 2° C (4° F) higher indicates a high fever. The normal adult pulse rate is 60 to 100 per minute (children 80 to 100, babies 100 to 140). You should know how to take a temperature and a pulse rate. As a general rule the pulse increases about 20 beats per minute for each ° C (2° F) rise in fever.

Respiration (breathing) rate is also an indicator of illness. Count the number of breaths per minute: between 12 and 20 is normal for adults and older children (up to 30 for younger children, 40 for babies). People with a high fever or serious respiratory illness (like pneumonia) breathe more quickly than normal. More than 40 shallow breaths a minute may indicate pneumonia.

Heat In northern and outback areas you can expect the weather to be hot between October and April, and travellers from cool climates may feel uncomfortable, even in winter. 'Hot' is a relative term, depending on what you are used to. The sensible thing to do on a hot day is to avoid the sun between mid-morning and mid-afternoon. Infants and elderly people are most at risk from heat exhaustion and heatstroke.

Water People who first arrive in a hot climate may not feel thirsty when they should; the body and 'thirst mechanism' often need a few days to adjust. The rule of thumb is that an active adult should drink at least four litres of water per day in warm weather, more when physically very active, such as when cycling or walking. Use the colour of your urine as a guide: if it's clear you're probably drinking enough, but if it's dark you need to drink more. Remember that body moisture will evaporate in the dry air with no indication that you're sweating.

Tap water is safe to drink in towns and cities throughout the Territory. In outback areas, bore water may not be fit for human consumption, so seek local advice before drinking it.

Always beware of water from rivers,

creeks and lakes, as it may have been infected by stock or wildlife. The surest way to disinfect water is to thoroughly boil it for 10 minutes.

Health Problems

Sunburn In the tropics, the desert or at high altitude you can get sunburnt surprisingly quickly, even through cloud. Use a sunscreen and take extra care to cover areas which don't normally see sun – such as your feet. A hat provides added protection, and you should also use zinc cream or some other barrier cream for your nose and lips. Calamine lotion is good for mild sunburn.

Remember that too much sunlight, whether it's direct or reflected (glare) can damage your eyes. If your plans include being near water, sand or snow, then good sunglasses are doubly important. Good quality sunglasses are treated to filter out ultraviolet radiation. However, poor quality lenses will actually do more harm than good. Since all sunglasses cause your pupils to dilate and tinted lenses don't filter out much of the UV radiation, your retinas will end up adsorbing more ultraviolet light than they would if no sunglasses were worn. Excessive ultraviolet light can damage your retinas.

Prickly Heat Prickly heat is an itchy rash caused by excessive perspiration trapped under the skin. It usually strikes people who have just arrived in a hot climate and whose pores have not yet opened sufficiently to cope with greater sweating. Keeping cool but bathing often, using a mild talcum powder or even resorting to air-conditioning may help until you acclimatise.

Heat Exhaustion Dehydration or salt deficiency can cause heat exhaustion. Take time to acclimatise to high temperatures and make sure you get sufficient liquids. Wear loose clothing and a broad-brimmed hat. Do not do anything too physically demanding.

Salt deficiency is characterised by fatigue, lethargy, headaches, giddiness and muscle cramps and in this case salt tablets may help. Vomiting or diarrhoea can deplete your liquid and salt levels. Anhydrotic heat exhaustion, caused by an inability to sweat, is quite rare. Unlike the other forms of heat exhaustion it is likely to strike people who have been in a hot climate for some time, rather than newcomers.

Heatstroke This serious, sometimes fatal, condition can occur if the body's heat-regulating mechanism breaks down and the body temperature rises to dangerous levels. Long, continuous periods of exposure to high temperatures can leave you vulnerable to heat stroke. You should avoid excessive alcohol or strenuous activity when you first arrive in a hot climate.

The symptoms are feeling unwell, not sweating very much or at all and a high body temperature (39°C to 41°C). Where sweating has ceased the skin becomes flushed and red. Severe, throbbing headaches and lack of coordination will also occur, and the sufferer may be confused or aggressive. Eventually the victim will become delirious or convulse. Hospitalisation is essential, but meanwhile get victims out of the sun, remove their clothing, cover them with a wet sheet or towel and then fan continually.

Fungal Infections Fungal infections, which occur with greater frequency in hot weather, are most likely to occur on the scalp, between the toes or fingers (athlete's foot), in the groin (jock itch or crotch rot) and on the body (ringworm). You get ringworm (which is a fungal infection, not a worm) from infected animals or by walking on damp areas, like shower floors.

To prevent fungal infections wear loose, comfortable clothes, avoid artificial fibres, wash frequently and dry carefully. If you do get an infection, wash the infected area daily with a disinfectant or medicated soap and water, and rinse and dry well. Apply an antifungal powder like the widely available Tinaderm. Try to expose the infected area to air and sunlight as much as possible and wash all towels and underwear in hot water as well as changing them often.

Motion Sickness Eating lightly before and during a trip will reduce the chances of motion sickness. If you are prone to motion sickness try to find a place that minimises disturbance – near the wing on aircraft, close to midships on boats, near the centre on buses. Fresh air usually helps; reading and cigarette smoke don't. Commercial motion-sickness preparations, which can cause drowsiness, have to be taken before the trip commences; when you're feeling sick it's too late. Ginger (available in capsule form) and peppermint (including mint-flavoured sweets) are natural preventatives.

Jet Lag Jet lag is experienced when a person travels by air across more than three time zones (each time zone usually represents a one-hour time difference). It occurs because many of the functions of the human body (such as temperature, pulse rate and emptying of the bladder and bowels) are regulated by internal 24-hour cycles called circadian rhythms. When we travel long distances rapidly, our bodies take time to adjust to the 'new time' of our destination, and we may experience fatigue, disorientation, insomnia, anxiety, impaired concentration and loss of appetite. These effects will usually be gone within three days of arrival, but there are ways of minimising the impact of jet lag:

* Rest for a couple of days prior to departure; try to avoid late nights and last-minute dashes for travellers' cheques, passport etc.
* Try to select flight schedules that minimise sleep deprivation; arriving late in the day means you can go to sleep soon after you arrive. For very long flights, try to organise a stopover.
* Avoid excessive eating (which bloats the stomach) and alcohol (which causes dehydration) during the flight. Instead, drink plenty of non-carbonated, non-alcoholic drinks such as fruit juice or water.
* Avoid smoking, as this reduces the amount of oxygen in the aeroplane cabin even further and causes greater fatigue.
* Make yourself comfortable by wearing loose-fitting clothes and perhaps bringing an eye mask and ear plugs to help you sleep.

Diarrhoea A change of water, food or climate can all cause the runs; diarrhoea caused by contaminated food or water is more serious. Despite all your precautions you may still have a mild bout of diarrhoea but a few rushed toilet trips with no other symptoms is not indicative of a serious problem. Moderate diarrhoea, involving half-a-dozen loose movements in a day, is more of a nuisance.

Dehydration is the main danger with any diarrhoea, particularly for children where dehydration can occur quite quickly. Fluid replacement remains the mainstay of management. Weak black tea with a little sugar, soda water, or soft drinks allowed to go flat and diluted 50% with water are all good. With severe diarrhoea a rehydrating solution is necessary to replace minerals and salts. Commercially available ORS (oral rehydration salts) are very useful. In an emergency you can make up a solution of eight teaspoons of sugar to a litre of boiled water and provide salted cracker biscuits at the same time. You should stick to a bland diet as you recover.

Lomotil or Imodium can be used to bring relief from the symptoms, although they do not actually cure the problem. Only use these drugs if absolutely necessary – eg if you *must* travel. For children under 12 years Lomotil and Imodium are not recommended. Under all circumstances fluid replacement is the most important thing to remember. Do not use these drugs if the person has a high fever or is severely dehydrated.

Viral Gastroenteritis This is caused not by bacteria but, as the name suggests, by a virus. It is characterised by stomach cramps, diarrhoea, and sometimes by vomiting and/or a slight fever. All you can do is rest and drink lots of fluids.

Worms These parasites are most common in rural, tropical areas and a stool test when you return home is not a bad idea. They can be present on unwashed vegetables or in meat which has been prepared on a farm and not been inspected by the proper authorities.

Infestations may not show up for some time, and although they are generally not serious, if left untreated they can cause severe health problems. A stool test is necessary to pinpoint the problem and medication is often available over the counter.

Tetanus This potentially fatal disease is found in undeveloped tropical areas. It is difficult to treat but is preventable with immunisation. Tetanus occurs when a wound becomes infected by a germ which lives in the faeces of animals or people, so clean all cuts, punctures or animal bites. Tetanus is also known as lockjaw, and the first symptom may be discomfort in swallowing, or stiffening of the jaw and neck; this is followed by painful convulsions of the jaw and whole body.

Sexually Transmitted Diseases Sexual contact with an infected sexual partner spreads these diseases. While abstinence is the only 100% preventative, using condoms is also effective. Gonorrhoea and syphilis are the most common of these diseases; sores, blisters or rashes around the genitals, discharges or pain when urinating are common symptoms. Symptoms may be less marked or not observed at all in women. Syphilis symptoms eventually disappear completely but the disease continues and can cause severe problems in later years. The treatment of gonorrhoea and syphilis is by antibiotics.

There are numerous other sexually transmitted diseases, for most of which effective treatment is available. However, there is no cure for herpes and there is also currently no cure for AIDS.

HIV/AIDS HIV, the Human Immunodeficiency Virus, may develop into AIDS, Acquired Immune Deficiency Syndrome. Any exposure to blood, blood products or bodily fluids may put a person at risk. Transmission in Australia is mostly through contact between homosexual or bisexual males, or via contaminated needles shared by IV drug users. Apart from abstinence, the most effective preventative is always to practise safe sex using condoms. It is impossible to detect the HIV-positive status of an otherwise healthy-looking person without a blood test.

HIV/AIDS can also be spread through infected blood transfusions, although in Australia all blood is screened for HIV. It can also be spread by dirty needles – vaccinations, acupuncture, tattooing and ear or nose piercing can potentially be as dangerous as intravenous drug use if the equipment is not clean.

Fear of HIV infection should never preclude treatment for serious medical conditions. Although there may be a risk of infection, it is very small indeed.

Cuts & Scratches Skin punctures can easily become infected in hot, humid weather and may be difficult to heal. Treat any cut with an antiseptic such as Betadine. Where possible avoid bandages and Band-aids, which can keep wounds wet. Coral cuts are notoriously slow to heal, as the coral injects a weak venom into the wound. Avoid coral cuts by wearing shoes when walking on reefs, and clean any cut thoroughly with sodium peroxide if available.

Bites & Stings Bee and wasp stings are usually painful rather than dangerous. Calamine lotion will give relief and ice packs will reduce the pain and swelling. There are some spiders with dangerous bites but antivenenes are usually available. Scorpion stings are notoriously painful. Scorpions often shelter in shoes or clothing.

Certain cone shells found in Australia can sting dangerously or even fatally. There are various fish and other sea creatures which can sting or bite dangerously or which are dangerous to eat. Again, local advice is the best suggestion.

For information on snakes and box jellyfish see the Dangers & Annoyances section later in this chapter.

Leeches & Ticks Leeches may be present in damp rainforest conditions; they attach themselves to your skin to suck your blood. Trekkers often get them on their legs or in their boots. Salt or a lighted cigarette end will make them fall off. Do not pull them off, as the bite is then more likely to become infected. An insect repellent may keep them away. You should always check your body if you have been walking through a potentially tick-infested area as ticks can cause skin infections and other more serious diseases.

If a tick is found attached, press down around the tick's head with tweezers, grab the head and gently pull upwards. Avoid pulling the rear of the body as this may squeeze the tick's gut contents through the attached mouth parts into the skin, increasing the risk of infection and disease. Smearing chemicals on the tick will not make it let go and is not recommended.

Women's Health

Poor diet, lowered resistance due to the use of antibiotics for stomach upsets and even contraceptive pills can lead to vaginal infections when travelling in hot climates. Keeping the genital area clean, and wearing skirts or loose-fitting trousers and cotton underwear will help to prevent infections.

Yeast infections, characterised by a rash, itch and discharge, can be treated with a vinegar or lemon-juice douche, or with yoghurt. Nystatin suppositories are the usual medical prescription. Trichomoniasis is a more serious infection; symptoms are a discharge and a burning sensation when urinating. Male sexual partners must also be treated, and if a vinegar-water douche is not effective medical attention should be sought. Metronidazole (Flagyl) is the prescribed drug.

Pregnancy Most miscarriages occur during the first three months of pregnancy, so this is the most risky time to travel as far as your own health is concerned. Miscarriage is not uncommon, and can occasionally lead to severe bleeding. The last three months should also be spent within reasonable distance of good medical care. A baby born as early as 24 weeks stands a chance of survival, but only in a good modern hospital. Pregnant women should avoid all unnecessary medication, but vaccinations and

malarial prophylactics should still be taken where possible. Additional care should be taken to prevent illness and particular attention should be paid to diet and nutrition. Alcohol and nicotine, for example, should be avoided.

WOMEN TRAVELLERS

The Northern Territory is generally a safe place for women travellers, although it's probably best to avoid walking alone late at night. Sexual harassment is unfortunately still second nature to many Aussie males, particularly in the Territory where the macho male image is still big. It's generally true to say your average Territory male is going to be fairly unenlightened about women's issues; you're far more likely to meet an ocker than a Snag!

Hitching is certainly not recommended for solo women, and even pairs should exercise care at all times (see the section on hitching in the Getting Around chapter.)

GAY & LESBIAN TRAVELLERS

While Australia in general is rapidly becoming a popular destination among gay and lesbian travellers, attitudes in the Territory are a good few years (light-years, some would say) behind those you find on the east coast and elsewhere – the predominant attitude you're likely to come across is that gay men are still 'bloody poofters' and that's that.

Graylink (PO Box 3826, Darwin, NT 0801 (☎ 8948 0089; fax 8948 1777) is a gay-friendly, Darwin-based company which coordinates independent travel and group tours through the Top End of Australia. It also operates a local tour booking agency and information centre by the international arrivals gate at Darwin Airport.

EMERGENCY

In the case of a life-threatening situation ☎ 000. This call is free from any phone and the operator will connect you with either the police, ambulance or fire brigade. To dial any of these services direct, check the inside

Northern Territory for the Disabled Traveller

The general level of disability awareness in Australia is encouraging, however, information about accessible accommodation and tourist attractions is fragmented and available on a regional basis only. The practical level of awareness is generally high and new accommodation must meet standards set down by law.

Information

The Australian Tourist Commission (see the Tourist Information section earlier in this chapter for contact details) publishes an information fact sheet *Travel in Australia for People with Disabilities* containing addresses of organisations which provide assistance to the disabled.

NICAN (National Information Communications Awareness Network), PO Box 407, Curtin, ACT 2605 (☎(06) 285 3713; fax 285 3714) is an Australia-wide directory providing information on accessible accommodation, sporting and recreational activities.

ACROD (Australian Council for the Rehabilitation of the Disabled), PO Box 60, Curtin, ACT 2605 (☎(06) 282 4333; fax 281 3488), can provide information about help organisations, accommodation and tour operators providing specialised tours.

Other sources to contact are the Northern Territory Visual Impairment Resource Unit (☎ 8981 5488) and the Deafness Association of the Northern Territory (☎ 8945 2016).

Publications to look for include:

Access in Alice published by the Disability Services Bureau (☎ 8951 6772)

Darwin – City Without Steps and *Free in Darwin – Places to Go*, available from the local council, Darwin Civic Centre, Harry Chan Ave (☎ 8982 2511) and from the Darwin Region Tourism Association, 33 Smith St (☎ 8981 4300) which also has a list of Darwin's wheelchair-accessible accommodation. Information is also available from the Community Care Centre for Disability Workers in Darwin (☎ 8989 2876)

Easy Access Australia – A Travel Guide to Australia ($24.80), a book researched and written by wheelchair users (order from PO Box 218, Kew, Victoria, 3101)

Smooth Ride Guides – Australia & New Zealand, published in the UK but available in Australia

A Wheelie's Handbook of Australia, another book written by a wheelchair user (order from Colin James, PO Box 89, Coleraine, Victoria 3315).

Organised Tours

Few tour operators are equipped for wheelchairs but in Darwin, Land-a-Barra Tours (☎ 8932 2543 or 8981 5233) operates a boat where a wheelchair can be anchored securely, providing a safe fishing session. Also in Darwin, Sahara Tours (☎ 8953 0881) runs tours in a wheelchair hoist-equipped bus.

---

front cover of the White Pages section of the telephone book.

For other telephone crisis and personal counselling services (such as sexual assault, poisons information or alcohol and drug problems), check the Community Information pages of the telephone book.

DANGERS & ANNOYANCES
Animal Hazards

There are a few unique and sometimes dangerous creatures, although it's unlikely that you'll come across many of them. Here's a rundown just in case.

Snakes The best-known danger in the Australian outback, and the one that captures visitors' imaginations, is snakes. Although there are many venomous snakes there are few that are aggressive, and unless you have the bad fortune to stand on one it's unlikely that you'll be bitten. Taipans and tiger snakes, however, will attack if alarmed. Sea snakes can also be dangerous.

Places to Stay

Accommodation in the Territory is generally good, the difficulty is finding out about it. Always ask at tourist offices for lists of wheelchair-accessible accommodation and tourist attractions.

Darwin and Alice Springs both have large hotels and a number of motels which provide accessible rooms. Motel chains such as Flag and Best Western are also well represented.

There are other accommodation providers which have accessible rooms and most proprietors will do what they can to assist you. The publication guides published by the state motoring organisations are very comprehensive and give wheelchair-access information. However, it is best to confirm that the facilities would suit your needs.

For campers there are wheelchair-accessible showers and toilets at Cooinda, Merl, Muirella Park, Gunlom and Yulara camp sites.

Getting Around

Air Travel by air is easy; Qantas and Ansett welcome disabled passengers. Qantas staff undergo disability training and Ansett has instituted ANSACARE, a system of recording your details once only eliminating repetition at booking and obviating the need for further medical certificates. Neither airline requires a medical certificate for long-term, stable disabilities. Darwin, Alice Springs and Yulara airports all have facilities for the disabled traveller; parking spaces, wheelchair access to terminals and accessible toilets. However, there are no air bridges at Alice or Yulara so the airlines use a forklift to raise an enclosed platform to transfer wheelchair passengers. Some Qantas jets have an accessible toilet on board.

Bus Long-distance bus travel is not yet a viable option for the wheelchair user.

Train The *Ghan*, which runs weekly between Alice Springs and Adelaide, has one compartment fitted out for wheelchair users.

Taxi Taxis in Darwin (☎freecall 131008 or 8981 8777) include three station wagons and one van converted to carry a wheelchair. In Alice (☎ 8952 1877) a modified stretch vehicle is available.

Car Rental Avis and Hertz offer hire cars with hand controls at no extra charge for pick up at the major airports, but advance notice is required.

Parking The international wheelchair symbol for parking in allocated bays is widely recognised.

Bruce Cameron

To minimise your chances of being bitten always wear boots, socks and long trousers when walking through undergrowth where snakes may be present. Don't put your hands into holes and crevices, and be careful when collecting firewood.

Snake bites do not cause instantaneous death and antivenenes are usually available. Keep the victim calm and still, wrap the bitten limb tightly, as you would for a sprained ankle, and then attach a splint to immobilise it. Then seek medical help, if possible with the dead snake for identification. Don't attempt to catch the snake if there is even a remote possibility of being bitten again. Tourniquets and sucking out the poison are now comprehensively discredited.

Spiders We've got a couple of nasty spiders too, including the funnel-web, the redback and the white-tail, so it's best not to play with any spider. Of these, only the redback is found in the Territory. For redback bites apply ice and seek immediate medical attention.

Insects Among the splendid variety of biting insects the mosquito and march fly are the most common.

Leeches are common in wet areas, and while they will suck your blood they are not dangerous and are easily removed by the application of salt or heat.

Crocodiles Saltwater crocodiles can be a real danger and have killed a number of people (travellers and locals). They are found in river estuaries and large rivers, sometimes a long way inland, so before diving into that inviting, cool water find out from the locals whether it's croc-free.

Box Jellyfish The box jellyfish, also known as the sea wasp or 'stinger', is present in Territory waters during summer and can be fatal. The stinging tentacles spread several metres away from the sea wasp's body; by the time you see it you're likely to have been stung. If someone is stung, they are likely to run out of the sea screaming and collapse on the beach, with weals on their body as though they've been whipped. They may stop breathing. Douse the stings with vinegar (always carry some with you when swimming at the beach), do not try to remove the tentacles from the skin, and treat as for snake bite. If there's a first-aider present, they may have to apply artificial respiration until the ambulance gets there. Above all, stay out of the sea when the sea wasps are around – the locals are ignoring that lovely water for an excellent reason.

Flies & Mosquitoes

For four to six months of the year you'll have to cope with those two banes of the Australian outdoors – the fly and the mosquito.

In the towns the flies are not too bad; it's in the country that it starts getting out of hand, and the further 'out' you get the worse the flies seem to be. In central Australia the flies start to come out with the warmer spring weather (late August), particularly if there has been any amount of spring rain, and last through until winter. They are such a nuisance that virtually every shop sells the Genuine Aussie Fly Net (made in Korea), which fits on a hat and is rather like a string onion bag but is very effective. It's either that or the 'Great Australian Wave' to keep them away. Repellents such as Aerogard and Rid go some way to deterring the little bastards.

Mossies too can be a problem, especially in the Top End – in Kakadu there are droves of them year round. Fortunately none of them are malaria carriers.

On the Road

Kangaroos and wandering stock can be a real hazard to the driver. A collision with one will badly damage your car and probably kill the animal. Unfortunately, other drivers are even more dangerous, particularly those who drink. Australia has its share of fatal road accidents, particularly in the countryside, so don't drink and drive, and please take care. The dangers posed by stray animals and drunks are particularly enhanced at night, so it's best to avoid travelling after dark. See the

Redback Spider

Getting Around chapter for more on driving hazards.

WORK

If you come to Australia on a 12-month 'working holiday' visa you can officially only work for three out of those 12 months, but working on a regular tourist visa is not on. Many travellers on tourist visas do find casual work, but with a national unemployment rate of around 9%, and youth unemployment as high as 40% in places, it can be difficult to find a job, legal or otherwise, in many areas.

With the current boom in tourism, casual work is often not too hard to find at the major tourist centres. Alice Springs and Darwin are both good prospects, but the opportunities are usually limited to the peak holiday seasons.

Other good prospects for casual work include factories, bar work, waiting on tables or washing dishes, other domestic chores at outback roadhouses, nanny work, fruit picking and collecting for charities.

Although many travellers do find work, if you are coming to Australia with the intention of working, make sure you have enough funds to cover you for your stay, or have a contingency plan if the work is not forthcoming.

The Commonwealth Employment Service (CES) has offices in Darwin, Katherine, Tennant Creek and Alice Springs, and the staff usually have a good idea of what's available where.

The various backpackers' magazines, newspapers and hostels are good information sources – some local employers even advertise on their notice boards.

Tax File Number It's important to apply for a Tax File Number (TFN) if you plan to work (or open a bank account – see the Money section earlier in this chapter for details) in Australia, not because it's a condition of employment, but without a TFN tax will be deducted from any wages you receive at the maximum rate, which is currently set at 48.5%! To get a TFN, contact the local branch of the Australian Taxation Office for a form. It's a straightforward procedure, and you will have to supply adequate identification, such as a passport and driving licence. The issue of a TFN takes about four weeks.

Paying Tax Yes, it's one of the certainties in life! If you have supplied your employer with a Tax File Number, tax will be deducted from your wages at the rate of 29% if your annual income is below $20,700. As your income increases, so does the tax rate, with the maximum being 48.5% for that part of an income over $50,000. For non-resident visitors, tax is payable from the first dollar you earn, unlike residents who have something like a $6000 tax-free threshold. For this reason, if you have had tax deducted at the correct rate as you earn, it is unlikely you'll be entitled to a tax refund when you leave.

If you have had tax deducted at 48.5% because you have not submitted a Tax File Number, you will be entitled to a partial refund. Once you lodge a tax return (which must include a copy of the Group Certificate all employers issue to salaried workers at the end of the financial year or within seven days of leaving a job), you will be refunded the extra tax you have paid. Before you can lodge a tax return, however, you must have a Tax File Number.

ACTIVITIES

There are plenty of activities that you can take part in while travelling through the Territory. Here is just an idea of what's available:

Bushwalking

One of the best ways of really getting away from it all in the Territory is to go bushwalking. There are many fantastic walks in the various national parks, particularly Kakadu, Litchfield and Watarrka (Kings Canyon). Willis's Walkabouts (☎ 8985 2134) is one company which offers extended bushwalks year round in both the Top End and the Centre.

Scuba Diving

There's great scuba diving in Darwin harbour on old WW II wrecks. See the Darwin section for details of companies offering dives and courses.

Cycling

You often see people cycling in the Northern Territory, but the stops between drinks can be uncomfortably long and you need to be well prepared. For the not so masochistic there are plenty of great day trips around Darwin and in the MacDonnell Ranges out of Alice Springs.

Camel Riding

For the more adventurous, camel riding has really taken off in the country around Alice Springs. If you've done it in India or Egypt or you just fancy yourself as the explorer/outdoors type, then here's your chance. You can take anything from a five-minute stroll to a 14-day expedition.

Hot-Air Ballooning

Hot-Air Ballooning is another popular adventure option in Alice Springs, with at least two companies offering early morning flights over the outback.

Fossicking

Fossicking is a popular pastime in the Northern Territory, although it is really only an option if you have a 4WD. About 30% of Australia's land area consists of basins which have been filled with sediments; with the notable exception of precious opal, these are poor in gemstones. Only about 15% has potential for fossickers and this lies in three interrupted zones that run roughly north-south across the continent. The central zone runs from Kangaroo Island off South Australia to Darwin and includes the northern Flinders Ranges, the Harts Range in central Australia and the Top End goldfields.

In order to fossick you must first obtain a fossicking permit. Permission to fossick on freehold land and mineral leases must usually be obtained from the owner or lease-holder. Sadly, the actions of the thoughtless minority in trespassing and abuse of property has brought the hobby into disrepute in many areas and fossickers are no longer always welcome.

Contact the Department of Mines & Energy in Darwin, Tennant Creek or Alice Springs for information on mining law, permits and the availability of geological maps, reports and fossicking guides.

Barramundi Fishing

For many visitors to the northern regions of Australia, one of the primary motivations for their visit is to land a 'barra' – Australia's premier native sport fish.

The barra is such a highly prized fish mainly because of its great fighting qualities: once it takes a lure or fly, it fights like hell to be free. As you try to reel one in, chances are it will play the game for a bit, then make some powerful runs, often leaping clear of the water and shaking its head in an attempt to throw the hook. Even the smaller fish (three to four kg) can put up a decent fight, but when they are about six kg or more you have a battle on your hands which can last several minutes.

Landing the barra is a challenge, but it's only half the fun; the other half is eating it. The barramundi is a prized table fish, although the taste of the flesh does depend to some extent on where the fish is caught. Those caught in saltwater or tidal rivers are generally found to have the sweetest flavour; those in landlocked waterways can have a muddy flavour and soft flesh if the water is a bit murky.

Naturally, everyone has their own theory as to where, when and how barramundi are most likely to be caught. The fish is found throughout coastal and riverine waters of the Top End. The best time to catch them is the post-Wet, ie around late March to the end of May. At this time the floods are receding from the rivers and the fish tend to gather in the freshwater creeks which are full of young fish. The best method is to fish from an anchored boat and cast a lure into a likely spot, such as a small creek mouth or flood-way.

The period from June to September is the Dry. While it's not the best season for barra, many roads and tracks which are impassable at other times of the year are open, and so the opportunities of finding a good spot are much enhanced. Trolling close to banks, snags or rock bars with lures is best at this time as the barra tend to stay deep and are relatively inactive as the water is cool.

The build-up to the Wet, from October to late December, is another good fishing time. The water temperature is on the rise, so the fish are more active. Coastal inlets and tidal rivers offer the best fishing at this time, and trolling lures is the best method, although live bait also gets good results.

During the Wet, from January to March, fishing is generally done from boats as many tracks and roads are flooded, making access by vehicle difficult. Casting lures into flood-water run-off or channels is the best method, but even fishing from a river bank or into large channels which feed the rivers is often successful.

In tidal rivers the barra seem to strike most

A lucky Barramundi fisherman sports his catch

during the last hour or so of the ebb tide, particularly if this is late in the day. The same applies to saltwater areas, although the first couple of hours of the rising tide are also good.

Life Cycle of the Barramundi Early in the Wet, the female barras spawn around the river mouths. The high tides wash the eggs into the coastal swamps. At the end of the Wet, juvenile fish migrate up the rivers to the freshwater areas. By the end of the first year, a barra weighs around half a kg and measures around 30 cm. Here they stay until they are three to four years old (around 3.5 kg and 65 cm), when they head for the tidal waters. Maturing males start to head downstream at the beginning of the Wet, and once in the open water, mature males undergo an amazing transformation – they turn into females and start spawning! By the time the fish are about seven years old they weigh upwards of seven kg (around 90 cm), and fish of up to 20 kg are not uncommon.

Bag & Size Limits It's in everyone's interest to follow the legal restrictions when fishing for barra. In the Northern Territory, the minimum size limit is 55 cm, and the bag limit is five fish in one day. They may not be retained on a tether line at any time. Certain areas of the Northern Territory are closed to fishing between 1 October and 31 January.

Good Fishing Practices Apart from following the legal restrictions, there are a number of things you can do to enhance the quality of barra fishing for yourself and others who follow.

When releasing undersized fish or those you don't need, try to remove the hook while the fish is still in the water, use a net to land the fish for de-hooking and weighing. Where it's necessary to handle the fish, grip it firmly by the lower jaw ensuring your fingers don't get under the gill cover.

To store fish in top condition, they should be killed and bled as soon as possible. Bleeding by cutting the gills or throat is the best method, and if the fish is then placed in ice water this reduces clotting and aids bleeding. Rapid cleaning also preserves the quality, and it's helpful if you can avoid cutting into the flesh surrounding the gut region or rupturing the intestines. Chill the cleaned fish as soon as possible, as this slows the rigor mortis process; when rigor mortis takes place rapidly, violent muscle contractions result in loss of natural juices and the flesh has a tendency to fall apart when filleted.

Clean and rinse fish in a container if possible; doing so in the river may attract crocodiles.

Information The following addresses may be useful:

Amateur Fishermen's Association of the Northern Territory, PO Box 1231, Darwin, NT 0810 (☎ 8989 2499)

Darwin Game Fishing Club, GPO Box 3629, Darwin, NT 0801 (☎ 8984 4327)

Northern Territory Game Fishing Association, GPO Box 128, Darwin, NT 0801 (☎ 8946 9846)

Recreational Fisheries Division, Department of Primary Industries & Fisheries (☎ 8999 4395)

Organised Fishing Trips & Charters There are a host of commercial operators offering fishing trips for barra and other sporting fish. Some of them include:

Barra Bash
    GPO Box 2253, Darwin, NT 0801 (☎ toll-free 1800 632 225). It does day trips out of Darwin.
Big Barra Fishing Safaris
    11 Bailey Circuit, Driver, NT 0830 (☎ 8932 1473). It offers one-day trips to the Mary River system east of Darwin, or extended tours in north-western Arnhem Land (one of only two operators to have permission to fish in Arnhem Land).
Croc-Spot Tours & Fishing Charters
    McArthur River Caravan Park, Borroloola, NT 0854 (☎ 8975 8721). It does day trips along the tidal waters of the McArthur River for barra and other sports fish, or extended offshore trips to Barranyi National Park for ocean fishing.
Land-a-Barra Tours
    10 Fagan Court, Gray, NT 0830 (☎ 8932 2543)

HIGHLIGHTS

The Territory is outdoor-adventure country. With such a variety of landscapes and climate, the main appeal lies in the wealth of natural attractions which rival anything else in Australia. The obvious attraction is Uluru (Ayers Rock), probably Australia's most readily identifiable symbol after Sydney's Opera House. There's also the UN World Heritage listed Kakadu National Park, with its abundant flora and fauna and superb wetlands; Litchfield National Park, with cool plunge pools and waterfalls; Nitmiluk National Park with the superb Katherine Gorge; and the spectacular Kings Canyon in Watarrka National Park. Other less visited parks, such as Gregory National Park in the Victoria River District and Rainbow Valley south of Alice Springs, are also well worth exploring, although you'll need a 4WD vehicle to fully appreciate them.

The Territory is also where Australia's Aboriginal cultural heritage is at its most accessible – the rock-art sites of Kakadu, and Aboriginal-owned and run tours of Arnhem Land, Manyallaluk (near Katherine), King's Canyon and Uluru are just a few of the possibilities.

The European history of the Territory is one of hardship and struggle in a hostile and unfamiliar environment. Relics of those days leave a strong impression – the Alice Springs Telegraph Station, the ghost town of Newcastle Waters, the Elsey Cemetery near Katherine and the ruins of Victoria Settlement on the Cobourg Peninsula are all vivid and poignant reminders that life in the Territory has never been easy.

The fishing opportunities are some of the best in the country, with the famed barramundi being the main prize. Places such as Borroloola on the Gulf and the settlement of Daly River both rely to a large degree on fishing-based tourism.

ACCOMMODATION

The four main cities and town in the Northern Territory are very well equipped with youth hostels, backpackers' hostels and caravan parks with camp sites – the cheapest shelter you can find. In addition to this there are plenty of motels.

A typical town will have a basic motel at

around $50 for a double, an old town centre pub with rooms (shared bathrooms) at say $30, and a caravan park probably with camp sites for around $10 and on-site vans or cabins for $35 for two. If there's a group of you, the rates for three or four people in a room are always worth checking. Often there are larger 'family' rooms or units with two bedrooms.

There are a couple of free backpackers' newspapers and booklets available at hostels around the country, and these have fairly up-to-date listings of hostels, although they give neither prices nor details of each hostel.

There's a wide variation in seasonal prices for accommodation. At peak times, school holiday in particular, prices are at their peak, whereas at other times useful discounts can be found. This particularly applies to the Top End, where the Wet season (summer) is the off season and prices can drop by as much as 30%. In this book high season prices are used unless indicated otherwise.

Bush Camping

Camping in the bush, either freelance or at designated spots in national parks and reserves, is for many people one of the highlights of a visit to Australia, and this is especially so in the Northern Territory where the national parks are a major attraction. Nights spent around a campfire under the stars are unforgettable.

In the Centre you don't even need a tent – swags are definitely the way to go. These ready made zipped canvas bedrolls, complete with mattress, are widely available as both singles and doubles, and are extremely convenient – it takes literally a few seconds to pack or unpack.

In the Top End it's still possible to use swags in the Dry, the only addition you'll need is a mosquito net. In the Wet sleeping out is a risky business and you basically need a tent.

There a few basic rules to camping in the wild:

- Most of the land in Australia belongs to someone, even if you haven't seen a house for 100 km or so.

They own it – it is their back yard. You need permission before you are allowed to camp on it. In national parks and on Aboriginal land you will need permits. On public land observe all the rules and regulations.

- Select your camping spot carefully. Start looking well before nightfall and choose a spot that makes you invisible from the road. You'll notice any number of vehicle tracks leading off the main road into the bush: explore a few and see what you find.
- Some trees (for instance, river red gums and ironwood) are notorious for dropping limbs. Know your trees, or don't camp under large branches.
- Ants live everywhere, and it's embarrassingly easy to set up camp on underground nests. Also beware of the wide variety of mean spiny seeds on the ground which can ruin your expensive tent groundsheet with pinprick holes – carry a tarpaulin or sheet of thick plastic to use as an underlay.
- Carry out all the rubbish you take in, don't bury it. Wild animals dig it up and spread it everywhere.
- Observe fire restrictions – where and when you can light a fire and make sure it is safe. Use a trench and keep the area around the fire clean of flammable material.
- Don't chop down trees or pull branches off living trees to light your fire. Don't use dead wood that's become a white-ant habitat (it won't burn well either). If the area is short of wood, go back down the track a little and collect some there. If that is not possible, use a gas stove for cooking.
- Respect the wildlife. This also means observing crocodile warnings and keeping away from suspect river banks.
- Don't camp right beside a water point. Stock and wildlife won't come in while you are there, and if it is the only water around they may die of thirst.
- Don't camp close enough to a river or stream to pollute it. In most parks the minimum distance is 20 metres.
- Don't use soap or detergent in any stream, river, dam or any other water point.
- Use toilets where they are provided. If there isn't one, find a handy bush, dig a hole, do the job and then fill in the hole. Bury all human waste well away from any stream.

Camping & Caravan Parks

In cities and towns, camping at caravan parks is the cheapest way of all, with nightly costs for two of around $8 to $15. There is a great number of caravan parks and you'll almost always find space available, especially if you only want an unpowered site. The exception is the camping ground at Yulara during school holidays when it's advisable to book in advance for any type of site, but especially a grassed one.

Australian caravan parks are well kept, conveniently located and excellent value. One of the drawbacks is that camp sites are often intended more for caravanners (house trailers for any North Americans out there) than for campers and the tent campers get little thought in these places. The fact that most of the sites are called 'caravan parks' indicates who gets most attention.

On-Site Vans & Cabins Most caravan parks have on-site vans which you can rent for the night. These give you the comfort of a caravan without the inconvenience of actually towing one of the damned things. On-site cabins are also widely available, and these are more like a small self-contained unit. They usually have one separate bedroom, or at least an area which can be screened off from the rest of the unit – just the thing if you have small kids. Cabins also have the advantage of having their own bathroom and toilet, although this is sometimes an optional extra. They are also much less cramped than a caravan, and the price difference is not always that great – say $25 to $30 for an on-site van, $30 to $50 for a cabin.

Hostels

YHA There are YHA or affiliate hostels in Alice Springs, Yulara, Darwin, Kakadu, Katherine, Mataranka and Tennant Creek.

YHA hostels provide basic accommodation, usually in small dormitories or bunk rooms although most provide twin rooms for couples. The nightly charges are very reasonable, usually between $12 and $18 a night and $2 more for non-members. To become a full YHA member in Australia costs $26 a year (there's also a $16 joining fee, although if you're an overseas resident joining in Australia you don't have to pay this). You can join at the YHA Travel Centre in Darwin (in the Transit Centre in Mitchell St) or at any of the other YHA hostels.

None of the hostels have the old fetishes for curfews and doing chores, and they don't kick you out during the day.

The YHA has the Aussie Starter Pack, whereby Australian residents joining the YHA receive two vouchers worth $8 each to use at a hostel in their state. International visitors joining the YHA at a hostel receive their first night at that hostel for free. The scheme has standardised the additional nightly fee charged to non-YHA members at $2 per night. When staying at a hostel non-members receive an Aussie Starter Card, to be stamped each night by the YHA. Once the card has been stamped 12 times, you are given a year's free membership.

You must have a regulation sheet sleeping bag or bed linen – for hygiene reasons a regular sleeping bag will not do. If you haven't got sheets they can be rented at many hostels (usually for $3), but it's cheaper, after a few nights' stay, to have your own. YHA offices and some larger hostels sell the official YHA sheet bag.

All hostels have cooking facilities and 24-hour access, and there's usually some communal area where you can sit and talk. There are usually laundry facilities and often excellent notice boards. Many hostels have a maximum-stay period because it would hardly be fair for people to stay too long when others are being turned away.

YHA members are also entitled to a number of handy discounts around the country on things such as car hire, activities and accommodation, and these are detailed in the *Discounts* booklet, published each year.

Backpacker Hostels There are backpacker hostels in Darwin, Katherine, Tennant Creek and Alice Springs. Most are purpose-built as backpackers' hostels and have a good range of facilities.

Prices at backpackers hostels are generally in line with YHA hostels, typically $12 to $18, although discounts can reduce this.

There's at least one organisation (VIP) which you can join where, for a modest fee (typically $15), you'll receive a discount card (valid for 12 months) and a list of participating hostels. This is hardly a great inducement to join but you do also receive useful discounts on other services, such as bus passes, so they may be worth considering.

Motels, Serviced Apartments & Holiday Flats

If you've got transport and want a modern place with your own bathroom and other facilities, then you're moving into the motel bracket. Motels cover the earth in Australia, just like in the USA, but they're usually located away from the city centres. Prices vary and with the motels singles are often not much cheaper than doubles. You'll sometimes find motel rooms for less than $40, but most places will be starting at $50.

Holiday flats and serviced apartments are much the same thing and bear some relationship to motels. A holiday flat is much like a motel room but usually has a kitchen or cooking facilities so you can fix your own meals. Usually holiday flats are not serviced like motels – you don't get your bed made up every morning and the cups washed out. In some holiday flats you actually have to provide your own sheets and bedding but others are operated just like motel rooms with a kitchen. Most motels provide at least tea and coffee-making facilities and a small fridge, but a holiday flat will also have cooking utensils, cutlery, crockery and so on.

Holiday flats are often rented on a weekly basis but even in these cases it's worth asking if daily rates are available. Paying for a week, even if you stay only for a few days, can still be cheaper than having those days at a higher daily rate. If there are more than just two of you, another advantage of holiday flats is that you can often find them with two or more bedrooms. A two-bedroom holiday flat is typically priced at about 1½ times the cost of a comparable single-bedroom unit.

FOOD

Meat, meat and more meat is the message in the Territory, where old habits die hard and cholesterol is something which only affects wimps down south. If you are into dinner-plate sized, inch-thick steaks, you've come to the right place. Exotic novelty meats such as kangaroo, camel, crocodile and buffalo also feature prominently, especially in places where tourists are the main patrons.

Fish, in particular the ubiquitous – and, I reckon, overrated – barramundi, is another local favourite.

At the bottom end of the food scale is the Australian meat pie. The standard pie is an awful concoction of anonymous meat and dark gravy in a soggy pastry case. You'll have to try one though; the number consumed in Australia each year is phenomenal, and they're a real part of Australian culture. In country towns where they are made by the local baker rather then being mass-produced, they can actually be pretty good.

Vegetarian Food

Vegetarians are not well catered for. In Darwin and Alice Springs there are a number of cafes with a few vegetarian dishes on the menu. Elsewhere you will have to resort to the fairly ordinary salad bars, or cook for yourself.

Shopping for Food

While a wide range of produce is sold in supermarkets, most of it has been trucked in from elsewhere and so is not always as fresh as it might be. The exception is beef, which is produced locally and is cheap and excellent. Despite the distances most food has travelled before hitting the local shelves, prices are not too out of line with what you pay elsewhere around the country.

Where to Eat

Takeaway Food In Darwin and Alice Springs you'll find all the well-known international fast-food chains – *Hungry Jack's, KFC, Pizza Hut* etc – all typically conspicuous.

On a more local level, you'll find a milk bar on (almost) every corner, and most of them sell pies, pasties, sandwiches and milkshakes. Then there are the local fish & chip shops or hamburger joints. Hamburgers and steak sandwiches from these places are generally very good, and can be very filling.

Most shopping centres have a pizza joint, and many of these do home deliveries.

Absolute rock-bottom is the kept-luke-warm-for-hours, vastly overpriced food found at roadhouses across the Territory. Give it a miss unless you have absolutely no choice.

Restaurants & Cafes Best value are the modern and casual cafes, where for less than $20 you can get an excellent feed. Unfortunately they are in short supply in this part of the world, and are pretty much limited to Darwin and, to a lesser extent, Alice Springs.

While eating out is a pleasure in the cities, in smaller country towns it can be something of an ordeal. The food will be predictable and unexciting, and is usually of the 'meat and three veg' variety.

Pubs Most pubs serve two types of meals: bistro meals, which are usually in the $10 to $15 range and are served in the dining room or lounge bar, where there's usually a self-serve salad bar; and bar (or counter) meals which are filling, simple, no-frills meals eaten in the public bar, and these usually cost less than $10, sometimes as little as $4.

The quality of pub food varies enormously, and while it's usually fairly basic and unimaginative, it's generally pretty good value. The usual meal times are from noon to 2 pm and from 6 to 8 pm.

Food Markets Where the climate allows there are often outdoor food stalls and markets, and these can be an excellent place to sample a variety of cuisines, with Asian being the most popular. Darwin's Thursday evening Mindil Beach Market is probably the largest of its type in the country, and the range of cuisines is very impressive.

DRINKS

In the non-alcoholic department Australians knock back Coke and flavoured milk like there's no tomorrow and also there's some excellent mineral water brands.

Beer

Beer drinking is as much part of the culture in the Territory as latte is down south, although it's part of the Territory image which local tourist authorities are trying, with difficulty, to shake off.

Australian beer will be fairly familiar to North Americans; it's similar to what's known as lager in the UK. It may taste like lemonade to the European real-ale addict, but it packs quite a punch. It is chilled before drinking.

Fosters is, of course, the best known international brand with a worldwide reputation, but there's a bewildering array of Australian beers. Among the most well known in the Territory are the beers made by Victoria's CUB – Fosters, Victoria Bitter (or VB) and Carlton Draught, which are known locally by the can colour – blue, green and white, respectively.

Other popular beers are XXXX (pronounced four-ex), and Tooheys Red. Recent additions to the stable of old favourites include Carlton Cold, Diamond Draught and lower alcohol beers like Tooheys Blue and Lite Ice, and styles other than your average Aussie lager, such as Blue Bock and Old Black Ale, both made by Tooheys.

The smaller breweries generally seem to produce better beer – Cascade (Tasmania) and Coopers (South Australia) being two examples. Coopers also produce a stout, which is popular among connoisseurs, and their Black Crow is a delicious malty, dark beer.

The only beer indigenous to the Territory is NT Draught, although it's not terribly popular.

Standard beer generally contains around 4.9% alcohol, although the trend in recent years has been towards low-alcohol beers, with an alcohol content of between 2% and 3.5%. Tooheys Blue is a particularly popular light beer.

And a warning: people who drive under the influence of alcohol and get caught lose their licences (unfortunately, drink-driving is a serious problem in Australia). The maximum permissible blood-alcohol concentration level for drivers in the Northern Territory is 0.08%.

While Australians in general and Territorians in particular are generally considered to be heavy beer drinkers, per capita beer has fallen quite considerably in recent years. In the past decade per capita consumption has decreased by 20%.

Excessive use of alcohol is a problem in many Aboriginal communities and for this reason many are now 'dry', and it is an offence to carry alcohol into these places. The problem has also led to restricted trading hours and even 'dry days' in some places – in Alice Springs, for instance, takeaway liquor outlets don't open until noon.

Wine

If you don't fancy Australian beer, then turn to wine like many Australians are doing. Australia has a great climate for wine producing and makes some superb wines that are cheap and readily available.

Wine is sold in 750-ml bottles or two and four-litre 'casks' – a great Australian innovation.

It takes a little while to become familiar with Australian wines and their styles, especially since the manufacturers are being forced to delete generic names from their labels as exports increase; the biggest victim is 'champagne', which is now called 'sparkling wine'. White wines are almost always drunk chilled, and in the outback many people chill their reds too.

Australia also produces excellent ports (perfect at a campfire) but only mediocre sherries.

ENTERTAINMENT
Cinema

In Darwin and Alice Springs there are at least a couple of commercial cinemas showing new-release mainstream movies. In other places one cinema may have survived, although the all-pervasive video shops have dealt what is in many cases a death-blow to country cinemas.

Discos & Nightclubs

These are pretty much limited to Darwin, where there's a reasonable choice. Admission charges range from around $6 to $12.

Some places have certain dress standards, but it is generally left to the discretion of the people at the door – if they don't like the look of you, bad luck.

Live Music

A few pubs in Darwin and Alice Springs have live music, and these are often great places for catching live bands.

The best way to find out about the local scene is to get to know some locals, or travellers who have spent some time in the place. Otherwise there are often comprehensive listings in newspapers, particularly on Friday.

Spectator Sports

Unfortunately the Territory doesn't offer a great deal to the armchair – or wooden bench – sports fan. Aussie Rules is the main game, although it is only played on local club level. Unlike down south when the football season is winter, in the Territory it is during the Wet.

During the other (non-football) half of the year there's cricket, although once again it is only played on a local level. Occasionally an interstate side will come up and play a couple of games for some out-of-season match practice.

Australia loves a gamble, and hardly any town of even minor import is without a horse-racing track or a Totalisator Agency Board (TAB) betting office. Most towns host at least one annual country race meeting, and these can be great fun. Darwin and the Alice both have racing carnivals. In addition to these are rodeos held in major towns throughout the Territory in winter.

THINGS TO BUY

There are lots of things definitely not to buy – like plastic boomerangs, fake Aboriginal ashtrays and T-shirts, and all the other terrible souvenirs which fill the tacky souvenir shops in the big cities. Most of them come from Taiwan or Korea anyway. Before buying an Australian souvenir, turn it over to check that it was actually made here!

Aboriginal Art

Aboriginal artwork has been 'discovered' by the international community, and prices are correspondingly high.

For most people the only thing remotely affordable are small carvings and some very beautiful screen-printed T-shirts produced by Aboriginal craft cooperatives. Dijeridus and boomerangs are also popular purchases, but just be aware that unless you pay top dollar, what you are getting is something made purely for the tourist trade – these are certainly not the real thing.

Australiana

The term 'Australiana' is a euphemism for souvenirs. These are the things you buy as gifts for all the friends, aunts and uncles, nieces and nephews, and other sundry bods back home. They are supposedly representative of Australia and its culture, although many are extremely dubious.

The seeds of many of Australia's native plants are on sale all over the place. Try growing kangaroo paws back home (if your own country will allow them in).

Also gaining popularity are 'bush tucker' items such as tinned witchetty grubs, or honey ants.

Opals

The opal is Australia's national gemstone and opals and jewellery made with it are popular souvenirs. It's a beautiful stone, but buy wisely and shop around – quality and prices can vary widely from place to place. There's a couple of shops in Alice Springs which specialise in opal jewellery.

Getting There & Away

AIR

Basically getting to Australia means flying, although it is sometimes possible to hitch a ride on a yacht to or from Australia.

The main problem with getting to Australia is that it's a long way from anywhere. Coming from Asia, Europe or North America there are lots of competing airlines and a wide variety of air fares, but there's no way you can avoid those great distances. Australia's current international popularity adds another problem – flights are often heavily booked. If you want to fly to Australia at a particularly popular time of year (the middle of summer, ie Christmas time, is notoriously difficult) or on a particularly popular route (like Hong Kong or Singapore to Sydney or Melbourne) then you need to plan well ahead.

In the Northern Territory the only international entry point is Darwin, and there are only limited options from here. The majority of visitors to the Northern Territory arrive here either by road or air from elsewhere in Australia.

Discount Tickets

Buying airline tickets these days is like shopping for a car, a stereo or a camera – five different travel agents will quote you five different prices. Rule number one if you're looking for a cheap ticket is to go to an agent, not directly to the airline. The airline can usually only quote you the absolutely by-the-rule-book regular fare. An agent, on the other hand, can offer all sorts of special deals particularly on competitive routes.

Ideally an airline would like to fly all its flights with every seat in use and every passenger paying the highest fare possible. Fortunately life usually isn't like that and airlines would rather have a half-price passenger than an empty seat. When faced with the problem of too many seats, they will either let agents sell them at cut prices, or occasionally make one-off special offers on particular routes – watch the travel ads in the press.

Of course what's available and what it costs depends on what time of year it is, what route you're flying and who you're flying with. If you're flying on a popular route (like from Hong Kong) or one where the choice of flights is very limited (like from South America or, to a lesser extent, from Africa) then the fare is likely to be higher or there may be nothing available but the official fare.

Similarly the dirt cheap fares are likely to be less conveniently scheduled, go by a less convenient route or be with a less popular airline. Flying London-Sydney, for example, is most convenient with airlines like Qantas, British Airways, Thai International or Singapore Airlines. They have flights every day, they operate the same flight straight through to Australia and they're good, reliable, comfortable, safe airlines. At the other extreme you could fly from London to an Eastern European or Middle Eastern city on one flight, switch to another flight from there to Asia, and change to another airline from there to Australia. It takes longer, there are delays and changes of aircraft along the way, the airlines may not be so good and, furthermore, the connection only works once a week and that means leaving London at 1.30 on a Wednesday morning. The flip side is it's cheaper.

Round-the-World Tickets

Round-the-World (RTW) tickets are very popular these days and many of these will take you through Australia. The airline RTW tickets are often real bargains and since Australia is pretty much at the other side of the world from Europe or North America it can work out no more expensive, or even cheaper, to keep going in the same direction right round the world rather than U-turn to return.

The official airline RTW tickets are

usually put together by a combination of two airlines, and permit you to fly anywhere you want on their route systems so long as you do not backtrack. Other restrictions are that you (usually) must book the first sector in advance and cancellation penalties apply. There may be restrictions on how many stops you are permitted and usually the tickets are valid from 90 days up to a year. A typical price for a South Pacific RTW ticket is around £760 or US$2500

An alternative type of RTW ticket is one put together by a travel agent using a combination of discounted tickets from a number of airlines. A UK agent like Trailfinders can put together interesting London-to-London RTW combinations including Australia for between £690 and £800.

Circle Pacific Tickets

Circle Pacific fares are a similar idea to RTW tickets which use a combination of airlines to circle the Pacific combining Australia, New Zealand, North America and Asia.

Air Travel Glossary

Apex Apex, or 'advance purchase excursion' is a discounted ticket which must be paid for in advance. There are penalties if you wish to change it.

Baggage Allowance This will be written on your ticket: usually one 20 kg item to go in the hold, plus one item of hand luggage.

Bucket Shop An unbonded travel agency specialising in discounted airline tickets.

Bumped Just because you have a confirmed seat doesn't mean you're going to get on the plane – see Overbooking.

Cancellation Penalties If you have to cancel or change an Apex ticket there are often heavy penalties involved, insurance can sometimes be taken out against these penalties. Some airlines impose penalties on regular tickets as well, particularly against 'no show' passengers.

Check In Airlines ask you to check in a certain time ahead of the flight departure (usually 1½ hours on international flights). If you fail to check in on time and the flight is overbooked the airline can cancel your booking and give your seat to somebody else.

Confirmation Having a ticket written out with the flight and date you want doesn't mean you have a seat until the agent has checked with the airline that your status is 'OK' or confirmed. Meanwhile you could just be 'on request'.

Discounted Tickets There are two types of discounted fares – officially discounted (see Promotional Fares) and unofficially discounted. The lowest prices often impose drawbacks like flying with unpopular airlines, inconvenient schedules, or unpleasant routes and connections. A discounted ticket can save you other things than money – you may be able to pay Apex prices without the associated Apex advance booking and other requirements. Discounted tickets only exist where there is fierce competition.

Full Fares Airlines traditionally offer first class (coded F), business class (coded J) and economy class (coded Y) tickets. These days there are so many promotional and discounted fares available from the regular economy class that few passengers pay full economy fare.

Lost Tickets If you lose your airline ticket an airline will usually treat it like a travellers' cheque and, after inquiries, issue you with another one. Legally, however, an airline is entitled to treat it like cash and if you lose it then it's gone forever. Take good care of your tickets.

No Shows No shows are passengers who fail to show up for their flight, sometimes due to unexpected delays or disasters, sometimes due to simply forgetting, sometimes because they made more than one booking and didn't bother to cancel the one they didn't want. Full fare passengers who fail to turn up are sometimes entitled to travel on a later flight. The rest of us are penalised (see Cancellation Penalties).

On Request An unconfirmed booking for a flight, see Confirmation.

Open Jaws A return ticket where you fly out to one place but return from another. If available this can save you backtracking to your arrival point.

Examples would be Qantas-Northwest Orient, Canadian Airlines International-Cathay Pacific and so on. As with RTW tickets there are advance-purchase restrictions and limits to how many stopovers you can take. Typically fares range between US$1760 and US$2240. Possible Circle Pacific routes include Los Angeles-Bangkok-Sydney-Auckland-Honolulu-Los Angeles or Los Angeles-Tokyo-Kuala Lumpur-Sydney-Auckland-Honolulu-Los Angeles.

To/From the UK

The cheapest tickets in London are from the numerous 'bucket shops' (discount-ticket agencies) which advertise in magazines and papers like *Time Out*, *Southern Cross* and *TNT*. Pick up one or two of these publications and ring round a few bucket shops to find the best deal. The magazine *Business Traveller* also has a great deal of good advice on air-fare bargains. Most bucket shops are trustworthy and reliable but the occasional sharp operator appears – *Time Out* and *Busi-*

Overbooking Airlines hate to fly empty seats and since every flight has some passengers who fail to show up (see No Shows) airlines often book more passengers than they have seats. Usually the excess passengers balance those who fail to show up but occasionally somebody gets bumped. If this happens guess who it is most likely to be? The passengers who check in late.

Promotional Fares Officially discounted fares like Apex fares which are available from travel agents or direct from the airline.

Reconfirmation At least 72 hours prior to departure time of an onward or return flight you must contact the airline and 'reconfirm' that you intend to be on the flight. If you don't do this the airline can delete your name from the passenger list and you could lose your seat. You don't have to reconfirm the first flight on your itinerary or if your stopover is less than 72 hours. It doesn't hurt to reconfirm more than once.

Restrictions Discounted tickets often have various restrictions on them – advance purchase is the most usual one (see Apex). Others are restrictions on the minimum and maximum period you must be away, such as a minimum of 14 days or a maximum of one year. See Cancellation Penalties.

Standby A discounted ticket where you only fly if there is a seat free at the last moment. Standby fares are usually only available on domestic routes.

Tickets Out An entry requirement for many countries is that you have an onward or return ticket, in other words, a ticket out of the country. If you're not sure what you intend to do next, the easiest solution is to buy the cheapest onward ticket to a neighbouring country or a ticket from a reliable airline which can later be refunded if you do not use it.

Transferred Tickets Airline tickets cannot be transferred from one person to another. Travellers sometimes try to sell the return half of their ticket, but officials can ask you to prove that you are the person named on the ticket. This is unlikely to happen on domestic flights, on an international flight tickets may be compared with passports.

Travel Agencies Travel agencies vary widely and you should ensure you use one that suits your needs. Some simply handle tours while full-service agencies handle everything from tours and tickets to car rental and hotel bookings. A good one will do all these things and can save you a lot of money but if all you want is a ticket at the lowest possible price, then you really need an agency specialising in discounted tickets. A discounted ticket agency, however, may not be useful for other things, like hotel bookings.

Travel Periods Some officially discounted fares, Apex fares in particular, vary with the time of year. There is often a low (off-peak) season and a high (peak) season. Sometimes there's an intermediate or shoulder season as well. At peak times, when everyone wants to fly, not only will the officially discounted fares be higher but so will unofficially discounted fares or there may simply be no discounted tickets available. Usually the fare depends on your outward flight – if you depart in the high season and return in the low season, you pay the high-season fare. ■

ness Traveller give some useful advice on precautions to take.

Trailfinders (☎ (0171) 938 3366) at 46 Earls Court Rd, London W8, and STA Travel (☎ (0171) 581 4132) at 74 Old Brompton Rd, London SW7, and 117 Euston Rd, London NW1 (☎ (0171) 465 0484), are good, reliable agents for cheap tickets.

The cheapest London to Sydney or Melbourne bucket-shop (not direct) tickets are about £385 one way or £638 return. Cheap fares to Perth are around £330 one way and £550 return. Such prices are usually only available if you leave London in the low season – March to June. In September and mid-December fares go up by about 30%, while the rest of the year they're somewhere in between. Average direct high-season fares to Sydney, Melbourne or Perth are £468 one way and £875 return.

Many cheap tickets allow stopovers on the way to or from Australia. Rules regarding how many stopovers you can take, how long you can stay away, how far in advance you have to decide your return date and so on, vary from time to time and ticket to ticket, but recently most return tickets have allowed you to stay away for any period between 14 days and one year, with stopovers permitted anywhere along your route. As usual with heavily discounted tickets the less you pay the less you get. Nice direct flights, leaving at convenient times and flying with popular airlines, are going to be more expensive than flying from London to Singapore or Bangkok with some Eastern European or Middle Eastern airline and then changing to another airline for the last leg.

From Australia you can expect to pay around A$1200 one way, and A$1800 return to London and other European capitals, with stops in Asia on the way. Again, all fares increase by up to 30% in the European summer and at Christmas.

To/From North America

There is a variety of connections across the Pacific from Los Angeles, San Francisco and Vancouver to Australia, including direct flights, flights via New Zealand, island-hopping routes and more circuitous Pacific rim routes via nations in Asia. Qantas, Air New Zealand and United all fly USA-Australia; Qantas, Air New Zealand and Canadian Airlines International fly Canada-Australia. An interesting option from the east coast is Northwest's flight via Japan.

One advantage of flying Qantas or Air New Zealand is that on the US airlines, if your flight goes via Hawaii, the west coast to Hawaii sector is treated as a domestic flight. This means that you have to pay for drinks and headsets – goodies that are free on international sectors.

To find good fares to Australia check the travel ads in the Sunday travel sections of papers like the *Los Angeles Times*, *San Francisco Chronicle-Examiner*, *New York Times* or *Toronto Globe & Mail*. You can typically get a one-way/return ticket from the west coast for US$830/1000, or US$1000/1400 from the east coast. At peak seasons, particularly the Australia summer/Christmas time, seats will be harder to get and the price will probably be higher. In the USA good agents for discounted tickets are the two student travel operators, Council Travel and STA Travel, both of which have lots of offices around the country. Canadian west-coast fares out of Vancouver will be similar to those from the US west coast. From Toronto fares go from around C$2230 return, from Vancouver C$1700.

If Pacific island-hopping is your aim, check out the airlines of Pacific island nations, some of which have good deals on indirect routings. Qantas can give you Fiji or Tahiti along the way, while Air New Zealand can offer both and the Cook Islands as well. See the Circle Pacific section for more details.

One-way/return fares available from Australia include: San Francisco A$1000/1360, New York A$1150/1660 and Vancouver $1000/1360.

To/From New Zealand

Air New Zealand and Qantas operate a network of trans-Tasman flights linking Auckland, Wellington and Christchurch in

New Zealand with most major Australian gateway cities. You can fly directly between a lot of places in New Zealand and a lot of places in Australia.

Fares vary depending on which cities you fly between and when you do it, but from New Zealand to Sydney you're looking at around NZ$450 one way and NZ$565 return, and to Melbourne NZ$529 one way and NZ$730 return. There is a lot of competition on this route, with United and British Airways both flying it as well as Qantas and Air New Zealand, so there is bound to be some good discounting going on.

Cheap fares to New Zealand from Europe will usually be for flights via the USA. A straightforward London-Auckland return bucket-shop ticket costs around £950. Coming via Australia you can continue right around on a Round-the-World (RTW) ticket which will cost from around £1050 for a ticket with a comprehensive choice of stopovers.

To/From Asia

Ticket discounting is widespread in Asia, particularly in Singapore, Hong Kong, Bangkok and Penang. There are a lot of fly-by-night operators in the Asian ticketing scene so a little care is required. Also the Asian routes have been particularly caught up in the capacity shortages on flights to Australia. Flights between Hong Kong and Australia are notoriously heavily booked while flights to or from Bangkok and Singapore are often part of the longer Europe-Australia route so they are also sometimes very full. Plan ahead. For much more information on South-East Asian travel and on to Australia see Lonely Planet's *South-East Asia on a shoestring*.

Typical one-way fares to Australia from Singapore are S$585 to Darwin (or Perth).

You can also pick up some interesting tickets in Asia to include Australia on the way across the Pacific. Qantas and Air New Zealand offer discounted trans-Pacific tickets.

From Australia return fares from Darwin to Singapore, Kuala Lumpur and Bangkok range from $800 to $1000.

The cheapest way out of Australia is to take one of the flights operating between Darwin and Kupang (Timor, Indonesia). Current one-way/return fares are $198/330. See the Darwin Getting There & Away section for full details.

To/From Africa

The flight possibilities between Africa and Australia have increased markedly in the last few years, and there is a number of direct flights each week between Africa and Australia, but only between Perth and Harare (Zimbabwe) or Johannesburg (South Africa). Qantas, South African Airways and Air Zimbabwe all fly this route.

Qantas and Malaysia Airlines (via Kuala Lumpur) are the only airlines with connections to Darwin.

To/From South America

Two routes operate between South America and Australia. The Chile connection involves Lan Chile's twice-weekly Santiago-Easter Island-Tahiti flight, from where you fly Qantas or another airline to Australia. Alternatively there is the route which skirts the Antarctic circle, flying from Buenos Aires to Auckland and Sydney, operated twice-weekly by Aerolineas Argentinas.

Departure Tax

There is a $27 departure tax when leaving Australia, but this is often incorporated into the price of your air ticket and so is not always paid as a separate tax.

Warning

This section is particularly vulnerable to change – prices for international travel are volatile, routes are introduced and cancelled, schedules change, rules are amended, special deals come and go, borders open and close. Airlines and governments seem to take a perverse pleasure in making price structures and regulations as complicated as possible and you should check directly with the airline or travel agent to make sure you understand how a fare (and ticket you may buy) works.

In addition, the travel industry is highly competitive and there are many lurks and perks. The upshot of this is that you should get quotes and advice from as many airlines and travel agents as possible before you part with your hard-earned cash. The details given in this chapter should be regarded only as pointers and cannot be any substitute for your own careful, up-to-date research.

LAND
Basically to get to the Territory you have to travel a bloody long way! The nearest state capital to Darwin is Brisbane, a distance of about 3500 km!

Train
The *Ghan* between Adelaide and Alice Springs costs $140 in coach class (no sleeper and no meals), $309 in holiday class (a sleeper with shared facilities and no meals) and $500 in 1st class (a self-contained sleeper and meals). Low season (February through June) fares are $140/278/450 respectively. For bookings phone ☎ 13 2232 during office hours.

The train departs from Adelaide on Thursday at 2 pm, arriving in Alice Springs the next day at 10.30 am. From Alice Springs the departure is on Friday at 2 pm, arriving in Adelaide the next day at 11.30 am. From April to December there's a second departure from Adelaide on Monday and Alice Springs on Tuesday.

You can also join the *Ghan* at Port Augusta, the connecting point on the Sydney to Perth route. Fares between Alice Springs and Port Augusta are $106 coach class, $279 holiday class and $464 1st-class sleeper ($106/250/416 low season).

You can transport cars between Alice Springs and Adelaide for $195, or between Alice Springs and Port Augusta for $185. Double-check the times by which you need to have your car at the terminal for loading: they must be there several hours prior to departure for the train to be 'made up'.

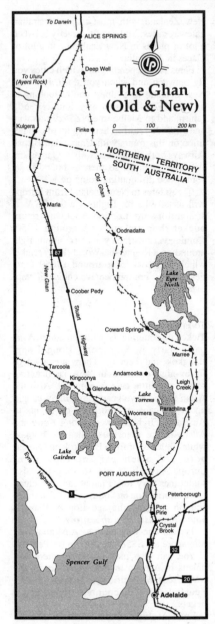

The Ghan (Old & New)

The Ghan

Australia's great railway adventure would have to be the *Ghan*. The *Ghan* went through a major change in 1980 and although it's now a rather more modern and comfortable adventure, it's still a great trip.

The *Ghan* saga started in 1877 when it was decided to build a railway line from Adelaide to Darwin. It took over 50 years to reach Alice Springs, and they're still thinking about the final 1500 km to Darwin more than a century later. The basic problem was that they made a big mistake right at the start, a mistake that wasn't finally sorted out until 1980. They built the line in the wrong place.

The grand error was a result of concluding that because all the creek beds north of Marree were bone dry, and because nobody had seen rain, there wasn't going to be rain in the future. In fact they laid the initial stretch of line right across a flood plain and when the rain came, even though it soon dried up, the line was simply washed away. In the century or so that the original *Ghan* line survived it was a regular occurrence for the tracks to be washed away.

The wrong route was only part of the *Ghan's* problems. At first it was built wide gauge to Marree, then extended narrow gauge to Oodnadatta in 1884. And what a jerry-built line it was – the foundations were flimsy, the sleepers were too light, the grading was too steep and it meandered hopelessly. It was hardly surprising that right up to the end the top speed of the old *Ghan* was a flat-out 30 km/h!

Early rail travellers went from Adelaide to Marree on the broad-gauge line, changed there to narrow gauge as far as Oodnadatta, then had to make the final journey to Alice Springs by camel train. The Afghani-led camel trains had pioneered transport through the outback and it was from these Afghanis that the *Ghan* took its name.

Finally in 1929 the line was extended from Oodnadatta to Alice Springs. Though the *Ghan* was a great adventure, it simply didn't work. At the best of times it was chronically slow and uncomfortable as it bounced and bucked its way down the badly laid line. Worse, it was unreliable and expensive to run. And worst of all, a heavy rainfall could strand it at either end or even in the middle. Parachute drops of supplies to stranded train travellers became part of outback lore and on one occasion the *Ghan* rolled in 10 days late!

By the early '70s the South Australian state railway system was taken over by the Federal government and a new line to Alice Springs was planned. The A$145 million line was to be standard gauge, laid from Tarcoola, north-west of Port Augusta on the transcontinental line, to Alice Springs – and it would be laid where rain would not wash it out. In 1980 the line was completed in circumstances that would be unusual for any major project today, let alone an Australian one – it was ahead of time and on budget.

In the late '80s the old *Ghan* made its last run and the old line was subsequently torn up. One of its last appearances was in the film *Mad Max III*.

Whereas the old train took 140 passengers and, under ideal conditions, made the trip in 50 hours, the new train takes twice as many passengers and does it in 24 hours. It's still the *Ghan*, but it's not the trip it once was. ∎

Bus

A great many travellers see Australia by bus because it's one of the best ways to come to grips with the country's size and the country's variety of terrain, and because the bus companies have such comprehensive route networks – far more comprehensive, in fact, than the railway system. The buses all look pretty similar and are similarly equipped with air-conditioning, toilets and videos.

There are two major bus companies in Australia – Greyhound Pioneer Australia (☎ toll-free 13 2030) and McCafferty's (☎ toll-free 13 1499), operating out of Brisbane. Both companies operate services into and out of the Territory on three routes – the Western Australian route from Broome,

Derby and Kununurra; the Queensland route through Mt Isa to Threeways; or straight up the Track from Adelaide.

Fares can vary a bit between the companies, but if one discounts a fare the other tends to follow quite quickly. Both companies have advance-purchase fares, and these can be as much as 50% off the normal fare if you book – usually 15 days. The fares quoted below are all full one-way fares.

Greyhound Pioneer and McCafferty's have a variety of passes available, and if you are travelling extensively in Australia they can be excellent value. The set-route passes are the most popular as they give you a set amount of time (usually 12 months) to cover a set route, and many of these include the highlights of the Territory – Uluru and Kakadu – as well Darwin, Alice Springs and all the towns along the Stuart Highway.

To/From Queensland On services from Queensland you often have to change buses

---

Interstate Quarantine
When travelling between states in Australia, whether by land or air, you may well come across signs (mainly in airports, interstate railway stations and at state borders) warning of the possible dangers of carrying fruit, plants and vegetables which may be infected with a disease or pest from one area to another.

The reason is that certain pests and diseases – such as fruit fly, cucurbit thrips, grape phylloxera and potato cyst nematodes, to name a few – are prevalent in some areas but not in others, and so for obvious reasons authorities would like to limit the spread of such problems.

Most quarantine control relies on honesty and the quarantine posts at the state/territory borders are not actually staffed. It's prohibited to carry most fruits and vegetables across the Northern Territory/Western Australia border in either direction; the controls with South Australia and Queensland are less strict, but some items are still suspect. Check at the borders. ■

---

at Threeways (or Tennant Creek) and Mt Isa. For example, you pay around $155 one way from Mt Isa to Darwin (21 hours), $250 from Brisbane (47 hours), and $237 from Cairns (40 hours). Cairns to Alice Springs costs $216 and takes 32 hours.

To/From Western Australia From Western Australia, Greyhound Pioneer and McCafferty's go to and from Perth daily through Kununurra, Broome and Port Hedland. All buses stop at Katherine, and go on to Darwin.

Some sample journey fares and times to Darwin: $90 from Kununurra (10 hours), $178 from Broome (22 hours) and $348 from Perth (57 hours).

To/From South Australia Coming up from Adelaide to Coober Pedy, you can go direct to Alice Springs, or get off at Erldunda and connect direct with services to Yulara and Uluru-Kata Tjuta National Park, 244 km to the west along the Lasseter Highway.

Greyhound Pioneer and McCafferty's have daily return services from Adelaide to Alice Springs for $142, and it takes about 20 hours. From Coober Pedy the fare is $70 and the journey takes about eight hours.

If you want to go direct to Uluru, the journey from Adelaide takes 22 hours and costs $152. From Coober Pedy it's eight hours and $66.

Other Bus Options The are a few companies which offer flexible transport options in various parts of the country, and are a good alternative to the big bus companies. The trips are generally aimed at budget travellers and so are good fun, and are a combination of straightforward bus travel and an organised tour. The buses are generally smaller and so not necessarily as comfortable as those of the big bus companies, but it's a much more interesting way to travel.

The only one operating in the Territory is the Wayward Bus (☎ toll-free 1800 882 823), an Adelaide-based company which offers transport between Adelaide and Alice Springs. The trips, which take eight days and cost $560), take in Flinders Ranges, the Oodnadatta Track, Uluru-Kata Tjuta and Watarrka (Kings Canyon) national parks. These trips include sight-seeing, meals and accommodation along the way.

Car & Motorbike
See the Getting Around chapter for details of road rules, driving conditions and information on buying and renting vehicles.

The main roads into the Territory are the Barkly Highway from Mt Isa and north Queensland; the Victoria Highway from the Kimberley in Western Australia; and the Stuart Highway from South Australia. All are bitumen roads in excellent condition, the main problem being the sheer distances involved.

Hitching
Hitching is never entirely safe in any country in the world, and we don't recommend it. Travellers who decide to hitch should understand that they are taking a small but potentially serious risk. However, many people do choose to hitch, and the advice that follows should help to make their journeys as fast and safe as possible.

Hitching is possible, but again, the distances involved make it difficult. Expect to be stuck for a day or so waiting for a ride. Katherine (where the Victoria Highway branches off west to WA) and Threeways (where the Barkly Highway heads east for Queensland) are renowned spots for this.

For more information on hitching in the Territory, see the Getting Around chapter.

Organised Tours
There are a number of tours which start in other states and end in the Northern Territory. One of these is the Wayward Bus (see Other Bus Options earlier in this chapter), which operates between Adelaide and Alice Springs.

Wilderness Challenge (☎ 8955 6504) offers eight-day 4WD trips between Broome and Darwin, although at $1295 these are not cheap.

Even more expensive is Australian Bushmans Tours (☎ toll-free 1800 027 917), a company providing 10-day trips from Cairns to Uluru (Ayers Rock) for $1899.

SEA
It is simply not possible to get to Darwin (or any other Australian port for that matter) on a scheduled shipping service. It may be possible to pick up a ride on a yacht in Indonesia or Singapore, but you'd have to be lucky.

Getting Around

For schedules of all land and sea transport services throughout the Northern Territory and the rest of Australia, there's the publication called *Travel Times*, which is published twice yearly and is available from newsagents ($7.95).

AIR

Australia is so vast (and at times so empty) that unless your time is unlimited you will probably have to take to the air sometime.

There are only two main domestic carriers within Australia, Qantas (which merged with Australian Airlines) and Ansett, despite the fact that the airline industry is deregulated. For 40-odd years Australia had a 'two-airline policy'; Australian and Ansett had a duopoly on domestic flights.

With this cosy cohabitation the airlines could charge virtually what they liked, and operate virtually identical schedules. All this meant that domestic airline travel within Australia was expensive and the choices of flights limited, particularly on the low-volume routes.

With deregulation came another player, Compass, and a fierce price war. The net result was that Compass folded (twice!) and for all intents we're back to a two-airline industry and relatively high prices, although discounting is now a regular feature of the domestic flights scene.

Unfortunately there is only limited discounting on flights into and out of the Northern Territory, so the advance-purchase deals are about the best you can hope for.

Note that all domestic flights in Australia are nonsmoking. Because Qantas flies both international and domestic routes, flights leave from both the international and domestic terminals at Australian airports. Flights with flight numbers from QF001 to QF399 operate from international terminals; flight numbers QF400 and above operate from domestic terminals.

Cheap Fares

Random Discounting A major feature of the deregulated air-travel industry is random discounting. As the airlines try harder to fill planes, they often offer substantial discounts on selected routes. Although this seems to apply mainly to the heavy volume routes, that's not always the case.

To make the most of the discounted fares, you need to keep in touch with what's currently on offer, mainly because there are usually conditions attached to cheap fares – such as booking 14 or so days in advance, only flying on weekends or between certain dates and so on. Also the number of seats available is usually fairly limited. The further ahead you can plan the better.

It is fair to say that on virtually any route in the country covered by Qantas or Ansett the full economy fare will not be the cheapest way to go. Because the situation is so fluid, the special fares will more than likely have changed by the time you read this. For that reason we list the full one-way economy fares throughout the book, although you can safely assume that there will be a cheaper fare available.

Discounts are generally greater for return rather than one-way travel.

Some Possibilities If you're planning a return trip and you have 14 days up your sleeve then you can save 45% to 50% by travelling Apex. You have to book and pay for your tickets 14 days in advance and you must stay away at least one Saturday night. Flight details can be changed at any time, but the tickets are nonrefundable. If you book seven days in advance the saving is 35% to 40% off the full fare.

For one-way travel, if you can book three days in advance a saving of around 10% is offered; for seven-day advance booking the discount is around 20%.

University or other higher education students under the age of 26 can get a 25%

discount off the regular economy fare. An airline tertiary concession card (available from the airlines) is required for Australian students. Overseas students can use their International Student Identity Card.

All nonresident international travellers can get up to a 40% discount on internal Qantas flights and 25% on Ansett flights simply by presenting their international ticket when booking. It seems there is no limit to the number of domestic flights you can take, it doesn't matter which airline you fly into Australia with, and it doesn't have to be on a return ticket. Note that the discount

applies only to the full economy fare, and so in many cases it will be cheaper to take advantage of other discounts offered. The best advice is to ring around and explore the options before you buy.

Air Passes
With discounting being the norm these days, air passes do not represent the value they did in pre-deregulation days. However, there are a few worth checking out if you plan to fly quite a bit in Australia. If the Territory is your only destination, a pass would be of no use at all.

Qantas Qantas offers two passes. The Australia Explorer Pass can only be purchased overseas and involves purchasing coupons for either short-haul flights at $170 one way, or for long-haul sectors (such as just about anywhere to Uluru) for $220. You must purchase a minimum of four coupons before you arrive in Australia, and once here you can buy up to four more.

There is also the Qantas Backpackers Pass, which can only be bought in Australia on production of identification such as a YHA membership or a VIP Backpackers or Independent Backpackers Card. You must purchase a minimum of three connecting sectors (such as Sydney-Uluru, Uluru-Darwin and Darwin-Cairns), and stay a minimum of two nights at each stop. The discount is quite substantial; a sample fare using this pass is Sydney to Uluru for $279 one way, as against the full economy fare of $505.

Ansett Ansett has its Kangaroo Airpass, which gives you two options – 6000 km with two or three stopovers for $949 ($729 for children) and 10,000 km with three to seven stopovers for $1499 ($1149 for children). A number of restrictions apply to these tickets, although they can be a good deal if you want to see a lot of country in a short period of time. You do not need to start and finish at the same place; you could start in Sydney and end in Darwin, for example.

Restrictions include a minimum travel

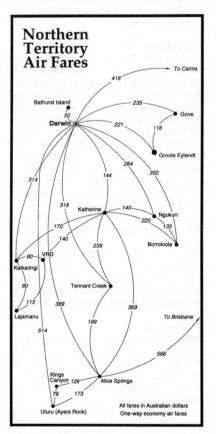

Northern Territory Air Fares

To Cairns 418
Bathurst Island 50
Darwin
235 — Gove
221 118
Groote Eylandt
284 350
314 144
319 Katherine 140 Ngukurr
170 220 135
140 239 Borroloola
80 VRD
Kalkaringi
80 Tennant Creek
115 389 369
Lajamanu 199 To Brisbane
514
566
Kings Canyon 129 Alice Springs
79 173
Uluru (Ayers Rock)

All fares in Australian dollars
One-way economy air fares

time (10 nights) and a maximum (45 nights). One of the stops must be at a non-capital-city destination and be for at least four nights, and you can only stay at each destination once. All sectors must be booked when you purchase the ticket, although these can be changed without penalty unless the ticket needs rewriting, in which case there's a $50 charge. Refunds are available in full before travel commences and not at all once you start using the ticket.

On a 6000-km air pass you could, for example, fly Sydney-Alice Springs-Cairns-Brisbane-Sydney. That gives you three stops and two of them are in non-capital cities. The regular fare for that circuit would be $1569, but with current discounts (seven day advance purchase) it's $1217, so you save $368. A one-way route might be Adelaide-Melbourne-Sydney-Alice Springs-Perth. There are three stops, of which one is a non-capital city. Regular cost for that route would be $1484, but with discounts it's $1187, so the saving is $238.

Other Airline Options
There is one secondary airline operating within the Northern Territory. Airnorth (☎ toll-free 1800 627 474) connects Darwin and Alice Springs with most places in the Territory, including Uluru, Bathurst Island, Borroloola, Gove, Kalkaringi, Katherine, Lajamanu, Kings Canyon, Tennant Creek and Victoria River Downs. See the chart for fare details.

The regional airline in Western Australia, Ansett WA, also connects Darwin with the Kimberley.

Airport Transport
There are private or public bus services at Darwin, Alice Springs and Uluru airports. In smaller places you'll probably be able to cadge a lift with airline staff, who often make a special trip to the airport/airstrip to meet the flight.

BUS
Greyhound Pioneer Australia (☎ toll-free 13 2030) and McCafferty's (☎ toll-free 13 1499), operating out of Brisbane, both have extensive services throughout the Northern Territory – see the Getting There & Away chapter for details of the fares and passes offered by the two companies.

CAR
Distances in the Northern Territory are large, and there are many places where access by public transport is either inconvenient or not possible, so the car is the accepted means of getting from A to B. More and more travellers are also finding it the best way to see the country. With three or four of you the costs are reasonable and the benefits many, provided of course you don't have a major mechanical problem.

Road Rules
Driving in the Territory holds few real surprises. Australians drive on the left-hand side of the road just like in the UK, Japan and most countries in south and east Asia and the Pacific. There are a few local variations from the rules of the road as applied elsewhere in the West. The main one is the 'give way to the right' rule – if an intersection is unmarked (unusual), you must give way to vehicles entering the intersection from your right.

The general speed limit in built-up areas is 60 km/h. On the open highway there is no speed limit outside of built-up areas.

All new cars in Australia have seat belts back and front and if your seat has a belt then you're required to wear it. You're liable to be fined if you don't. Small children must be belted into an approved safety seat.

Although overseas licences are acceptable in Australia for genuine overseas visitors, an International Driving Permit is preferred.

On the Road
Road Conditions The Territory is not crisscrossed by multilane highways. There simply is not enough traffic and the distances are too great to justify them. All major highways are bitumen roads engineered to a pretty high standard.

A number of secondary roads are just a single-lane strip of bitumen, and are known as 'beef roads'. By 1975 the Commonwealth government had spent $30 million dollars on 2500 km of roads in an effort to promote the beef cattle industry. One of these single-lane bitumen roads is the Delamere Road, which runs from the Victoria Highway to Wave Hill station, another is the Carpentaria Highway from the Stuart Highway to Borroloola.

You don't have to get very far off the beaten track, however, to find yourself on dirt roads, and anybody who sets out to see the country in reasonable detail will have to do some dirt-road travelling. If you seriously want to explore, then you'd better plan on having four-wheel Drive (4WD) and a winch. A few useful spare parts are worth carrying if you're travelling on highways in the Northern Territory. A broken fan belt can be a damn nuisance if the next service station is 200 km away.

Drink-Driving Drink-driving is a serious problem, especially in country areas. Serious attempts have been made in recent years to reduce the road toll – random breath tests are not uncommon in built-up areas. If you're caught with a blood-alcohol level of more than 0.08% then be prepared for a hefty fine and the loss of your licence.

Fuel Fuel (super, diesel and unleaded) is available from stations sporting the well-known international brand names. Prices vary from place to place and from price war to price war but generally it's in the 70c to 80c a litre range. In the outback the price can soar and some outback service stations are not above exploiting their monopoly position. Distances between fill-ups can be long in the outback.

Hazards Cows and kangaroos are two common hazards on country roads, and a collision is likely to kill the animal and seriously damage your vehicle. Kangaroos are most active around dawn and dusk, and they travel in groups. If you see one hopping across the road in front of you, slow right down – its friends are probably just behind it. Many Australians try to avoid travelling

altogether between 5 pm and 8 am, because of the hazards posed by animals. Finally, if one hops out right in front of you, hit the brakes and only swerve to avoid the animal if it is safe to do so. The number of people who have been killed in accidents caused by swerving to miss an animal is high. It's better to damage your car and probably kill the animal than kill yourself and others with you.

Another thing to watch for are the road trains found on roads throughout the Territory. These consist of a prime mover and two, or usually three, trailers. On dual-lane highways they pose few problems, although you do need to allow a surprisingly long distance when overtaking. On single-lane bitumen roads you need to get right off the road if one approaches, because you can be damn sure it won't! On dirt roads you also need to pull over, and often stop altogether while you wait for the dust cloud to clear. Overtaking road trains on these roads is hazardous. Often it's best just to have a break for a while and let the road train get well ahead of you.

Outback Travel If you really want to see outback Australia there are still lots of roads where the official recommendation is that you report to the police before you leave one end, and again when you arrive at the other. That way if you fail to turn up at the other end they can send the search parties. Nevertheless many of these tracks are now much better kept than in years past and you don't need 4WD or fancy expedition equipment to tackle them. You do need to be carefully prepared and to carry important spare parts, however. Backtracking 300 km to pick up some minor malfunctioning component or, much worse, to arrange a tow, is unlikely to be easy or cheap. When travelling to really remote areas it is advisable to travel with a high-frequency outpost radio transmitter which is equipped to pick up the Royal Flying Doctor Service bases in the area.

You will need to carry a fair amount of water in case of disaster – around 20 litres a person is sensible – stored in more than one container. Food is less important and the space might be better allocated to an extra spare tyre.

The Automobile Association of the Northern Territory can advise on preparation and supply maps and track notes. Most tracks have an ideal time of year. In the Centre it's not wise to attempt the tough tracks during the heat of summer (November-March) when the dust can be severe, chances of mechanical trouble are much greater and water will be scarce and hence a breakdown more dangerous. Similarly in the north travelling in the Wet may be hindered by flooding and mud.

If you do run into trouble in the back of beyond, stay with your car. It's easier to spot a car than a human from the air, and you wouldn't be able to carry your 20 litres of water very far anyway.

For the full story on safe outback travel, get hold of Lonely Planet's *Outback Australia*. Some of the favourite tracks in the Territory are:

Simpson Desert Crossing the Simpson Desert from Birdsville (Qld) to the Stuart Highway is becoming increasingly popular but this route is still a real test. A 4WD vehicle is definitely required and you should be in a party of at least three or four vehicles equipped with long-range two-way radios.

Warburton Road/Gunbarrel Highway This route runs west from Uluru (Ayers Rock) by the Aboriginal settlements of Docker River and Warburton to Laverton in Western Australia. From there you can Drive down to Kalgoorlie and on to Perth. The route passes through Aboriginal reserves and permission to enter them must be obtained in advance if you want to leave the road. A well-prepared conventional vehicle can complete this route although ground clearance can be a problem and it is very remote. From the Yulara resort at Uluru to Warburton is 567 km, and it's another 568 km from there to Laverton. It's then 361 km on sealed road to Kalgoorlie. For 300 km near the Giles Meteorological Station the Warburton Road and the Gunbarrel Highway run on the same

route. Taking the old Gunbarrel (to the north of the Warburton) all the way to Wiluna in Western Australia is a much rougher trip requiring 4WD. The Warburton Road is now commonly referred to as the Gunbarrel – just to make life simple.

Tanami Track Turning off the Stuart Highway just north of Alice Springs the Tanami Track (or Road) goes north-west across the Tanami Desert to Halls Creek in Western Australia. It's a popular short-cut for people travelling between the Centre and the Kimberley. The road has been extensively improved in recent years and conventional vehicles are quite OK although there are occasional sandy stretches on the WA section. Be warned that the Rabbit Flat roadhouse in the middle of the desert is only open from Friday to Monday.

Plenty Highway & Sandover Highway These two routes run east from the Stuart Highway, to the north of Alice Springs, to Mt Isa in Queensland. They're suitable for robust conventional vehicles.

Travel Permits

If you wish to travel through the outback on your own, you may need special permits to pass through or visit Aboriginal land or to camp in national parks.

Aboriginal Land Permits A glance at any up-to-date land-tenure map of the Northern Territory shows that vast portions are Aboriginal land. Generally this has either government-administered reserve status or it may be held under freehold title vested in an Aboriginal land trust and managed by a council or corporation. With either format, the laws of trespass apply just as with any other form of private land, but the fines attached can be somewhat heftier.

In some cases permits won't be necessary if you stay on recognised public roads that cross Aboriginal territory. However, as soon as you leave the main road by more than 50 metres, even if you're 'only' going into an Aboriginal settlement for fuel, you may need a permit. If you're on an organised tour, the operator should take care of any permits, but this is worth checking before you book.

Applications To make an application, you have to write to the appropriate land council as outlined below, enclosing a stamped, self-addressed envelope and giving all details of your proposed visit or transit. In general, the following information is required: the names of all members of the party; the dates of travel; route details; purpose of the visit; the make, model and registration number of the vehicle; and contact address and telephone number.

Allow plenty of time: the application process may take one or two months as the administering body generally must obtain approval from the relevant community councils before issuing your permit. Keep in mind also that there is no guarantee that you'll get one. It may be knocked back for a number of reasons, including the risk of interference with sacred sites, or disruption of ceremonial business. As well, some communities simply may not want to be bothered by visitors.

The Central Land Council administers all Aboriginal land in the southern and central regions of the Territory. Write to the Permits Officer (☎ 8951 6320; fax 8953 4345) at PO Box 3321, Alice Springs, NT 0871.

A transit permit is required for the Yulara-Docker River road, but not for either the Tanami Track or the Sandover Highway where these cross Aboriginal land. Travellers may camp overnight without a permit within 50 metres of the latter two routes. On the Tanami Track, you can call in to Yuendumu and fuel up without a permit.

Arnhem Land and other northern mainland areas are administered by the Northern Land Council. Write to the Permits Officer (☎ 8920 5172; fax 8945 2633) at PO Box 42921, Casuarina (Darwin), NT 0811.

Visitors to Bathurst and Melville islands also need permits. Apply in advance to the Tiwi Land Council, Unit 9, Wingate Centre, Winnellie, Darwin, NT 0800 (☎ 8947 1838).

National Park Permits You sometimes need a permit to camp in a national park or even to visit, such as for Gurig National Park, and such a permit must be obtained in advance. It often includes maps and other useful information. Details of required permits are provided in the relevant sections in this book. If you're visiting Kakadu more than once in a year, it pays to buy a season pass, which costs $60 and covers the vehicle and all its occupants.

Car Rental

If you've got the cash there are plenty of car-rental companies ready and willing to put you behind the wheel. Competition in the car-rental business is pretty fierce so rates tend to be variable and lots of special deals pop up and disappear again. Whatever your mode of travel on the long stretches, it can be very useful to have a car for some local travel. Between a group it can even be reasonably economical. There are some places, like around Alice Springs, where if you haven't got your own transport you really have to choose between a tour and a rented vehicle since there is no public transport and the distances are too great for walking or even bicycles.

The four major companies are Budget, Hertz, Avis and Territory Rent-a-Car, with offices or agents in most towns. Then there is a number of local firms or firms with just one outlet. People assume that the big operators generally have higher rates than the local firms but it ain't necessarily so, so don't jump to conclusions.

The big firms have a number of big advantages, however. First of all they're the ones at the airports – Avis, Budget, Hertz and Territory are represented at Darwin and Alice Springs airports. If you want to pick up a car or leave a car at the airport then they're the best ones to deal with.

The major companies offer a choice of deals, either unlimited km or a flat charge plus so many cents per km. On straightforward off-the-card city rentals they're all pretty much the same price. It's on special deals, odd rentals or longer periods that you find the differences. Weekend specials, usually three days for the price of two, are usually good value. If you just need a car for three days make it the weekend rather than midweek. Budget offer 'stand-by' rates and you may see other special deals available.

Daily rates are typically about $50 a day for a small car (Holden Barina, Ford Festiva, Daihatsu Charade, Suzuki Swift), about $75 a day for a medium car (Mitsubishi Magna, Toyota Camry, Nissan Pulsar) or about $100 a day for a big car (Holden Commodore, Ford Falcon), all including insurance. You must be at least 21 to hire from most firms.

There is a whole collection of other factors to bear in mind about this rent-a-car business. For a start, if you're going to want it for a week, a month or longer then they all have lower rates. If you're in the really remote outback (places like Darwin and Alice Springs are only vaguely remote) then the choice of cars is likely to be limited to the larger, more expensive ones.

And if in Darwin, don't forget the 'rent-a-wreck' companies. They specialise in renting older cars and have a variety of rates, typically around $35 a day. If you just want to travel around the city, or not too far out, they can be worth considering.

One thing to be aware of when renting a car in the Northern Territory is that if you are travelling on *any* dirt road you are generally not covered by insurance. So if you have an accident, you'll be liable for *all* the costs involved. This applies to all companies, although they don't always point this out. This condition does not apply to 4WD vehicles.

4WD Rental Having a 4WD vehicle enables you to get right off the beaten track and out to some of the great wilderness and outback places, to see some of the Australian natural wonders that most travellers don't see.

Renting a 4WD vehicle is within the budget range if a few people get together. Something small like a Suzuki or similar costs around $100 per day; for a Toyota Landcruiser you're looking at around $150, which should include insurance and some free km (typically 100 km per day). Check

the insurance conditions, especially the excess, as they can be onerous – $4000 is typical, although this can often be reduced to around $1000 on payment of an additional daily charge (around $20). Even in a 4WD the insurance cover of most companies does not cover damage caused when travelling 'off-road', which basically means anything that is not a maintained bitumen or dirt road. Make sure you know exactly what you are covered for, and that it applies to the areas you intend visiting.

Hertz and Avis have 4WD rentals, with one-way rentals possible between the eastern states and the Northern Territory. Budget also rents 4WD vehicles from Darwin and Alice Springs. Brits:Australia (☎ toll-free 1800 331 454) is a company which hires fully equipped 4WD vehicles fitted out as campervans. These have proved extremely popular in recent years, although they are not cheap at $120 per day for unlimited km, plus Collision Damage Waiver ($15 per day). They have offices in Darwin, Alice Springs and all the mainland capitals, so one-way rentals are also possible.

Buying a Car

If you want to explore Australia by car and haven't got one or can't borrow one, then you've either got to buy one or rent one. Australian cars are not cheap – another product of the small population. Locally manufactured cars are made in small, uneconomic numbers and imported cars are heavily taxed so they won't undercut the local products. If you're buying a second-hand vehicle reliability is all important. Mechanical breakdowns way out in the outback can be very inconvenient (not to mention dangerous) – the nearest mechanic can be a hell of a long way down the road.

Shopping around for a used car involves much the same rules as anywhere in the Western world but with a few local variations. First of all, used-car dealers in Australia are just like used-car dealers from Los Angeles to London – they'd sell their mother into slavery if it turned a dollar. You'll probably get any car cheaper by buying privately through newspaper small ads rather than through a car dealer. Buying through a dealer does give the advantage of some sort of guarantee, but a guarantee is not much use if you're buying a car in Darwin and intend setting off for Perth next week.

The further you get from civilisation, the better it is to be in a Holden or a Ford. New cars can be a whole different ball game of course, but if you're in an older vehicle, something that's likely to have the odd hiccup from time to time, then life is much simpler if it's a car for which you can get spare parts anywhere from Bourke to Bulamakanka. When your fancy Japanese car goes kaput somewhere back of Borroloola it's likely to be a two-week wait while the new bit arrives fresh from Fukuoka. On the other hand, when your rusty old Holden goes bang there's probably another old Holden sitting in a ditch with a perfectly good widget waiting to be removed. Every scrap yard in Australia is full of good old Holdens.

Note that third-party personal injury insurance is always included in the vehicle registration cost. This ensures that every vehicle (as long as it's currently registered) carries at least minimum insurance. You're wise to extend that minimum to at least third-party property insurance as well – minor collisions with Rolls-Royces can be amazingly expensive.

When you come to buy or sell a car there are usually some local regulations to be complied with. In the Northern Territory safety checks are compulsory every year when you come to renew the registration. Stamp duty has to be paid when you buy a car and, as this is based on the purchase price, it's not unknown for buyer and seller to agree privately to understate the price! It's much easier to sell a car in the same state or territory that it's registered in, otherwise it has to be re-registered in the new state. It may be possible to sell a car without re-registering it, but you're likely to get a lower price.

Finally, make use of the Automobile Association of Australia (AANT). They can advise you on any local regulations you

should be aware of, give general guidelines about buying a car and, most importantly, for a fee (from $85 to $100 for members and affiliate members depending on the type of vehicle) will check over a used car and report on its condition before you agree to purchase it. They also offer car insurance to their members.

MOTORBIKE

Motorbikes are a very popular way of getting around. The climate is just about ideal for biking much of the year, and the many small trails from the road into the bush often lead to perfect spots to spend the night in the world's largest camping ground.

The long, open roads are really made for large-capacity machines above 750 cc, which Australians prefer once they outgrow their 250 cc learner restrictions. But that doesn't stop enterprising individuals – many of them Japanese – from tackling the length and breadth of the continent on 250 cc trail bikes. Doing it on a small bike is not impossible, just tedious at times.

If you want to bring your own motorcycle into Australia you'll need a *carnet de passages*, and when you try to sell it you'll get less than the market price because of restrictive registration requirements (not so severe in the Northern Territory). Shipping from just about anywhere is expensive.

However, with a little bit of time up your sleeve, getting mobile on two wheels is quite feasible, although the small population of the Territory means that there is not a great deal of choice. You'll get a much better range of machines and more competitive prices in the other state capitals, particularly Sydney and Melbourne.

You'll need a rider's licence and a helmet. A fuel range of 350 km will cover fuel stops up the Centre. Beware of dehydration in the dry, hot air – force yourself to drink plenty of water, even if you don't feel thirsty.

The 'roo bars' (outsize bumpers) seen on large trucks and many outback cars tell you one thing: never ride on the open road from early evening until after dawn. Marsupials are nocturnal, sleeping in the shade during the day and feeding at night, and road ditches often provide lush grass for them to eat. Cows and sheep also stray onto the roads at night. It's wise to stop riding by around 5 pm.

It's worth carrying some spares and tools even if you don't know how to use them, because someone else often does. If you do know, you'll probably have a fair idea of what to take. The basics include: a spare tyre tube (front wheel size, which will fit on the rear but usually not vice versa); puncture repair kit with levers and a pump (or tubeless tyre repair kit with at least three carbon dioxide cartridges); a spare tyre valve, and a valve cap that can unscrew same; the bike's standard tool kit for what it's worth (after-market items are better); spare throttle, clutch and brake cables; tie wire, cloth tape ('gaffer' tape) and nylon 'zip-ties'; a handful of bolts and nuts in the usual emergency sizes (M6 and M8), along with a few self-tapping screws; one or two fuses in your bike's ratings; a bar of soap for fixing tank leaks (knead to a putty with water and squeeze into the leak); and, most important of all, a work-shop manual for your bike (even if you can't make sense of it, the local motorcycle mechanic can). You'll never have enough elastic straps (octopus or 'ocky' straps) to tie down your gear.

Make sure you carry water – at least two litres on major roads in central Australia, more off the beaten track. And finally, if something does go hopelessly wrong in the back of beyond, park your bike where it's clearly visible and observe the cardinal rule: **don't leave your vehicle**.

BICYCLE

Whether you're hiring a bike to ride around a city or wearing out your Bio-Ace chain-wheels on a Melbourne-Darwin marathon, you'll find that Australia is a great place for cycling. There are bike tracks in Darwin and Alice Springs, and in the country you'll find thousands of km of good roads which carry so little traffic that the biggest hassle is waving back to the drivers. Especially appealing is that in many areas you'll ride a very long way without encountering a hill.

Bicycle helmets are compulsory wear in all states and territories. It's rare to find a reasonably sized town that doesn't have a shop stocking at least basic bike parts.

If you're coming specifically to cycle, it makes sense to bring your own bike. Check your airline for costs and the degree of dis-mantling/packing required. Within Australia you can load your bike onto a bus or train to skip the boring bits. Note that bus companies require you to dismantle your bike, and some don't guarantee that it will travel on the same bus as you.

You can buy a good steel-framed touring bike in Australia for about $400 (plus pan-niers). It may be possible to rent touring bikes and equipment from a few of the com-mercial touring organisations.

You can get by with standard road maps, but as you'll probably want to avoid both the highways and the low-grade unsealed roads, the Government series is best. The 1:250,000 scale is the most suitable but you'll need a lot of maps if you're covering much territory. The next scale up, 1:1,000,000, is adequate. They are available in Darwin and Alice Springs.

Until you get fit you should be careful to eat enough to keep you going – remember that exercise is an appetite suppressant. It's surprisingly easy to be so depleted of energy that you end up camping under a gum tree just 10 km short of a shower and a steak. No matter how fit you are, water is still vital. Dehydration is definately no joke and can be life-threatening.

It can get very hot in summer, and you should take things slowly until you're used to the heat. Cycling in 35°C-plus tempera-tures isn't too bad if you wear a hat and plenty of sunscreen, and drink *lots* of water.

Of course, you don't have to follow the larger roads and visit towns. It's possible to fill your mountain bike's panniers with muesli, head out into the mulga, and not see anyone for weeks. Or ever again – outback travel is very risky if not properly planned. Water is the main problem in the 'dead heart', and you can't rely on it where there aren't settlements. That tank marked on your map may be dry or the water from it unfit for humans, and those station buildings probably blew away years ago. That little creek marked with a dotted blue line? Forget it – the only time it has water is when the country's flooded for hundreds of km.

Always check with locals if you're heading into remote areas, and notify the police if you're about to do something particularly adventurous. That said, you can't rely too much on local knowledge of road conditions – most people have no idea of what a heavily loaded touring bike needs. What they think of as a great road may be pedal-deep in sand or bull dust, and cyclists have happily ridden along roads that were officially flooded out.

HITCHING

Hitching is never entirely safe in any country in the world. It is in fact illegal in most states of Australia (which doesn't stop people doing it) and we don't recommend it. Travellers who decide to hitch should understand that they are taking a small but potentially serious risk. Before deciding to hitch, talk to local people about the dangers, and it is a good idea to let someone know where you are planning to hitch to before you set off. If you do choose to hitch, the advice that follows should help to make your journey as fast and safe as possible.

Factor one for safety and speed is numbers. More than two people hitching together will make things very difficult, and solo hitching is unwise for men as well as women. Two women hitching together may be vulnerable, and two men hitching together can expect long waits. The best option is for a woman and a man to hitch together.

Factor two is position – look for a place where vehicles will be going slowly and where they can stop easily. A junction or freeway slip road is a good place if there is stopping room. Position goes beyond just where you stand. The ideal location is on the outskirts of a town – hitching from way out in the country is as hopeless as from the centre of a city. Take a bus out to the edge of town.

Factor three is appearance. The ideal appearance for hitching is a sort of genteel poverty – threadbare but clean. Don't carry too much gear because if it looks like it's going to take half an hour to pack your bags aboard you'll be left on the roadside.

Factor four is knowing when to say no. Saying no to a car-load of drunks is pretty obvious, but you should also be prepared to abandon a ride if you begin to feel uneasy for any reason. Don't sit there hoping for the best; make an excuse and get out at the first opportunity.

It can be time-saving to say no to a short ride that might take you from a good hitching point to a lousy one. Wait for the right, long ride to come along. On a long haul, it's pointless to start walking as it's not likely to increase the likelihood of your getting a lift and it's often an awfully long way to the next town.

Trucks are often the best lifts but they will only stop if they are going slowly and can get started easily again. Thus the ideal place is at the top of a hill where they have a downhill run. Truckies often say they are going to the next town and if they don't like you, will drop you anywhere. As they often pick up hitchers for company, the quickest way to create a bad impression is to jump in and fall asleep.

It's also worth remembering that while you're in someone else's vehicle, you are their guest and should act accordingly. Many drivers no longer pick up people because they have suffered from thoughtless hikers in the past. It's the hitcher's duty to provide entertainment!

Of course people do get stuck in outlandish places but that is the name of the game. If you're visiting from abroad a nice prominent flag on your pack will help, and a sign announcing your destination can also be useful. University and hostel notice boards are good places to look for hitching partners. The main law against hitching is 'thou shalt not stand in the road' so when you see the law coming, step back.

Just as hitchers should be wary when accepting lifts, drivers who pick up fellow travellers to share the costs should also be aware of the possible risks involved.

ORGANISED TOURS

There are all sorts of tours around, including some interesting camping tours and 4WD safaris in the Territory. Some of these go to places you simply couldn't get to on your own without large amounts of expensive equipment. You can also walk, boat, raft, canoe, ride a horse or camel, or even fly.

There are plenty of tour operators, a number of which are aimed at backpackers, and the emphasis is on active, fun tours. Particularly popular are the tours out of Darwin to Kakadu and Litchfield national parks, and from Alice Springs to Watarrka (Kings Canyon) and Uluru-Kata Tjuta national parks. Other interesting options are tours to the Tiwi Islands off the coast of Darwin, extended bushwalking trips in Kakadu and elsewhere in the Top End, and camel trips through the beautiful central Australian bush.

Tours on Aboriginal Land

There are a number of tourist operations, some of them Aboriginal owned, running trips to visit Aboriginal land and communities in the Northern Territory. This is the best way to have any meaningful contact with Aboriginal people, even though you may feel that by being on a tour what you're getting is not the 'real thing'. The fact is that this is the way the Aboriginal owners of the land want tourism to work, so that they have some control over who visits what and when.

Arnhem Land offers the most options, mainly because of its proximity to Kakadu. The tours here generally only visit the very western edge of Arnhem Land, and take you to Oenpelli and other places which are normally off limits. Some of the tour operators include Umorrduk Safaris, AAT-Kings and Davidson's Arnhem Land Safaris (see the Kakadu and Arnhem Land sections for more details).

Other places in the Top End with similar operations include Tiwi Islands, and the Litchfield and Katherine areas, while in the Centre they are at Kings Canyon and Uluru. See those sections for details.

Darwin

• *Population: 78,100*

The 'capital' of northern Australia comes as a surprise to many people. It's a lively, modern place with a young population, an easy-going lifestyle, a great climate and a cosmopolitan atmosphere.

In part this is thanks to Cyclone Tracy, which did a comprehensive job of flattening Darwin on Christmas Day in 1974. People who were there during the reconstruction say a new spirit grew up with the new buildings, as Darwinites, showing true Top End resilience, took the chance to make their city one of which to be proud. Darwin became a brighter, smarter, sturdier place.

More recently it has been the city's proximity to Asia which has become the focus of interest as Australia looks increasingly to the region for trade and business opportunities. This should come as no surprise really: after all, Darwin is closer to Jakarta than it is to Canberra! The potential is there for Darwin to become Australia's major link with Asia, especially if the rail link south to Alice Springs actually becomes a realty. The number of Asians who have settled in Darwin in recent years has also increased markedly and this has greatly enhanced the cultural blend – between 45 and 60 ethnic groups are represented in the city, depending on who you listen to. Asian and European accents are almost as thick in the air as the Aussie drawl.

Despite its burgeoning sophistication, in many ways Darwin still retains a small-town atmosphere. It's a long way from any other major Australian city and even today the remoteness gives it a distinct 'far off' feel. A lot of people only live here for a year or two – it's surprising how many people you meet elsewhere in Australia who used to live in Darwin. It's reckoned you can consider yourself a 'Territorian' if you've stuck it for five years.

From the traveller's point of view Darwin is a major stop. There is a constant flow of

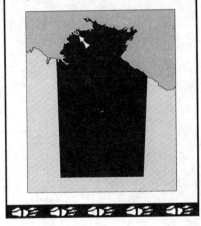

HIGHLIGHTS

- Delve into the history of the Territory at the Museum & Art Gallery
- Take a cruise on Darwin Harbour
- Sample an array of food at Mindil Beach's open-air market

travellers coming and going from Asia, or making their way around Australia. Darwin is an obvious base for trips to Kakadu and other Top End natural attractions, such as Litchfield Park. It's a bit of an oasis too – whether you're travelling south to Alice Springs, west to Western Australia or east to Queensland, there are a lot of km to be covered before you get anywhere, and having reached Darwin many people rest a bit before leaving.

HISTORY

The Darwin peninsula had been the preserve of the Larakia Aboriginal clan for thousands of years prior to the arrival of Europeans in the 18th century. (The word 'larakia' is actually trade-Malay for 'lead-in', used in reference to vessels turning into the wind as

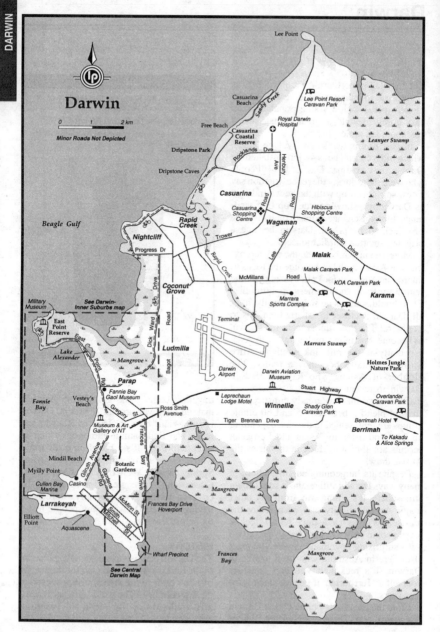

Darwin

0   1   2 km

Minor Roads Not Depicted

Lee Point

Casuarina Beach

Sandy Creek

Lee Point Resort Caravan Park

Royal Darwin Hospital

Free Beach

Casuarina Coastal Reserve

Rocklands Dve

Henbury Ave

Leanyer Swamp

Dripstone Park

Dripstone Caves

Casuarina

Beagle Gulf

Rapid Creek

Nightcliff

Progress Dr

Casuarina Shopping Centre

Hibiscus Shopping Centre

Lee Point Road

Wagaman

Vanderlin Drive

Trower

Malak

Malak Caravan Park

Rapid Creek

McMillans

Road

KOA Caravan Park

Coconut Grove

Karama

Military Museum

See Darwin-Inner Suburbs map

Dick Ward Drive

Marrara Sports Complex

East Point Reserve

Lake Alexander

East Point Rd

Mangrove

Ludmilla

Bagot Road

Terminal

Marrara Swamp

Holmes Jungle Nature Park

Parap

Darwin Airport

Darwin Aviation Museum

Fannie Bay

Vestey's Beach

Gregory St

Fannie Bay Gaol Museum

Ross Smith Avenue

Leprechaun Lodge Motel

Stuart   Highway

Overlander Caravan Park

Winnellie

Shady Glen Caravan Park

Berrimah Hotel ▼

Frances Bay

Tiger Brennan Drive

Berrimah

To Kakadu & Alice Springs

Museum & Art Gallery of NT

Mindil Beach

Myilly Point

Glfurth Avenue

Botanic Gardens

Gardens Rd

McMinn St

Frances Bay Drive Hoverport

Mangrove

Cullen Bay Marina

Casino

Larrakeyah

Elliott Point

Aquascene

Smith St

Mitchell St

Frances Bay Drive Hoverport

Wharf Precinct

Frances Bay

Mangrove

See Central Darwin Map

they anchor.) With the arrival of Europeans they were forced to vacate their traditional lands and inevitably came into violent conflict with the new arrivals, despite attempts by the first administration under George Goyder to avoid conflict.

From the early 19th century the British were keen to establish a major base in northern Australia. However, it took a long time to decide on Darwin as the site for the region's main centre and, even after the city was established, growth was slow and troubled. Early attempts to settle the Top End were mainly due to British fears that the French or Dutch might get a foothold in Australia. Between 1824 and 1829 Fort Dundas on Melville Island and Fort Wellington on the Cobourg Peninsula, 200 km north-east of Darwin, were settled and then abandoned. Victoria, settled in 1838 on Cobourg's Port Essington harbour, survived a cyclone and malaria, but was abandoned in 1849.

In 1845 the Austrian explorer Ludwig Leichhardt reached Port Essington overland from Brisbane, and in 1862 Charles McDouall Stuart crossed the continent from south to north, arousing prolonged interest in the Top End. The region came under the control of South Australia in 1863, and more ambitious development plans were made. A settlement in the Top End was needed to service the pastoral boom which the South Australian government was pinning its hopes on for colonising the Northern Territory. It had put on the market half a million acres in 160-acre plots and these were sold both at home, many to ministers in the government, and in London, where wealthy ex-colonists took up the offers. This left the South Australian government with the problem of surveying the land and marking out the plots. To this end a settlement was established in 1864 by Boyle Travers Finniss, an ex-British army officer who went on to become a prominent politician in South Australia, at Escape Cliffs on the mouth of the Adelaide River, about 50 km north-east of Darwin's present location. However, as it was surrounded by huge mangrove and melaleuca swamps, and reefs made shipping treacherous, it was a poor choice. In the words of explorer John McKinlay (who led the search for Burke & Wills in 1861): 'A greater sense of waste and desolation is unimaginable. As a seaport and a city this place is worthless.' It was finally abandoned in 1866.

Finally, South Australian Surveyor-General George Goyder was sent north in 1869 to have a go at settling and surveying the area. He headed straight for the city's current location, Port Darwin, having read the 1839 journals of John Lort Stokes who sailed into the harbour in 1839 aboard the *Beagle* and named it Port Darwin after a former shipmate, the evolutionist Charles Darwin. The settlement was officially called Palmerston, however, everyone knew the location's original name of Port Darwin, and in 1911 the name was officially changed to Darwin. The city was laid out on a grid pattern and many of the streets in the city centre were named after South Australian surveyors – McLachlan, Smith, Bennett, Knuckey, McMinn and Mitchell.

Palmerston's early prospects were not good, as the prospective landholders down south proved reluctant to make the move north and settle. Most forfeited their holding and demanded refunds, as it had taken longer than the stipulated five years to survey the plots, mainly due to time wasted trying to establish the settlement at Escape Cliffs. A saviour was urgently needed and it came in the form of the submarine telegraph cable which was to connect Australia with Britain. In 1871 Palmerston was chosen as the Australian landfall point and the South Australian government contracted to build an overland telegraph link to Adelaide. At this time the settlement still had a population of less than 500 and a small collection of buildings, which included a Government House, a police barracks, some weatherboard shops and a few log huts.

Activity in the area increased with the discovery of gold at Pine Creek about 200 km south. By 1874 the town had 1700 residents (although only about 50 of them were women), its own newspaper, the *Northern Territory Times & Government Gazette*, and plots of land which had been almost worthless only a few years before but were now fetching prices of up to £500.

But once the gold fever had run its course Palmerston slipped into a period of stagnation, due to the oppressive climate (including occasional cyclones), its poor communications with other Australian states, and the conflict between the various ethnic groups. Many people left the settlement and by 1880 the population had dwindled to less than 500, of whom 300 were Chinese labourers who had been encouraged to immigrate in the hope that they would provide a source of cheap labour.

The discovery of pearlshell in Port Darwin in 1884 led to the development of a small industry which lasted for 70 years and became a vital part of the local economy. By the turn of the century there were more than 50 luggers operating out of Port Darwin, most of them employing Indonesian or Japanese divers.

Despite the hardships, development continued and during the 1880s a number of important buildings were built, some of which still stand today: a new jail at Fannie Bay (today the Fannie Bay Gaol Museum); the current Commonwealth Bank building on Bennett St (at the time it was the finest nongovernment building in the settlement although its owner, the Town & Country Bank, failed only two years later); a termite-proof town hall; and the Victoria Hotel. The construction of a railway line south to Pine Creek to service the goldfields also boosted hopes but by the time it was finished in 1889 the gold was exhausted and the state government had incurred a massive debt. Any hopes that pastoralists might use the railway to transport their stock was unfounded as the nearest cattle markets were in the Kimberley region of WA and in Queensland.

In 1897 Palmerston was hit by a devastating cyclone – one of a number which have hit the town over the years, and probably the most destructive prior to Tracy in 1974. Hardly a building survived undamaged, and many were destroyed completely. Again in 1937 the city of Darwin was badly damaged by a cyclone.

When the Commonwealth Government assumed control of the Northern Territory in 1911 there was a brief flurry of building activity, but this was shortlived and for the next 20 years the city slipped back into inactivity.

WW II put Darwin permanently on the map when the town became an important base for Allied action against the Japanese in the Pacific. As early as the mid-1930s the strategic importance of the city had been identified and fortifications installed to protect the city's huge oil storage tanks against possible attack. The oil tanks were installed in the early '30s as Darwin became the navy's northern refuelling base when the switch from coal to oil was made.

When things started hotting up in Europe in the late '30s Darwin became the focus of military activity in Australia with the establishment of the Darwin Mobile Defence Force in 1939, the construction of an anti-submarine boom net across the harbour in 1940, and the stationing of an entire air force squadron at the civil airfield.

As the Japanese advanced rapidly through South-East Asia in late 1941 an attack on Darwin seemed more and more likely. Consequently women and children were evacuated so that by the time the first raid hit on 18 February 1942 only 63 women and children remained in the city. The raid was launched from five aircraft carriers in the Timor Sea, and within an hour a force of 188 fighters and bombers attacked the city virtually unopposed. Despite the preparations against exactly such a raid there was heavy loss of life and property. This first attack on Australia by a hostile power was followed almost immediately by another, which was delivered by 54 heavy bombers which were stationed in Ambon and Sulawesi.

These early raids led to a mass evacuation of the city as everyone headed south by whatever means possible. The road south at that stage only went as far as Adelaide River, 100 km away, and the little town was soon swamped with evacuees. In all, Darwin was attacked 64 times during the war and 243 people lost their lives; it was the only place in Australia to suffer prolonged attacks.

At the end of the war the city's administrators seized the chance to rebuild the city into something it had never been – attractive. The Chinatown area of Cavenagh St was seen as the major problem and so instead of handing the buildings back to their former owners the government bulldozed the lot.

The late 1940s was a period of stagnation for Darwin while the rest of the country enjoyed a post-war boom. The main reason was that the government's dream of rebuilding meant that no long-term leases could be approved as existing buildings were supposed to make way for the new ones in a few short years. As a result business confidence slumped and banks were unwilling to risk their money over such a short term. The situation was resolved when the plan was modified in 1949 to cause as little disturbance as possible.

During the 1950s and '60s Darwin was rebuilt and expanded rapidly. New homes and buildings shot up everywhere, although carelessness crept in and the cyclone threat was disregarded. Consequently when the worst happened, and it did on 24 December 1974, the devastation was far worse than it should have been. Cyclone Tracy ripped through Darwin, seriously damaging 95% of its domestic dwellings and killing 49 people. For the second time in 50 years the city was virtually rebuilt.

Modern Darwin has an important role as the front door to Australia's northern region and as a centre for administration and mining. Its modern port facilities mean it is well placed to become the main connection between Australia and Asia.

ORIENTATION

Darwin's centre is a fairly compact area at the end of a peninsula. The Stuart Highway does a big loop entering the city and finally heads south to end under the name Daly St. The city-centre peninsula stretches southeast from here, and the main city centre shopping area, Smith St and its mall, is about half a km from Daly St.

Long-distance buses arrive right in the city centre at the transit centre at 69 Mitchell St, and there is accommodation a few minutes walk away. Most of what you'll want in central Darwin is within two or three blocks of the transit centre or Smith St Mall.

The suburbs spread a good 12 to 15 km away to the north and east. Larrakeyah is immediately north of the centre and then the Botanic Gardens and the golf course form a buffer between the centre and the old suburbs of Parap and Fannie Bay, the latter with its old jail and the East Point Reserve.

North again are the cities newer northern suburbs such as Nightcliff and Rapid Creek, although these are separated from the Fannie Bay area by mangrove swamps right on the coast and the airport directly inland.

The Stuart Highway to Alice Springs swings off to the east through the light-industrial suburbs of Winnellie and Berrimah, and eventually to Palmerston, a new satellite town 20 km from the city centre.

The city is well endowed with open spaces and parks, and has an excellent series of bicycle tracks. The best beaches are to the north of the city.

INFORMATION
Tourist Office

The Darwin Regional Tourism Association Information Centre (☎ 8981 4300; fax 8981 7346) is at 33 Smith St, in the mall. It's open from 8.15 am to 5 pm from Monday to Friday, from 9 am to 3 pm on Saturday and from 10 am to 3 pm on Sunday. It has several decent booklets, displays dozens of brochures and can book just about any tour or accommodation in the Territory. There's also a DRTA tourist information desk at the airport (☎ 8945 3386).

The NT Government Publications Centre (☎ 8999 7152; fax 8999 7972) at 13 Smith St, open Monday to Friday from 9 am to 4 pm, supplies government publications. These are mostly of dry documents detailing laws and local regulations, but if you're interested in delving into a particular aspect of the Northern Territory it may be able to help.

There are good notice boards in the mall (a couple of doors from the tourist office) and in the backpacker hostel. These are useful for buying and selling things (like vehicles) or looking for rides.

Publications There are a couple of free publications which have some useful detail but they are far from comprehensive. *Darwin & the Top End Today* is published twice yearly and has information on Darwin and the surrounding area. Possibly of more use is *This Week in Darwin* as it has listings of what's happening on a weekly basis.

The *Daily Plan It* is a free monthly newspaper which is sometimes helpful. The Friday edition of the *Northern Territory News* newspaper has its *Avagoodweegend* (ugh!) lift-out with details of theatres, live bands and cinemas.

The *Backpackers Bible to the Northern Territory* is a free booklet produced locally every year, and it's also worth getting hold of.

Post & Telecommunications
The Darwin GPO is on the corner of Cavenagh and Edmunds Sts. The poste restante is computerised and efficient; a computer-generated list of all mail held is printed each morning and is available by the poste restante counter. This saves you queuing for mail only to find there's nothing there. You'll need some form of identification to collect any mail.

Useful Organisations
The Automobile Association of the Northern Territory (☎ 8981 3837; fax 8941 2965) has its office in the MLC Building at 81 Smith St. It stocks a good range of maps, and has current information about the status of various Top End roads which are sporadically closed in the Wet due to heavy rain.

Parks & Wildlife (☎ 8999 5511) prints an excellent range of free leaflets covering all the main national parks and reserves (with the exception of Kakadu) of the Top End.

The head office is way out in Palmerston but there's also a desk (☎ 8999 3881; fax 8981 0653) in the main tourist office in the Smith St Mall. This is also the place to come if you want to organise a permit to visit Gurig National Park.

The Australian Nature Conservation Agency (☎ 8981 5299; fax 8981 3497) is the body which, along with the traditional owners, administers Kakadu and Uluru national parks. The office is in the MLC Building at 81 Smith St. The agency prints a number of worthwhile books and brochures about the parks, although these are all available at the parks themselves.

For good maps of the Territory try the map sales office of the Department of Land, Planning & Environment (☎ 8999 7032) on the corner of Cavenagh and Bennett Sts.

The National Trust (☎ 8981 2848) is at 52 Temira Crescent in Myilly Point – pick up a copy of its Darwin Heritage Guide leaflet (also available from the tourist office). The National Trust also publishes a series of handy booklets ($2 each) on Trust-classified places throughout the Territory.

The Department of Mines & Energy (☎ 8999 5461) is in the Centrepoint Tower in the Smith St Mall. For fishing information, the Department of Primary Industry & Fisheries (☎ 8999 4321) has its office in the Harbour View Plaza on the corner of Bennett and McMinn Sts.

For reference material and other information on just about anything to do with the Northern Territory, visit the State Library (☎ 8999 7177) in the new Parliament House. As well as the excellent Northern Australia Collection there's a fully catalogued collection of images available for viewing on CD-rom. It's open Monday to Saturday from 10 am to 6 pm.

Permits to visit Arnhem Land are issued by the Northern Land Council (☎ 8920 5100; fax 8945 2633) at 9 Rowling St, Casuarina, behind the Casuarina Shopping Centre. Tiwi Island permits are available from the Tiwi Land Council (☎ 8947 1838) at the Windgate Centre, Sadgroves Cres, Winnellie.

Foreign Consulates

For a list of consulates in Darwin, see Visas & Embassies in the Facts for the Visitor chapter.

Travel Agents

There's no shortage of agents in Darwin. STA (☎ 8941 2955) have an office in the Galleria shopping centre in Smith St Mall, while the Flight Centre (☎ 8945 3815) is another high-volume, low-price specialist with an office on Cavenagh St.

Natrabu Travel (☎ 8981 3695), in the arcade behind the Vic Hotel on the Smith St Mall is the agent for Merpati, the Indonesian feeder airline which flies to Kupang (Timor) twice weekly.

Jalan Jalan Tours & Travel is a small travel agent on Knuckey St which specialises in tickets to Indonesia.

Freight Agents

If you need to get some gear freighted overseas, Perkins Shipping (☎ 8981 4688) at Frances Bay Dve are used to handling anything from a backpack up.

Within Australia, try TNT Darwin Express (☎ 8984 3822) at Berrimah Rd, Berrimah.

Bookshops

Bookworld (☎ 8981 5277) on Smith St Mall is a good bookshop, as is Angus & Robertson (☎ 8941 3489) in the Galleria shopping centre, also in the Smith St Mall. They also have a shop in the Casuarina Shopping Centre in the northern suburbs.

For maps, the NT General Store (☎ 8981 8242) on Cavenagh St has a good range, or try the Department of Lands, Planning & Environment (see Useful Organisations earlier in this chapter).

Other Shops

Camping Gear For general camping equipment one of the best places is the NT General Store on Cavenagh St, and they also have a shop in the Hibiscus Shopping Centre in Leanyer. For specialist lightweight tents and bushwalking gear, try Snowgum (☎ 8948

1717) at 269 Bagot Rd in Coconut Grove. Also in this area is Barbecues Galore (☎ 8985 4544), 301 Bagot Rd, which stocks larger tents, portable fridges and camping gear.

For sales and repairs of portable car fridges, try Keepikool (☎ 8984 3733) at 7/63 Winnellie Rd in Winnellie.

Bicycle Sales & Repairs Darwin has a couple of large bicycle sales/repair shops. Wheelman Cycles (☎ 8981 6369) is centrally located at 64 McMinn St, or there's Bikes to Fit (☎ 8948 1128) at 5/8 Totem Rd, Coconut Grove.

Medical & Emergency Services

There are various medical and emergency services in Darwin and they include:

Vaccinations
> The federal Department of Health runs an International Vaccination Clinic (☎ 8981 7492) at 43 Cavenagh St. It is open on weekdays from 9 am to 5 pm. There's a $20 consultation fee, plus charges for whatever vaccinations you have.

Medical Treatment
> For emergency medical treatment phone the Royal Darwin Hospital on ☎ 8922 8888. It is located in the northern suburb of Tiwi. There's also a Marine Stinger Emergency Line on ☎ toll-free 1800 079 909.

Counselling
> Lifeline Crisis Line (☎ 8981 9227, or toll-free 1800 019 116)
> AIDS Hotline (☎ toll-free 1800 011 144)
> AIDS Council of NT (☎ 8941 1711)
> Rape & Sexual Assault Referral Centre (☎ 8922 7156)

Dental
> For emergency dental treatment up until 9 pm try the Night & Day Medical & Dental Surgery (☎ 8927 1899), Shop 31, Casuarina Shopping Centre.

Chemist
> For prescription filling up until 9 pm there's the Trower Rd Night & Day Pharmacy (☎ 8927 7857).

Ambulance
> For ambulance attendance phone ☎ 000 or 8927 9000.

Police
> For emergency police assistance phone ☎ 8927 8888 or 000.

THINGS TO SEE
City Centre

Despite its shaky beginnings and the destruction caused by WW II and Cyclone Tracy, Darwin has a number of historic buildings.

One of the most famous city landmarks is the **Victoria Hotel** on Smith St Mall. The 'Vic' was originally built in 1890 and badly damaged by Cyclone Tracy. The building on the corner of the mall and Bennett St only dates from 1981 but it does incorporate the colonnade of the 1884 stone **Commercial Bank building**, which at the time was one of the finest buildings in the city. It was known locally as the 'stone bank', to distinguish it from the 'tin bank', a termite-proof, prefabricated structure imported by the English, Scottish & Australian Chartered Bank and erected on Smith St around the same time.

The **old town hall** on Smith St was also built during the gold boom of the 1880s. It was occupied by the navy during WW II and later by the Museums Board. Unfortunately it was virtually destroyed by Tracy, despite its solid Victorian construction. Today only remnants of its walls remain.

Across the road, **Brown's Mart**, a former mining exchange dating from 1885, was badly damaged in the fierce cyclone of 1897 and again by Tracy, but was restored on both occasions and now houses a theatre.

The 1884 **police station** and **old courthouse** at the corner of Smith St and the Esplanade were in use by the navy up until 1974. They were badly damaged, but have been restored and are now used as government offices. A small plaque in the garden bed on the Smith St side of the building marks the spot where the first Telegraph Station stood.

Right across the road from here, perched on the edge of the escarpment, is the **Survivors' Lookout**, a reminder of the wartime bombing raids over Darwin. The lookout has a number of interesting interpretive signs and some old photos, and a staircase leads from here down to the harbour and Wharf Precinct (see below).

A little further along the Esplanade, **Government House**, built in stages from 1870, was known as the Residency until 1911 when the Territory came under the control of the Commonwealth Government. Initially it was little more than a large room with hand-cut stone walls and canvas roof. George Scott, the Resident in 1873, described it as 'an ill-devised dilapidated barn'. He added a second storey in 1874, but virtually the whole lot had to be rebuilt soon after as the termites had made a mess of things and there was a real danger of collapse. The current building dates from 1877 and, although damaged by virtually every cyclone since, it is in fine condition today. It is opened to the public once a year in July-August.

Almost opposite Government House is a new memorial housing an old plaque which used to mark the spot where the original telegraph cable from Banyuwangi in Indonesia was brought up the cliffs to the Telegraph Station. This cable put Australia into instant communication with Britain for the first time. The original cairn was removed to make way for the new **Parliament House** building, the $120 million looming white monstrosity which dominates this edge of the cityscape and was opened in 1994. From the outside it looks like something from 1960 Moscow and has been criticised for lacking outback ambience. Fortunately the interior is much more pleasing and is worth a wander around – it includes dining rooms, a gymnasium, ministers' suites and reading rooms.

On the corner of the Esplanade and Herbert St is the agreeably tropical **Hotel Darwin**, built during the 1940s and still a great place.

Further along is the **Old Admiralty House** at the corner of Knuckey St, one of the few 1930s Burnett buildings still standing in Darwin (see Myilly Point for details of the work of B C G Burnett, the Northern Territory government architect in the 1930s). Up until 1984 it was used by the navy; it now houses the Greening Australia shop and cafe.

On the opposite corner of Knuckey St is the old stone building known as the **British-Australian Telegraph Residence (Lyons Cottage)**. The cottage was built in the 1920s as an executive residence for the British Australian Telegraph Company, the company which laid the submarine cable between Java and Australia. It was later the family home of John Lyons, a prominent mayor of Darwin. These days the building is an excellent little museum with photographic displays of early Darwin. Focus of the exhibits is the Guy Middleton collection of photographs. Middleton came to the Territory in the 1920s and travelled widely in his job as a bookkeeper for the international Vesteys Brothers company. Entry is free and it's open daily from 10 am to noon and 12.30 to 5 pm.

The Esplanade is fronted by **Bicentennial Park**, a very pleasant expanse of grass and trees, with some excellent views out over the harbour. Also in the park are a number of memorials.

Almost opposite the Hotel Darwin is the **Anzac Memorial**, with plaques to commemorate all those who fought in WW I and other campaigns. Further along is a memorial to the scientist and explorer **Ludwig Leichhardt**, and further again is a **lookout** over the harbour.

There's a modern **Chinese temple** on the corner of Woods and Bennett Sts.

Wharf Precinct

The Darwin Wharf Precinct centres around the old Stokes Hill Wharf, below the cliffs at the southern end of the city centre. The aim here has been to turn what was basically the city's ugly port facilities into something attractive which will draw the tourists. To a large extent this has been achieved and it's well worth spending a morning wandering around this area. A shuttle bus operates between the Wharf Precinct sites and the northern end of Smith St Mall, or it's a short stroll down from the Survivors' Lookout at the end of Smith St.

Right at the outer end of the jetty is an old warehouse, now known as the Arcade, which houses a good food centre with numerous places to eat – great for an alfresco lunch or cool afternoon beer (see Places to Eat for details).

Indo-Pacific Marine & Australian Pearling Exhibition Probably the focal point of the precinct is this excellent marine aquarium. It's a successful attempt to display living coral and its associated life. Each small tank is a complete ecosystem, with only the occasional extra fish introduced as food for some of the carnivores such as stonefish or angler fish. They sometimes have box jellyfish, as well as more attractive creatures like sea horses, clown fish and butterfly fish. The living coral reef display is especially impressive.

Housed in the same building is the Pearling Exhibition, which deals with the history of the pearling industry in this area. While pearling around Darwin doesn't have the importance it has in places like Broome (WA), quite a bit still goes on in the Territory, mainly on the Cobourg Peninsula in Arnhem Land. The exhibition has excellent displays and informative videos.

Both displays are housed in the former Port Authority garage at the Wharf Precinct, which has been completely renovated and air-conditioned. The Indo-Pacific Marine is open daily from 9 am to 5 pm (last entry 4 pm) and costs $10 ($4 for children), and the Pearling Exhibition hours are from 8 am to 5 pm weekdays, 10 to 6 pm on weekends and it costs $5.50 ($3 children).

WW II Oil-Storage Tunnels The Wharf Precinct also features a series of eight concrete oil-storage tunnels which were dug into the cliff face below the city centre during WW II. It doesn't sound all that exciting, but in fact is well worth a look.

The early air raids on Darwin destroyed the above-ground tanks near the Stokes Hill Wharf so it was decided that oil should be stored in these underground concrete tunnels. It was an ambitious project but one which failed to take into account things such as the high water-table and the amount of seepage; the latter prevented the tunnels from ever being used. Tunnels 5 and 6 (177 metres long) are open to the public, and on the walls are a series of interesting photos of Darwin during the war.

The tunnels are open from 10 am to 2 pm Tuesday to Sunday, and entry is $3.

Aquascene

At Doctor's Gully, near the corner of Daly St and the Esplanade, fish come in for a feed every day at high tide, and have been since the 1950s. Half the stale bread in Darwin gets dispensed to a horde of milkfish, diamond-scaled mullet, scats, catfish and butterfish. Some are quite big such as the milkfish who grow to over a metre and will demolish a whole slice of bread in one go. It's a great sight and children love it – the fish will take bread right out of your hand. Feeding times depend on the tides (☎ 8981 7837 for tide times, or check *Darwin & the Top End Today*). Admission is $4 ($2.50 children); the bread is free. As you can stand on a concrete ramp right in the water, it's not a bad idea to wear bathers, particularly for kids.

In the early days of commercial aviation the Qantas Catalina flying boats used Doctors Gully as their base.

Myilly Point Historic Precinct

Right at the far northern end of Smith St is this small but important historic precinct of houses built in the 1930s. The houses were designed specifically for the tropical climate by the Northern Territory Principal Architect, Beni Carr Glynn Burnett, who came to Darwin in 1937 after spending many years working as an architect in China. The small elevated point was a prime residential spot as it had fine views and enjoyed any sea breezes, and so it was here that the top civil and military officials were housed.

The buildings were all elevated, and featured asbestos-cement louvres and casement windows, so the ventilation could be regulated according to the weather conditions at the time. Internal walls were only three-quarter height and also featured lower louvres to allow cross-ventilation. The eaves were also left open to aid ventilation.

Fortunately the houses have survived, although at one stage in the early 1980s it looked as though they would be flattened to make way for the casino, which was eventually built on lower ground to the north. The buildings are now on the Register of the National Estate; one house, now called Burnett House, is the home of the National Trust (☎ 8981 2848), while another is a gallery and cafe.

Cullen Bay

At the end of Myilly Point is the new Cullen Bay Marina. What was once a public beach and a site of historical importance for local Aboriginal people has been turned into an exclusive marina with permanent boat moorings and a rash of up-market apartments. A two-stage lock separates the marina from the main harbour, and it is from the jetty here that the jet boats to Mandorah leave. A regular shuttle bus runs between Cullen Bay and the north end of the Smith St Mall.

Botanic Gardens

The 42-hectare Botanic Gardens site was first used in the 1870s when a German immigrant, Maurice Holtze, was employed as Darwin's (at the time Palmerston) official gardener to establish a major fruit and vegetable plantation in an effort to make the settlement less dependent on unreliable shipments.

Unfortunately cyclones have a devastating effect on tress and in 1974 Cyclone Tracy destroyed 80% of the trees and shrubs in the gardens. Fortunately, vegetation grows fast in Darwin's climate and the Botanic Gardens, with their noteworthy collection of tropical flora, have been restored.

Many of the plant varieties in the gardens were traditionally used by local Aboriginal people, and a self-guided Aboriginal Plant Use walk has been set up within the gardens. There's also a small pocket of monsoon vine forest, and another of riverine forest.

There's a coastal habitat section of the gardens, over the road, between Gilruth Ave and Fannie Bay, which features sand dunes, a small wetland and numerous mangroves.

It's an easy two-km bicycle ride out to the gardens from the centre along Gilruth Ave and Gardens Rd, or there's another entrance off Geranium St, which runs off the Stuart Highway in Stuart Park. The Gardens Rd gate is open from 7 am to 7 pm daily; the Geranium St access is 24 hours.

Museum & Art Gallery of the Northern Territory

This excellent museum and art gallery is on Conacher St at Fannie Bay, about four km from the city centre. It's bright, well presented and not too big, but full of interesting displays. A highlight is the Northern Territory Aboriginal art collection, with just the right mix of exhibits and information to introduce visitors to the purpose of this art, and its history and regional differences. It's particularly strong on carvings and bark paintings from Bathurst and Melville islands and Arnhem Land.

There's also a good collection on the art of the Pacific and Asian nations closest to Australia, including Indonesian *ikat* (woven cloth) and gamelan instruments, and a sea gypsies' *prahu* (floating home) from Sabah, Malaysia.

Pride of place among the stuffed Northern Territory birds and animals undoubtedly goes to 'Sweetheart', a five-metre, 780-kg saltwater crocodile, who became quite a Top End personality after numerous encounters with fishing dinghies on the Finnis River south of Darwin. Apparently he had a taste for outboard motors. He died when captured in 1979. You can also see a box jellyfish, safely dead in a jar.

The non-Aboriginal Australian art collection includes works by top names like Nolan, Lindsay and Boyd. The museum has a good little bookshop and outside, but under cover, there is an excellent maritime display with a number of vessels, including an old pearling lugger and a Vietnamese refugee boat.

Admission to the museum (☎ 8989 8211) is free and it's open from Monday to Friday from 9 am to 5 pm, Saturday and Sunday from 10 am to 5 pm. The Nos 4 or 6 buses will drop you close by, or you can get there on the Tour Tub (see Getting Around) or along the bicycle path from the city centre. The museum also has an excellent licensed restaurant which makes a great spot for lunch (see Places to Eat).

Fannie Bay Gaol Museum

Another interesting museum is a little further out of town at the corner of East Point Rd and Ross Smith Ave. This was Darwin's main jail from 1883 to 1979, when a new maximum security lock-up opened at Berrimah. You can look round the old cells and see the gallows used in the Territory's last hanging in 1952. There are also good displays on Cyclone Tracy, transport and technology. The museum is open weekdays from 9 am to 5 pm and on weekends from 10 am to 5 pm; admission is free. Bus Nos 4 and 6 from the city centre go very close to the museum, and it's also on the Tour Tub route.

East Point Reserve

This spit of undeveloped land north of Fannie Bay is good to visit in the late afternoon when wallabies come out to feed, cool breezes spring up and you can watch the sunset across the bay. There are some walking and riding trails as well as a road to the tip of the point.

On the northern side of the point is a series of wartime gun emplacements and the **Military Museum** (☎ 8981 9702), devoted to Darwin's WW II activities, open daily from 9.30 am to 5 pm ($5). The large, circular concrete structure is the emplacement for the 9.2-inch gun. The gun was the largest of a number of armaments placed on East Point from the mid-1930s. The installation of the 9.2-inch gun started in 1941 but because of interruptions caused by the Japanese air raids it was not installed and tested until 1945, by which time the war was all but over! Ironically, the gun was sold for scrap to a Japanese salvage company in 1960.

Also part of the East Point Reserve is **Lake Alexander**. This small, recreational saltwater lake was made so that people could enjoy a swim year-round without having to worry about nasties such as box jellyfish. There's a small 'beach' at one end, and windsurfing and other watersports are also permitted. From the carpark at the northern

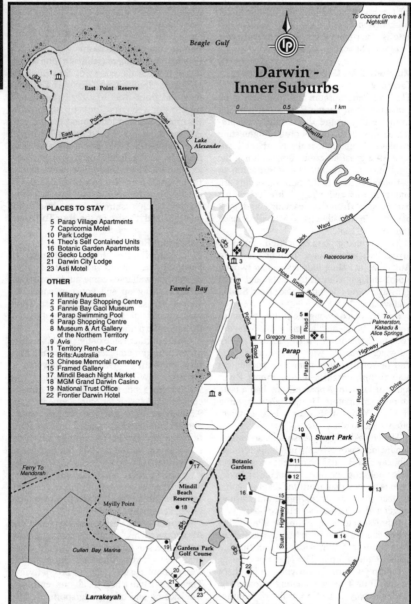

Beagle Gulf

To Coconut Grove & Nightcliff

Darwin - Inner Suburbs

0   0.5   1 km

East Point Reserve

East Point Road

Lake Alexander

Dick Ward Drive

Leanyer Creek

Fannie Bay

Racecourse

Ross Smith Avenue

To Palmerston, Kakadu & Alice Springs

Fannie Bay

East Point Road

Gregory Street

Parap

Parap Road

Stuart Highway

PLACES TO STAY

5 Parap Village Apartments
7 Capricornia Motel
10 Park Lodge
14 Theo's Self Contained Units
16 Botanic Garden Apartments
20 Gecko Lodge
21 Darwin City Lodge
23 Asti Motel

OTHER

1 Military Museum
2 Fannie Bay Shopping Centre
3 Fannie Bay Gaol Museum
4 Parap Swimming Pool
6 Parap Shopping Centre
8 Museum & Art Gallery
   of the Northern Territory
9 Avis
11 Territory Rent-a-Car
12 Brits:Australia
13 Chinese Memorial Cemetery
15 Framed Gallery
17 Mindil Beach Night Market
18 MGM Grand Darwin Casino
19 National Trust Office
22 Frontier Darwin Hotel

Stuart Park

Woolner Road

Tiger Brennan Drive

Ferry To Mandorah

Botanic Gardens

Myilly Point

Mindil Beach Reserve

Stuart Highway

Francis Bay Drive

Cullen Bay Marina

Gardens Park Golf Course

Larrakeyah

end of the lake a **boardwalk** leads down to the mangroves, which are best viewed at low tide.

Vehicles are permitted in the reserve, and there's also a good bicycle track and footpath. Bus Nos 4 and 6 will take you five km from the city centre to the corner of East Point Rd and Ross Smith Ave; from there it's three km to the tip of the point, or you can take the Tour Tub.

Holmes Jungle Nature Park
This 250-hectare park in Darwin's eastern suburbs features a small remnant of monsoon rainforest which is sustained by a small permanent spring. This patch of forest is typical of the monsoon forest which once covered much of the Darwin area. Banyan trees, various palms, vines and ferns form the monsoon habitat, while the woodland area is dominated by eucalypts and grevilleas.

The area has long been a popular recreational spot for Darwin residents, and was used as a stock-agistment area by the early European owner of the land, Felix Holmes. During WW II the army built a convalescent camp here, but this was removed in the 1960s. Also removed were all non-indigenous plant species, in an effort to encourage natural regeneration.

There are a couple of walking tracks through the park, as well as picnic facilities and a lookout.

Darwin Aviation Museum
Darwin's aviation museum would be unspectacular were it not for the American B52 bomber. This truly mammoth aircraft, one of only two displayed outside the USA, dominates the other displays, which include the wreck of a Japanese Zero fighter shot down in 1942 and other items of historical interest.

The museum is on the Stuart Highway in Winnellie, about eight km from the centre. It is open daily from 8.30 am to 5 pm; entry is $6 ($3 children). Bus Nos 5 and 8 run along the Stuart Highway.

ACTIVITIES
Beaches
Darwin has plenty of beaches, but you'd be a fool to venture into the water during the October to May wet season because of the deadly box jellyfish. Popular beaches include **Mindil** and **Vestey's** on Fannie Bay, and **Mandorah**, across the bay from the city (see the Around Darwin chapter).

In north Darwin, there's a stinger net protecting part of **Nightcliff** beach off Casuarina Dve, and a stretch of the seven-km **Casuarina** beach further east is an official nude beach. This is a good beach but at low tide it's a long walk to the water's edge.

Swimming Pools
In addition to the beaches and Lake Alexander (see East Point Reserve earlier in this chapter), Darwin has four public swimming pools. These are at Casuarina Dve, Nightcliff (☎ 8985 1682); Ross Smith Ave, Parap (☎ 8981 2662); Gsell St, Casuarina (☎ 8927 9091); and at the Palmerston Leisure Centre (☎ 8932 3474) on Tilston Ave, Palmerston. The pool at Parap is the main one and it has the obligatory waterslide.

Scuba Diving
Cullen Bay Dive (☎ 8981 3049; fax 8981 4913) at the Cullen Bay Marina takes divers out to wrecks in the harbour throughout the year. The cost is $29 per dive, plus $20 for equipment hire, which includes protective gear to guard against box jellyfish stings. They also do full-day diving trips at $79.

Other companies which do dives out of Darwin include Coral Divers (☎ 8981 2686) in Stuart Park, and Fathom Five Pro Charters (☎ 8985 4288) in Millner.

Cycling
Darwin has an excellent series of bicycle tracks, the main one runs from the northern end of Cavenagh St to Fannie Bay, Coconut Grove, Nightcliff and Casuarina. At Fannie Bay a side track heads out to the East Point Reserve. See the Getting Around section later in this chapter for details of bicycle hire.

Golf

The nine-hole Gardens Park Golf Course (☎ 8981 6365) is centrally located on Gilruth Ave near the Botanic Gardens. It is open to the public from 7 am to 7 pm daily and a round costs $8.

Sailing

The Winter School of Sailing (☎ 8981 9368) has a 12-metre sloop which takes six passengers on three-hour cruises around the harbour. These operate throughout the year, and the cost is $45 per person.

Longer cruises can also be arranged, and the cost for these is $200 per person per day, which includes all meals.

Abseiling & Rockclimbing

NT Adventure Activities (☎ 8927 7567) is a small company which does four-hour sunset abseiling trips on Darwin's sea cliffs for beginners for $40.

Helicopter Flights

For a view of Darwin from the air, Heli North (☎ /fax 8981 2002) will whisk you over the city for $55 ($40 for children under 10) for 15 minutes or $90 ($50) for a half-hour flight.

The helipad is almost opposite the WW II Oil-Storage Tunnels near Stokes Hill Wharf.

ORGANISED TOURS

There are innumerable tours in and around Darwin offered by a host of companies. The Information Office in the mall is the best place for information on what's available. Many tours go less frequently (if at all) in the wet season. Some of the longer or more adventurous ones have only a few departures a year; enquire in advance if you're interested.

Aboriginal Cultural Tours

If Darwin is your only chance to delve into Aboriginal culture, there are a few options. The Frontier Darwin Hotel (☎ toll-free 1800 891 101; fax 8981 3173) has Aboriginal corroborees three times a week at 7.45 pm.

The charge of $38 ($20 children) includes a barbecue.

You may get a more authentic feel for Aboriginal culture on the four-hour White Crane Dreaming tour operated by Northern Gateway (☎ 8941 1394; fax 8941 2815). This tour includes a 25-minute flight to the homelands of the Kuwuma Djudian people, and a chance to sample bush tucker. The cost is $215 ($175 children aged three to 12).

Better are the full-day tours to Bathurst and Melville islands, operated by Tiwi Tours (☎ 8981 5115; fax 8981 5391). The cost is $230 ($184 children) which includes the flight to the islands, a boat trip between the two islands and a visit to a pukumani burial site.

Other day tours operate to Umorrduk in Arnhem Land ($440 per person) and Peppimenarti at the Daly River ($300 per person flying, $200 by 4WD).

City Sights

Among the Darwin city tours, Darwin Day Tours (☎ 8981 8696; fax 8981 1777) four-hour trip at 8.15 am daily is pretty comprehensive ($29 adults, $15 children). The same company also does a 4½-hour Sunset Tour for $32 ($16). Keetleys Tours (☎ 81-4422; fax 8941 1341) does similar tours for slightly less. All these day tours pick-up and drop off at your accommodation.

The Tour Tub (☎ /fax 8985 4779) is an open-sided minibus which tours around the various Darwin sights throughout the day (see Getting Around later in this chapter), and you can either stay on board and do a full circuit or get on and off at the various stops. The cost is $14 ($7 for children).

Harbour Cruises

Darwin Hovercraft Tours (☎ 8941 2233; fax 8981 8852) operates one-hour, 35-km hovercraft flights around the harbour from the Frances Bay Dve hoverport for $35 ($25 children), and these can be a lot of fun.

For something a little more sedate Darwin Duchess Cruises (☎ /fax 8978 5094) leaves Stokes Hill Wharf at 2 pm Wednesday to

Sunday for a two-hour cruise around the harbour ($22 adults, $12 children), and again at 5.30 pm for a two-hour sunset cruise.

Fishing Tours

The Tour Tub (☎ /fax 8985 4779) has a five-metre punt which is available for half-day fishing trips on the harbour, departing at 8 am and 1 pm daily. The cost is $55 ($40 children). Full-day trips cost $100 ($85) including lunch.

Barra Bash (☎ toll-free 1800 632 225) and NT Sportfishing Safaris (☎ 8945 5338) also do one-day fishing trips out of Darwin.

Tours Further Afield

A number of operators do trips to the jumping crocodiles at Adelaide River, the Crocodile Farm and to the Territory Wildlife Park on the Cox Peninsula road. For Adelaide River try Adelaide River Queen Cruises (☎ 8988 8144; fax 8988 8130), which does half-day trips at 7 am for $55 ($40 children), which includes the two-hour boat ride on the Adelaide River and a visit to Fogg Dam.

Darwin Day Tours (☎ 8981 8696; fax 8981 1777) does a three-hour trip to the Crocodile Farm at 12.30 pm ($25 adults, $13 children), six-hour trips to the Territory Wildlife Park ($30, $16) departing at 7.30 am, and an eight-hour trip which covers the two for $51 ($29).

Keetleys Tours (☎ 8981 4422; fax 8941 1341) combines the Territory Wildlife Park and the jumping crocodiles in an eight-hour trip which leaves Darwin at 7.30 am and costs $88 ($78 children).

FESTIVALS

Darwin has plenty of colour and flair when it comes to local festivals. Most of these take place in the Dry, especially during July and August.

Beer Can Regatta

An utterly insane and typically Territorian festival which features races for boats made entirely out of beer cans. It takes places at Mindil Beach in July/August and is a good fun day (☎ 8927 5775).

Festival of Darwin

This is mainly an outdoor arts and culture festival held each year in August which highlights Darwin's unique position in Australia with its high Asian and Aboriginal populations (☎ 8989 7333).

Royal Darwin Show

Every July the showgrounds in Winnellie are the scene for the agricultural show. Activities include all the usual rides, as well as demonstrations and competitions.

Darwin Cup Carnival

The Darwin Cup racing carnival takes place in July and August of each year, and features eight days of racing and associated social events. The highlight is the running of the Darwin Cup.

Darwin to Ambon Yacht Race

Darwin is the starting point for the highly regarded and fiercely contested Darwin to Ambon Yacht Race, which takes place in July/August. It draws an international field of contestants and there is a real feeling of anticipation in Darwin in the few days leading up to the event.

Darwin Rodeo

Yee ha! August.

PLACES TO STAY

Darwin has backpacker hostels, guest-houses, motels, holiday flats, and a clutch of up-market hotels. There's also half a dozen or so caravan parks/camp sites, but unfortunately none of these are close to the city centre.

Places to Stay – bottom end

Camping & Caravan Parks Sadly, Darwin takes no advantage of what could be fine camp sites on its many open spaces. East Point, for instance, would be superb. To camp or get an on-site van you must go to

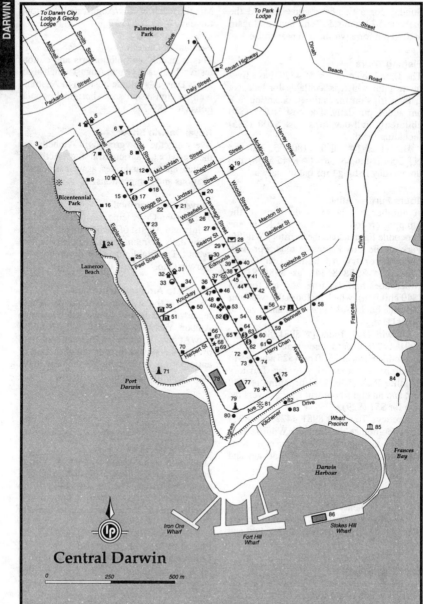

Central Darwin

0   250   500 m

one of the privately run caravan parks in the outer city. A second drawback is that a number of the more conveniently situated caravan parks don't take tent campers.

If you're going to be staying for a few days it's worth enquiring about weekly rates, as these are usually significantly cheaper, and can be better value even if you're not staying a full seven days.

Shady Glen Caravan Park (☎ 8984 3330), 10 km east, is at the corner of Stuart Highway and Farrell Crescent, Winnellie. This is the closest park to the city centre but it's very cramped, the swimming pool is tiny and the amenities blocks are way past it. There is, however, plenty of shade. Camp sites are $12 for two ($16 with power), or there are small on-site vans at $36 for two.

Lee Point Resort (☎ 8945 0535) is at Lee Point, 15 km north of the city on Lee Point Rd. This is a

PLACES TO STAY

2	Alatai Holiday Apartments
4	Banyan View Lodge
5	Elke's Inner City Backpackers
7	Top End Hotel
8	Marrakai Serviced Apartments
9	Darwin Travelodge
10	Ivan's Backpackers Hostel
11	Fawlty Towers
16	Beaufort Hotel
19	Frogshollow Backpackers
20	Mirrambeena Tourist Resort
25	Novotel Atrium Hotel
26	Tiwi Motel
31	Melaleuca Lodge
32	Darwin City Youth Hostel
34	Value Inn
39	Air Raid City Lodge
56	Don Hotel
66	Darwin Plaza Hotel
70	Hotel Darwin

PLACES TO EAT

6	Thai Garden and Uncle Sam's
14	Peppi's
21	Lindsay St Cafe
23	Sizzler
29	Guiseppe's
37	Swiss Cafe & Restaurant
38	Cafe Capri and Hana Sushi Bar
41	Pancake Palace
42	Night Tokyo Restaurant
43	Raymond's
44	Lam Saigon Restaurant
54	Hog's Breath Cafe
55	Victoria Hotel & Arcade
67	Knife & Fork and Hanuman restaurants
86	The Arcade

OTHER

1	Frontier Darwin Hotel
3	Aquascene
12	Thrifty Rent-a-Car
13	Rent-a-Rocket
15	Performing Arts Centre
17	National Bank
18	Rent a Dent
22	ANCA & AANT
24	Leichhardt Memorial
27	International Vaccination Clinic
28	Main Post Office
30	Time Disco
33	Transit Centre
35	Lyons Cottage
36	Jalan Jalan Tours & Travel
40	NT General Store
45	Raintree Gallery
46	Paspalis Centrepoint & Singapore Airlines
47	Indigenous Creations
48	Darwin Plaza
49	Galleria Shopping Centre
50	Malaysia Airlines
51	Old Admiralty House
52	Darwin Regional Tourism Association Office
53	Ansett Anthony Plaza & Star
55	Garuda
57	Chinese Temple
58	Harbour View Plaza
59	Department of Land, Planning & Environment
60	Qantas
61	City Bus Depot
62	Commonwealth Bank
63	Westpac Bank
64	Bookworld
68	Police Station
69	Petty Sessions Bar
71	Anzac Memorial
72	NT Government Publications Centre
73	Old Town Hall
74	Brown's Mart
75	Christ Church Cathedral
76	Old Police Station & Courthouse
77	Supreme Court Building
78	Parliament House
79	Telegraph Cable Memorial
80	Government House
81	Survivors Lookout
82	WW II Oil Storage Tunnels
83	Helipad
84	Deckchair Cinema
85	Indo-Pacific Marine & Australian Pearling Exhibition

DARWIN

new and spacious park close to the beach at Lee Point. The facilities are excellent although the shade trees are still a little small. Unpowered sites cost $14, or with power it's $17.

Malak Caravan Park (☎ 8927 3500) and the adjacent *KOA Caravan Park* (☎ 8927 2651) on McMillans Rd near the airport are actually just one place. It's for caravans only but it's well maintained and not too far from the centre.

Overlander Caravan Park (☎ 8984 3025) is 12 km east of the centre at 1064 McMillans Rd, Berrimah. Camp sites here are $12 for two ($14 powered), and there are on-site vans at $30 to $35.

Palms Caravan Park (☎ 8932 2891) is 17 km southeast of the city on the noisy Stuart Highway at Berrimah. Camp sites are $14 for two ($16 powered), or there are on-site vans at $36 and cabins for $68.

Also consider camping at Howard Springs, 26 km out, where there are two caravan parks which take campers (see the Around Darwin chapter).

Hostels – City Centre There's a host of choices in this bracket, with several of the cheapest places on or near Mitchell St, conveniently close to the transit centre. Most places have guest kitchens, and the showers and toilets are almost always communal. As always, competition is fierce so it's always worth asking about discounts for first night (currently $2 at some hostels), for a weekly rate (usually seventh night free) if you plan to stay that long, or during the Wet when things are likely to be slack.

Very popular among travellers is the purpose-built *Frogshollow Backpackers* (☎ 8941 2600; fax 8941 0758) at 27 Lindsay St, about 10 minutes walk from the transit centre but still close to the centre of town. It's a modern, spacious and clean place, and has a swimming pool and two spas in the small garden. The charge is $13.50 a night in a fan-cooled, eight-bed dorm, and there are good sized double rooms with fridge and fan for $30, or $35 with air-con and $40 with air-con and attached bath. It has a well-appointed kitchen, common area with TV and travel information and, as with other hostels, it does pick-ups from the transit centre (and airport on demand). It also

organises free trips for guests out to East Point at sunset, which are popular.

Ivan's Backpackers Hostel (☎ toll-free 1800 800 798) at 97 Mitchell St is another popular place. There's a pool, two kitchens, frequent barbecues and a good travel desk. A dormitory bunk is $13 in a four to seven-bed room complete with fridge and bathroom. All rooms are air-conditioned at night, and there's a very popular bar with cheap meals in the evening. There are also free bicycles for guests to use. Double rooms are available for $45 with attached bath.

Right across the road from Ivan's, at 88 Mitchell St, is *Fawlty Towers* (☎ toll-free 1800 068 886), a friendly and informal place in one of the few surviving elevated tropical houses in the city centre. There's a small swimming pool and the dorms are air-conditioned at night. A bed in a four-bed dorm costs $14, or there are doubles for $38.

The *Darwin City Youth Hostel* (☎ 8981 6344; fax 8981 6674) is at 69A Mitchell St and is part of the recently remodelled transit centre. Its rooms are all fan-cooled twins and cost $16 per person, or $14 for YHA members. The building has been extensively renovated, so the facilities are as good as any you'll find in the city and the location is great. They also have a comprehensive travel booking service.

Right across the road from the transit centre is the *Melaleuca Lodge* (☎ toll-free 1800 623 543), which has recently been transformed from one of Darwin's accommodation low points into a fresh, new backpacker hostel. Dorm beds are $14 (in four to 10-bed rooms), or there are doubles with TV and fridge for $40 and triples for $50. All rooms are air-conditioned at night, the kitchen facilities are good and there's a travel desk and swimming pool.

Hostels – Elsewhere Still on Mitchell St, but just north of Daly St, is *Elke's Inner City Backpackers* (☎ toll-free 1800 808 365; fax 8981 4401) at No 112. The hostel is actually in a couple of recently renovated adjacent houses, and it has much more of a garden feel to it than those right in the heart of the city.

There's a new pool and spa between the two buildings, and there's a travel desk and fax service. Dorm beds are $14.50 in four to six-bed dorms, or twin rooms are $35.

Further north at 151 Mitchell St, about a 10-minute walk from the centre, is the family-run *Darwin City Lodge* (☎ toll-free 1800 808 151; fax 8941 0106). Formerly a family home, this place is one of the Cyclone Tracy survivors and is certainly a bit rough around the edges. However, it's clean, the atmosphere is good, there's a pool and the owners are friendly. The cost is $14 in a dorm, or there's a separate building nearby which has twin rooms for $35. Some of the rooms are air-conditioned. This place offers substantial discounts during the wet season.

In the same area is the *Gecko Lodge* (☎ toll-free 1800 811 250) at 146 Mitchell St. This is another smaller hostel in an old house, and there's a pool and a common room. Dorm beds cost $14, or there are twin rooms for $40, and at night all rooms are air-conditioned.

The big YWCA *Banyan View Lodge* (☎ 8981 8644; fax 8981 6104) is at 119 Mitchell St. It takes women and men and has no curfew. Rooms have fans and fridges, and are clean and well kept; there's two TV lounges, a kitchen and an outdoor spa. The charge is $15 per person in a twin share room, $25/37 for singles/doubles, or $28/40 with air-con.

Places to Stay – middle

Guesthouses Darwin has a number of good small guesthouses, and these can make a pleasant change from the hostel scene, especially if you're planning a longer stay. Among those which aren't too far from the centre is the friendly, quiet and airy *Park Lodge* (☎ 8981 5692; fax 8981 3720) at 42 Coronation Dve in Stuart Park, only a short cycle or bus ride from the city centre. All rooms have fan, air-con and fridge; bathrooms, kitchen, sitting/TV room and laundry are communal. Air-con singles/doubles cost $35/40, and this includes breakfast of toast and jam and tea/coffee. Numerous city buses, including Nos 5 and 8, run to this part

of Darwin along the highway; ask the driver where to get off.

Further out from the centre at 19 Harcus Crt, Malak, close to the airport is *Robyn's Nest* (☎ /fax 8927 7400). Two rooms on the ground floor of this family home are let out to guests, and the cost is $58 per room with attached bath. Both are air-conditioned, with TV, fridge and tea/coffee-making facilities, and there's a pool and spa.

Right in the city centre there's the *Air Raid City Lodge* (☎ 8981 9214) at 35 Cavenagh St which has air-con rooms with attached bath, TV and tea/coffee-making facilities for $50/60. It's not bad value although there's no garden or outdoor area.

Hotels Good value in this range is the charming old *Hotel Darwin* (☎ 8981 9211; fax 8981 9575), right in the heart of the city on the Esplanade. There's a good range of facilities and a lush garden, which is a rarity in an inner-city hotel. The rooms are comfortable, and all are air-conditioned and have attached bath, TV, phone and fridge. The room rates are $82/105, and this includes a light breakfast. Wet season rates are about 25% less.

Also good is the new, air-con *Value Inn* (☎ 8981 4733), on Mitchell St opposite the transit centre. The rooms are comfortable but small, and have fridge, colour TV and attached bath. The price is $55 for up to three people.

At the other end of the city centre is the lively *Top End Hotel* (☎ 8981 6511; fax 8941 1253) on the corner of Daly and Mitchell Sts. Rooms in this modern two-storey hotel cost $100/110, and there's a 10% discount in the Wet.

The *Don Hotel* (☎ 8981 5311) is also in the centre at 12 Cavenagh St, and air-con rooms with TV and fans cost $60/70 including a light breakfast.

Apartments & Holiday Flats There are plenty of modern places in Darwin, but prices in this range often vary immensely between the Dry and the cheaper Wet. Many of them give discounts if you stay a week or more – usually of the seventh-night-free variety. Typically these places have air-con and swimming pools.

Good value here and well located is the *Peninsular Apartment Hotel* (☎ toll-free 1800 808 564; fax 8941 2547) at 115 Smith St, just a short walk from the city centre. The studios have a double and a single bed, and cost $99 ($84 in the Wet), while the two-bedroom apartments accommodate four people and cost $125 ($94.50). All rooms are air-conditioned, have a microwave and a cooker, fridge, TV and attached bath. There's also a shaded swimming pool.

The *Alatai Holiday Apartments* (☎ toll-free 1800 628 833; fax 8981 8887) are modern, self-contained apartments at the northern edge of the city centre on the corner of McMinn and Finniss Sts. The three-storey block is built around a swimming pool and licensed cafe, and there's also a restaurant featuring Singaporean and Malaysian food. Two-bed studio apartments cost $99 ($89 in the Wet), while two-bedroom apartments are $142 ($128) and for three-bedrooms it's $241 ($217). The studios only have a microwave and electric frypan for cooking; the larger apartments also have a stove.

Also in the city centre is the *Mirrambeena Tourist Resort* (☎ 8946 0111) at 64 Cavenagh St. This large place has 90-odd units which cost from $95/103 for a single/double, and $150 with cooking facilities.

Further from the city centre and with a great location right by the Botanic Gardens at 17 Geranium St in Stuart Park are the *Botanic Gardens Apartments* (☎ 8946 0300; fax 8981 0410), a block of two-bedroom, self-contained apartments which cost $146 ($125 in the Wet) for up to four people. All apartments are air-conditioned, and have a balcony, full cooking facilities and a washing machine and drier.

Also in Stuart Park are *Theo's Self Contained Units* (☎ 8981 2700; fax 8981 7166) at 20 Gothenburg Crescent. The two-bedroom units accommodate up to four people and cost $100 per night ($80 in the Wet), and there's an outdoor spa.

In Parap, a little further again from the centre there's another option, the *Parap Village Apartments* (☎ toll-free 1800 620 913; fax 8941 3465) at 39 Parap Rd. All apartments have their own balcony and laundry, and outside there's two pools and a children's play area. The rates are $145 for a two-bedroom apartment ($130 in the Wet) and $165 ($150) for a three-bedroom apartment.

A cheaper alternative is the *Coolibah Resort* (☎ 8985 4166; fax 8985 4979) at 91 Aralia St, Nightcliff, which costs $59/69/79 for single/double/triple one-bedroom apartments ($49/55/60 in the Wet), or there are two-room apartments which accommodate up to seven people at $105 ($89).

Motels Motels in Darwin tend to be expensive. Conveniently central is the *Asti Motel* (☎ toll-free 1800 063 335; fax 8981 8038) on the corner of Smith and Packard Sts just a couple of blocks from the city centre. Rooms cost $54, and there are some four-bed family rooms for $90.

Also in the centre and reasonably priced is the *Tiwi Lodge Motel* (☎ 8981 6471) on Cavenagh St, where rooms cost $61.

The *Tops Boulevard Motel* (☎ 8981 1544) at 38 Gardens Rd, the continuation of Cavenagh St beyond Daly St, is a comfortable modern motel. Double rooms cost $86, or studio rooms with cooking facilities are $115 (these sleep three people). All rooms have private bathroom, fridge and TV. There's also a pool, tennis court and restaurant.

For motel accommodation in Fannie Bay there's the *Capricornia Motel* (☎ 8981 4055; fax 8981 2031) at 44 East Point Rd, with rooms at $55/65.

Places to Stay – top end
Hotels Darwin's few up-market hotels are on the Esplanade, making best use of the prime views across the bay. The modern *Beaufort Hotel* (☎ 8982 9911) is part of the Performing Arts Complex, and has rooms for $225, and suites from $250.

Close by is the *Novotel Atrium Hotel* (☎ 8941 0755), which does indeed have an atrium, complete with lush tropical plants, and rooms for $155 and up. Also on the Esplanade is the *Darwin Travelodge* (☎ 8981 5388) with rooms from $160.

One block back from the Esplanade but still with the fine views is the city's only five-star hotel, the *Darwin Plaza Hotel* (☎ 8982 0000) at 32 Mitchell St. It has all the facilities you'd expect, including some non-smoking floors. Rooms here start at $205 for a single/double.

The new *Holiday Inn* should by now be taking shape on the Esplanade, behind the revamped Transit Centre.

Serviced Apartments For self-contained accommodation at this end of the market there's the *Marrakai Serviced Apartments* (☎ 8982 3711) at 93 Smith St in the city centre. The two-bedroom suites here all have cooking facilities and a dishwasher, and cost $185 for a double and $220 for a triple.

PLACES TO EAT
Darwin's proximity to Asia is obvious in its large number of fine Asian eateries. Take-away places, a growing number of lunch spots in and around the Smith St Mall and the excellent Asian-style markets, held two or three times a week at various sites around the city, are the cheapest options. There's also a good selection of more expensive restaurants offering a variety of cuisines.

A number of eateries around town, particularly the pubs, offer discount meals for backpackers. Keep an eye out for vouchers at the hostels.

City Centre
Cafes & Takeaways One of the best options for cheap food used to be the open-air Banyan Food Stalls next to the Transit Centre on Smith St. These should have been retained in the recent redevelopment of the Transit Centre and hopefully still offer a cheap alternative right in the city centre. The popular Mexican *Coyote's* stall is extremely popular with travellers and has reputation which spans the country. Also good here is the *Payao Thai Cafe*.

A host of snack bars and cafes in Smith St Mall offer lots of choice during the day – but, except for Thursday, the late shopping night, they're virtually all closed from about 5 pm and on Saturday afternoon and all day Sunday.

There's a good collection of fast-food counters in Darwin Plaza towards the Knuckey St end of the mall – *Omar Khayyam* for Middle Eastern and Indian, *La Veg* for health food, lasagne and light meals, *Ozzy Burgers* for, well, burgers, and *Rose-land* for yoghurt, fruit salads and ice cream.

Further up the mall the Galleria shopping centre has a few good places: *Satay King* specialises in Malaysian food and serves that excellent Nonya dish, curry laksa; *Mamma Bella* serves predictable Italian food; *Al Fresco* has gourmet sandwiches and ice cream; and the *Galleria* is a straightforward burger place. There's a good seating area in the centre, although at lunch times it can be difficult to find a spare table.

Further up the mall is Anthony Plaza where the *French Bakehouse* is one of the few places you can get a coffee and snack every day.

In the Victoria Arcade behind the Victoria Hotel the *Satay House* has good cheap Indonesian fare, while *Harrisons Coffee Studio* is a popular spot for coffee and snacks.

Right opposite the Vic is the *Hog's Breath Cafe* (☎ 8941 3333), a popular American-style grill which prides itself on its 18-hour tenderised rib steaks. There's also a wide range of burgers, as well as Mexican and seafood dishes.

Simply Foods, at 32 Smith St, is a busy health-food place. It's a good spot with appealing décor, music and friendly service.

At 2 Lindsay St there's the very popular open-air *Lindsay St Cafe* (☎ 8981 8631) in the garden of a typical elevated tropical house. The menu is varied, with a tendency towards Asian cooking. Main courses are around $15.

Cafe Capri (☎ 8981 0010) on Knuckey St is a chic new spot which has a good following. Pastas and salads are the go at the lunchtime, while in the evening the meals are

DARWIN

a bit more sophisticated, featuring dishes such as venison. Main meals are around $18 in the evening, less at lunchtimes.

For excellent Malay food head for the no-frills *Rendezvous Cafe*, in the Star Village Arcade off the Smith St Mall. While the ambitious menu covers the full range of cafe dishes, it's the Malay food which stands out in this excellent little place.

In the new Supreme Court Building at the southern end of the city centre, *Rumpoles* is a ritzy cafe serving coffee, gourmet sandwiches and cakes.

At the end of Stokes Hill Wharf at the Wharf Precinct, the Arcade is a small, Asian-style food centre with a number of different shops offering a variety of cuisines. This is a great spot for an alfresco fish & chips lunch washed down with a cool beer, or a cappuccino and cake.

Restaurants The *Pancake Palace* (☎ 8981 5307), on Cavenagh St near Knuckey St, is open daily for lunch and in the evening until 1 am. Conveniently close to many of Darwin's night spots, it has sweet and savoury pancakes from $8, as well as meaty offerings such as buffalo and beef steaks.

Also on Cavenagh St is the agreeably rowdy *Guiseppe's*, one of the few good Italian pasta places in Darwin. Main dishes are in the $12 to $15 range, or there's pizza from $12.

An unusual find is the *Swiss Cafe & Restaurant* (☎ 8981 5079) tucked away in the Harry Chan Arcade off 58 Smith St. For good, solid European food you can't beat this place, and it's reasonably priced with main dishes around $12 to $15. Offering similar fare is the *Knife & Fork Restaurant* (☎ 8981 8877), on Mitchell St, just behind the Hanuman Restaurant. Here the cuisine is predominantly German and Russian, and main course are in the $15 to $23 range.

On Cavenagh St, *Raymonds* (☎ 8981 2909) is a good, long-running place which relies heavily on pasta dishes. Main course are around $15.

The *Sizzler* restaurant (☎ 8941 2225) on Mitchell St is one of the chain found Aus-tralia-wide. It's amazingly popular, with queues out onto the footpath every night in the Dry. The reason is that it's very good value: for around $15 you can fill your plate from a wide range of dishes, and have a dessert too.

One of the best restaurants in the city centre area is *Peppi's* at 84 Mitchell St. It's fully licensed and a two-course meal for two will set you back around $80 with drinks.

Also excellent is *Christo's on the Wharf* (☎ 8981 8658), out on the Stokes Hill Wharf. Here you have the choice of eating outdoors or in the air-con *Gilligans Piano Bar*. Not surprisingly given the location, seafood is the specialty, but the style is mainly Greek.

Asian As you would expect in a city with a sizeable Asian population, there's a range of restaurants featuring Asian cuisine. The *Hanuman* (☎ 8941 3500) at 28 Mitchell St near the Darwin Plaza Hotel is an excellent spot. The chef here hails from a well-known Thai restaurant in Melbourne, and the food, which also includes Indian and Malay dishes, is excellent. Expect to pay around $17 for a main course.

For something different there's the *Lam Saigon Restaurant* (☎ 8981 7808) at 21 Cavenagh St. The seafood hotpot is popular, or if there's four people you can try the buffet at $18 per person. Other main meals are around $13, although it's cheaper at lunchtime.

The *Jade Garden* on the Smith St Mall (upstairs, roughly opposite the Victoria Arcade) offers a nine-course meal for $12 a head.

On Knuckey St the *Hana Sushi Bar* (☎ 8981 0414) is the city's newest Japanese restaurant. You can eat here in traditional style, or takeaway service is also available. The *Night Tokyo Restaurant* (☎ 8981 9292) on the 2nd floor of the Jape Plaza on Cavenagh St is a Japanese tepanyaki restaurant where, if the mood strikes, you can also indulge in karaoke (oh joy!).

Hotels The more expensive hotels all have at least one major restaurant, and some of these can be fine places to eat, although they're far from cheap.

One of the best of these is *Siggi's* (☎ 8982 9911) at the Hotel Beaufort. The menu is a mixture of classic French-influenced dishes and unusual local food, such as salmon marinated in green ants! Main courses are around $25. For a buffet lunch the *Brasserie* here charges $10 on weekdays for a soup, salad and a main course. The evening barbecue buffet is a lavish affair (as it should be at $32.50) and on Friday and Saturday evenings seafood is the go. The breakfast buffet here is also a gut-buster, at $12 for a continental or $18 for the full-on cholesterol trip.

The Plaza Hotel has *Dundee's* (☎ 8982 0000), where 'Northern Territory cuisine' is also featured. This usually translates to the full range of wild meats – crocodile, barramundi, buffalo and camel – and is indeed the case here. Also of interest here is the 2nd floor *Iguana Restaurant*, with yet more interesting Australian dishes.

At the Atrium Hotel there's the well-regarded *Castaways Restaurant* (☎ 8941 0755). This dry-season alfresco restaurant is a very pleasant place to eat, with the emphasis on barbecued food. Inside on the ground floor at the Atrium is the *Corellas Restaurant*, which has an extensive à la carte menu throughout the week, a $10 lunchtime buffet on weekdays and excellent weekend evening buffets for $23.

Out of the Centre

The pickings are pretty slim as you move away from the city centre.

On Smith St, just beyond Daly St, the *Thai Garden Restaurant* serves not only delicious and reasonably priced Thai food but pizzas too! It has a few outdoor tables. There's a takeaway 'Aussie-Chinese' place across the road, and the 24-hour *Uncle Sam* fast-food joint next door. In the small shopping centre here is the *All Sorts Cafe*, a relaxed BYO cafe-restaurant.

Out at Fannie Bay, the *Dolly Pot Inn* (☎ 8981 1288), at 7 Keith Lane behind the Fannie Bay shops, serves a range of 'Aussie tucker'. The original Dolly Pot restaurant is

in Tennant Creek and is something of an institution. This second outlet has recently opened in Darwin.

The licensed *Cornucopia* at the Museum & Art Gallery in Fannie Bay serves superb and reasonably priced food, and you can sit outside under the swishing fans on the verandah close to the sea, or inside with the air-conditioning.

Markets Easily the best all-round eating experience in Darwin is the bustling Asian-style market at Mindil Beach on Thursday night during the dry season. People begin arriving from 5.30 pm, bringing tables, chairs, rugs, grog and kids to settle under the coconut palms for sunset and decide which of the tantalising food-stall aromas has the greatest allure. It's difficult to know whether to choose Thai, Sri Lankan, Indian, Chinese, Malaysian, Brazilian, Greek or Portuguese. You'll even find Indonesian black rice pudding. All prices are reasonable at around $2 to $5 for a meal. There are cake stalls, fruit-salad bars, arts and crafts stalls, and sometimes entertainment in the form of a band or street theatre.

Similar food stalls can be found at the Parap market on Saturday morning, the one at Rapid Creek on Sunday morning, and in the Smith St Mall in the evening (except Thursday), but Mindil Beach is the best for its atmosphere and proximity. It's about two km from the city centre, off Gilruth Ave. During the Wet, it transfers to Rapid Creek. Bus Nos 4 and 6 go past Mindil Beach: No 4 goes on to Rapid Creek, No 6 to Parap.

ENTERTAINMENT

Darwin is a lively city with bands at several venues and a number of clubs and discos. More sophisticated tastes are also catered for, with theatre, film, concerts and a casino.

The best source of what's on around town is probably the *Avagoodweegend* liftout in the Friday edition of the *NT News*.

Bars & Live Music

Live bands play upstairs at the *Victoria Hotel* from 9 pm Wednesday to Saturday. The *Bil-*

labong Bar in the Atrium Hotel, on the corner of the Esplanade and Peel St, has live bands on Friday and Saturday nights until 1 am. Take a look at the hotel's spectacular seven-storey glass-roofed atrium while you're there.

The Hotel Darwin is pleasant in the evening for a quiet drink. There's a patio section by the pool. It's livelier on Friday night when there's a band in the *Green Room*, or on Wednesday to Saturday nights in the *Pickled Parrot Piano Bar*, and there's often bands playing in *The Driveway*, the pub's former drive-in bottle shop which has been turned into a small venue.

The *Jabiru Bar* in the Atrium Hotel is the venue on Wednesday evening for Crab Races. It's all very light hearted and there are prizes for the winners.

There's also live music in the evenings at *Sweetheart's Bar* at the casino.

Nightclubs & Discos

The *Brewery Bar* in the Top End Hotel on the corner of Mitchell and Daly Sts is a popular evening venue. The *Beachcomber* bar at the rear is a popular disco and nightclub (Wednesday to Saturday), while the *Sportsmens Bar* at the front on Mitchell St offers entertainment of the 'prawns and porn' variety – cheap food and strip shows to attract the lunchtime punters.

Petty Sessions on the corner of Mitchell and Bennett Sts is a combination winebar, nightclub and disco. It's quite a popular place and stays open to 2 am.

On the small street which runs between Smith and Cavenagh Sts one block from Knuckey St is the *Time* disco. It's probably the most popular nightspot in the city, and stays open until the early hours.

Another late night venue is *Caesars* nightclub at the Don Hotel on Cavenagh St.

Folk & Country Music

For something a bit more laid back there's the *Top End Folk Club* which meets every second Sunday of the month at the Northern Territory University Social Club, The Breezway at the Casuarina uni campus. Visitors

are welcome. Phone ☎ 8988 1301 for more details.

If you're into country & western music, the NT Country Music Association meets every second Wednesday at the Driver Primary School out in Palmerston. This is the place for bootscooters! Contact ☎ 8932 1030 for details.

Jazz

On Sunday afternoon at the MGM Grand Darwin casino there's *Jazz on the Lawns*, where you can eat, watch the sunset and listen to some fairly sedate jazz.

Theatre

The *Performing Arts Centre* (☎ 8981 1222) on Mitchell St, opposite McLachlan St, hosts a variety of events, from fashion-award nights to plays, rock operas, pantomimes and concerts.

The Darwin Theatre Company (☎ 8981 8424) often has play readings and other performances around the city.

The old Brown's Mart (☎ 8981 5522) on Harry Chan Ave is another venue for live theatre performances.

Cinema

There are several cinemas in town and the *Darwin Film Society* (☎ 8981 2215) has regular showings of offbeat/arthouse films at the Museum Theatrette in the Museum of Arts & Sciences, Conacher St, Bullocky Point. The film society also runs the unusual *Deckchair Cinema* (☎ 8981 0700) near Stokes Hill Wharf. Here you can watch the movie under the stars while reclining in a deckchair. Screenings are listed in the newspapers, or on flyers around town.

Casino

Finally, there's the *MGM Grand Darwin* casino on Mindil Beach off Gilruth Ave – as long as you're 'properly dressed'. That means no thongs, and long socks for men wearing shorts!

Spectator Sports

There's quite a bit happening on the local

sports scene but very little in the way of interstate (let alone international) events.

The Northern Territory Football League is the local Australian Rules league, and there are matches most weekends in the Dry season. Phone ☎ 8945 2224 for venues and match details.

Rugby Union matches are played at Rugby Park in Marrara (☎ 8981 1433), while Northline Speedway (☎ 8984 3469) is where the petrol heads cut loose.

THINGS TO BUY

Aboriginal art is generally cheaper in Alice Springs, but Darwin has greater variety. The Raintree Gallery at 29 Knuckey St is one of a number of places offering a range of art work – bark paintings from Arnhem Land, and interesting carvings by the Tiwi people of Bathurst and Melville islands and by the peoples of central Australia.

T-shirts printed with Aboriginal designs are popular but quality and prices vary. Riji Dij at 11 Knuckey St has a large range of T-shirts for $25. They are printed by Tiwi Designs and Territoriana, both local companies using Aboriginal designs and, to a large extent, Aboriginal labour. It stocks Tiwi printed fabric and clothing made from fabric printed by central Australian Aboriginal people. Another place worth trying is Indigenous Creations on the Smith St Mall.

Another excellent place is Framed, a gallery on the Stuart Highway in Stuart Park which is heavily into Aboriginal art. There are some fine works here, with prices to match.

You can find Balinese and Indian clothing at Darwin's markets – Mindil Beach (Thursday evening, dry season only), Parap (Saturday morning) and Rapid Creek (Sunday morning, and Thursday evening in the wet season). Local arts and crafts (the market at Parap is said to be the best), jewellery and bric-a-brac are on sale too.

GETTING THERE & AWAY
Air

Darwin is becoming increasingly busy as an international and domestic gateway. The airport is only a short bus or taxi ride from the city centre.

On the international scene, there are flights to Brunei, Indonesia (Bali and Timor), Malaysia, Singapore and Thailand.

Domestically Darwin is not so well served. Ansett and Qantas Australian fly direct to Adelaide, Alice Springs, Brisbane, Broome, Kununurra and Sydney, but the number of flights is limited and there is very little discounting as it's not a heavy traffic route.

On a more local level, Airnorth fly daily to Katherine ($144), Tennant Creek ($319), Alice Springs ($389) and to various other smaller settlements in the Top End.

See the Getting There & Away and Getting Around chapters for full details of flights in and out of Darwin.

Airlines The main airline offices in Darwin include:

Airnorth
    Darwin Airport (☎ toll-free 1800 627 474; fax 8945 3559)
Ansett
    19 Smith St Mall (☎ 13 1300)
    Casuarina Shopping Centre (☎ 8945 1233)
Garuda
    9 Cavenagh St (☎ 8981 6422)
Malaysia Airlines
    38 Mitchell St (☎ 8941 3055)
Merpati
    Natrabu Travel, 12 West Lane (☎ 8981 3695)
Qantas
    19 Smith St Mall (☎ 13 1313)
    Casuarina Shopping Centre (☎ 8982 3327)
Royal Brunei Airlines
    22 Cavenagh St (☎ 8941 1394)
Singapore Airlines
    Smith St Mall (☎ 8941 1799)

Bus

Greyhound Pioneer (☎ 13 2030; fax 8981 6659) and McCafferty's (☎ 13 1499; fax 8941 0928) both operate out of the transit centre on Mitchell St in the city centre.

Again, see the Getting There & Away and Getting Around chapters for details of routes and fares.

Car Rental

Darwin has numerous budget car-rental operators, as well as all the major national and international companies.

Rent-a-Rocket and Nifty Rent a Car offer similar deals on their mostly 1970s and early 1980s cars. Costs depend on whether you're staying near Darwin, or going further afield to Kakadu, Katherine, Litchfield Park and so on. For local trips with Rent-a-Dent you pay around $35 a day, depending on the vehicle, and must stay within 70 km of Darwin. This includes 150 free km, but with these deals you can't go beyond Humpty Doo or Acacia Store (about 70 km down the Track). The prices drop for longer rentals.

Value Rent a Car has vehicles from $37, but this doesn't include any free km.

Territory Rent-a-Car is far and away the biggest local operator and is probably the best value. Discount deals to look for include cheaper rates for four or more days' hire, weekend specials (three days for roughly the price of two), and one-way hires (to Jabiru, Katherine or Alice Springs). Daily charges start at around $45 daily for a small car, including 100 free km per day.

There are also plenty of 4WD vehicles available in Darwin, but you usually have to book ahead, and fees and deposits can be hefty. The best place to start looking is probably Territory, which has several different models – the cheapest, a Suzuki four-seater, costs around $95 a day including insurance, plus 28c a km over 100 km. Territory also has camping equipment packages at $25 per vehicle per day.

Brits:Australia also rents 4WDs and campervans.

Rental companies, including the cut-price ones, generally operate a free towing or replacement service if the vehicle breaks down. But (especially with the cheaper operators) check the paperwork to see exactly what you're covered for in terms of damage to vehicles and injuries to passengers. The usual age and insurance requirements apply in Darwin and there may be restrictions on off-bitumen driving, or on the distance you're allowed to go from the city. Even with the big firms the insurance does not cover you when driving off the bitumen, so make sure you know exactly what your liability is in the event of an accident.

Most rental companies are open every day and have agents in the city centre to save you trekking out to the Stuart Highway. Territory, Budget, Hertz and Thrifty all have offices at the airport.

Avis
    145 Stuart Highway, Stuart Park (☎ toll-free 1800 225 533; fax 8981 3155)
Brits:Australia
    Stuart Highway, Stuart Park (☎ toll-free 1800331 454; fax (03) 9416 2933)
Budget
    69 Mitchell St (☎ toll-free 1800 805 627; fax 8981 1777)
Hertz
    Cnr Smith & Daly Sts (☎ toll-free 1800 891 112; fax 8981 0288)
Nifty Rent a Car
    10 McLachlan St (☎ 8981 2999; fax 8941 0662)
Rent-a-Rocket
    McLachlan St (☎ 8941 3733)
Territory Rent-a-Car
    64 Stuart Highway, Parap (☎ toll-free 1800 891 125; fax 8981 5247)
Thrifty
    Cnr Smith & McLachlan Sts (☎ 8981 8555; fax 8981 1697)
Value Rent a Car
    Mitchell St (☎ 8981 5599)

GETTING AROUND
To/From the Airport

Darwin's busy airport terminal, only about six km from the centre of town, handles international flights as well as domestic ones. Hertz, Budget, Thrifty and Territory Rent-a-Car have desks at the airport. The taxi fare into the centre is about $12.

There is an airport shuttle bus (☎ 8941 5000) for $6, which will pick up or drop off almost anywhere in the centre. When leaving Darwin book a day before departure.

Bus

City Bus Darwin has a fairly good city bus service operating Monday to Friday. On Saturday, services cease around lunch time and on Sunday and holidays they shut down completely. The city services start from the small terminal (☎ 8989 6540) on Harry Chan Ave, near the corner of Smith St. Buses enter the city along Mitchell St and leave along Cavenagh St.

Fares are on a zone system – shorter trips are $1 or $1.40, and the longest cost $1.90. Bus No 4 (to Fannie Bay, Nightcliff, Rapid Creek and Casuarina) and No 6 (Fannie Bay, Parap and Stuart Park) are useful for getting to Aquascene, the Botanic Gardens, Mindil Beach, the Museum & Art Gallery, Fannie Bay Gaol Museum and East Point. Bus Nos 5 and 8 go along the Stuart Highway past the airport (but not near the terminal building) to Berrimah, from where No 5 goes north to Casuarina and No 8 continues along the highway to Palmerston.

Tour Tub The Tour Tub (☎ 8985 4779) is a private bus which does a circuit of the city, calling at the major places of interest, and you can hop on or off anywhere. In the city centre it leaves from Knuckey St, at the end of the Smith St Mall. The set fare is $14, and the buses operate hourly from 9 am to 4 pm. Sites visited include Aquascene (only at fish-feeding times), Indo-Pacific Marine and Wharf Precinct, MGM Grand Darwin casino, the Museum & Art Gallery, Military Museum, Fannie Bay Gaol Museum, Parap markets (Saturday only) and the Botanic Gardens.

Bicycle

Darwin has an extensive network of excellent bike tracks. It's a pleasant ride out from the city to the Botanic Gardens, Fannie Bay, East Point or even, if you're feeling fit, all the way to Nightcliff and Casuarina.

Many of the backpackers' hostels have bicycles, and these are often free for guests to use, otherwise there's a small rental charge.

Around Darwin

There are numerous places of interest close to Darwin. Litchfield Park, a national park to the south of Darwin, has become very popular amongst locals in the last few years, while the Territory Wildlife Park is an excellent place to get a look at, and photograph, a wide variety of animals, both native and introduced.

Just off the Arnhem Highway (the main access route into Kakadu National Park from Darwin), there are a couple of interesting little wildlife reserves, and the new Mary River National Park which is set to become the next major attraction of the Top End.

All the places listed in this chapter are easily accessible by car and are only a few hours at the most from Darwin. Organised day tours run to most of these places, usually combining a number of attractions in one hit.

It's well worth spending a few days exploring this area as it offers a wealth of things to do.

MANDORAH

This popular beach resort on the tip of Cox Peninsula is about 125 km by road from Darwin, the last 30 km or so of which is unsealed, or only 10 km across the harbour by boat.

Places to Stay & Eat

The *Mandorah Hotel* (☎ 8978 5044) is right by the beach and has 18 air-con units at $65 for a double with attached bath, and there's quite a reasonable restaurant.

Getting There & Away

The Mandorah Jet Shuttle (☎ 8981 7600) operates about eight times in each direction, with the first departure from the Cullen Bay Marina in Darwin at 6.15 am, the last at 6.05 pm. The journey takes about 20 minutes, and the cost is $15 return ($8 children).

LITCHFIELD NATIONAL PARK

This 146-sq-km national park, 115 km south

HIGHLIGHTS

- Visit spectacular Litchfield National Park
- View the native fauna at the truly excellent Territory Wildlife Park
- See the jumping crocodiles at Adelaide River Crossing
- Cruise the superb Mary River wetlands

of Darwin, encloses much of the spectacular Tabletop Range, a wide sandstone plateau mostly surrounded by cliffs. Four waterfalls, which drop off the edge of this plateau, and their surrounding rainforest patches, unusual termite mounds, curious sandstone formations and a wide variety of fauna are the park's main attractions, but the beautiful country, excellent campsites, and the 4WD, bushwalking and photography opportunities are also highlights. It's well worth a few days, although weekends can get crowded – the local saying in Darwin is 'Kaka-don't, Litchfield-do'.

There are two routes to Litchfield Park, both about a two-hour drive from Darwin. One, from the north, involves turning south off the Berry Springs to Cox Peninsula road onto a well-maintained dirt road, which is suitable for conventional vehicles except in the wet season. The second, and more popular, approach is along a bitumen road from Batchelor into the east of the park. The two access roads join up so it's possible to do a loop from the Stuart Highway.

History

The Wagait Aboriginal people lived in this area, and the many pools and waterfalls and other prominent geographical features had great significance.

In 1864 the Finniss Expedition explored the Northern Territory of South Australia, as it was then called. Frederick Litchfield was a member of the party, and some of the features in the park still bear the names he gave them.

In the late 1860s copper and tin were discovered, and this led to a flurry of activity with several mines operating in the area. The ruins of two of these are still visible today – at Bamboo Creek (which operated from 1906 to 1955) and Blyth Homestead.

The area was then opened up as pastoral leases, and these were in existence right up

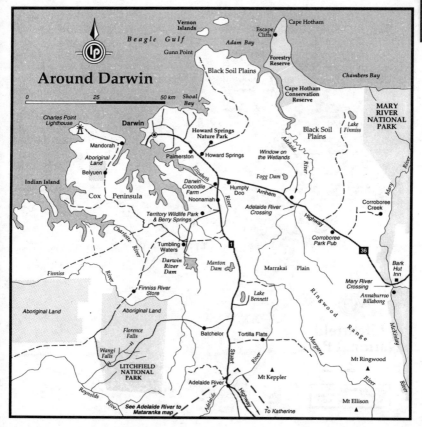

to the proclamation of the national park in 1986.

Information

Permits are not required to enter the park, unless you plan to walk and camp in remote areas. There is a ranger stationed near the northern entrance to the park, but there is no information or visitor centre. In an emergency the ranger can be contacted on ☎ 8976 0282. If you have an FM radio, Parks & Wildlife broadcasts an eight-minute commentary on the park on 88 MHz.

Parks & Wildlife also publish a very good map of the park. If more detail is required, the topographic sheet maps which cover the park are the 1:100,000 Reynolds River (5071) and the 1:50,000 Sheets NO 5071 (I-IV). These are available from the Department of Land, Planning & Environment in Darwin.

Pets and firearms are prohibited.

Flora & Fauna

The dominant trees of the open forest are the Darwin woollybutt (*Eucalyptus miniata*) and the Darwin stringybark (*E. tetrodonta*), while below these sand palms, banksias,

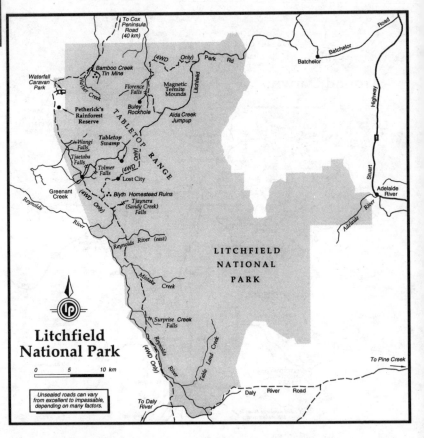

Litchfield National Park

cycads, acacias and grevilleas form the lower level. Around the waterfalls and permanent springs are pockets of surprisingly thick monsoon rainforest.

The more open plains are covered with the high spear grass (*Sorghum intrans*) which is so common throughout much of the Top End.

The wildlife of the park is another of its attractions, with the birdlife being especially abundant. Two of the most commonly sighted birds are the distinctive red-tail black cockatoo (*Calyptorhynchus magnificus*) and the sulphur-crested cockatoo (*Cacatua galeria*). Smaller parrots such as the very beautiful rainbow lorikeet (*Trichoglossus haematodus*), northern rosella (*Platycerus venustus*) and the lovely red-winged parrot (*Aprosmictus erythropterus*) are also often seen.

The jabiru, or more correctly the black-necked stork (*Xenorhynchus asiaticus*), is found in the flooded areas of the park during the Wet, and predatory birds such as black kites (*Milvus migrans*), whistling kites (*Haliastur indus*) and wedge-tail eagles (*Aquila audax*) are often seen soaring in the thermals above the plateau, especially in the dry season.

The wetland areas of the park, fed by the Finniss, Daly and Reynolds river systems, are home to the magpie goose (*Anseranas semipalmata*) and lots of saltwater crocodiles.

The antilopine wallaroo is the largest mammal in the park, but dingos are also sighted from time to time. Most of the smaller mammals are nocturnal, and so are not often seen. These include the northern quoll (rare), the northern brown bandicoot and the northern brushtail possum.

Magnetic Termite Mounds

About 15 km from the eastern boundary of the park is the first major batch of these curious grey termite mounds. A small boardwalk takes you out close to some of the mounds, and there's an excellent information display.

The mounds here are formed by the activity of the magnetic termite (*Amitermes*

meridionalis). These termites are only active on floodplains and their way of dealing with the flooding is to build these distinctive mounds. Whereas other termites head underground to escape extremes of temperature, the magnetic termites build mounds with a climate-control system. The mounds are thin, wide and up to two metres high, and all lie roughly north-south. This means that the eastern face heats up during the morning, but remains in the shade during the heat of the afternoon and so the termites move closer to this side. At night as the face cools down the termites move back to the centre of the mound.

Not all termite mounds face exactly the same direction, as local climatic and physical conditions, such as wind and shade, dictate just how much sun the mound should receive. So how do termites know how to align their mound? Scientists don't know, but it is thought that there is some sort of genetic coding which is inherited.

Florence Falls & Buley Rockhole

Almost immediately after the termite mounds the road climbs the escarpment up the Aida Creek Jump-up and after six km you come to the Florence Falls turn-off on the eastern edge of the plateau. The falls lie in a pocket of monsoon forest five km off the road along a good track. They were named by the South Australian surveyor, George Goyder, as his party passed through here after establishing a camp on Darwin harbour in 1869.

Florence Falls has a walking track (with wheelchair access) which leads to a spectacular lookout, while a steeper path heads down to the excellent swimming hole. The track completes a loop back to the carpark.

Buley Rockhole is another popular swimming spot, and there's a walking trail to the Tabletop Range escarpment.

There are two camp sites here, one accessible only by 4WD. These are pleasant sites and are far less heavily used than Wangi Falls (see Facilities later in this chapter).

From Florence falls a 4WD track takes you north across the Florence Creek and swings around to the east to join the main Litchfield Park Road near the park's eastern boundary.

Lost City

Back on the main road it's another 4.2 km to the turn-off to the Lost City, 10.5 km south of the road along a 4WD track. The feature here is the large sandstone block and pillar formations which, with a little imagination or a good joint, resemble ruined buildings. It's rather a fanciful proposition really but the area is undeniably atmospheric.

This track continues another 3.5 km along a *very* rough section as it comes down off the range, to the **Blyth Homestead Ruins**. This section of track should not be attempted by inexperienced drivers.

Tabletop Swamp

About five km past the Lost City turn-off is the track on the left to the Tabletop Swamp. This small wetland lies just off the road, and is a good spot for spotting waterbirds. There's a short walking track and picnic tables.

Tolmer Falls

It's a further five km to the Tolmer Falls turn-off. Access to the falls themselves has been restricted to protect the habitat of various bats, but a 400-metre walking track (with wheelchair access) leads to a lookout with spectacular views of the falls. You can continue along this track to complete a 1.5-km loop back to the carpark. This takes you past some excellent small rock pools above the falls. You are not permitted to swim in the rock pools directly behind the falls, but those further back up the creek are fine.

Blyth Homestead Ruins & Tjaynera Falls

It's another two km along the main road to **Greenant Creek**, where there's a picnic area and a 1.8-km walking trail to **Tjaetaba Falls** on the north side of the road.

Just beyond Greenant Creek is the turn-off to Tjaynera (Sandy Creek) Falls, which lie nine km off the road along an incredibly corrugated 4WD track. From the end of the

track it's a 1.7-km walk to the falls from the car park and camp site along a track lined with lofty paperbark trees. The pool here is deep and cool, and is far less crowded than Wangi.

On the way to the falls from the main road, there's a turn-off to the north after 5.5 km, and this is the southern end of the Lost City track (see the Lost City section earlier). The Blyth Homestead is 1.5 km along this track. This 'homestead' was built in 1929 by the Sargent family, and it's hard believe now but it remained in use up until the area was declared a national park in 1986.

After another two km the main track forks, the left (eastern) fork heading to the falls (1.5 km), the right (southern) fork continues right down through the isolated southern reaches of the park, to a camp site on the east branch of the **Reynolds River** (six km), and then another at **Surprise Creek Falls** (13 km). Don't be tempted to swim here as salties may be lurking. The track crosses the Reynolds River and eventually links up with the Daly River road, 17 km beyond Surprise Creek. From this intersection you can head east to the Stuart Highway or south-west to Daly River. This track through the south of the park is impassable during the Wet.

Wangi Falls

The main road through the park continues from the Tjaynera turn-off another 6.5 km to the turn-off to the most popular attraction in Litchfield – Wangi Falls (pronounced 'wong-gye'), two km along a side road.

The falls here flow year-round and fill a beautiful plunge pool, which is great for swimming. Although the pool looks safe enough, the currents can be strong if the flow of water into the pool is large enough and the level high. On the edge of the pool a large multi-language sign points out the dangers, and markers indicate when the water is considered to be too high to be safe. There's an emergency telephone at the car park here – every year a few people get into difficulty while swimming in the pool.

There are also extensive picnic and camping areas by the pool. This area can really become overrun on weekends. A marked three km, 1½-hour **walking trail** takes you up and over the top of the falls, but it's quite a steep walk.

Petherick's Rainforest Reserve

From the Wangi turn-off it's 5.5 km to Petherick's Rainforest Reserve, a small freehold forest reserve which actually lies outside the park. There's waterfalls, some thermal springs and monsoon rainforest, as well as the wreckage of an old Spitfire. An entry fee of $3 is charged, but this is waived if you camp here.

Walker & Bamboo Creeks

From Petherick's the road loops back into the park, and after about six km there's a turn-off to Walker Creek, not far off the road, where there's more rock pools and a camp site. At Bamboo Creek, reached along a short 4WD track just north of the Walker Creek side road, remnants of the tin mines which operated here in the 1870s can still be seen.

It's only another three km to the northern boundary of the park, and from there it's around 40 km of dirt road to the Cox Peninsula road.

Activities

During the winter months the rangers conduct a number of activities aimed at increasing your enjoyment and knowledge of the park. On Tuesday at 10 am there's a guided walk to Tolmer Falls, on Wednesday at 8 pm a slide show at the Wangi picnic area, and on Thursday at 10 am the magnetic termite mounds are the feature of a talk.

Organised Tours

There are plenty of companies offering day trips to Litchfield from Darwin. Woolly Butt (☎ 8941 2600), which operates out of Frogshollow Backpackers in Darwin is popular. The price is $65 including morning tea and lunch.

Facilities

Parks & Wildlife maintains a number of camp sites within the park. Those at Florence Falls (separate 2WD and 4WD areas), Buley Rockhole and Tjaynera Falls have facilities such as toilets, showers and fireplaces, while the bush camps in the south of the park are very basic. The cost is $2 at Florence Falls 2WD, and $1 at the others.

At Wangi the camping area is relatively small and does get crowded. In the dry season it is very dusty underfoot and it is often full by late afternoon. There is an amenities block with showers and toilets. If you want to have a fire here (fireplaces are provided), collect wood before you get to the camp site as there is very little in the vicinity. It costs $4 per person to camp here.

It's also possible to camp at *Petherick's Rainforest Reserve*, on the western edge of the park, for $5 per person, but it's a pretty unattractive proposition as the facilities are basically non-existent.

A much better bet is the *Waterfall Caravan Park* (☎ 8978 2678) about two km north of Petherick's and also outside the park. This friendly place has grass and shade for camping, and the owners can take guests on guided walks to areas of the range which are otherwise inaccessible. The cost is $3 per person.

Batchelor The small town of Batchelor lies just outside the park's eastern boundary and is the nearest place for supplies and fuel. There's a caravan park (with on-site vans and cabins), a motel, a well-stocked store, a pub (no accommodation) and a service station. See the Batchelor section later in this chapter for details.

DARWIN CROCODILE FARM

On the Stuart Highway, 40 km south of Darwin, the crocodile farm (☎ 8988 1450) has around 7000 saltwater and freshwater crocodiles. This is the residence of many of the crocodiles which have been taken out of Northern Territory waters because they've become a hazard to people. But don't imagine they're here out of human charity. This is a farm, not a rest home, and around 2000 of the beasts are killed each year for their skins and meat – you can find crocodile steaks or even crocodile burgers in a number of Darwin eateries.

The farm is open from 10 am to 4 pm daily. Feedings are the most spectacular times to visit and these occur daily at 2 pm, and again on Monday, Wednesday and weekends at noon. Entry is $9.50 (children $5). Many of the day trips from Darwin include the croc farm on their itinerary.

TERRITORY WILDLIFE PARK & BERRY SPRINGS
The turn-off to Berry Springs is 48 km down the Track from Darwin, then it's 10 km along the Cox Peninsula road to the Territory Wildlife Park and the adjoining Berry Springs Nature Park, both of which are managed by Parks & Wildlife.

Territory Wildlife Park
Situated on 400 hectares of bushland, the Territory Wildlife Park (☎ 8988 6000) has some excellent enclosures featuring a wide variety of Australian birds, mammals, reptiles and fish, some of which are quite rare, and there's even one of feral animals.

In addition to its role as a native animal showcase for visitors, the park has wildlife conservation as one of its major objectives. There's a very successful captive breeding program, and the Animal Care Centre where orphaned, sick or injured animals are cared for and raised.

Highlights of the park are the large, walk-through **nocturnal house**, where you can observe nocturnal native fauna such as bilbies, water rats and bats in a variety of habitats; the 12 small aviaries each representing a different habitat, from mangroves to monsoon forest, and the huge walk-through aviary; and the arthropod and reptile exhibit, where snakes, lizards, spiders and insects do their thing.

Also worth the effort is walking along the raised boardwalk through the Monsoon Forest. Interpretive signs along the walk describe the various features of the forest.

The park is very well set up, and all the exhibits are on a four-km perimeter road, which you can either walk around or hop on and off the little shuttle trains which run every 15 minutes and stop at all the exhibits.

There are a number of free talks and activities given by the staff each day at the various exhibits, and these are listed on noticeboards at the main entrance. It's well worth the $10 entry fee ($5 children) and you'll need half a day to see it all. The park is open daily from 8.30 am to 4 pm (gates close at 6 pm).

Berry Springs Nature Park
Close by is the Berry Springs Nature Park which is a great place for a swim and a picnic. There's a warm thermal waterfall, spring-fed pools ringed with paperbarks and pandanus palms, and abundant bird life. The lower reaches of the creek are inhabited by saltwater crocodiles, but the springs keep the upper reaches fresh and therefore free of salties.

The park is open daily from 8 am to 6.30 pm, and there's no entry fee.

Places to Stay The *Lakes Resort Caravan Park* (☎ 8988 6277) is on the Cox Peninsula road 2.5 km east of the wildlife park. It has a good range of amenities, including a pool with water slide, and a variety of cabins from $42 to $55. Camp sites cost $13.50, or $16 with power.

Close by is the *Tumbling Waters Deer & Van Park* (☎ 8988 6255), on the Tumbling Waters Road, with cabins at $45 and camp sites for $12 ($15 powered).

HOWARD SPRINGS NATURE PARK
The 383-hectare Howard Springs Nature Park, with crocodile-free swimming in a spring-fed pool, is 35 km from Darwin. Turn-off 24 km down the Stuart Highway, beyond Palmerston.

The springs and the river of the same name were named after a Captain Howard, the captain of a vessel which, in the 1860s, used to take settlers to Escape Cliffs, the predecessor to Darwin. The aboriginal name for the area was Wargan, and it was known as this up until 1936. This reliable source of water so close to Darwin was used during WW II to supplement Darwin's drinking water supply, and a weir was built at the springs.

The forest-surrounded swimming hole can get uncomfortably crowded because it's so convenient to the city. Nevertheless on a quiet day it's a pleasant spot for an excursion and there are short walking tracks and lots of bird life.

A variety of fish and turtles can usually be spotted from the path across the weir, and agile wallabies graze quite unafraid of humans. Goannas also frequent the picnic area scrounging for hand-outs. They can get aggressive so it's best not to feed them.

The park is open daily from 8 am to 8 pm.

Places to Stay

There are two nearby caravan parks. The *Howard Springs Caravan Park* (☎ 8983 1169; fax 8983 2487) on Whitewood Rd has powered ($14) and unpowered ($12) sites. There's also on-site vans at $30.

The *Coolalinga Caravan Park* (☎ 8983 1026) is actually on the Stuart Highway, and it is not as close to the springs. Unpowered sites are $10, with power it's $13.

MANTON DAM

The scenic Manton Dam, about 80 km south of Darwin along the Track, is a popular recreational area for Darwin residents, especially in the wet season when the ocean is off-limits due to the presence of box jellyfish.

The dam is another reminder of the demands which WW II placed on the Top End, as fresh water was in short supply in Darwin. It was built in 1940 to supplement that supply, and is still an emergency source of water today.

As well as watersports enthusiasts, the lake is starting to attract those keen on hooking a barramundi – 100,000 fingerlings were released into the dam a few years ago and they would now have reached the 55 cm minimum legal size.

Facilities consist of a boat ramp, grassed picnic area, fireplaces and toilets. The dam is open from 9 am to 5 pm weekdays and 8 am to 7 pm on weekends.

LAKE BENNETT

About 10 km south of Manton Dam is Lake Bennett, another small artificial lake which lies 10 km off the Stuart Highway. This one was originally built for irrigation purposes but is now used solely for recreation. Small boats can be hired at the Holiday Park.

The *Lake Bennett Holiday Park* (☎ 8976 0960), on the lake shore, has camp sites at $6 ($8 with power) and on-site tents at $15/24. There's a barbecue but nothing else in the way of cooking facilities, so you'll need to be fairly self-contained.

BATCHELOR

This small town of 650 people lies 14 km west of the Stuart Highway. Although a small settlement had evolved here during this century, it was only the establishment of the Rum Jungle uranium mine nearby in the 1950s which really put it on the map. Earlier, it had been a defence-force base during WW II. The small airstrip here was extended in 1941 to take the large B-17 Flying Fortresses of the US Airforce which were stationed here following the bombing of Pearl Harbour early the same year. This in itself was unremarkable except for the fact that the extended runway had a railway crossing on it.

Uranium mining ceased in the 1960s, but it was actually the early '70s before the stockpile was exhausted and operations ceased. These days Batchelor owes its existence to the Aboriginal Teacher Training

---

WW II Airstrips

One feature of the Stuart Highway between Darwin and Batchelor is the number of old airstrips right by the side of the road. These date back to WW II when American and Australian fighter aircraft were stationed in the Top End. Due to the threat of Japanese bombing raids these squadrons were based along the highway rather than in Darwin itself. Strips such as Strauss, Hughes and Livingstone are all signposted by the highway. ■

College, and the fact that it is the main access point for Litchfield National Park.

The Rum Jungle Lake, five km west of town, is a popular boating and swimming spot.

Places to Stay & Eat

The *Batchelor Caravillage* (☎ 8976 0166) has camp sites at $14 ($18 powered), a couple of on-site vans for $42, and one cabin at $60. The *Rum Jungle Motor Inn* (☎ 8976 0123) has rooms at $88.

For meals try the pub (the Rum Jungle Recreation Club) or the motel.

Arnhem Highway

The Arnhem Highway branches off towards Kakadu National Park 34 km south of Darwin. The eastern boundary of Kakadu is 160 km from the Stuart Highway, and there are a number of interesting stop-offs and detours along the way. Most people, however, tend to belt along here at a great rate of knots, intent on reaching Kakadu in the shortest possible time.

HUMPTY DOO

Only 10 km along this road you come to the small town of Humpty Doo. The *Humpty Doo Hotel* is a colourful pub with some real character, and it does counter lunches and teas all week. Sunday, when local bands usually play, is particularly popular. **Graeme Gow's Reptile World** (☎ 8988 1681) has a big collection of Australian snakes and a very knowledgable owner (open daily from 8.30 am to 6 pm).

FOGG DAM CONSERVATION RESERVE

About 15 km beyond Humpty Doo is the turn-off to Fogg Dam, which lies six km north of the highway. This is a great place for watching water birds, there's some excellent stands of paperbark trees and a viewing platform out over the wetlands, which form part of the Adelaide River floodplain.

Although the dam's function these days is

primarily as a waterbird habitat, it does have an interesting history. In the 1950s investors pumped a load of money into a scheme to turn the Adelaide River floodplains into a major rice-growing enterprise, the Humpty Doo Rice Project. It lasted just a few short years, one of the main causes of its demise was the flocks of magpie geese which used to fly in and feast on the ripening crop. Other contributing factors were the poor engineering of the dam and channels which meant the water supply was unsatisfactory, and the presence of salt in the ground.

The road into the reserve goes right across the old dam wall, although with the massive growth of water plants it's hard to tell on which side of the low wall was the actual dam. On the western side of the wall is an elaborate two-storey viewing platform with interpretive signs.

On the eastern side of the wall as you enter the reserve is a 3.6-km walking track which takes you through the monsoon forest.

Another feature of the reserve is the high number of mosquitoes – be prepared.

Fauna

The birds you are most likely to see in greatest number are the previously mentioned magpie geese, especially in the late dry season as other water sources dry up. Other birds commonly seen are brolgas, jabirus, white-breasted sea eagles, kingfishers, ibis and herons.

In the same reserve is a patch of monsoon rainforest, and here you're likely to come across numerous birds and animals, including scrub fowls and pittas. The reserve also holds large numbers of water pythons, which feed almost exclusively on the large population of dusky rats.

Agile wallabies can also be seen in large numbers grazing on the lush grass of the floodplain.

ADELAIDE RIVER CROSSING

A further eight km along the Arnhem Highway is the Adelaide River Crossing. The main attraction here are the amazingly popular river cruises where saltwater croco-

An Adelaide River croc jumping for its dinner

should be a reality by now. The area covers the Mary River wetlands which extend north and south of the Arnhem Highway. The park is scheduled to include a handful of existing conservation reserves which take in a series of billabongs and lagoons along the river. These include the Mary River Crossing Reserve, the Wildman River Reserve, Shady Camp, Mary River Conservation Reserve, Stuart's Tree Historical Reserve and Swim Creek.

This area offers excellent fishing and wildlife-spotting opportunities, and because there is not much in the way of infrastructure it is far less visited than nearby Kakadu, to which in many ways it is very similar.

Flora & Fauna

Like other wetland areas of the Top End, the Mary River is teeming with birdlife, and the numbers increase as the dry season wears on. Brolgas, storks, white-headed burdekin ducks, cormorants, magpie geese and egrets are all found in numbers throughout the system.

Mammals commonly found in the park area include the wallabies, bandicoots, possums and various species of bat. Feral pigs and dingoes also live in the area, and the picture is completed by the emus which inhabit the woodland areas.

The fishing fraternity is of course interested chiefly in the barramundi which is found in the Mary River waterways. And in case you had any ideas about swimming, the waterways which come within the park boundaries are home to the highest concentration of saltwater crocodiles in the world! There's also a significant population of freshies.

Information

Although the park did not officially exist at the time of writing, the visitor centre had already been built. The **Window on the Wetlands** centre (☎ 8978 8904) is an ultra-modern creation atop Beatrice Hill, a small hill by the Arnhem Highway just a few km east of the Fogg Dam turn-off.

The centre has some excellent 'touchy-

diles jump for bits of meat held out on the end of poles. The whole thing is a bit of a circus really, but it is quite an amazing sight; it's not often you see crocodiles doing anything other than sunning themselves on a river bank or gliding menacingly through the water.

The cruises are run by Adelaide River Queen Cruises (☎ 8988 8144), and their jetty and office/shop is right by the bridge. The main vessel, the *Adelaide River Queen* has a fully enclosed air-con lower deck, from where you can get some spectacular pictures of crocs jumping right outside the window, and an open upper deck. The cost is $28 ($15 children) for a two-hour cruise (daily at 2 pm), or $24 ($15) for a 1½-hour trip (daily at 9 and 11.30 am) on a slightly smaller boat.

MARY RIVER NATIONAL PARK

Although only proposed at the time of writing, the Mary River National Park feely' displays which give some great detail on the wetland ecosystem, as well as the history of the local Aboriginal people and the European pastoral activity which has taken place in the area over the years. There's also great views out over the Mary River system.

The Park
There are plans to increase the infrastructure once the park has been fully established, although there are already a number of places where you can camp and get out on the water. Currently access is via the Point Stuart Road, a good dirt road which heads north off the Arnhem Highway about 22 km west of Annaburroo.

Mary River Crossing This small reserve is right by the highway near the Bark Hut Inn. The boat ramp here provides access to the river, and there's also a picnic ground.

Couzens Lookout & North Rockhole Another dirt road 16 km north of the Arnhem Highway heads west to the Mary River 16 km away. Couzens Lookout offers some great views, and North Rockhole, also on the river but six km away, has a boat ramp and a shady but basic camp site.

Brian Creek Monsoon Forest About nine km beyond the North Rockhole turn-off another road heads west, this one leading to the Wildman River Wilderness Lodge (see Facilities later in this chapter). Less than one km along this road is the turn-off to this small pocket of dense rainforest, which comes as a surprise being in the middle of a woodland area.

Shady Camp This is another popular fishing and camping area right on the Mary River, about 40 km north of the Arnhem Highway.

Organised Tours
From Darwin As the popularity of this area increases so does the number of tour operators accessing the park. Already a number of companies operating out of Darwin combine a trip to Kakadu with a detour to the Mary River wetlands. Holiday AKT (☎ toll-free 1800 891 121), Crocodylus Back to Basics (☎ toll-free 1800 645 533) and Southern Cross Safaris (☎ 8981 6473) all visit this area.

River Cruises There are a couple of private concessions within the park, and these offer both accommodation (see Facilities later in this chapter) and trips out on the river. The Wildman River Wilderness Lodge runs two-hour river trips from North Rockhole daily at 9.30 am and 4 pm, at a cost of $18 ($9 children). From the Point Stuart Wilderness Lodge, three-hour wetland tours cost $22 ($15), and there are departures at 9 am and 4 pm daily.

Shady Camp Crocodylus (☎ toll-free 1800 645 533) runs excellent three-hour jet boat trips for $45.

Facilities
Apart from the camp sites at North Rockhole and Shady Camp, the only other accommodation options are two wilderness lodges.

The *Wildman River Wilderness Lodge* (☎ 8978 8912; fax 8981 5391) charges $80 for a double room, or $150 including all meals. The lodge has a beautiful position on the edge of the floodplains, and has good facilities including a swimming pool and a licensed dining room.

The other choice is the *Point Stuart Wilderness Lodge* (☎ 8978 8914; fax 8981 372890) a little further north and a few km off the main track. The lodge is actually part of an old cattle station, and there's the ruins of an old abattoir here, but don't let this deter you as the setting is quite nice and the facilities are very good. There's a good grassy camping area and a swimming pool. It costs $6 to camp, there are dorm beds for $17, and four-bed self-contained units at $74.

The *Bark Hut Inn* (☎ 8978 8988) is just outside the proposed park boundary, two km east of the Mary River Crossing. It's a pleasant enough place for a stop, but there's little reason to do so. Camping costs $10 for a site with or without power, or there's basic accommodation at $20 per person.

The turn-off to the *Annaburroo Billabong Caravan Park* (☎ 8978 897891) on a billabong about one km off the road, is right opposite the Bark Hut, and it too offers camping and basic accommodation.

Getting There & Away

The turn-off to Cooinda along the Old Darwin Road is 19 km beyond the Bark Hut.

This is an unsealed road, often impassable in the Wet, and it's easier to continue along the sealed highway. The entrance to Kakadu National Park is a further 19 km along the highway. Some Darwin city buses go out as far as Humpty Doo. There are also Greyhound Pioneer and McCafferty's bus services along the Arnhem Highway (see the Kakadu National Park Getting There & Around section in the Kakadu & Arnhem Land chapter).

Kakadu & Arnhem Land

East of Darwin lies Kakadu National Park, without doubt the biggest attraction of a visit to the Top End and probably Australia's second most visited national park after Uluru in central Australia.

Further east again, across the East Alligator River, lies the vast expanse of Arnhem Land. This entire area is Aboriginal owned and is only accessible with a permit, and then only in limited areas and usually only with an organised group.

Lying off the coast of the two are two more Aboriginal-owned areas, the islands of Bathurst and Melville. Both have very little in the way of tourist facilities, but can be visited on organised tours.

HIGHLIGHTS

- Spend a minimum of three days exploring Kakadu National Park, probably Australia's finest tropical park
- View the Aboriginal rock-art sites in Kakadu
- Explore the ruins of a British settlement at the remote Gurig National Park in north-western Arnhem Land

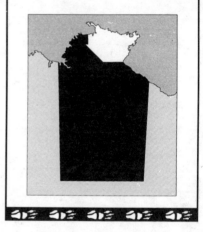

Kakadu National Park

Kakadu National Park is one of the natural marvels not just of the Northern Territory, but of Australia. The longer you stay, the more rewarding it is. It encompasses a variety of habitats, including some stunning wetlands, boasts a mass of wildlife and the area has been home to Aboriginal people for the past 50,000 years, and they have left some significant Aboriginal rock-art sites. All these combine to make it one of the top tourist destinations in the country, and have also gained it unique World Heritage Listing as an area of both cultural and ecological importance.

The name Kakadu comes from the language of the Gagadju people, the traditional owners of the area. Much of Kakadu is Aboriginal land, leased to the government for use as a national park. The park is jointly managed by the Australian Nature Conservation Agency (ANCA) and the traditional Aboriginal owners, 10 of whom sit on the 14-member board of management. There are around 300 Aboriginal people living in several Aboriginal settlements in the park and in the township of Jabiru, and about one third of the park rangers are Aboriginal people. In addition, a number of the Aboriginal elders are employed to advise staff on management issues.

The traditional owners are represented through the Gagadju Association, which owns a number of the park's material assets – the hotels at Jabiru and Cooinda, the Border Store and the Yellow Water cruise operation – and the Ranger Uranium Mine Lease. The owners currently receive around $1.2 million per year from mining royalties, and this is either invested or goes to providing services for the local community.

Some of the southern areas within the park

are subject to a land claim under the Native Title Act by the Jawoyn people of the Katherine region. Should the claim be successful, the land will be leased back to the ANCA for continued use as a national park.

HISTORY

Kakadu, at nearly 22,000 sq km, is the largest national park in Australia. It was proclaimed a national park in three stages. Stage One, the eastern and central part of the park including Ubirr, Nourlangie, Jim Jim Falls, Twin Falls and Yellow Water Billabong, was declared in 1979. Stage Two, in the north, was declared in 1984 and gained World Heritage listing for its natural importance. Stage Three, in the south, was finally listed in 1991, bringing virtually the whole of the South Alligator River system within the park.

Aboriginal Heritage

It is known that Aboriginal people have lived in the Kakadu area for the past 50,000 years.

Artefacts such as stone tools, ochre and grindstones have been found at a number of occupation sites throughout the park, indicating that Aboriginal people were constantly in the area.

As elsewhere in Australia, they led a hunter-gatherer existence, with the men doing the hunting and the women the gathering of vegetable foods and seeds. They moved through the country as necessary, but never aimlessly, and along defined paths which had been used for generations in the search for food, water or other natural resources such as ochre or bark.

The rocky nature of the rugged countryside which typifies much of the park today offered excellent shelter to the Aboriginal people, and many of these shelters bear art sites of world importance.

Today the park is occupied by a number of different Aboriginal groups (or clans), each with a different language and often different traditional practices as well.

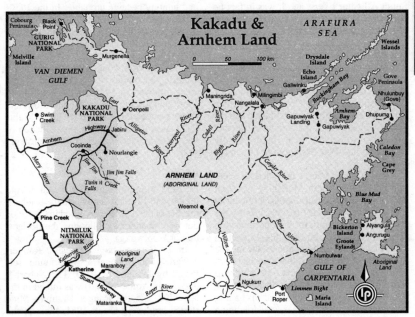

Although many of these traditional practices have been modified or lost altogether in the years since contact with Europeans, the traditional owners today still have strong personal and spiritual links with the land.

The languages still spoken by Aboriginal people in the park are Gundjehimi and Kunwinjku by the people living in the vicinity of the Arnhem Land escarpment, and Jawoyn, which is spoken by the people in the southern reaches of the park. Gagadju was the dominant language in the park area early this century, but it is no longer in widespread use.

European Exploration

Although a number of European vessels had sailed along the coast on exploratory voyages since the mid-17th century, it wasn't until Captain Phillip King came along on a number of voyages between 1818 and 1822 that any of the hinterland was investigated. King travelled up the East Alligator and South Alligator rivers, and it was in fact he who named them, having mistaken the many saltwater crocs for alligators.

The first European to come through this area overland was the remarkable Prussian naturalist Ludwig Leichhardt, who set out from the Darling Downs in Queensland in October 1844 for the British settlement of Port Essington on the Cobourg Peninsula. He crossed the Arnhem Land plateau and the South Alligator River many months later and somewhat worse for wear, before finally staggering into Port Essington in December 1845.

Some 20 years later, a party led by experienced explorer John McKinlay was sent out by the South Australian government to find a better site than Escape Cliffs by the Adelaide River mouth for their northern settlement. McKinlay botched the expedition somewhat by not setting out until the middle of the wet season, which that year had been particularly severe. The party took months to travel just the relatively short distance to the East Alligator River, and ended up bailing out by shooting their horses, constructing a makeshift horse-hide raft and floating all the way back to Escape Cliffs.

In the 1870s the surge of Europeans to the goldfields at Pine Creek led to increased activity in the Kakadu area, and this was followed by the commencement of pastoral activity following the granting of the first lease in 1876.

In the 1890s a few Europeans started to make a living from shooting buffalo for hides in the Alligator rivers region. Foremost among these men was Paddy Cahill, who dominated European settlement in this area up until 1925 when the Church Missionary Society was given permission by the government to establish a mission at Oenpelli, one of a number throughout the Arnhem Land Aboriginal Reserve, which had been established in 1921. By this stage any attempts to set up pastoral properties had failed and parts of the area had become vacant crown land.

The buffalo industry continued throughout the first half of this century, but with the introduction of synthetics demand fell away and hunting became unviable. In the 1950s a fledgling buffalo safari hunting industry developed, with the clients being mainly Americans who were flown in to shoot.

In 1969 and 1972 the precursors to Kakadu, the Woolwonga and Alligator rivers wildlife sanctuaries, were declared. These were followed in 1978 by the granting of some land titles to the traditional Aboriginal owners under the Aboriginal Land Rights (NT) Act of 1976, and the proclamation of the Kakadu National Park the following year.

Mining

In 1953 uranium was discovered in the region, and 12 small deposits in the southern reaches of the park were worked in the 1960s but were abandoned following the declaration of Woolwonga.

In 1970 three huge deposits, Ranger, Nabarlek and Koongarra, were found, followed by Jabiluka in 1973. The Nabarlek deposit (in Arnhem Land) was mined in the late '70s, and the Ranger Uranium Mine started producing ore in 1981. Most of the

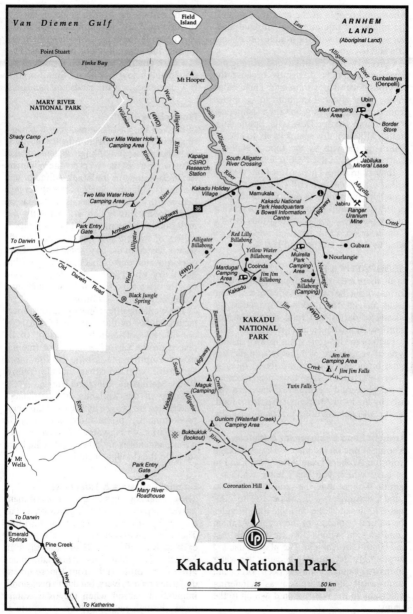

Kakadu National Park

0   25   50 km

Aboriginal people of the area were against the mining of uranium on traditional land, but were enticed with the double lure of land title and royalties.

Currently the Jabiluka and Koongarra deposits are on hold, mainly because the previous federal government's Three-Mine Policy only allowed uranium to be mined from three sites at any one time (Nabarlek, Ranger and Roxby Downs in South Australia), although this seems likely to change following the win by the Liberal-National Party coalition in the 1996 federal election.

It was partly the Three-Mine Policy which killed off Coronation Hill (Guratba), a proposed uranium mine in the south of the park in 1991. Up until then the southern reaches of the park (Stage Three) had only been a Conservation Zone, until it was decided what to do with Coronation Hill.

GEOGRAPHY & FLORA

In all, there are six major topographical landforms within the park: the sandstone Arnhem Land plateau, the riverine floodplains, the coastal estuaries and tidal flats, monsoon rainforests, lowlands, and the southern hills.

Each of the landforms has its own distinct type of vegetation, and this in turn dictates what birds and animals are found in each. Over 1600 plant species have been recorded in the park, and a number of them are still used by the local Aboriginal people for food, bush medicine and other practical purposes.

Arnhem Land Escarpment & Plateau

A straight line on the map separates Kakadu from the Arnhem Land Aboriginal Land to its east, which you can't enter without a permit. The meandering sandstone Arnhem Land escarpment, a dramatic 100 to 200-metre-high sandstone cliff line that provides the natural boundary of the rugged Arnhem Land plateau, winds 500 km through east and south-east Kakadu. The plateau itself is surprisingly dry, mainly because the water drains away quickly into the deep gorges and tumbles off the escarpment as thundering waterfalls in the wet season down on to the plains.

The soil on the plateau is also relatively shallow and low in nutrients, and so the vegetation is confined to species which can tolerate the generally poor conditions. This is a stark contrast to the rich growth of the floodplains below the plateau. Spinifex grass is widespread, as is the sandstone pandanus.

Floodplains

In the Wet the vast floodplains of Kakadu's four north-flowing rivers turn the north of the park into a kind of huge, vegetated lake. From west to east the rivers are the Wildman, the West Alligator, the South Alligator and the East Alligator. Such is the difference between dry and wet seasons that areas on river floodplains which are perfectly dry underfoot in September will be under three metres of water a few months later. As the waters recede in the Dry, some loops of wet season watercourses become cut off, but don't dry up. These are billabongs, and they're often carpeted with water lilies and are a magnet for water birds.

The wetlands offer some of the most spectacular sights of the park, and have been considered sufficiently important to be placed on the List of Wetlands of International Importance. Some of the more accessible wetland areas include Yellow Water, Mamukala, Ubirr and Bubba.

Many of the wetlands and permanent waterholes are fringed by stands of tall trees, predominantly broadleafed and weeping paperbarks. Freshwater mangroves and water pandanuses are other plants which are suited to the floodplain environment.

Coastal Estuaries & Tidal Flats

The coastal zone has long stretches of mangroves, important for halting erosion and as a breeding ground for marine and bird life. There are 29 mangrove species known to exist in Australia, and 21 of these grow in Kakadu. The tidal flats behind the mangroves are quite rich from the sediment deposited by the rivers, but due to occasional inundation caused when the tidal waters break through natural levees, plant life is restricted to those which can tolerate salt water.

Monsoon Rainforest

Isolated pockets of monsoon rainforest appear throughout the park, and are of one of two types: coastal and sandstone. Coastal monsoon rainforest is dominated by banyan, kapok and milkwood trees, and generally appears along river banks or other places where there is permanent water – either above or below ground.

Sandstone monsoon rainforest occurs along the gorges of the escarpment, such as at Jim Jim Falls.

Lowlands

About half the park, predominantly the southern section, is dry lowlands with open grassland or woodland. The main tree of the woodland, and one which dominates much of the Top End, is the Darwin woollybutt eucalypt. Other eucalypts include Cooktown ironwoods and Darwin stringybarks. Below the canopy provided by these trees pandanus palms and other small trees grow, while the ground is covered by annual grasses. Naturally enough these grasses are the dominant form of vegetation in the grasslands, and after the Wet can shoot up to two metres high making the most of the moisture before the ground dries up during the Dry.

Much of the Arnhem Highway from the Stuart Highway into Jabiru passes through lowland country.

Southern Hills

The hills in the southern part of the park are different from those elsewhere, such as the Arnhem Land plateau, in that the rocks are of volcanic origin. Erosion of this material has led to different soil types than elsewhere in the park, this in turn giving rise to distinctive flora and fauna types. One of the most noticeable and widespread eucalypts found here, especially in the Gunlom vicinity, is the instantly recognisable northern salmon gum, with its smooth-pink trunk. Other common trees include scarlet gums, variable-barked bloodwoods and the Darwin box.

Introduced Plants

A large number of non-native plants are known to exist in Kakadu, although the vast majority pose no threat. Two exceptions to this, however, are the mimosa (*Mimosa pigra*) and salvinia or water hyacinth (*Salvinia molesta*), both of which can spread to cover huge areas.

Mimosa The mimosa is a thorny shrub, native to Central America. It grows up to four metres high and spreads rapidly due to its production of large amounts of very hardy seeds, and its tolerance of both flood and drought. It is widespread across the Top End, but has been brought under control within the park.

Salvinia This is a noxious little aquatic fern native to Brazil. It is free-floating and reproduces at an incredible rate – it can double in size every 10 days. The Magela Creek and East Alligator River systems are both threatened by the weed, and in fact access to the Magela Creek system has now been prohibited in an attempt to stop the spread any further – you'll see the fenced off areas and signs all along the left side of the road when driving between the Arnhem Highway and Ubirr.

The saviour was meant to come in the form of a small weevil which was going to spread like crazy and gobble the lot. Although this method of control has proved effective elsewhere, it seems the weevil is not partial to the weed in Kakadu.

CLIMATE

The great change between the Dry and the November-to-March Wet makes a big difference to visitors to Kakadu. Not only is the landscape transformed as the wetlands and waterfalls grow, but Kakadu's lesser roads become impassable in the Wet, cutting off some highlights, such as Jim Jim Falls. The

KAKADU & ARNHEM LAND

local Aboriginal people recognise six seasons in the annual cycle.

Gunmeleng
> This is the 'build-up' to the Wet, which starts in mid-October. Humidity and the temperatures rise (to 35°C or more) – and the number of mosquitoes, always high near water, rises to near plague proportions. By November the thunderstorms have started, billabongs start to be replenished and the water birds and fish disperse. Traditionally this is when the Aboriginal people made the seasonal move from the floodplains to the shelter of the escarpment.

Gudjuek
> The Wet proper continues through January, February and March, with violent thunderstorms and an abundance of plant and animal life thriving in the hot, moist conditions. Around 1300 mm of rain falls in Kakadu, most of it during this period.

Banggereng
> April is the season when storms (known as 'knock 'em down' storms) flatten the spear grass, which during the course of the Wet has shot up to two metres in height.

Yekke
> From May to mid-June, is the season of mists,

when the air starts to dry out. It is quite a good time to visit – there aren't too many other visitors, the wetlands and waterfalls still have a lot of water and most of the tracks are open.

Wurrgeng & Gurrung
> This is the late Dry, July and August, and the most comfortable to visit Kakadu. It is when wildlife, especially birds, congregates in big numbers around the shrinking billabongs and watercourses, but it's also when most tourists come to the park.

FAUNA
Kakadu has about 25 species of frog, 60 types of mammals, 51 freshwater fish species, 75 types of reptile, 280 bird species (one-third of all those native to Australia) and at least 4500 kinds of insect. There are frequent additions to the list, and a few of the rarer species are unique to the park.

You'll only see a tiny fraction of these creatures in a visit to the park since many of them are shy, nocturnal or few in number. Take advantage of talks and walks led by park rangers, mainly in the Dry, to get to know and see more of the wildlife (see Activities later in this chapter).

Fire as a Management Tool
One of the things which strikes the first-time visitor to the Top End in the Dry is the amount of smoke in the sky from large bushfires. In a country where bushfires are normally associated with enormous damage and loss of life, it sometimes seems as though huge tracts of the Top End are being reduced to ashes. In fact the truth is that the fires, although uncontrolled, are deliberately lit and are rejuvenating the country.

For thousands of years Aboriginal people have used fire as a hunting and an environmental-management tool, and they have been doing it for so long that many plant species have now evolved so that they can survive fires, and in fact rely on them for seedling regeneration. The usual practice was that fires were lit in the early dry season, and would only burn the lower shrubs and spear grass which grows so prolifically after the Wet. Fires late in the Dry were avoided as they could burn out of control over huge areas. The fires in the early dry season would burn over a fairly small area, and the result was a mosaic of burnt and unburnt areas.

Since European settlement of the Top End and the decline in Aboriginal people leading a traditional existence, the burning patterns have changed. This led to the accumulation of unburnt material on the ground and any fires late in the dry season would destroy huge areas.

In the last decade or so the benefits of the traditional methods of environmental management have been recognised by the Australian Nature Conservation Agency (ANCA), which jointly manages Kakadu with the assistance of the traditional owners. They are now trying to recreate the mosaic burn pattern. ■

Mammals

Nine types of kangaroo and wallaby inhabit the park, mostly in the open forest and woodland areas, or on the fringes of the floodplains. Those commonly seen include are the agile wallaby and the antilopine wallaroo. Others, such as the black wallaroo, narbarlek and the short-eared rock-wallaby, are found on the escarpment and so not often sighted.

Nocturnal northern brushtail possums, sugar gliders and northern brown bandicoots are also common in the woodlands. Kakadu is home to 26 bat species and is a key refuge for four endangered varieties.

Also found within the park are a number of native rodents and dingoes.

Birds

Kakadu's abundant water birds, and their beautiful wetland setting, make a memorable sight. The park is one of the chief refuges in Australia for several species, among them the magpie goose, green pygmy-goose and burdekin duck. Other fine water birds include pelicans, darters and the jabiru stork, with its distinctive red legs and long straight beak. Herons, egrets, ibis and cormorants are common.

The stands of paperbark trees which fringe many of the waterholes attract many birds such as the lemon-breasted flycatcher, brush cuckoos and rufous-banded honeyeaters.

The open woodlands are home to yet more birds. You're quite likely to see rainbow bee-eaters and kingfishers (of which there are six types in inland Kakadu), as well as parrots, cockatoos (especially the yellow-tailed and red-tailed black cockatoos), hawks, pigeons, quails and honeyeaters. Majestic white-breasted sea eagles are often seen near inland waterways too, and wedge-tailed eagles, whistling kites and black kites are common. At night you might hear barking owls calling – they sound just like dogs.

The mangrove colonies of the coastal zone provide perfect roosts for many species, including mangrove kingfishers, chestnut rails and red-headed honeyeaters.

Reptiles

The park has both types of Australian crocodile. Both Twin and Jim Jim falls, for instance, have resident freshwater crocodiles, which are considered harmless, while there are also plenty of the dangerous saltwater (or Estuarine) variety in the park. You're sure to see a few if you take an East Alligator River or Yellow Water cruise.

Kakadu's other reptiles include several types of lizard, such as the spectacular frilled lizard (seen only in the Wet), and five freshwater turtle species, of which the most common is the northern snake-necked turtle. There are many snakes, including four highly poisonous types (taipans, death adders, king brown and western brown) but you're unlikely to see any. Oenpelli pythons, probably unique to the Kakadu escarpment, were only discovered by Europeans in 1973.

Fish

You can't miss the silver barramundi, which creates a distinctive swirl near the water surface. It can grow to well over a metre long and changes its sex from male to female at the age of five or six years. Other fish found in the billabongs include saratoga, rainbow fish and catfish.

Insects

Mosquitoes seem to be the most noticeable insect in the park, although they become less of a menace as you move south, and so they are worse at Ubirr than at Cooinda.

Feral Animals

Feral animals – non-native animals which have gone wild – have caused great damage to the environment and decimated the native fauna not only in Kakadu, but throughout the Territory. The main offenders in the park are water buffalo, but pigs, Balinese cattle (banteng), as well as cats and dogs which are also a problem.

The dreaded cane toads have not yet reached the park, although they have been reported on the southern edge of Arnhem Land near Roper, so it is inevitable that they will eventually turn up here. When that happens they could have a disastrous impact on the delicate environment of Kakadu.

Buffalo The water buffalo, which ran wild after being introduced to the Top End from Timor by European settlers in the first half of the 19th century, quickly adapted to the climate and bred like mad. Being heavy, hard-hoofed animals they caused huge damage to the wetlands as they made wallows, muddied the water, and created 'swim channels' between lagoons which allowed salt water intrusion. The result was that much of the native flora died, and this led to a huge reduction in the number of birds which visited the wetlands.

In the last decade or so the government put in place the BTEC (brucellosis and tuberculosis eradication campaign) programme, which aimed to wipe out these bovine diseases. Buffaloes were major carriers and so were quickly targeted. Buffalo hunters were also encouraged to remove live buffs from the park for slaughter or for commercial farming.

The overall result is that since 1979 over 100,000 buffaloes have been killed or removed from the park, and the damage they caused is rapidly recovering – in fact it's hard to see any evidence at all of their presence. It is thought there is still around 200 buffs in the park, but these have been left here at the request of the Aboriginal owners, who feel that hunting buffalo is a part of their culture they would like to maintain. These remaining buffaloes are fitted with radio transmitters and their movements closely monitored by park staff. The traditional owners also keep a domesticated herd of around 500 buffalo for milk and meat production, but these have been declared disease free and are kept fenced in.

ABORIGINAL ART

Kakadu is an important repository of rock art collections – there are over 5000 sites, which date from 20,000 years old right up to those from the 1960s. Two of the finest collections are the galleries at Ubirr and Nourlangie.

The paintings have been classified to fall into three roughly defined periods: Pre-estuarine, which is from the earliest paintings up to around 6000 years ago; Estuarine, which covers the period from 6000 to around 2000 years ago, when the valleys flooded due to the rising sea levels caused by the melting polar ice caps; and Freshwater, from 2000 years ago up until the present day. (See the section on Aboriginal art in the Facts About the Northern Territory chapter for a full discussion of the various styles).

For the local Aboriginal people the rock-art sites are a major source of traditional knowledge, their historical archives if you like, given that they have no written language. The most recent paintings, some executed as recently as the 1980s, connect the local community with the artists, while the older paintings are believed by many Aboriginal people to have been painted by spirit people, and depict stories which connect the people with creation legends and the development of Aboriginal law.

The majority of rock-art sites open to the public are relatively recent, and some visitors feel somewhat cheated when they learn that the paintings were only done in the 1960s. Many people are also surprised to learn that the old paintings they are seeing have actually been touched up by other Aboriginal people quite recently. In fact this was not uncommon, although the repainting could only be done by a specific person who knew the story that was being depicted. What also comes as a surprise to many people is the way the paintings in a particular site are often layered, with newer paintings being placed right over the top of older ones.

The conservation of the Kakadu rock-art sites is a major part of the park management task. As the paintings are all done with natural, water-soluble ochres, they are very susceptible to water damage from drip lines running across the rock. To prevent this sort of damage small ridges of clear silicon rubber have been made on the rocks above the paintings, so the water flowing down the rock is diverted to either side, or actually drips right off. Buffaloes also did their bit to damage the lower down paintings as they

RAY STAMP

HUGH FINLAY

HUGH FINLAY

Darwin
Top Left: Juvenile crocodiles at the Darwin Crocodile Farm
Top Right: Thousands of fish come at high tide to be fed by hand, Doctors Gully
Bottom: The Old Courthouse and Police Station are among the oldest buildings
in the city centre

nankeen
night heron

paperbark swamp

magnetic
termite mound

pied heron

agile wallaby

glossy ibis

magpie goose

red lotus lily

Tropical

The tropical wetlands of northern Australia witness remarkable seasonal change. Growing, flowering, feeding and breeding are all governed by the annual cycle of Wet and Dry. Towards the end of the Dry, the receding swamps and lagoons attract thousands of water birds; noisy flocks of whistling ducks and magpie geese are joined by fish-hunting jabiru and pied heron. A series of spectacular storms precedes the Wet. By the end of

pig-nosed turtle

pandanus

jabiru

brolga

plumed
whistling duck

swamphen

waterlily

Wetland

December heavy rains have arrived, signalling the estuarine crocodile to nest and forcing the antilopine wallaroos to higher ground. In the warm, wet environment, plant growth is rapid. Many water birds now nest among the rushes and wild rice. Further storms flatten the tall grasses, and by about May, the Wet is over. As the land dries, natural fires and Aboriginal hunting fires continue to shape this environment.

salt-water crocodile

Kakadu National Park
  Top: Nourlangie Rock at sunset
Bottom: Darter drying its wings

loved to rub against the walls of the rock shelters. The dust raised by hundreds of tourists tramping past these sites on a daily basis didn't help either. Today most of the accessible sites have boardwalks which not only keep the dust down but also keep people at a suitable distance from the paintings.

ORIENTATION

From where the Arnhem Highway to Kakadu turns east off the Stuart Highway, it's 120 km to the park boundary and another 90 km east across the park to Jabiru; it's sealed all the way.

A turn-off to the north, a few km past the northern entrance station on the Arnhem Highway, leads to camp sites at Two Mile Water Hole (eight km) and Four Mile Water Hole (38 km) on the Wildman River, which is popular for fishing. The track is not suitable for conventional vehicles except in the Dry, and then only as far as Two Mile Water Hole.

About 35 km further east along the highway, a turn-off to the south, again impassable to conventional vehicles in the Wet, leads to camp sites at Alligator and Red Lily billabongs, and on to the Old Darwin Road.

South Alligator River Crossing is on the highway 45 km into the park, about two km past the Kakadu Holiday Village. The cruises on the tidal river here are a good opportunity for crocodile-spotting.

Seven km east of South Alligator a short side road to the south leads to Mamukala, with views over the South Alligator flood plain, an observation building, a three-km walking trail and bird-watching hides.

From Mamukala it's 29 km to the turn-off to one of the major sites in the park, Ubirr, 36 km away in the northern part of the park near the East Alligator River. This road also gives access to Oenpelli, Arnhem Land and the Cobourg Peninsula, but note that a permit is needed to enter Arnhem Land (inquire at the Northern Land Council in Jabiru).

The township of Jabiru is right on the eastern edge of the park, just a few km beyond the Ubirr turn-off. The Kakadu Highway to the Park Headquarters and Bowali Visitors Centre (2.5 km), the Nourlangie turn-off (21 km), Muirella turn-off (28 km), Jim Jim Falls turn-off (41 km), Cooinda turn-off (47 km), the southern entrance to the park (137 km) and Pine Creek on the Stuart Highway (202 km) turns south off the Arnhem Highway shortly before Jabiru. It is bitumen for all but 20 km just north of the southern park gate.

INFORMATION
Bowali Information Centre

The excellent Bowali Information Centre (☎ 8938 1121; fax 8938 1115), which is on the Kakadu Highway a couple of km south of the Arnhem Highway, is open daily from 8 am to 5 pm. Here you'll find informative and interesting displays, including a few to keep the kids happy, a high-tech theatrette showing a 25-minute audio-visual presentation on the park (screened on the hour), plenty of leaflets on various aspects of the park, a cafe, gift shop and excellent resource centre with a comprehensive selection of reference books. There is another dozen or so videos featuring various documentaries made about Kakadu in the last few years, and these are also shown throughout the day (on the half hour).

In Darwin you can get information on Kakadu from the Australian Nature Conservation Agency. Top End tourist offices usually have copies of the *Kakadu Visitor Guide* leaflet, which includes a good map.

Warradjan Aboriginal Cultural Centre

This new centre near Cooinda gives an excellent insight into the culture of the park's traditional owners. The building itself is circular, which is a symbol for the way the Aboriginal people sit in a circle when having a meeting; the shape is also reminiscent of the *warradjan* (pig-nosed turtle), hence the name of the centre.

Inside, the displays depict creation stories when the Nayuhyunggi (first people) laid out the land and the laws, and the winding path you follow through the display symbolises

KAKADU & ARNHEM LAND

the way the Rainbow serpent moves through the country.

It's an excellent display, with crafts made by the local people, as well audio-visual displays. There's also a craft shop selling locally made items such as dijeridus and T-shirts.

Entry Fees

Entry to the park is $15 (children under 16 free). This entitles you to stay in the park for 14 days. The fee is payable at the park gates as you enter. If there's a few of you and you plan camping in the park, it works out cheaper to get a yearly ticket for $60. This covers one vehicle and all its occupants, as well as camping fees at the Mardugal, Muirella Park, Merl and Gunlom camp sites, which usually cost $7 per person per night.

ACTIVITIES
Walks

Kakadu is excellent but tough bushwalking country. Many people will be satisfied with the marked tracks. For the more adventurous there are infinite possibilities, especially in the drier south and east of the park, but take great care and prepare well. Tell people where you're going and don't go alone. You need a permit from the Bowali Information Centre to camp outside the established camp sites.

Kakadu by Foot is a helpful guide to the marked walking trails in Kakadu. It is published by ANCA ($1.95) but is not always available at the visitor centre.

Marked Tracks in the Park There are some excellent marked tracks within the park. They range from one km to 12 km long and are all fairly easy. Many of the ranger-led activities involve a guided walk along various tracks, and there's usually a Park Notes facts sheet for each walk so you can do a self-guided walk. These sheets are available from the visitor centre, and usually from a box at the start of each track.

Ubirr There are four tracks in the Ubirr area in the north of the park:

Ubirr Art Site
  This is an easy one-km walk which takes you around the rock-art galleries, and there's a short but steep side track to a lookout with great views over the East Alligator River floodplain. Allow one hour for the round trip.
Manngarre Monsoon Rainforest Walk
  This flat, 1.5-km walk starts by the downstream

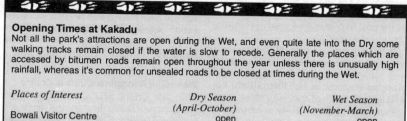

Opening Times at Kakadu

Not all the park's attractions are open during the Wet, and even quite late into the Dry some walking tracks remain closed if the water is slow to recede. Generally the places which are accessed by bitumen roads remain open throughout the year unless there is unusually high rainfall, whereas it's common for unsealed roads to be closed at times during the Wet.

Places of Interest	Dry Season (April-October)	Wet Season (November-March)
Bowali Visitor Centre	open	open
Nourlangie	open	usually open
Ubirr	open	usually open
Yellow Water	open	open
Walking tracks	most open	some open
Look-outs	open	open
Boat cruises	running	running
Jim Jim & Twin falls	opens May/June	closed
Maguk	opens May/June	closed
Gunlom	open	sometimes closed

boat ramp near the Border Store, and for much of the way is along a raised boardwalk. It takes about one hour.

Bardedjilidji Sandstone Walk

This is a slightly longer walk (2.5 km) starting from the upstream picnic area car park. It takes in wetland areas of the East Alligator River and some interesting eroded sandstone outliers of the Arnhem Land escarpment. It takes about 1½ hours.

Rock Holes Sandstone Walk

This is an extension of the Bardedjilidji Walk, taking in more of the same country. It's a total of nine km, and takes around three hours return.

South Alligator

This part of the park, where the Arnhem Highway crosses the South Alligator River, is not quite as heavily used as other areas such as Ubirr and Nourlangie and so you're less likely to see other walkers.

Mamukala Wetlands Walk

This easy path leads to a hide overlooking the wetlands. Late in the Dry you can expect to see masses of water birds, including magpie geese. There's three options here, but even the longest is only three km and takes less than three hours.

Gu-ngarre Monsoon Rainforest Walk

This is a flat and easy 3.5 km walk which includes not only monsoon rainforest but also woodlands and a waterhole. It's an excellent walk for learning about Aboriginal plant use. It takes about 1½ hours.

Muirella Park Area

Muirella Park is an excellent camping area in the central part of the park. It is convenient as a base for visiting Nourlangie, 25 km away, and for visiting Cooinda/Yellow Waters which is about 30 km south along the Kakadu Highway.

Bubba Wetlands Walk

This five-km walk skirts the edge of the Bubba Wetlands, and starts near the camp site (signposted). It makes an easy two-hour stroll, and there are wooden benches at intervals around the edge. This walk is closed in the Wet.

Mirrai Look-Out Walk

This look-out is just off the Kakadu Highway, four km south of the Muirella Park turn-off. The track is only a bit under one km each way, and it scales the dizzy heights of Mt Cahill (120 metres).

Iligadjarr Wetlands Walk

On this interesting four-km walk you can learn something of the uses the Aboriginal people of the area had for the various wetland plants. Allow 1½ hours, and don't try it in the Wet.

Nourlangie

Nourlangie is probably the most visited part of the park, and there are six walking trails in the immediate vicinity.

Nourlangie Art Site Walk

This is a 1.5-km walk taking in the excellent rock-art sites around the base of Nourlangie Rock. The Anbangbang Rock Shelter is the main gallery, and is accessible by wheelchair. Elsewhere the track is steep in parts, but you could still whip around it in half an hour or less; to have a good look at the paintings allow at least one hour. There are fine views out over the East Alligator floodplains and the Arnhem Land escarpment from a lookout just beyond the art sites.

Nawulandja Look-Out Walk

This is just a short walk up a gradual slope, but it gives excellent views of the Nourlangie Rock area.

Anbangbang Billabong Walk

This pretty billabong lies close to Nourlangie, and the picnic tables dotted around its edge make it a popular lunch spot. The track loops right around the billabong, a total distance of 2.5 km; allow one hour. You won't get far on this walk in the Wet.

Nanguluwur Gallery Walk

The Nanguluwur gallery sees far fewer visitors than Anbangbang simply because it's further to walk (four km return) and the gravel access road, which leads off the Nourlangie Rock road, can't handle buses and other large vehicles. The walk itself is flat and takes an easy two hours.

Gubara Springs Walk

Further along the same road from Nanguluwur is the Gubara walk, a six-km walk which skirts some clear pools in a patch of monsoon rainforest. Allow two hours return.

Barrk Sandstone Bushwalk

This is the most strenuous of the short day walks within the park, and involves some steep climbing up onto the top of Nourlangie Rock. The track starts at the Nourlangie car park, and you need to allow a full day to complete it.

Jim Jim Falls

Sixty km off the Kakadu Highway are the spectacular Jim Jim Falls. It's a popular destination, even though a 4WD vehicle is required to get in here.

Jim Jim Falls Walk
    This is more of a scramble than a walk, as you
    climb over and around boulders of increasing
    size as you approach the falls. It is definitely not
    suitable for small children unless you can carry
    them. It's about one km each way, and you need
    to allow at least half an hour in each direction,
    and another hour for a swim in the fantastic
    plunge pool at the foot of the falls.
Budjmii Look-Out Walk
    There are excellent escarpment views on this
    one-km walk, which is fairly rugged in places.

Cooinda This is the most accessible wetland
in the park, and also has the boat cruises on
it, and so is far and away the busiest part of
the park.

Yellow Water Walk
    The one walk here is little more than a stroll along
    a raised boardwalk out to a small viewing plat-
    form over the wetland. Nevertheless, it's a very
    pretty area with birds everywhere, and you can
    get some great photos at sunset (just be liberal
    with the mosquito repellent).
Mardugal Walks
    Close by at Mardugal camping area are two short
    walks which take you around the Mardugal Bil-
    labong.

Southern Area There are two short walks in
the southern part of the park.

Maguk Walk
    This flat walk takes you to a plunge pool at the
    base of a small waterfall, which flows year round.
    It's one km each way; allow 1½ hours, more if
    you want to swim.
Gunlom Waterfall Walk
    This is a short but steep walk which takes you to
    the top of the Gunlom Waterfall, above the
    plunge pool. It has great views and is worth the
    effort. It's about one km each way and you should
    allow about an hour for the round trip.

Walking Information A bushwalking permit
is needed if your walk is for more than one
day. These are available from the Bowali
Information Centre, or the ANCA in Darwin.
It's a good idea to allow a few days for the
permit to be issued.

Topographic maps are necessary for
extended walks, and these are available in
Darwin from the Department of Land, Planning & Environment; there's nothing available in Kakadu itself.

The Darwin Bushwalking Club (☎ 8985
1484) welcomes visitors and may be able to
help with information too. It has walks most
weekends, often in Kakadu. Or you could
join a Willis' Walkabouts guided bushwalk
(see the Activities section in the Facts for the
Visitor chapter).

Guided Walks & Talks

In the Dry season there's a variety of free
activities put on by the park staff. These take
the form of guided art-site talks, guided
walks along some of the walking tracks
already mentioned and evening slide shows
at the various camping grounds. It's well
worth going along to some of these activities
as it's a great opportunity to learn some more
about various aspects of the park.

The schedule of activities differs somewhat from one season to the next, but the
following outline gives you a rough idea of
what's on. Full details are given on a leaflet
which you will be given on entering the park.

Art-Site Talks These are held at the various
rock-art sites at Ubirr (six daily) and
Nourlangie (six daily).

Guided Walks These are held at Ubirr (three
times weekly), Muirella Park (twice
weekly), Yellow Water (three times weekly),
Maguk (twice weekly), Gunlom (four times
weekly) and Jim Jim Falls (once a week).

Slide Shows These are held in the early
evening once a week at various venues: the
Hostel Kakadu at Ubirr, the Frontier Kakadu
Lodge in Jabiru, Muirella Park campground,
Kakadu Holiday Village at South Alligator,
Cooinda Caravan Park, Mardugal camping
area, Jim Jim Falls camping area and
Gunlom camping area.

River Trips

Yellow Water The boat rides on the Yellow
Water wetlands which operate throughout
the dry season are probably the most popular
activity within the park. They do give you an

opportunity to get right out into the water-ways, and get surprisingly close to the water birds and crocs. Many people reckon the dawn trip is the best, and the sunrise is without doubt quite a sight, but the other trips throughout the day can be equally good. Apply mosquito repellent liberally if you opt for the dawn trip.

The trips are not particularly cheap, however. The 1½-hour trips depart daily at 11.15 am, and 1 and 2.45 pm, and cost $19.50 ($10.50 for children aged four to 12); the two-hour cruises leave at 6.45 and 9 am, and 4.30 pm, and cost $22.50 ($11.50). During the Wet there's a 3½-hour tour daily at 7 am and 3 pm, and this travels from the Yellow Water billabong along the South Alligator system. The cost is $35.50 ($18.50).

All tours are operated by Yellow Water Cruises and are booked through the travel desk at Cooinda (☎ 8979 0111). A shuttle bus connects the lodge with Yellow Water for the cruises, or you can make your own way. It's a good idea to make reservations, especially during the Dry, and especially for the dawn trip.

East Alligator River Aboriginal-guided Guluyambi river trips are held on the East Alligator River near the Border Store in the north of the park. These are excellent trips with the emphasis on Aboriginal culture and their relationship with the land. The boats are quite a bit smaller than those used at Yellow Water which makes for a more personal experience.

The Guluyambi tours leave from the upstream boat ramp at 9 and 11 am, and at 1 and 3 pm, cost $22.50 ($11 children four to 14) and last just under two hours. A free shuttle bus runs between the boat ramp and the Border Store and Merl camp site. For information and bookings ☎ toll-free 1800 089 113.

Scenic Flights
If you can afford it, the view of Kakadu from the air is spectacular. Kakadu Air Services (☎ 8979 2411) at Jabiru runs half-hour flights on the hour throughout the day for $55, or hour-long flights for $100.

Rotor Services (☎ 8945 0944) operates half-hour helicopter rides at $100 per person.

UBIRR

This spectacular rock-art site lies 36 km north of the Arnhem Highway. The rock-art site is open daily from 8.30 am to sunset from June to November.

Shortly before Ubirr you pass the Border Store. Nearby are a couple of walking trails close to the East Alligator River, which forms the eastern boundary of the park here. There is a backpackers' hostel and camp site nearby.

An easily followed path from the Ubirr car park takes you through the main galleries and up to a lookout with superb views. There are paintings on numerous rocks along the path, but the highlight is the main gallery with a large array of well-executed and pre-served x-ray-style wallabies, possums, goannas, tortoises and fish, plus a couple of *balanda* (white men) with hands on hips. Also of major interest here is the Rainbow Serpent painting, and the picture of the

The Rainbow Serpent
The story of the Rainbow Serpent is a common subject in Aboriginal traditions across Australia, although the story varies from place to place.

In Kakadu the serpent is a woman, Kuringali, who painted her image on the rock wall at Ubirr while on a journey through this area. This journey forms a creation path which links the places she visited: Ubirr, Manngarre, the East Alligator River and various places in Arnhem Land.

To the traditional owners of the park, Kuringali is the most powerful spirit. Although she spends most of her time resting in billa-bongs, if disturbed she can be very destructive, causing flood and earthquakes, and one local story has it that she even eats people. ■

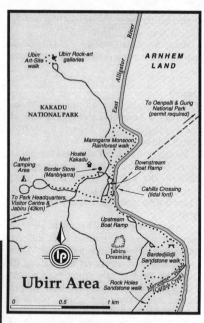

Ubirr Area

The Namarkan Sisters

The story of the Namarkan Sisters is told to warn young children about the dangers of crocodiles. It seems the sisters were sitting together by a billabong one day when one dived into the water, changed into a crocodile, then paddled back and frightened the life out of her sister. She then changed herself back and returned to her sister, who related how she had been terrified by a crocodile.

The first sister got such a kick out of this, that she repeated it over and over. Finally the other sister realised what was going on, and retaliated in the same way. The sisters then realised that if they were to turn themselves into crocodiles permanently, they could scare and eat anyone they pleased.

Today the Namarkan Sisters are present in all crocodiles, evident in the lumps behind the eyes and their great skill and cunning as hunters. ■

Namarkan Sisters, shown with string pulled taut between their hands.

The Ubirr paintings are in many different styles. They were painted during the period from over 20,000 years ago right up to the 20th century. Allow plenty of time to seek out and study them.

JABIRU

The township of Jabiru (population 1750) was built to accommodate the Ranger mine workers when the mine first started in the early 1980s. The intention was that it would be only a temporary settlement, but it has developed into the major service centre for Kakadu.

It's a pleasant enough little town, and it's the only place in the vicinity to buy supplies.

Information

The shopping centre in the town centre is where activity is concentrated. The post office is in the newsagency here. There's a branch of the Westpac Bank, with an ATM outside. If you want to withdraw cash using EFTPOS, this facility is available at the supermarket and the Mobil service station on Leichhardt St.

For permits to visit Oenpelli, across the East Alligator River, contact the Northern Land Council (☎ 8979 2410) on Flinders St near the shopping centre. The office is open weekdays from 8 am to 4.21 pm! There's also a travel agent, Jabiru Travel Centre (☎ 8979 2548), in the shopping centre.

The medical centre (☎ 8979 2018) is also in the main group of shops, and doctors are available for consultations from 8 am to 4 pm weekdays (except Wednesday when it closes at 2.30 pm). On weekends you can call the duty sister. A dentist only calls on Jabiru about once every six weeks.

The police station (☎ 8979 2122) is in the centre on Tasman Crescent.

For fuel, mechanical repairs, camping gas and ice there's the Mobil service station (☎ 8979 2001) on Leichhardt St, which is open from 7 am to 8.30 pm daily.

The supermarket in the shopping centre is

open 9 am to 5 pm weekdays, to 1.30 pm on Saturday and from 10 am to 2 pm Sunday.

The only liquor outlet is the Jabiru Sports & Social Club (☎ 8979 2326) down by the lake, behind the service station.

If you feel like a dip there's an Olympic sized public swimming pool just off Civic Dve. It's open daily from 9 am to 7 pm.

For car hire, Territory Rent-a-Car has a desk at the Gagudju Crocodile Hotel (☎ 8979 2552).

Things to See

'Not much' sums it up. About the only option is a tour of the **Ranger Uranium Mine** east of the town. These are operated by Kakadu Parklink (☎ 8979 2411) daily at 10 am, and again at 1.30 pm during the dry season. The 90-minute bus tours leave from the Jabiru Airport, and the cost is $10 ($5 children).

Places to Stay & Eat

The *Kakadu Frontier Lodge* (☎ 8979 2422) has a very well-equipped caravan park, complete with a swimming pool and a restaurant. Shady and grassed powered sites cost $20, or there are dusty unpowered sites for $16. In the lodge section there are beds in four-

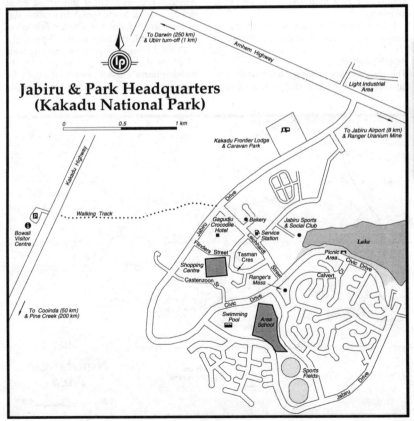

Jabiru & Park Headquarters
(Kakadu National Park)

KAKADU & ARNHEM LAND

bed air-con dorms for $22, but the only cooking facilities are a few barbecues by the swimming pool. The poolside bistro serves reasonable pub-style meals for around $12.

The *Gagudju Crocodile Hotel* (☎ 8979 2800) is probably most famous for its design – it's set out in the shape of a crocodile, although this is only really apparent from the air. There's nothing very exotic about the hotel itself, although it is comfortable enough. Room prices start at $189 for a double.

Apart from the restaurants at the two hotels, there's the *Golden Bowl Restaurant* at the sports club. It does a pretty standard range of Chinese food, and you can eat in or takeaway.

Lastly there's a cafe in the shopping centre, and a bakery near the fire station.

NOURLANGIE

The sight of this looming, mysterious, isolated outlier of the Arnhem Land escarpment makes it easy to understand why it has been important to Aboriginal people for so long. Its long, red, sandstone bulk, striped in places with orange, white and black, slopes up from surrounding woodland to fall away at one end in sheer, stepped cliffs, at the foot of which is Kakadu's best-known collection of rock art.

The name Nourlangie is a corruption of *nawulandja*, an Aboriginal word which refers to an area bigger than the rock itself. The Aboriginal name for part of the rock is Burrunggui. You reach it at the end of a 12-km sealed road which turns east off the Kakadu Highway, 21 km south of the Arnhem Highway. Other interesting spots nearby make it worth spending a whole day in this corner of Kakadu. The last few km of the road are closed from around 5 pm daily.

From the main car park a round-trip walk of about 1.5 km takes you first to the **Anbangbang shelter**, which was used for 20,000 years as a refuge from heat, rain and

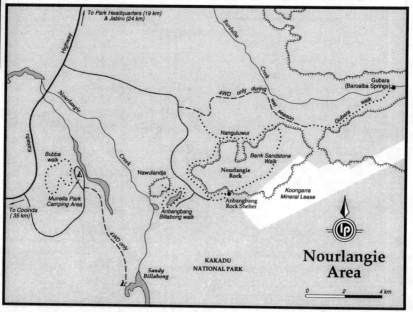

Nourlangie Area

the area's frequent wet-season thunderstorms. The shelter may have housed up to 30 people of the Warramal clan. Archaeological finds have revealed that the shelter was in almost constant use from about 6000 years ago to the time of contact. The gallery here was repainted in the 1960s by Nayambolmi (also known as Barramundi Charlie), a respected artist, fisherman and hunter.

The major character in the main gallery at Nourlangie is **Namondjok** ('na-mon-jock'), who committed incest with one of his clan sisters. Next to Nahmondjok is **Namarrgon** ('na-mad-gon'), or the Lightning Man. He is responsible for all the spectacular electrical storms which occur during the Wet, and here is depicted surrounded by an arc of lightning. **Barrginj** ('bar-geen'), is the wife of Namarrgon, and is the small female figure just to the left and below Namondjok. Their children are called the Alyurr, also known as Leichhardt's grasshoppers. These are orange and blue grasshoppers which are only seen just before the onset of the Wet.

From the gallery you can walk on to a lookout where you can see the distant Arnhem Land escarpment, which also includes Namarrgon Djadjam, the home of Namarrgon.

Heading back towards the highway you can take three turn-offs to further places of interest. The first, on the left about one km from the main car park, takes you to **Anbangbang Billabong**, with its picnic site and dense carpet of lilies. The second, also on the left, leads to a short walk up to **Nawulandja Lookout** with good views back over Nourlangie Rock.

The third turn-off, a dirt track on the right, takes you to another outstanding, but little visited, rock-art gallery, **Nanguluwur**. Here the paintings cover most of the styles found in the park, including a good example of 'contact art', a painting of a two-masted sailing ship towing a dinghy.

A further six km along this road, followed by a three-km walk, brings you to **Gubara (Baroalba Springs)**, an area of shaded pools set in monsoon forest, and a major breeding ground for freshwater fish such as saratoga.

JIM JIM & TWIN FALLS

These two spectacular waterfalls are along a 4WD dry-season track that turns south off the Kakadu Highway between the Nourlangie Rock and Cooinda turn-offs. It's about 60 km to Jim Jim Falls, with the last km on foot, and 70 km to Twin Falls, where the last few hundred metres are through the water up a snaking, forested gorge – great fun on an inflatable air bed. Jim Jim, a sheer 215-metre drop, is awesome after the rains, but its waters can shrink to nothing at the end of the Dry. Even so, the gorge itself is impressive at any time, and the plunge pool makes a great swimming hole. There's even a brilliant-white sandy beach.

Twin Falls is possibly more impressive for most visitors as it flows year round. The track to Twin Falls is often blocked until well into the Dry by the Jim Jim Creek at the Jim Jim camping area. Markers indicate the depth in the middle of the creek but these should be used as a very rough guide only as wheel tracks in the sandy creek bed can mean the water is deeper than you think. If you're unsure, wait for a tour vehicle or someone else with local knowledge to cross before attempting it.

Unfortunately few of the organised tours out of Darwin go to Jim Jim or Twin Falls. They'll try to convince you with the line that Jim Jim is dry, and therefore not worth seeing (wrong), and that Twin Falls is simply not worth it, full stop (wrong again!).

YELLOW WATER & COOINDA

The turn-off to the Cooinda accommodation complex and the superb Yellow Water wetlands, with their big water bird population, is 47 km down the Kakadu Highway from its junction with the Arnhem Highway. It's then 4.5 km to the Warradjan Cultural Centre (see the Information section earlier in this chapter), a further km to the Yellow Water wetland turn-off, and about another km again to Cooinda.

A boat trip on the wetlands is one of the highlights of most people's visit to Kakadu. (See the Activities section earlier in this chapter for details.)

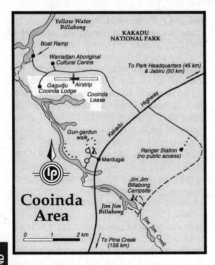

Yellow Water is also an excellent place to watch the sunset, particularly in the dry season when the smoke from the many bushfires which burn in the Top End at this time of year turns bright red in the setting sun. Bring plenty of insect repellent as the mosquitoes are voracious.

COOINDA TO PINE CREEK

Just south of the Yellow Water and Cooinda turn-off the Kakadu Highway heads south-west out of the park to Pine Creek on the Stuart Highway, about 160 km from Cooinda. Although there's about 20 km of gravel and the road crosses numerous creeks, it remains passable throughout the year.

About 45 km south of the Cooinda turn-off is the turn-off to **Maguk**, a fine little camp site on the Barramundie Creek 12 km off the highway along a 4WD track. A short walk along the creek brings you to the plunge pool at the foot of a small waterfall.

A further 32 km south along the highway is the **Bukbukluk** lookout, which gives great views over the park's southern hills.

After another eight km a road to the left (east) leads the 37 km (mostly gravel) to **Gunlom (Waterfall Creek)**, another superb

escarpment waterfall and plunge pool, and the only one accessible by conventional (non-4WD) vehicle. There are also camping and picnic areas, and plenty of distinctive northern salmon gums providing shade.

ORGANISED TOURS

There are hosts of tours to Kakadu from Darwin, a few that start inside the park itself, and yet more which operate from Katherine. Don't forget that the park entry fee of $15 is generally not included in tour prices.

From Darwin

Two-day tours typically take in Nourlangie, Ubirr and the Yellow Water cruise, and cost from around $170. Longer tours usually cover most of the main sights plus a couple of extras. Companies which aim at backpackers and seem to be popular include: Hunter Safaris (☎ 8981 2720; fax 8981 2757); All Terrain (☎ 8941 0070; fax 8981 3053); and Backpacking Australia Tours (☎ 8945 2988; fax 8941 0758). This last company has four-day 4WD trips which cover just about everything, including Jim Jim and Twin Falls, for $380.

Territory Style Tours (☎ 8941 0070; fax 8981 3053) is one company which does two-day 4WD trips out of Darwin which take in Jim Jim and Twin falls, plus Nourlangie and Yellow Water cruise, for $170.

A one-day tour to Kakadu from Darwin is really too quick, but if you're short of time it's better than nothing. You could try Australian Kakadu Tours (☎ 8981 5144), which will whiz you to Yellow Water for a two-hour cruise (included) and Nourlangie Rock and back to Darwin for $75 ($85 including lunch), plus the $15 park entry fee.

Willis' Walkabouts (☎ 8985 2134; fax 8985 2355) organises bushwalks guided by knowledgable Top End walkers following your own or preset routes of two days or more. (See the Activities section in the Facts for the Visitor chapter for more details.)

From Jabiru & Cooinda

You can take 10-hour, 4WD tours to Jim Jim and Twin Falls from Jabiru or Cooinda

($115, YHA members $110, children $90) with Kakadu Gorge & Waterfall Tours (☎ 8979 0111). Lord of Kakadu (☎ 8979 2567; fax 8979 2970) does the same trip for $120, and AAT-Kings (☎ 8947 1207; fax 8947 1324) charge $135.

Kakadu Park Connection (☎ 8979 0111) has half-day, 4WD trips from Cooinda for $55, but these really only visit Maguk. Full-day trips cost $105 and head into Gunlom in the south of the park.

Northern Adventure Safaris (☎ 8981 3833; fax 8979 2930) operates good two-day trips out of Jabiru, visiting Ubirr, Nourlangie and Yellow Water, for $203 ($160 for Greyhound Pioneer pass holders). Three-day trips also include Jim Jim and Twin falls, and cost $310 ($265).

For day trips to Ubirr, which include the Guluyambi river cruise and a visit to the Ranger mine, tours are run by Kakadu Parklink (☎ 8979 2411; fax 8979 2303) for $100 ($80 children) from Jabiru. It also does day trips down to Nourlangie and Yellow Water for the same price.

If you want to give fishing a go you could try the half-day trips operated by Kakadu Fishing Tours (☎ 8979 2025). These depart from Jabiru and cost $180 for one person, $220 for two and $330 for three.

From Katherine

Katherine Adventure Tours (☎ toll-free 1800 808 803; fax 8971 1176) is popular, charging $450 for five days, finishing up in Darwin.

Into Arnhem Land

A couple of outfits offer trips into Arnhem Land from Kakadu, although they only nip across the East Alligator River to Oenpelli. Aboriginal-owned Inkiyu Tours (☎ 8979 2474) runs half-day tours from the Border Store.

Lord of Kakadu Tours (☎ 8979 2567) does one-day trips from Jabiru for $135.

PLACES TO STAY

Accommodation prices in Kakadu can vary tremendously depending on the season –

dry-season prices (given here) are often as much as 50% above wet-season prices.

See the earlier Jabiru section in this chapter for details of accommodation options in Jabiru.

Camping

There are a number of National Parks sites with varying levels of facilities ranging from pit toilets to full amenities blocks with hot showers, although there's no electricity at any of them. There are also some commercial sites with more facilities, such as restaurants and swimming pools, attached to the various hotels/resorts.

National Park Camp Sites There are four main National Parks camp sites. They all have hot showers, flushing toilets, and drinking water and the fee is $7 per person. These are the only sites which are really suitable for caravans.

Merl This is close to Ubirr and the Border Store in the north of the park. There's plenty of shade, but the mosquitoes are thick, and it's closed in the Wet.

Muirella Park Muirella Park is six km off the Kakadu Highway, a few km south of the Nourlangie Rock turn-off. It's situated right on paperbark-lined billabong, and is actually on a reclaimed airstrip which used to be part of a 1950s safari camp, where clients were flown in. There's a reasonable amount of shade, although parts of the site can be flooded during the Wet.

Mardugal Just off the Kakadu Highway, 1.5 km south of the Cooinda turn-off, Mardugal is the only site unaffected by the Wet.

Gunlom This site is in the south of the park, and is accessed by a gravel road from the Kakadu Highway. It's a great site as it is close to the Gunlom (Waterfall Creek) plunge pool, and is surrounded by shady salmon gums.

Other Sites The National Parks provides 12

KAKADU & ARNHEM LAND

more basic camp sites around the park, and at these there is no fee. They have fire places, some have pit toilets, and at all you'll need to bring your own drinking water. To camp away from these you need a permit from the park information centre.

South Alligator

Just a couple of km west of the South Alligator River on the Arnhem Highway is the *Kakadu Holiday Village* (☎ 8979 0166; fax 8979 0147), which has singles/doubles from $120, and family rooms at $142. The hotel has a restaurant and a basic shop, as well as a swimming pool, restaurant and bar.

Sites in the grassed camping area cost $16, or $20 with power.

Ubirr

The popular *Hostel Kakadu* (☎ 8979 2232) behind the Border Store is the only place in Kakadu that offers budget accommodation and decent facilities. The budget accommodation at the resort hotels is a bit of an afterthought and there's not much in the way of cooking facilities. It's open year round (as long as the road remains open) and has dorm accommodation (one with air-con) at $14 per person. The Border Store has supplies and snack food, and is open daily until 5 pm.

Cooinda

This is by far the most popular place to stay, mainly because of the proximity of the Yellow Water wetlands and the early-morning boat cruises. It gets mighty crowded at times, mainly with camping tours. The *Gagudju Lodge Cooinda* (☎ 8979 0145; fax 8979 0148) has some comfortable units for $126 single or double, and much cheaper and more basic air-con 'budget rooms', which are just transportable huts of the type found on many building sites and more commonly known in the Territory as 'demountables' or 'dongas'. For $15 per person they are quite adequate, if a little cramped (two beds per room), although there are no cooking facilities.

The bistro restaurant in the bar serves unexciting but good-value meals at around $11 to $15, and a full breakfast at $7.50.

The large camping area is OK with plenty of shade, although the facilities are over-stretched at times. It costs $3.50 for a site, or $6.50 with power.

GETTING THERE & AROUND

Ideally, take your own 4WD. The Arnhem Highway is sealed all the way to Jabiru. The Kakadu Highway is sealed or gravel from its junction with the Arnhem Highway, near Jabiru, all the way to Pine Creek, with the exception of a 20-km stretch just inside the park's southern boundary. Sealed roads lead from the Kakadu Highway to Nourlangie, to the Muirella Park camping area and to Ubirr. Other roads are mostly dirt and blocked for varying periods during the Wet and early Dry.

Bus

Greyhound Pioneer runs daily buses from Darwin to Katherine via Jabiru and Cooinda, and vice versa. This saves backtracking all the way to Darwin. In both directions the buses stop at the Yellow Water wetland in time for the 1 pm cruise, and wait here for 1½ hours until the cruises finish. The south-bound buses leave Darwin at 6.30 am, Jabiru at 9.55 am and Cooinda at 2.30 pm, arriving in Katherine at 5.15 pm. From Katherine they leave at 7.15 am, Cooinda at 2.30 pm, Jabiru at 4.20 pm, arriving in Darwin at 7 pm.

Taipans are one of the four types of poisonous snakes found in Kakadu

The cost is $65, Darwin to Katherine including two stopovers. To travel one way from Darwin to the park costs $25; from Katherine it's $35.

McCafferty's have a daily service from Darwin to Jabiru ($25) and on to Ubirr ($30). The inbound service leaves Darwin at 10 am and Jabiru at 1.40 pm, arriving at the Border Store at 2.20 pm. In the opposite direction it leaves the Border Store at 2.35 pm, Jabiru at 5 pm, arriving in Darwin at 8 pm.

Bathurst & Melville Islands

These two large, flat islands about 80 km north of Darwin are the home of the Tiwi Aboriginal people.

The Tiwi people's island homes kept them fairly isolated from mainland developments until this century, and their culture has retained several unique features. Perhaps the best known are the pukumani burial poles, carved and painted with symbolic and mythological figures, which are erected around graves. More recently the Tiwi have turned their hand to art for sale – bark painting, textile screen printing, batik and pottery, using traditional designs and motifs.

The main settlement on the islands is **Nguiu** in the south-east of Bathurst Island, which was founded in 1911 as a Catholic mission. On Melville Island the settlements are **Pularumpi** and **Milikapiti**.

Most Tiwi live on Bathurst Island and follow a non-traditional lifestyle. Some go back to their traditional lands on Melville Island for a few weeks each year. Melville Island also has descendants of the Japanese pearl divers who regularly visited here early this century, and people of mixed Aboriginal and European parentage who were gathered here from around the Territory under government policy half a century ago.

History

Unlike other Aboriginal groups in Arnhem Land, the Tiwi had generally poor relations with the Macassan fisherpeople who came from the island of Celebes (now Sulawes) in search of the trepang, or sea cucumber, from the 17th century. This earned them a reputation for hostility which stayed with them right through the colonial era.

In their efforts to colonise the north of Australia, in 1824 the British established a settlement at Fort Dundas, near Pularumpi on Melville Island. Like the other British settlements in the north, initial hopes were high as the land seemed promising, but these hopes soon gave way to depression as the oppressive climate, isolation, disease, the absence of expected maritime trade and, to a degree, the hostility of the local people, took their toll. The settlement was abandoned within 18 months and the British had another attempt at settling the north, this time at Raffles Bay near Croker Island. (It too was unsuccessful.)

In the late 19th century two South Australian buffalo shooters spent a couple of years on Melville Island and, with the help of the Tiwi, reputedly shot 6000 buffaloes. The Tiwi speared one of the shooters; the other, Joe Cooper, fled to Cape Don on the Cobourg Peninsula, but returned in 1900 and spent the next 16 years with the Tiwi.

Efforts by the Catholic church to establish a mission on Melville in 1911 met with resistance from Joe Cooper, so the mission was set up on Bathurst Island. The Tiwi were initially extremely suspicious as the missionaries had no wives, but the situation improved in 1916 when a number of French nuns joined the mission!

Information

You need a permit to visit the islands and the only realistic option is to take a tour as there is no commercial accommodation or transport on the islands. In fact you won't be issued a permit unless you have a tour booked. Tiwi Tours (☎ 8981 5115), a company which employs many Tiwi among its staff, is the main operator, and its tours have been recommended.

KAKADU & ARNHEM LAND

Organised Tours

A full-day Tiwi Tours trip costs $210 and includes the necessary permit, a flight from Darwin to Nguiu, visits to the early Catholic mission buildings and craft workshops, a boat crossing of the narrow Apsley Strait to Melville Island, swimming at Turacumbie Falls, a trip to a pukumani burial site and the flight back to Darwin from Melville. Tiwi Tours also offers three-day tours to the islands, staying at a tented camp, for $591 ($545 for children aged five to 12). The tours are available from May to October.

Holiday AKT (☎ toll-free 1800 891 121; fax 8981 5391) also offer daytrips, but these are serious money at $499 per person.

Arnhem Land

The entire eastern half of the Top End is the Arnhem Land Aboriginal Reserve, which is spectacular, sparsely populated and the site of some superb Aboriginal art. It's virtually closed to independent travellers apart from a few isolated pockets: Gove Peninsula, the peninsula at the north-east corner; Oenpelli, just across the East Alligator River near Ubirr in Kakadu National Park; and the already mentioned Cobourg Peninsula.

Access to Oenpelli and Cobourg Peninsula is across the East Alligator River from Ubirr in Kakadu. Acces to the north-eastern section of Arnhem Land is from Katherine.

OENPELLI

Oenpelli is a small Aboriginal town 15 km into Arnhem Land across the East Alligator River from the Border Store in Kakadu. There's not much of interest in the town itself, the main reason to visit being an opportunity to buy locally made arts and crafts at the Injalak Arts & Crafts centre (☎ 8979 0190) at prices well below what you have to pay in Kakadu itself. Injalak is both a workplace and shopfront for artists and craftspeople who produce traditional paintings on bark and paper, dijeridus, pandanus weavings and baskets, and screenprinted fabrics. All sales benefit the community.

The trip from the East Alligator River to Oenpelli is also spectacular as it crosses the beautiful Magela wetlands.

Before you can visit Oenpelli you must first go through the rigmarole of obtaining a permit from the Northern Land Council in Jabiru. These can take a day or so to issue, although some people have reported getting them in as little as half an hour.

COBOURG PENINSULA

This remote wilderness, 200 km north-east of Darwin, includes the **Cobourg Marine Park** and the Aboriginal-owned **Gurig National Park**.

Both parks are on the UN register of Wetlands of International Importance as they are the habitat of a variety of waterfowl and other migratory birds. The coastline here is beautiful and there are some excellent beaches, although it's frustrating not to be able to swim in them as the water is full of nasties. Gurig is also home to a wide variety of introduced animals – Balinese banteng cattle, buffalo, Indian Sambar deer and pig – all imported by the British when they attempted to settle the Top End last century.

As it's not really possible to explore the inland parts of the park as there are virtually no tracks within the park apart from the main access track, the focus here is on water-based activities. Unless you bring your own boat there's not a great deal to do, apart from wander along the deserted beaches gathering shells – of which there is an amazing variety and number.

The park is jointly managed by Parks & Wildlife and the local Aboriginal inhabitants through the Cobourg Peninsula Sanctuary Board.

History

Although European navigators had explored along this coastline, it was the British who tried to make a permanent settlement. After two unsuccessful attempts (at Melville Island and then Raffles Bay on the Cobourg Peninsula), a third attempt was made at Port

Essington in 1838. The garrison town was named Victoria Settlement, and at its peak was home to over 300 people. The British intention was that it would become the base for major trade between Australia and Asia, but by 1849, after the settlement had survived a cyclone and malaria outbreaks, the decision was made to abandon it.

Information
Entry to Gurig is by permit. You have to pass through Arnhem Land and the Aboriginal owners there severely restrict the number of vehicles going through – only 15 are allowed in at any one time – so you're advised to apply up to a year ahead for the necessary permit (fee $10) from the Parks & Wildlife desk in the Darwin Regional Tourism Association office in the Smith St Mall in Darwin (☎ 8989 3881; fax 8981 0653).

At Black Point there is a ranger station and visitor centre (☎ 8979 0244), which has an interesting section dealing with the Aboriginal, European and Maccassan people, and also has a brochure detailing the history of Victoria Settlement and a mud-map of the ruins.

Victoria Settlement
Victoria Settlement at Port Essington, a superb 30-km-long natural harbour on the northern side of the peninsula, is well worth a visit but it is only accessible by boat. The ruins still visible include various chimneys and wells, the powder magazine, and parts of the hospital. A charter-boat service (☎ 8979 0263) is usually available from the Gurig Store at Black Point, but the boat was wrecked on rocks during the 1994-95 wet season and may not have been replaced.

Facilities
There's a shady camp site with 15 sites about 100 metres from the shore at Smith Point. It's run by Parks & Wildlife and facilities include a shower, toilet and barbecue. There's no electricity and generators are not allowed to be used at night. The charge is $4 per site for three people, plus $1 for each additional person.

At Black Point there's the small Gurig Store (☎ 8979 0263), which is open weekdays from 3 to 5 pm only. It sells basic provisions such as ice, camping gas and fuel (diesel, super, unleaded, outboard mix), and basic mechanical repairs can be undertaken. Be warned that credit cards are not accepted here.

There's an airstrip at Smith Point which is serviced by charter flights from Darwin.

The fully equipped, four-bed *Cobourg Cottages* (☎ 8979 0263) at Smith Point overlooking Port Essington costs $100 for the whole cottage, but you need to bring your own supplies.

The only other accommodation option is the *Seven Spirit Bay Resort* (☎ 8979 0277), set in secluded wilderness at Vashon Head outside the national park and accessible only by air or boat. It charges $249 per person for single/double accommodation, but this includes three gourmet meals.

Accommodation is in individual open-sided, hexagonal 'habitats', each with semi-outdoor private bathroom! Activities available (at extra cost) include day trips to Victoria Settlement, guided bushwalks and fishing. Return transfer by air from Darwin costs $275 per person.

Getting There & Away
The track to Cobourg starts at Oenpelli and is accessible by 4WD vehicle only – and it's closed in the wet season. The 288-km drive to Black Point from the East Alligator River crossing takes about six hours and the track is in reasonable condition, the roughest part coming in the hour or so after the turn-off from Murgenella. The trip must be completed in one day as it's not possible to stop overnight on Aboriginal land.

Straight after the Wet, the water level at Cahills Crossing on the East Alligator River near the Border Store can be high, and you can only drive across the ford about an hour either side of the low tide. A tide chart is included with your permit, or the Bowali Information Centre in Kakadu has a list of tide times.

EASTERN ARNHEM LAND

The eastern part of Arnhem Land that is of interest to visitors is the Gove Peninsula.

Groote Eylandt, a large island off the east Arnhem Land coast, is also Aboriginal land, with a big manganese-mining operation. The main settlement here is Alyangula (population 670).

History

Early Dutch navigators in the 17th century were followed by Englishman, Matthew Flinders, who named the area after one of the earlier Dutch ships.

Early overland visitors to Arnhem Land were the explorer Ludwig Leichhardt in 1845 and the South Australian surveyor David Lindsay in 1883.

During the late 19th century cattle stations covered much of the area, although the land was largely unsuitable for stock, and there were a number of Christian missions.

In 1931 the area was proclaimed an Aboriginal reserve on the recommendations of an investigation into the Aboriginal people of the Northern Territory by the federal government.

The Aboriginal people of Yirrkala (population 590) made an important step in the land rights movement in 1963 when they protested at the plans for this mining on their traditional land. They failed to stop it, but forced a government inquiry and won compensation, and their case caught the public eye.

Permits

Travelling overland through eastern Arnhem Land is complicated by the fact that you have to have a permit, not to actually travel the road, but to allow you to stop and camp overnight along it. Even this is only a possibility at the designated campsites along the main road.

While obtaining permits to travel to Gove *should* be a straightforward matter, the Northern Land Council, which issues the permits, is notorious for being less than 100% cooperative. The best idea is to plan well ahead, and in the first instance contact the Gove Regional Tourist Association (☎ 8987 1985; fax 8987 2214) who can get you on the right track to start with.

If you are flying in to Gove no permit is needed, but to venture outside the town – even to the beaches close by – you need to get a recreational permit from the traditional owners through the local Dhimurru Land Management & Aboriginal Corporation (☎ 8987 3992) in Nhulunbuy (a formality).

Nhulunbuy

At Nhulunbuy (population 3500), on the Gove Peninsula, there is a bauxite-mining centre with a deep-water export port. The township itself was built in the 1970s to service the mine.

It's worth visiting the Yirrkala Arts & Crafts Museum, and you can buy locally made crafts at the Nambara Arts & Crafts Aboriginal gallery.

On Thursday morning there are tours of the alumina mine and plant, which is located 15 km from the town.

You can hire vehicles in Nhulunbuy to explore the coastline (there are some fine beaches, but beware of crocodiles).

Places to Stay Nhulunbuy has two motels and one resort hotel on the beachfront, all of which provide accommodation, and there are designated camp sites.

Getting There & Away

Air Ansett has almost daily flights between Darwin and Gove, and from there to Cairns. Air North flies between Darwin and outstations in eastern Arnhem Land such as Maningrida ($160), Ngukurr ($284), Numbulwar ($314) and Ramingining ($170).

Land Access to Gove is via the gravel road which leaves the Stuart Highway 52 km south of Katherine and cuts north-east across Arnhem Land the 700-odd km to Gove. Locals do the trip in as little as nine hours, although it's much more sensible to take your time and do it in a couple of days. This road is only open during the Dry.

ORGANISED TOURS

There are a number of tours into Arnhem Land, but these usually only visit the western part.

The Aboriginal-owned-and-operated Umorrduk Safaris (☎ 8948 1306; fax 8948 1305) has a two-day fly-in/fly-out tour from Darwin to the remote Mudjeegarrdart airstrip in north-western Arnhem Land. The highlight of the trip is a visit to the 20,000-year-old Umorrduk rock-art sites. The cost is $500 per person.

Another operator is Davidson's Arnhemland Safaris (☎ 8927 5240). Max Davidson has been taking people into Arnhem Land for years and has a concession at Mt Borradaile, north of Oenpelli, where he has set up his safari camp. The cost of staying at the camp is $300 per person per day, which includes accommodation, all meals, guided tours and fishing; transfers from Darwin can be arranged.

AAT-Kings (☎ toll-free 1800 334 009) has two-day coach trips operating out of Darwin which take you through Kakadu and on to Davidson's Safari Camp. The cost of these trips is $499 ($424 for children aged three to 14).

Darwin to Katherine

The Stuart Highway is the bitumen artery which connects Darwin on the coast with Alice Springs, 1500 km to the south in the heart of the Red Centre. In the Top End it is a busy road with plenty of stops to break the monotony.

Once past Palmerston, Darwin's satellite suburb, you pass the Arnhem Highway turn-off to Kakadu to the east, and soon after in quick succession the Crocodile Farm and the Cox Peninsula Road which leads to Mandorah, the Territory Wildlife Park, Berry Springs and Litchfield National Park.

Continuing on the highway there's Manton Dam and Lake Bennett, both popular places for watersports, before you get to the turn-off to Batchelor and the southern entrance to Litchfield National Park, 86 km south of Darwin.

All these destinations are dealt with in the Around Darwin chapter.

ADELAIDE RIVER

This sleepy settlement of 350 people on the Stuart Highway, 110 km south of Darwin, is today little more than a refuelling and refreshment stop for travellers on the Track. It does, however, have a long history, with its beginnings going back to the days of the Overland Telegraph Line and the North Australia Railway last century. The town was also an important rest camp and supply depot during WW II, and it's worth spending at least a few hours having a poke around.

The town comes alive during June when the Adelaide River Show, Rodeo, Campdraft & Gymkhana are held at the showgrounds.

Things to See

The former railway station Refreshment Room building on the southern edge of town is owned by the National Trust and is now the **Adelaide River Railway Historic Museum**. At one time this building was also the town's pub, and during WW II was taken over by the military as a wet canteen. Today

it houses some interesting wartime memorabilia.

Just a few km off the highway is the well-signposted **Adelaide River War Cemetery**. This small cemetery, set in an immaculate garden, is the largest war cemetery in the country and contains the graves of those killed in the 1942 Japanese air raids over Darwin.

Places to Stay

The basic *Shady River View Caravan Park* (☎ 8976 7047) has grassy sites at $12, or $15 with power. This is also the *Adelaide River*

Inn, which has single/double rooms for $35/65.

It's also possible to camp at the town's showgrounds, a km or so along the old Stuart Highway (now the road to Daly River), for $5 per person.

OLD STUART HIGHWAY

From Adelaide River the Stuart Highway runs straight and boring south-east the 100 km or so to the historic town of Pine Creek. It's a lot more relaxing to take the old highway, which is only slightly longer, but is infinitely more interesting and lacks the speeding traffic of the main highway. It's just a single lane of bitumen which winds lazily through typical Top End open woodland.

The old highway also gives access to the Daly River road, which leads to the mellow little settlement of Daly River, a popular fishing spot on the river of the same name, about 80 km from the main road (see later in this chapter for details), and to two small hot-spring reserves.

Robyn Falls

The turn-off to these small waterfalls is about 15 km along the highway from Adelaide River. From the car park it's a 15-minute scramble along a rocky path to the small plunge pool at the base of the falls. Although it's not a designated camp site, people have obviously taken advantage of the grass and running water at the car park here.

Douglas Hot Springs & Butterfly Gorge

To reach Douglas Hot Springs Nature Park, turn south off the old highway just before it rejoins the Stuart Highway and continue on for about 35 km. The nature park here includes a section of the Douglas River, a pretty camping area with shady paperbarks, and several hot springs – a bit hot for bathing at 40 to 60°C, but there are cooler pools. There are a number of Aboriginal sacred sites in the area, and the reserve is actually owned by the Wagaman people, and managed on their behalf by Parks & Wildlife. Don't be tempted to swim in the river itself unless you want to tangle with a saltie.

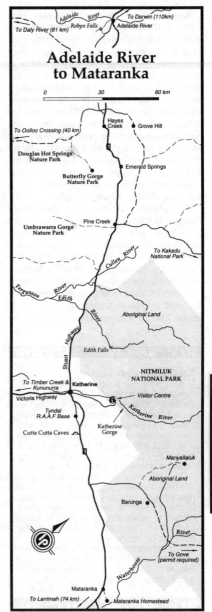

Adelaide River to Mataranka

About 17 km beyond Douglas Hot Springs, **Butterfly Gorge Nature Park** is along a 4WD road which is closed in the Wet. True to its name, common crow butterflies sometimes swarm in the gorge, which is reached via a short walking track from the car park. The gorge itself is a 70-metre-deep gash which has been cut into the sandstone escarpment by the Douglas River. There are numerous rock pools, the large one at the base of the gorge being a popular swimming hole. There are no saltwater crocs this far up the river, although you may well see freshies. The paperbark forest features some of the largest trees of this type in the Territory – some are close to 50 metres high.

The gravel road continues south from Douglas Hot Springs for about 45 km to the Daly River (the river, not the township), famed for its good fishing, and there are a couple of spots to stay along the way. The *Corn Patch Holiday Park* (☎ 8978 2479) is about five km south of Douglas Hot Springs.

A further 40 km brings you to the end of the road at **Ooloo Crossing**, at the Daly River. There's accommodation here in the

form of *Lukies Farm* (☎ 8978 2411), where you can bush-camp for $10 per vehicle. You need to be completely self-sufficient, but this is an excellent and fairly isolated fishing spot.

Grove Hill

Where the old highway rejoins the Stuart Highway it's possible to cross straight over and do a loop on the east side of the highway before rejoining it at Pine Creek. This well-maintained road is mostly gravel, and follows the line of the old railway. This is in fact the original 'north road', which was in use before the 'new road' (now the Old Stuart Highway!) was built. It's a worthwhile detour to see the old corrugated-iron pub at Grove Hill.

The *Grove Hill Heritage Hotel* (☎ 8978 2489) is part museum and part hotel. It lies right on the route of both the old railway line and the Overland Telegraph Line. It was built by the Lucy family in the 1930s and is completely original, even down to the corrugated iron accommodation wing at the back. It used to be a pub with no beer, but even that situation has been remedied recently. A bed in the twin-share rooms costs $15, or you can camp outside, although there is little shade.

DALY RIVER

The settlement of Daly River (population 300) lies 81 km west of the old Stuart Highway along a bitumen and good gravel road. With its setting on the Daly River, it's one of the most idyllic spots in the Territory. It's just far enough away from Darwin (240 km) to put it out of day-tripping reach, and so for most of the season it remains pleasantly uncrowded. The big draw here is the chance of hooking a barra in the river, but even if you're not into fishing it can be a very pleasant spot to while away a few days.

History

The first European to venture through this way was our old friend John MacDouall Stuart in 1862. He named the river after the then Governor of South Australia, Sir Dominick Daly, and a settlement of the same

North Australian Railway

In the 1880s the South Australian government decided to build a railway line from Darwin (Palmerston) to Pine Creek. This was partly to improve the conditions on the Pine Creek goldfields, as the road south from Darwin was often washed out in the Wet, but was also partly spurred by the dream – and it is still a dream – of a transcontinental railway line linking Adelaide and Darwin.

The line was built almost entirely by Chinese labourers, and was eventually pushed south as far as Larrimah. It continued to operate right up until 1976 when it was forced to close due to a lack of funds because of Cyclone Tracy's drain on the Northern Territory's resources.

The transcontinental link is still the subject of much discussion in the Territory, although it is still seemingly no nearer to reality than it was a century ago. ■

name was slowly established. In the 1880s there was a brief flurry of activity when a rich copper find was made by two prospectors. They were joined by three mates and together they mined and stockpiled the ore. In September of 1884 the men were attacked by local Aboriginal people who, up until that time, had been considered friendly – one of the attackers had even worked for the miners for some time prior to the attack. Four of the five died of the wounds they received, and the attack sparked a vicious response from the Resident in Palmerston. A punitive party was dispatched and it seems they went completely overboard, and massacred men, women and children at will. When the incident became public there was a major outcry. The leader of the party, Corporal George Montagu, and other members were quizzed by a board of inquiry established by the South Australian government, but they were all cleared of any wrongdoing.

The late 1880s saw the Jesuit missionaries move into the area, and they soon established four missions. Three of these folded fairly quickly, and the last was finally closed in 1899, bringing to an end nearly two decades of relative peace between the European and Aboriginal communities. From the Jesuits' point of view, however, it was time spent for little reward. It was around this time also that the bulk of the copper-mining activities ceased, although there was still one mine operating in 1915.

Pastoral ventures over the years have generally met with little success. In the 1880s it was sugar cane, which came and went quickly, in 1915 a dairy herd was brought in, and taken out again just a year later, while in the 1920s peanut farming was favoured. This last activity at least managed to survive into the 1950s.

These days it is the surviving cattle runs and the increasing tourism industry which keeps the area alive.

Information

The bulk of the population are part of the Nauiya Nambiyu Aboriginal community, about six km away from the rest of the town.

There's a well-stocked general store, service station and medical clinic (☎ 8978 2412), and visitors are welcome without a permit, although note that this is a dry community. Also here is Merrepen Arts, a resource centre which is also an outlet for locally made arts and crafts. Each year in June/July there's the **Merrepen Arts Festival**. Several Aboriginal communities from around the district, such as Wadeye, Nauiyi and Peppimenarti, display their arts and crafts.

The rest of the town consists largely of the colourful Daly River Pub, and the police station (☎ 8978 2466).

Things to See & Do

The main activity is getting out on the river and dangling a line. If you don't have your own, boat hire is available at the Mango Farm and Woolianna tourist outfits (see Places to Stay later in this chapter). At the Mango Farm you can hire a 3.6-metre dinghy with outboard motor for $16 per hour, $60 for a half day and $90 for a full day, or take a river cruise at $20 per person. Woolianna has two-person boats at $55/80 for a half/full day, as well as three-person ($65/90) and four-person boats ($70/100). Both places also operate guided fishing trips on request.

Places to Stay & Eat

The best options here involve camping. Just half a km from town on the road which takes you to the Mango Farm is the Daly River crossing, which has a huge sandbar which is a popular, although dusty, camping spot. There are a only couple of good spots with shade.

Further along this road, and well signposted seven km from the river crossing, is the *Mango Farm* (☎ 8978 2464), right on the banks of the river. This was the site of one of the Jesuit missions in the area, and it has a grove of absolutely giant mango trees, which were planted over 90 years ago by an agriculturalist. You can camp in the shade of these massive trees for $7 per person, $1 more with power, or there are twin-share safari tents at $13 per person, and a fully equipped, two-bedroom family unit which sleeps nine and costs $100. This place is well set up and has a swimming pool, and meals can be supplied on request.

Right in the town itself is the *Daly River Pub* (☎ 8978 2418) which has a shady little campsite at $7 per site ($10 with power), and you are of course right by the only watering hole for miles.

About five km before you actually get to Daly River a gravel road heads west for 15 km to *Woolianna on the Daly Tourist Park* (☎ 8978 2478), another low-key caravan park right on the banks of the Daly River. There's a beautiful shady green lawn for camping, and an in-ground swimming pool. Camping here costs $15 for a site ($18 powered), and there's a kiosk with basic grocery items. It's a good spot.

Getting There & Away
The Nauiya Nambiyu community runs a three-times weekly dry-season minibus service between Daly River and Darwin. It departs Daly River at 8.30 am and Darwin at 3 pm on Monday, Wednesday and Friday; the cost is $70 return (☎ 8978 2422 for details).

PINE CREEK
This small town (population 450), 245 km from Darwin, is one of only a handful of towns in the Territory that have great atmosphere – it was the scene of a gold rush in the 1870s and some of the old timber and corrugated-iron buildings survive. As it lies a km or so off the highway it also manages to retain an old-world, unhurried atmosphere undisturbed by the thundering road trains belting up and down the highway.

Pine Creek is also where the Kakadu Highway branches north-east off the Stuart Highway to Kakadu National Park.

History
In the early 1870s labourers working on the Overland Telegraph Line found gold here, sparking a gold rush which was to last nearly 20 years. A telegraph station was opened in 1874, and around the same time there was a large influx of Chinese workers, who were brought in by the Europeans to do all the tough work on the goldfields. It wasn't long before more Chinese began arriving under their own steam to work the goldfields themselves. Such was the Chinese influx that by the mid-1880s Chinese outnumbered Europeans 15 to one in Pine Creek.

Not all the Chinese who arrived to work on the goldfields were labourers; many were merchants and businesspeople with money behind them. Pine Creek boasted a number of Chinese stores, although all but one of them were destroyed by a fire in 1892. Once the gold ran out the population of Pine Creek dwindled; many Chinese returned home in the 1890s, driven away by the depression and the racism they were subject to.

Everyone coming to Pine Creek in the hope of striking it rich faced a difficult journey from Palmerston (Darwin). There was no road to the diggings, and the government was unwilling to spend money on building one. Although a person on horseback could do the journey in a few days in the Dry, a fully laden wagon could take up to six weeks. Finally the decision was made to build a railway, and in 1889 Pine Creek became the terminus of the North Australian Railway.

The pastoral industry has been the mainstay of the town throughout this century, although recently gold has regained a place in the town's economy as an open-cut mine has been established right on the edge of town.

Information
The old railway station residence now houses the local information centre, although it is open very irregular hours.

The ANZ on Railway Terrace is the only bank in town.

Things to See
The **railway station** is worth a quick wander. There are a number of old buildings still standing, as well as an old steam loco and a couple of carriages. Next to the station is the **Miners' Park** which has a number of old bits of equipment scattered about, and some fairly dry information boards.

More interesting perhaps is the **Pine Creek Museum**, which is housed in the old mining warden's residence, a prefabricated steel building which was moved here from Burrundie, a town close by, in 1913. The building is on Railway Terrace and is now owned by the National Trust. It is supposedly open from 11 am to 3 pm on weekdays during the Dry, but don't be surprised if it's not.

For an excellent **view** over the town and the open-cut mine, follow the signs on Main Terrace to a lookout. Also on Main St, across from the football oval, is the former **Playford Club Hotel**, a corrugated-iron relic of the gold rush days and mentioned in the famous novel *We of the Never Never*. For nearly 70 years it was the town's only pub; these days it's a private residence.

Places to Stay

The *Pine Creek Caravan Park* (☎ 8976 1217) is in the centre of town on Moule St, opposite the pub. It has sites at $10 ($15 with power), or there is air-con dormitory accommodation at $18.50 including linen.

The other alternative is the *Pine Creek Hotel* (☎ 8976 1288) on Moule St. It has air-con rooms which are a snip at $63/74.

UMBRAWARRA GORGE NATURE PARK

About three km along the Stuart Highway south of Pine Creek is the turn-off to Umbrawarra Gorge Nature Park, 22 km south-west along a dirt road (often impassable in the Wet). It's an excellent little spot with some fine Aboriginal rock-art sites, yet it sees few visitors.

The gorge takes its name from the Umbrawarra tin mine, which in 1909 was the Territory's largest. Little ore was ever removed, however, as a malaria epidemic swept through the area and left many miners dead. As the European miners left for better prospects, Chinese miners moved in and about 150 of them worked the area up until about 1925. The former mine site is now the car park area.

In Aboriginal legend, the gorge is the dreaming site of *Kuna-ngarrk-ngarrk*, the

white-bellied sea-eagle. Here he caught and ate a barramundi; the white flakes in the granite rock are said to be the scales of the barra, the quartz outcrops are eagle's shit.

Marked walking tracks lead from the car park to swimming holes in the gorge, or you can swim/scramble right along the gorge's five-km length. The area is home to the short-eared rock wallaby, and you're quite likely to see them leaping among the granite boulders.

There's a camp site with pit toilets and fireplaces.

Katherine

• *Population: 9200*

Apart from Tennant Creek, this is the only town of any size between Darwin and Alice Springs. It's a bustling little place where the Victoria Highway branches off to the Kimberley and Western Australia. The town's population has grown rapidly in recent years, partly because of the establishment of the large Tindal air-force base just south of town.

Katherine has long been an important stopping point, since the river it's built on and named after is the first permanent running water if you're coming north from Alice Springs. The town includes some historic old buildings, such as the Sportsman's Arms, featured in *We of the Never Never*, Jeannie Gunn's classic novel of turn-of-the-century outback life. The main interest here, however, is the spectacular Katherine Gorge 30 km to the east – a great place to camp, walk, swim, canoe, take a cruise or simply float along on an air mattress.

History

The Katherine area is the traditional home of the Jawoyn and Dagoman Aboriginal people, and following land claims in recent years they have received the title to large parcels of land in the area, including Nitmiluk (Katherine Gorge) National Park.

The first Europeans through the area were

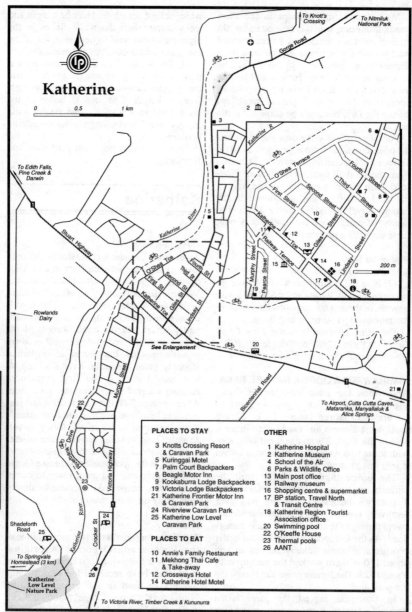

Katherine

To Knott's Crossing
To Nitmiluk National Park
Gorge Road

To Edith Falls, Pine Creek & Darwin

Katherine River

Rowlands Dairy

See Enlargement

To Airport, Cutta Cutta Caves, Mataranka, Manyallaluk & Alice Springs

Shadeforth Road

To Springvale Homestead (3 km)

Katherine Low Level Nature Park

To Victoria River, Timber Creek & Kununurra

Enlargement:
Katherine R.
O'Shea Terrace
First Street, Second Street, Third Street, Fourth Street
Katherine Tce
Railway Terrace
Giles Street
Lindsay Street
Murphy Street
Pearce Street
0 200 m

DARWIN TO KATHERINE

PLACES TO STAY
3 Knotts Crossing Resort & Caravan Park
5 Kuringgai Motel
7 Palm Court Backpackers
8 Beagle Motor Inn
9 Kookaburra Lodge Backpackers
19 Victoria Lodge Backpackers
21 Katherine Frontier Motor Inn & Caravan Park
24 Riverview Caravan Park
25 Katherine Low Level Caravan Park

PLACES TO EAT
10 Annie's Family Restaurant
11 Mekhong Thai Cafe & Take-away
12 Crossways Hotel
14 Katherine Hotel Motel

OTHER
1 Katherine Hospital
2 Katherine Museum
4 School of the Air
6 Parks & Wildlife Office
13 Main post office
15 Railway museum
16 Shopping centre & supermarket
17 BP station, Travel North & Transit Centre
18 Katherine Region Tourist Association office
20 Swimming pool
22 O'Keeffe House
23 Thermal pools
26 AANT

those in the expedition of Ludwig Leichhardt in 1844. The river was named the Catherine by John McDouall Stuart in 1862, but for some reason the current spelling was adopted. As was so often the case with Territory towns, it was the construction of the Overland Telegraph Line and the establishment of a telegraph station (at Knott's Crossing, a few km along the gorge road from the current town) which really got the town going.

Pastoral ventures soon followed, one of the most notable being that of Alfred Giles, who established Springvale station in 1878. Although his attempts at sheep and cattle farming were not outrageously successful, he did lay the foundations for the cattle industry which is important in the Katherine region today. The stone homestead Giles built still stands, about eight km from the town, and it's the heart of a thriving tourism venture.

The town found its current site when the railway bridge over the Katherine River was built in 1926. WW II saw Katherine become a major defence-force base, and it even received a bit of attention from the Japanese when nine bombers raided the town in March 1942.

The town now survives largely on the tourism generated by Katherine Gorge and the business from Tindal.

Orientation

Katherine's main street, Katherine Terrace, is also the Stuart Highway as it runs through town. Coming from the north-west, you cross the Katherine River Bridge just before the town centre. The Victoria Highway to Western Australia branches off a further 300 metres on. After another 300 metres Giles St, the road to Katherine Gorge, branches off in the opposite direction.

Information

At the south-eastern end of the town centre on the Stuart Highway is the Katherine Region Tourist Association office (☎ 8972 2650; fax 8972 2969) which is open Monday to Friday from 8.45 am to 5 pm, Saturday to 3 pm, and on Sunday from 9.30 am to 4 pm. The helpful staff here have an excellent range of printed material. Also of interest is the local newspaper, the *Katherine Times*. Tourism information is also broadcast on 88 MHz FM.

Diagonally opposite, at the 24-hour BP station, is Travel North (☎ 8972 1044), a major tour operator in the area, and this is also the transit centre where the long-distance buses pull in.

The GPO is on the corner of Katherine Terrace and Giles St. There are branches of the ANZ, Commonwealth and Westpac banks in Katherine.

In case of emergency the hospital (☎ 8973 9294) is on Giles St, about 2.5 km north of the town centre. Also on Giles St, but closer to the centre, there's a Parks & Wildlife office (☎ 8973 8770).

Annual events in Katherine include the Katherine Show (July), the Katherine Rodeo (July) and the Fabulous Flying Fox Festival, which runs throughout October and features local artists and performers.

Mimi Arts & Crafts on Pearce St is an Aboriginal-owned-and-run shop selling products made over a wide area, from the deserts in the west to the Gulf coast in the east.

Things to See

The railway arrived in 1926 as an extension of the line which until then had terminated at Pine Creek. Katherine's old railway station is now the **Railway Museum**, owned by the National Trust, and is on Railway Terrace, tucked away behind the Shell station on Katherine Terrace. It has been restored and now houses a display on railway history. It is open Monday to Friday from 10 am to noon and from 1 to 3 pm in the Dry season.

The small **Katherine Museum** is in the old airport-terminal building on Gorge Rd (the continuation of Giles St), about three km from the centre of town. There's a good selection of old photos and other bits and pieces of interest, including the original Gypsy Moth biplane flown by Dr Clyde Fenton, the first Flying Doctor. It is open

DARWIN TO KATHERINE

weekdays from 10 am to 4 pm, Saturday from 10 am to 2 pm and Sunday from 2 to 5 pm.

A few km beyond the museum and signposted off Gorge Rd is **Knott's Crossing**, the site of the original Katherine River crossing. The building here was formerly the Sportsmans Arms & Pioneer Cash Store. A little further again, and visible from the road, is one of the original pylons of the **Overland Telegraph**.

On Riverbank Dve, near the Victoria Highway, is **O'Keeffe House**, one of the oldest buildings in the town. It was originally built of simple bush poles, corrugated iron and flywire mesh by the army in 1943 as a recreation hut, and then became the officers' mess. After WW II the building passed through a number of hands, until it was bought in 1963 by Olive O'Keeffe, a nursing sister who became well known for her work in a number of places throughout the Territory over many years. The building was bought by the National Trust after 'Keeffie's' death in 1988.

The **School of the Air** on Giles St offers an opportunity to see how remote outback kids are taught. There are guided tours on weekdays during the school term.

Katherine has a good public **swimming pool** beside the highway on the Stuart Highway, about 750 metres past the information centre towards Mataranka. There are also some pleasant **thermal pools** beside the river, about two km south of town along the Victoria Highway.

The 105-hectare **Katherine Low Level Nature Park** is five km from town, just off the Victoria Highway. It's a great spot on the Katherine River, taking in four km of its shady banks, and the swimming hole by the weir is very popular in the Dry season; in the Wet flash-flooding can make it dangerous. Facilities provided here include picnic tables, toilets and gas barbecues. There are large colonies of little red-and-black flying foxes in the trees along the banks, while the water is the home of the northern snapping turtle. There's also plenty of the legendary barramundi and black bream.

Organised Tours

Tours are available from Katherine, taking in various combinations of the town and Springvale Homestead attractions, the Gorge, Cutta Cutta Caves, Mataranka and Kakadu. Most accommodation places can book you on these and you'll be picked up from where you're staying, or ask at the tourist office or Travel North.

There are excellent **Aboriginal tours** at Manyallaluk (see the Around Katherine section later in this chapter for details) and Jankanginya Tours (☎ toll-free 1800 089 103) take you out onto traditional Aboriginal land, sometimes referred to as Lightning Brothers country. Here you learn about bush tucker, crafts and medicine, and hear some of the stories associated with the rock art of the area. Accommodation is in a bush camp. The cost is $99 ($50 for children five to 15) for a one-day trip, or $240 ($120) for two days.

On the outskirts west of town, **Rowlands Dairy**, signposted off the road to Springvale Homestead, (☎ 8972 2122), is the Territory's only dairy farm, and the cows are kept in air-con comfort! On guided tours you can see the milk being processed at 10 am on Monday, Tuesday and Thursday, and see the milking daily at 3.30 pm. At $8 ($4 for children) it can be an expensive little outing.

Springvale Homestead, eight km south-west of town (turn right off the Victoria Highway after 3.8 km), claims to be the oldest cattle station in the Northern Territory. Today it's also a tourist-accommodation centre, and free half-hour tours around the old homestead are given once or twice daily. Throughout the year evening crocodile-spotting cruises ($33) are run from here, and three nights a week there are Aboriginal corroborees with demonstrations by the local Jawoyn people of fire making, traditional dance and spear throwing ($29.50 including barbecue). There's also horse riding and cattle musters by horseback.

For a trip along the Katherine River, Gecko Canoeing (☎ 8972 2224; fax 8972 2811) has excellent three-day safaris for $395. Springvale Homestead also has canoe hire at $8 per hour, $18 for a half day and $30 for a full day.

To Kakadu Travel North has two-day camping trips, which include Yellow Water, for $169. These include the park-entry fee, and end in Darwin.

Katherine Adventure Tours (☎ toll-free 1800 808 803; fax 8971 1176) has five-day trips (leaving Katherine on Tuesday) which include all the major park highlights, including Jim Jim and Twin falls, at a cost of $450. This tour also ends in Darwin.

Places to Stay

Camping There are several possibilities here. One of the nicest is *Springvale Homestead* (☎ 8972 1355; fax 8972 3201), right on the Katherine River. Shady camp sites cost $10 ($12 with power). It also has air-con budget units with fridge and attached bath at $39/48 for singles/doubles, and there is a licensed restaurant and a kiosk for snacks. It's eight km out of Katherine; turn right off the Victoria Highway after 3.8 km and follow the signs.

On the road to Springvale, five km from town, is the *Katherine Low Level Caravan Park* (☎ 8972 3962; fax 8972 2230), a good place close to the Low Level Nature Park. Camp sites are $12 for two, or $16 with power. On-site vans here cost $36.

Closer to town, on the Victoria Highway, is the *Riverview Caravan Park* (☎ 8972 1011), which has reasonably comfortable cabins for $40/45 singles/doubles and tent sites at $12 ($14 with power). The thermal pools are five minutes walk away.

The *Katherine Frontier Caravan Park* (☎ toll-free 1800 891 101; fax 8972 2790), four km south of town on the Stuart Highway, has camp sites at $16, plus a pool, barbecue area and licensed restaurant. This is actually part of the Frontier Katherine Motor Inn (see Motels).

The *Knott's Crossing Resort* (☎ 8972 2511; fax 8972 2628) on Giles St on the way out of town has a good range of facilities, and

sites at $14 ($17.50 powered). They also have a range of rooms (see Motels).

Hostels Katherine is also well supplied with hostels. All have a courtesy bus and do pick-ups from the bus station. None have a swimming pool.

Pick of the bunch is the *Kookaburra Lodge Backpackers* (☎ 8971 0257), on the corner of Lindsay and Third Sts, just a few minutes walk from the transit centre. It consists of air-con units with between six and 10 beds and costs $13 a night, or there are some twin rooms for $40. With so many people in each unit the bathroom and cooking facilities can get overcrowded at times, but it's a friendly and well-run place, and they also do canoe hire and transport out to Katherine Gorge (see that section later in the chapter for details).

Just around the corner is the *Palm Court Backpackers* (☎ 8972 2722), on the corner of Third and Giles Sts. It's in the most horrendously tasteless building, but the air-con rooms are uncrowded and have their own TV, fridge and bathroom. The problem here is that the communal cooking facilities are inadequate. The cost is $11 per person, $44 for double and $52 for a whole room (four beds).

Lastly, there's the *Victoria Lodge* (☎ 8972 3464) at 21 Victoria Highway, not far from the main street. It's a reasonable place with six-bed rooms at $13 per person, doubles at $35 and four-bed rooms for $65.

Motels Among the motels, the *Beagle Motor Inn* (☎ 8972 3998; fax 8972 3725) at the corner of Lindsay and Fourth Sts is one of the cheapest in Katherine, with 'budget' singles/doubles/triples at $30/40/50. These are pretty good value with air-con and fridge, although they do have common facilities. Rooms with attached bath cost $50/60.

On Giles St the *Kuringgai Motel* (☎ 8971 0266) has air-con units, some with cooking facilities, at $49/59.

The *Knotts Crossing Resort* (☎ 8972 2511) on Giles St also has air-con budget rooms with fridge, TV and attached bath at

$55. Standard rooms also have limited cooking facilities, and cost $64/72.

For something a bit better there's the *Katherine Frontier Motor Inn* (☎ toll-free 1800 891 101; fax 8972 2790) on the Stuart Highway. The rooms here also have cooking facilities and cost $112 for a double.

Places to Eat

Basically, Katherine has one or two of each of the usual types of Aussie eatery. Over the road from the transit centre, which has a 24-hour cafe, there's a *Big Rooster* fast-food place. The *Katherine Hotel Motel*, just up the main street, has counter meals as well as *Aussie's Bistro*, which is open for lunch and dinner daily and is pretty good value with main courses around $8 to $10. Also here is the more formal *Kirby's Restaurant*.

Over the road there's the *Golden Bowl* Chinese restaurant. A block further up on the corner of Warburton St, the *Crossways Hotel* does good counter meals for around $7.

Alfie's on the main street does good pizzas from $12.50 as well as other meaty main courses for around $10. This place is also open for breakfast from 6 to 10 am.

On the corner of Katherine Terrace and the Victoria Highway (Murphy St) is the *Mekhong Thai Cafe & Take-away*. This is an unusual find in an outback country town, and it has an extensive menu with entrees at $3 and main courses $8 to $11.

Over on First St there's *Annie's Family Restaurant*, a bright little place with main courses (steak/chicken/fish) for $15, including a self-serve salad bar. During the Dry it also does a full roast dinner for $14 or a soup and pasta lunch for $8.

Rusty's Creperie in Katherine Arcade is open from 9 am to 5 pm during the week. Meals here are served in a crêpe or on rice, and cost around $6.

Getting There & Away

Air Katherine Airport is eight km south of town, just off the Stuart Highway. You can fly to Katherine daily from Darwin ($144) and Alice Springs ($369) with Airnorth (☎ toll-free 1800 627 474). They also have

flights to Borroloola ($220, thrice weekly), Kalkaringi ($170, twice weekly) and Tennant Creek ($239, daily except Sunday).

Kakadu Air Services (☎ toll-free 1800 089 113) has daily flights between Katherine and Kakadu for $100, or a full-day tour including park entry and a Yellow Water cruise for $250.

Bus All buses between Darwin and Alice Springs, Queensland or Western Australia stop at Katherine, which means two or three daily to and from Western Australia, and usually four to and from Darwin, Alice Springs and Queensland. Typical fares from Katherine are: Darwin $40 ($20 advance purchase with Greyhound Pioneer), Alice Springs $131 ($66), Tennant Creek $65 ($33), Cairns $206 ($115) and Kununurra $50 ($25).

Greyhound Pioneer also has daily services to Kakadu ($30), from where you can connect to Darwin.

Car Rental There are a few car rental agencies in town. Avis (☎ 8971 0520) is at Hobbitts Auto Electrical at 47 Victoria Highway. Territory Rent-a-Car (☎ 8972 3183) is at 6 Katherine Terrace, and Hertz (☎ 8941 0944) is at Knott's Resort on Giles St.

Getting Around

You can rent bicycles at the Kookaburra Lodge, or there's bikes and mopeds for hire

from Katherine Moped & Bicycle Hire (☎ 8971 0727) at 67 Second St.

Travel North (☎ 8972 1044) has a bus service six times a day from the transit centre to the Gorge for $15 return, the first at 8.15 am, the last at 4.15 pm. The first return trip from the Gorge is at 9 am, the last at 5 pm.

Around Katherine

NITMILUK (KATHERINE GORGE) NATIONAL PARK

The Nitmiluk (Katherine Gorge) National Park lies just to the east of Katherine, and the highlight here is the spectacular Katherine Gorge, probably one of the most visited sites in the Northern Territory.

Strictly speaking, Katherine Gorge is 13 sandstones gorges, separated from each other by rapids of varying length. The gorge walls aren't high, but it is a remote, beautiful place. It is 12 km long and has been carved out by the Katherine River, which rises in Arnhem Land. Further downstream it becomes the Daly River before flowing into the Timor Sea 80 km south-west of Darwin. The difference in water levels between the Wet and Dry is staggering. During the dry season the gorge waters are calm, but from November to March they can become a raging torrent.

The Jawoyn Aboriginal people gained ownership of the former Katherine Gorge National Park in 1989 following a land claim hearing. The name was changed to Nitmiluk and the land leased back to Parks & Wildlife (at that time known as the Conservation Commission). It is managed by the Nitmiluk Board of Management. Nitmiluk is the Jawoyn name for the cicada dreaming, which takes in the area from the park headquarters up to the end of the first gorge.

Flora & Fauna

Most of the 3000-sq-km park features typical Top End woodland, with the dominant Darwin woollybutt and salmon gums, but there are also a number of endangered native plants found within the park, such as the endemic *Acacia helicophylla*.

Once again, the fauna within the park is also typical of the Top End. Large goannas are a common sight around the boat-ramp area, and various species of wallabies inhabit the cliff tops surrounding the gorge.

Birdlife is also abundant, one of the park's most valued inhabitants being the rare and endangered gouldian finch.

Information

It's 30 km by sealed road from Katherine to the visitor centre and the camp site, and nearly one km further to the car park where the gorge begins and the cruises start. The visitor centre (☎ 8972 1886) has displays and information on the national park, which includes extensive back country and Edith Falls to the north-west, as well as Katherine Gorge itself. There are details of a wide range of marked walking tracks starting here that go through the picturesque country south of the gorge, descending to the river at various points (see below). Some of the tracks pass Aboriginal rock paintings up to 7000 years old. The visitor centre is open daily from 7.30 am to 3 pm, and from 6 to 6.30 pm for de-registration of hikers.

The Katherine Gorge Canoe Marathon, organised by the Red Cross, takes place in June.

In line with the desires of the traditional owners, there's no entry fee to the park, although this is to some degree built into the price you pay for cruises.

Activities

Swimming Swimming in the gorge is safe in the Dry season. In the Wet the gorge is closed to boats and canoes. The only crocodiles around are the freshwater variety and they're more often seen in the cooler months.

Bushwalking There are some excellent bushwalks in the park, ranging from short day walks to a full five-day wilderness trek to Edith Falls. Walkers setting out on any walk (apart from the short walk to the lookout at the gorge and to Leilyn Loop at

Edith Falls) must register and de-register at the visitor centre at the gorge. If you plan to walk to Edith Falls there is a $50 refundable deposit payable at the start. This is just to ensure that people de-register at Edith (and get their $50 back) and don't involve many people in a time-wasting search just because they neglected to let someone know they'd finished the walk:

The main walks, all of which are clearly marked, are listed here. Note that all distances and timings are one way only.

Edith Falls
This 66-km walk takes five days and climbs the Arnhem Land escarpment. It takes in features such as the swamp-fed Biddlecombe Cascade (11.5 km from the Visitor Centre), the 30-metre Crystal Falls (20.5 km), the Amphitheatre Rainforest (31 km) and the Sweetwater Pool (61.5 km).

Butterfly Gorge
A two-hour, 5.5-km walk to a pocket of monsoon rainforest midway along the second gorge. There

are often large numbers of crow butterflies here, hence the name.

Lily Ponds
This three-hour walk takes you seven km along the gorge to the Lily Ponds Falls at the far end of the third gorge. This swimming hole can usually be used throughout the Wet season when swimming in the gorge itself is not an option.

Smitt's Rock
This rugged overnight trek which takes you the 11 km to Smitt's Rock near the start of the fifth gorge. There are excellent gorge views along the way, and you can swim and camp at Dunlop Swamp.

Eighth Gorge
Yep, this one goes to the eighth gorge, 16 km and one-day's walk from the visitor centre. Most of the way the trail is actually well away from the edge of the gorge, only coming down to it at the end.

Canoeing At the boat ramp by the main car park, about 500 metres beyond the visitor centre, you can rent canoes for one, two or three people (☎ toll-free 1800 808 211 or call at Kookaburra Lodge in Katherine). These

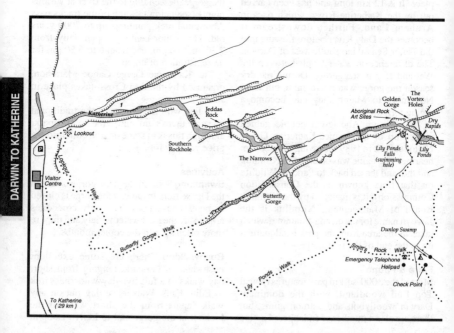

cost $20/28/36 for a half-day, or $27/42/57 for a whole day. This is a great way of exploring the gorge, although you need to be prepared to rough it a bit as the canoes have to be dragged over the rock bars which separate the gorges. The price includes the use of a waterproof drum for cameras and other gear, and life jackets if you feel the need.

You can also be adventurous and take the canoes out overnight, but you must book as only a limited number of people are allowed to camp out in the gorges. You get a map with your canoe showing things of interest along the gorge sides – Aboriginal rock paintings, waterfalls, plant life, and so on.

Organised Tours

Gorge Cruises The alternative and much less energetic way to get out onto the water is a cruise. These depart daily and there's a variety to choose from, none of them particularly cheap but bear in mind that part of the fee goes to the traditional owners in lieu of a

park-entry fee. During the season there's up to 1000 people coming through here each day, so it's no surprise that bookings on some cruises can be tight. It's a good idea to make a reservation the day before on ☎ toll-free 1800 089 103 or 8972 1253.

The two-hour run goes to the second gorge and includes a visit to some gorge-side rock paintings. These leave daily at 9 and 11 am, and at 1 and 3 pm; the cost is $25 ($10 children aged five to 15). The four-hour trip goes to the third gorge for $38 ($19.50), leaving at 9 and 11 am, and 1 pm. Finally, there's an eight-hour trip which takes you up to the fifth gorge, and also involves walking about four km. The cost is $65, and it departs daily at 9 am.

During the Wet only the four-hour 9 am cruise runs, and this only when the water is not too wild.

Guided Tours Every day at 1.30 pm there's a 2½-hour Aboriginal-guided bush tour

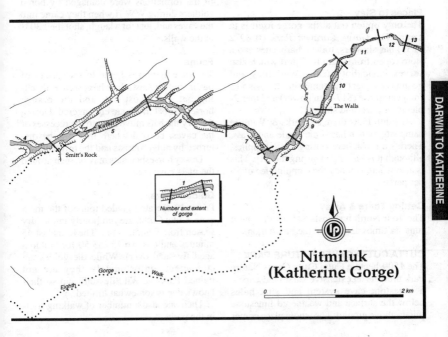

**Nitmiluk
(Katherine Gorge)**

DARWIN TO KATHERINE

which gives you an opportunity to learn a bit about the Jawoyn people and their traditional way of life. The tours leave from the boat ramp, from where you travel by boat to 17 Mile Creek, where the tour itself begins. The cost is $18 ($10 for children five to 15), and you can make reservations with Travel North in Katherine (☎ 8972 1044).

Scenic Flights You can also take half-hour light-aircraft flights with Brolga Air (☎ 8971 0700), which cost $47 ($38 for children aged four to 12), or helicopter flights with Gorge Helitours (☎ 8972 1253) at $60 for 15 minutes and $100 for half an hour.

Edith Falls

The Edith Falls are in the western corner of the park, and can be accessed by car from the Stuart Highway, 40 km north of Katherine. There's a beautiful plunge pool here for swimming, and a ranger is stationed here throughout the year.

Places to Stay

The only option out at the gorge itself is to camp. The *Gorge Caravan Park* (☎ 8972 1253) has showers, toilets, barbecues and a store (open from 7 am to 7 pm) which also serves basic hot meals. Wallabies and goannas frequent the camp site. It costs $13 for a camp site ($17 with power) and there's plenty of grass and shade.

At Edith Falls there's a Parks & Wildlife camp site, which has some shade and grass. There's a kiosk here selling basic supplies, although it is only open during the Dry. This is also where you pay the camping fee of $5 per person.

Getting There & Away

The Tour North bus costs $15 return, and it runs six times daily from the bus station.

CUTTA CUTTA CAVES NATURE PARK

The 1500-hectare Cutta Cutta Caves Nature Park protects an extensive karst landscape – a limestone-cave system and sink holes below the surface and weathered limestone pillars above ground. The whole place comes

as something of a surprise, as at first glance the grassy woodland landscape appears no different from anywhere else.

The caves are closed during the Wet, as electric lights tend to do spectacular things when they come into contact with water!

Geology

Geologically, the cave system is part of the Tindall Limestone formation, which was formed about 500 million years ago. The underground cavities have been formed by the limestone being diluted with rainwater which had become acidic from the soil. After millions of years caves are formed, and in these are typical limestone-cave calcite formations – stalactites, stalagmites, shawls and flowstones. While these caves do not compare in size with others elsewhere in Australia, they are interesting in that they are found in a region where it only rains for less than half the year, so that in the Dry season they are in fact quite dry. Unfortunately some of the formations were damaged by bored soldiers during WW II when they came into the caves and, just for a laugh, shot their 303s at the walls.

Fauna

The cave system is home to six species of bat, including Australia's largest cave-dwelling bat, the ghost bat, and the orange horseshoe bat. Both are endangered. During the Dry the bats move far into the recesses of the caves, beyond where they can be disturbed by noisy tourists and the bright lights.

Dusky horseshoe bats may be seen around the main cave area.

Guided Tours

Privately operated guided tours of the main cave, Cutta Cutta, are run hourly in the dry season from 9 am to 3 pm. The tours last 45 minutes and cost $6.75 ($3.50 for children aged five and over). While the guides are competent, unfortunately they are not trained Parks & Wildlife staff and so their knowledge is somewhat limited.

There are also a number of walking trails in the park.

MANYALLALUK

Manyallaluk is the former 3000-sq-km Eva Valley cattle station which abuts the eastern edge of the Nitmiluk (Katherine Gorge) National Park, the southern edge of Kakadu and the western edge of Arnhem Land. These days it is owned by the Jawoyn Aboriginal people, and the community here is showing the way when it comes to Aboriginal tourism – it has won at least one Brolga Award (the NT government's tourism awards) for its tours, and people generally speak very highly of them.

The name Manyallaluk comes from a Frog Dreaming site found to the east of the community, and on it are members not only of the Jawoyn but also from the Mayali, Ngalkbon and Rembarrnga language groups, with whom the Jawoyn share some traditions.

While it's possible to just rock up to the community and camp, the real reward comes in taking one of the tours offered by the community. Unlike many tourist operations in the Top End, these run throughout the year. The community is around 100 km from Katherine, and 35 km off the main track in to Arnhem Land. This 35-km stretch is along a well-maintained, all-season gravel road.

There is a reasonably well-stocked community store, which also sells some very reasonably priced locally made artifacts. Note that this is a dry community and alcohol is prohibited.

Organised Tours

There's a variety of tours to choose from, all operated by and from the community, although they do also make pick-ups in Katherine.

The one-day trip includes transport to and from Katherine, lunch, billy tea and damper, and you learn about traditional bush tucker and medicine, spear throwing and playing a dijeridu; the two-day trip adds swimming and rock-art sites. The day trip operates on Monday, Wednesday and Saturday from Katherine, and costs $95 ($63 for children aged five to 12), or with your own vehicle you can camp at Manyallaluk ($15 for two)

and take the day tour from there, which costs $63 ($42). It is possible just to camp without taking the tour, but you are restricted to the camping area. The cost for the two-day trip is $199 ($147).

There are also five-day trips out of Darwin, which take in either Litchfield or Kakadu in addition to Manyallaluk and Katherine Gorge, and these cost $825.

Bookings for the tours can be made through the community on ☎ 8975 4727; fax 8975 4724.

Places to Stay

It costs $15 for two to stay in the grassy camp site, or there are basic, four-bed mudblock units at $10 per person.

BARUNGA

Barunga is another Aboriginal community, 13 km along the Arnhem Land track beyond the Manyallaluk turn-off. Entry to the community is basically by permit only, but every year over the Queen's Birthday long weekend in June the settlement really comes alive for the Barunga Wugularr Sports & Cultural Festival.

For four days Aboriginal people come from all over the Territory for activities such as dancing and athletics, and arts and crafts also feature highly. On the Sunday there are demonstrations of traditional kills such as fire-lighting and the throwing of spears and boomerangs.

Permits are not required to visit Barunga during the festival, but you will need your own camping gear.

MATARANKA

Mataranka (population 160) is 103 km south-east of Katherine on the Stuart Highway. The town itself is just a stop on the highway; the real interest lies in the hot springs, seven km off the highway just south of town.

The first European explorers through this region were Leichhardt (1845) and John McDouall Stuart (1862). When A C Gregory came through in 1856 on his exploratory journey from Victoria River Depot (Timber

Creek), he came across a creek, which he named Elsey Creek, after Joseph Elsey, a young surgeon and naturalist in his party. The name went on to became famous, as Elsey station (established in 1881 and named after the creek) was the setting for the story *We of the Never Never*.

During WW II the town was another in a string of supply bases for the defence forces, and it had a camp hospital, although one member of the infantry battalion stationed here during the war remembers it as 'a disorganised convalescent camp, situated right in the middle of several extremely well-organised two-up schools.'

Information
The town has the usual gaggle of roadhouses, a police station (☎ 8975 4511) and a pub. The Stockyard is a souvenir shop and tea rooms.

Places to Stay & Eat
Although there are camping facilities in Mataranka itself, much better alternatives exist at Mataranka Hot Springs and Elsey National Park, both only a few km from town.

There's camping at the *Shell Roadhouse Caravan Park* (☎ 8975 4571) on the highway, with sites at $4 ($12 powered).

Somewhat more sophisticated is the *Territory Manor Caravan Park* (☎ 8975 4516), 300 metres off the highway, which is more of a holiday resort aimed at caravanners, and so all sites have power and en-suite bathrooms ($18). There's also a motel section here, with air-con units at $65/72.

The *Old Elsey Roadside Inn* (☎ 8975 4512) has just five rooms with air-con and attached bath at $45/55.

MATARANKA POOL NATURE PARK
The turn-off to the springs is just a couple of km south of Mataranka, and then it's eight km along a bitumen road.

The crystal-clear thermal pool here, in a pocket of pandanus palms, is a great place to wind down after a hot day on the road, though it can get crowded as it's very popular

among the tour groups. There's no need to worry about the freshness of the water though, as it comes out of the ground at more than 16,000 litres per minute at a temperature of 34°C.

The pool is just a short walk from the car park, which is at the very touristy Mataranka Homestead Tourist Resort. A couple of hundred metres away is the **Waterhouse River**, where you can walk along the banks, or rent canoes and rowing boats for $5 an hour.

Outside the homestead entrance is a replica of the **Elsey Station Homestead** which was made for the filming of *We of the Never Never*. There are interesting historical displays inside the replica.

Organised Tours
Two-hour horse rides are run twice daily by Hoofbeats & Bushtucker for $25. Enquire at the Mataranka Homestead.

Scenic flights in Tiger Moth aircraft are popular, and the cost is $50 for 10 minutes, or thrillseekers can go for the 20-minute aerobatics flight at $90.

For a taste of cattle-station life there are daily tours to Gorrie Station, which cost $90 including lunch.

Places to Stay & Eat
The *hostel* at Mataranka Homestead (☎ 8975 4544; fax 8975 4580) is quite comfortable and has some single and twin rooms, though the kitchen is small. It costs $15 per person ($13 with YHA card) including linen.

There's a large *camp site* at the homestead, with plenty of grass and shade, and decent facilities. Camping is $14 for a site ($18 with power), and air-con motel rooms with private bathroom are $74 for two. In between there are self-contained budget cabins which cost $60 for two or three people, $70 for four or five people. There's a store where you can get basic groceries, a bar with snacks and meals (not cheap), or you can use the camp site barbecues. There's often live entertainment here on weekend evenings during the Dry.

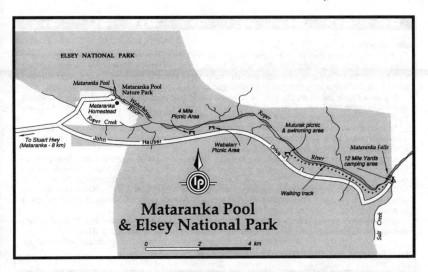

Mataranka Pool
& Elsey National Park

Getting There & Around

Long-distance buses travelling up and down the Stuart Highway make the eight-km detour to call at the homestead.

ELSEY NATIONAL PARK

The 138-sq-km national park abuts the Mataranka Pool Nature Park, and is accessed along John Hauser Drive, which leaves the Mataranka access road a couple of km before the homestead.

The park takes in the long stretch of the Roper River, which has some excellent monsoon forest along its banks. If you're coming up from the south this is the first really good example of this type of habitat. Also within the park are colourful tufa limestone formations, such as at the Mataranka Falls on the eastern edge of the park. (These formations crumble easily so take care not to damage them.)

While the park doesn't have the thermal pools, neither does it have the masses of people which flock to them, and it's a much more peaceful and low-key place.

Flora & Fauna

In addition to the lush tropical vegetation along the river banks, there are stands of large pandanus palms south of the river.

In the river you may well see snake-necked turtles. You definitely won't see barramundi unless there's one on the end of your line.

Activities

There are some good **swimming spots** along the river, one of the best being at the 12 Mile Yards camping area, where there's a couple of pontoons.

A four-km **walking track** takes you along the bank of the Roper River between the Mulurark day-use area and the Mataranka Falls at the eastern edge of the park.

Canoe hire is available from the 12 Mile Yards camp site.

Facilities

The *12 Mile Yards camp site* has lots of grass and shade, and good facilities, including a kiosk and solar hot showers, although there is no electricity. Camping here costs $5 for adults ($1 for children). There's also a boat ramp.

Jeannie Gunn

Probably the most widely known women's name in the Territory is that of Jeannie Gunn. Originally from Melbourne, where she had run a school for young ladies, she arrived in the Territory in 1902 with her husband, Aeneas, who had already spent some years in the Territory and was returning to take up the manager's position at Elsey Station.

It was a brave move on the part of Jeannie, as at that time there were very few European women living in the Territory, especially on isolated cattle stations. The trip from Darwin to Elsey station was made during the Wet and took several weeks.

Station life was tough, but Jeannie adapted to it and eventually gained the respect of the men working there. She also gained a good understanding of the local Aboriginal people, a number of whom worked on the station.

Only a year after their arrival at Elsey, Aeneas contracted malarial dysentery and died. Jeannie returned to Melbourne and soon after recorded her experiences of the Top End in the novel *We of the Never Never* in 1908. While at the station she had been a keen observer of the minutiae of station life, and was able to record these observations in her book in a way which captured the imagination of the people down south who led such a different existence. These days her depiction of Aboriginal people seems somewhat patronising.

Jeannie went on to become involved with the RSL, and in 1939 was awarded an OBE for her services to Australian literature. She died in Melbourne in 1961 at the age of 91.

Her book remains one of the classics of outback literature, recording in detail the lives of the early pioneers, and was made into a film in 1981. ■

ELSEY CEMETERY

The Elsey Cemetery lies a few km off the Stuart Highway on a section of old highway, five km south of the Roper Highway turn-off. It is here that a number of the characters who appeared in the novel *We of the Never Never* are buried.

During WW II, the army was given the task of locating the bodies of these people. A number of them, including Henry Ventlia Peckham ('The Fizzer'), were located and their remains moved to the small Elsey Cemetery. Also buried here is Aeneas Gunn, the manager of the station and husband of Jeannie Gunn, who died of malarial dysentery just a year after they moved here from Melbourne.

The site of the original homestead, as near as can be determined, is half a km or so beyond the cemetery, by the bridge over the Elsey Creek. A plaque and cairn mark the spot.

The Barkly Region

The Barkly region occupies a huge area of the Territory, and is the transition zone – from the green of the Top End to the distinctive red ochre of the centre. The Stuart Highway splits the region neatly down the middle – with the Barkly Tableland plateau and Gulf region to the east, the rich Victoria River pastoral district to the west, which gradually gives way to the spinifex-dotted expanses of the Tanami Desert south of it. It is predominantly cattle country.

As might be expected in the transition zone between the tropical Top End and the arid centre, the rainfall in this region varies markedly, from around 400 mm in the south to over 1000 mm along the coast, but is less predictable than elsewhere in the Top End. This in turn means that the typical Top End eucalypt woodland is less suited to the climate, and the area is instead dominated by open Mitchell and kangaroo grass plains. It is these grasses which make the Victoria River district such good pastoral country.

Victoria River District

The Victoria River itself, one of the largest in northern Australia, starts out in rugged country on the northern fringes of the Tanami Desert and winds its way north through some of the Territory's best pastoral land before entering the sea in the Joseph Bonaparte Gulf.

Travellers to the area today tend to just pass along the Victoria Highway, which bisects the region, connecting Katherine on the Stuart Highway with Kununurra over the border in Western Australia. The main attractions of the region are found along the highway. These are two of the state's less visited national parks, the Gregory and Keep River national parks, and the historic town of Timber Creek.

It's 513 km on the Victoria Highway from

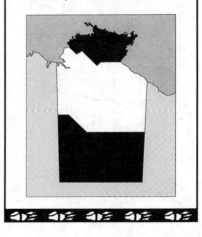

Katherine to Kununurra in Western Australia. The road is bitumen but still only one vehicle wide in places, although it's rapidly being widened.

As you approach the Western Australian border you start to see the boab trees found in much of the north-west of Australia. There's a 1½-hour time change when you cross the border. There's also a quarantine inspection post, and all fruit, vegetables and some other foodstuffs such as honey must be left here when travelling from the Territory

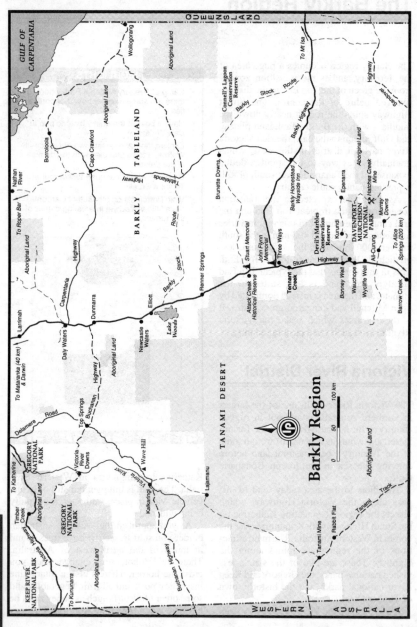

Barkly Region

to Western Australia. When entering the Territory from WA, there's also a variety of fruits and vegetables which must be deposited here. For more details, contact the NT Department of Primary Industries & Fisheries in Darwin (☎ 8981 8733).

History

European exploration first came when the British naval vessel, the HMS *Beagle* was surveying the north coast in 1839, having recently completed a five-year worldwide journey with a young naturalist on board by the name of Charles Darwin. The *Beagle* negotiated the difficult mouth of the Victoria River (named by the *Beagle's* captain, John Wickham, in honour of Queen Victoria) and sailed 200 km up the river to its navigable limit, which today is the site of Timber Creek.

In the 1850s the Colonial Office in London, with the prompting of the Royal Geographic Society, funded an expedition which was to travel from the Victoria River east to the Gulf of Carpentaria. The expedition was led by a young surveyor, Augustus Gregory, and the party landed at, and named, Timber Creek, when their ship, the *Tom Tough*, ran aground in shallows and was repaired with local timber.

For the next six months Gregory and his party surveyed the area extensively, and it was largely thanks to his glowing reports of the region that pastoral activity and European settlement followed. His reports also prompted the South Australian government's demand that the northern part of Australia should come within its borders.

The 1880s saw a pastoral boom, and it was during this time that the major stations of the Victoria River district were established – Victoria River Downs (the so-called 'Big Run' or plain VRD), Wave Hill, Bradshaw, Auvergne and Willeroo.

The cattle industry became the backbone of the Territory economy, and in the post-war recovery period of the 1950s there was strong worldwide demand for meat, but particularly from Britain. This led to the development of the infrastructure across the

Once or twice a year the livestock are mustered for sale or to check on their welfare

Territory and Queensland, but particularly in the Victoria River district where cattle were so important. Vesteys, a huge British company which owned more than 100,000 sq km of stations in the Territory, developed the 'road train' for cattle haulage, and the Commonwealth government started pouring money into 'beef roads'. By 1975, $30 million had been spent on 2500 km of roads. One of these single-lane bitumen roads is the Delamere Road, which runs from the Victoria Highway to Wave Hill station (a Vesteys property).

In 1966 the area became the focus for the Aboriginal land rights issue, when 200 Gurindji Aboriginal workers and their families on Wave Hill station, led by Vincent Lingiari, walked off the job in protest against poor living and working conditions. It wasn't until 1975, when the Whitlam Labor government was in power in Canberra, that the Gurindji received title to 3200 sq km of claimed land at Wave Hill, and it was 1986 before full ownership was granted.

VICTORIA RIVER CROSSING

The spot where the Victoria Highway crosses the Victoria River, 192 km south-west of Katherine, is known, not surprisingly, as Victoria River Crossing (on some maps it's simply marked Victoria River).

The setting here is superb. The crossing is snug among sandstone gorges, and the high cliffs and flat-top range are quite a sight. Much of the area around the crossing, either side of the road, forms the eastern section of the **Gregory National Park** (see that section later in this chapter), and there are picnic facilities at **Sullivans Creek**, about 10 km east of the crossing.

The settlement basically consists of just one roadhouse, the *Victoria River Wayside Inn* (☎ 8975 0744), which has a very pleasant camping area ($4 for a site, $5 with power), or air-con motel units with fridge and tea/coffee making facilities at $36/46. It also has a well-stocked store, a bar, dining room with decent pub-type meals from around $10, and is open daily from 7 am to 11 pm.

TIMBER CREEK

Almost exactly 100 km west of Victoria River Crossing is Timber Creek (population 120), really the only town between Katherine and Kununurra. It is close to the Victoria River at the foot of the rugged Newcastle Ranges.

Today the town relies almost entirely on passing trade as people stop to rest and refuel, but it's worth stopping for longer as the area is steeped in history, and amply repays any time spent here.

Timber Creek is also the best place to stock up with supplies and fuel before heading off into the Gregory National Park.

History

In 1839 the *Beagle* negotiated the river to a spot about eight km from town which came to be known as the Victoria River Depot. The depot was established to service the new pastoral leases which had opened up the country to the south.

Race relations were an early problem, and a police station was set up here at the turn of the century to establish order and help control the 'hostile' Aboriginal people. These days the police station is a museum.

Information

The town has a supermarket and a store (both with fuel), medical clinic (☎ 8975 0727), police station (☎ 8975 0733), pub, caravan park and motel.

There's also a Parks & Wildlife office (☎ 8975 0888) about one km west of town on the highway, and it has some informative displays on the region, and good wallmaps of Gregory National Park. There's no bank, but the roadhouses have EFTPOS facilities.

Boat hire is available from Fogarty's store and there's a boat ramp nearby.

The colourful Timber Creek Races are held over three days in the first weekend of September, the highlight being the Saturday night Ball.

Things to See

Behind the new police station, which is about two km west of town, is the **Police Station**

Museum. This station was built in 1908 to replace the 1898 original, and is worth a browse. It's open from 3 to 5 pm daily.

A few km beyond the museum is the **Victoria River Depot Historical Reserve**, the site of the original port/depot that initially serviced the area. Also in this area is the **Gregory's Tree Historical Reserve**, which protects a boab tree which has the initials of the European who first opened up this area, A C Gregory, carved into it.

Organised Tours

Max Fogarty, local character and proprietor of Fogarty's Store, runs Max's Victoria River Tours. The tours include a two-hour trip on the Victoria River, and you'll be shown fresh and saltwater crocodiles, fish and turtles being fed, and you can try billy tea, play the dijeridu and light a fire using fire sticks. Max has a good knowledge of the flora and fauna and local history. The tours leave daily at 8 am during the Dry, and cost $35 ($20 for children seven to 14) and bookings can be made at Max's information centre in Timber Creek (☎ /fax 8975 0850).

Places to Stay & Eat

The *Circle F Caravan Park* (☎ 8975 0722), by the Timber Creek Hotel/Fogarty's Store, has sites at $7.50 ($11 with power), or single, air-con bunkhouse rooms at $18 with linen and towel supplied. There are also four-bed, self-contained cabins at $55. The caravan park is also the site of the motel, and there are five units at $60 for up to three people.

Much the same is offered next door at the *Timber Creek Wayside Inn* (☎ 8975 0732), with camping at $3 per person ($11 per site with power), rooms with common facilities at $28/42/55 for single/double/quad, and motel rooms at $75.

The *Wayside Inn* and the pub both do meals.

At Big Horse Creek, on the river only a few km west of town, there's a *camp site* maintained by Parks & Wildlife.

Getting There & Away

The long-distance buses call through on the route between Darwin and Perth.

GREGORY NATIONAL PARK

The Gregory National Park, at nearly one million hectares it's the second largest in the Territory, and sees remarkably few visitors, yet has some superb gorge country, reminders of the early European pioneering efforts and links to the region's Aboriginal people – the Wardaman, Ngariman, Ngaliwurri,

---

The Duracks

The Duracks are firmly linked with cattle and the opening up of interior Australia. Brothers Patrick (Patsy) and Michael Durack took up land on Cooper Creek in western Queensland in the 1860s, and they were soon joined by members of their extended family.

With the discovery of good pastoral land in the Kimberley, the Duracks secured land in the Ord River in 1882. Having taken up the land, a huge cattle muster was organised and in June 1863 four parties of drovers with a total of 7500 head of cattle set off from the Cooper Creek area. On the map the trip was a neat 4000 miles (6440 km), but in 'drover's miles', meandering from water hole to water hole and grassland to grassland, it was much further.

It took two years and four months to make the journey, and both the men and cattle suffered greatly along the way – at one point they were held up at a water hole for months waiting for the drought to break. Many cattle were lost to pleuropneumonia and tick fever. Nevertheless, the party reached the Ord in September 1885 and still had enough cattle to establish three stations – Rosewood, Argyle and Lissadel.

Patsy Durack's granddaughter, Mary, became a popular author and many of her novels were set in the Kimberley. Her most well-known work is *Kings in Grass Castles*, and in it she describes the great trek. ■

Nungali, Jaminjung and Karrangpurra groups.

The park was gazetted in 1990 and has at its core the former Bullita station, but it also includes parts excised from neighbouring stations, including Victoria River Downs, Humbert River, Delamere, Auvergne and Innesvale. The park actually consists of two separate sectors: the eastern sector, known as the Victoria River section, which surrounds the Victoria River Crossing (see that section earlier in this chapter), and the much larger western sector, the Bullita sector, south of Timber Creek. The two areas are separated

by the Stokes Range Aboriginal land. Bullita was originally an outstation of the Durack family properties.

The park offers a chance to really get off the track. There's excellent fishing, bush camping and a 4WD track which tests both vehicle and driver.

Flora & Fauna

The flora of the park varies with the terrain and landforms. The northern part consists of grassy woodland, with pockets of monsoon forest, while the southern hills are dominated by spinifex grass, which explorer Ernest

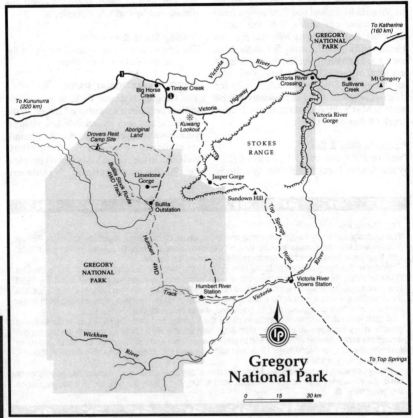

Gregory National Park

0   15   30 km

Giles dubbed 'that abominable vegetable production'. Less common plants found within the park include: the Victoria palms, a livistona palm that grows on the sandstone escarpments, and the northern grey box, a eucalypt endemic to the park.

There is not a great deal of animal life to be seen, although wallabies are reasonably common. What the park lacks in animals it makes up for with birds – lorikeets, parrots, budgerigars and mannikins are all active during the Dry.

Information
Information on the park can be obtained from the Parks & Wildlife office in Timber Creek (☎ 8975 0888), or from the Bullita ranger station (☎ 8975 0833).

To travel on either of the 4WD tracks (see below) you need a permit from the Timber Creek office, and on the Bullita Stock Route track there is a book at each end of the track which you sign.

The Bullita sector of the park is sometimes closed during the Wet. Both the 4WD tracks are closed from October to May.

Bullita Outstation
The old homestead here still has the original timber stockyards, and the name of one of the Duracks is carved in a boab tree nearby. The homestead is 52 km from the Victoria Highway along a well-maintained gravel road suitable for conventional vehicles.

Limestone Gorge
Limestone Gorge is nine km off the main Bullita access track, and it offers excellent swimming due to the absence of saltwater crocs that are found elsewhere in the park. There's also a Limestone Ridge walk which is marked by red flashes and takes about 1½ hours, and a camp site.

Bullita Stock Route 4WD Track
This 90-km track follows part of an old stock route into the western part of the park through some beautiful limestone-gorge country as far as the Drovers Rest camp site (50 km from Bullita Outstation), then loops

back to join the main Bullita access track, 27 km from the Victoria Highway.

Cattle were taken from Bullita and Humbert River stations along this track to the Auvergne Stock Route further north, and from there on to the meatworks in Wyndham (WA). The Spring Creek Yards (13 km from Bullita Outstation) were typical of yards used during cattle drives, when up to 500 head may be moved.

At the junction of the Spring Creek and East Baines River (21 km), a huge boab was obviously the site of a regular drovers' camp – 'Oriental Hotel' is carved into it and still clearly visible.

Humbert 4WD Track
This 112-km track along an old packhorse trail is an alternative entry or exit point for the park. It connects Bullita with Humbert River Station, just outside the south-western edge of the park and 30 km west of Victoria River Downs. The track was originally a supply trail for Humbert River from Victoria River Depot. It passes through some superbly scenic and quite isolated country, and it takes about six hours from Bullita to Humbert River.

Facilities
There are good *camp sites* at both Bullita and Limestone Gorge, which have fireplaces and pit toilets. A fee of $1 per person is payable into an honesty box at each site.

KEEP RIVER NATIONAL PARK
From Timber Creek the Victoria Highway continues west the 188 km to the WA border. The 570-sq-km Keep River National Park abuts the border, on the northern side of the highway.

The park has some stunning geological sandstone formations and within it are a number of significant Aboriginal rock-art sites. This region of the Territory is the tribal area of the Mirriwung and Gadjerong Aboriginal people.

Information
There's a rangers' station (☎ (091) 67 8827)

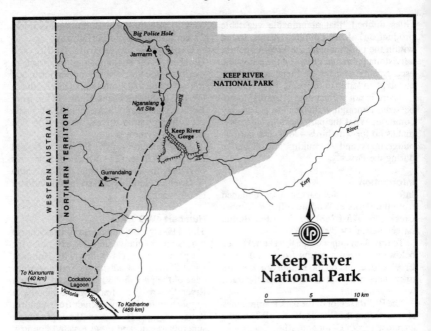

**Keep River
National Park**

0   5   10 km

three km into the park from the main road, although this is only a residence, not a visitor centre.

Bushwalkers intending to camp overnight in the park away from the designated camp sites need to obtain permits from the rangers, and preferably carry a topographic map (1:100,000 Keep 4766) and a compass. Reliable water is only available from a source near Cockatoo Lagoon near the park entrance, and summer temperatures of 37°C can make it very unpleasant for walking.

Things to See
The four-km long **Keep River Gorge** in the centre of the park makes an excellent walk, and there are some Aboriginal paintings along its walls. In the southern part of the park the **Gurrandalng Walk** heads off from the camping area through some varied country, and there are excellent views along the way. Just three km from the highway near the ranger station is the easy **Cockatoo**

Lagoon Walk, which has a bird-hide overlooking a lagoon.

From the car park at Nganalang, in the north of the park mid-way between Gurrandalng and Jarrnarm, it's only a 10-minute walk to a **rock-art site** on a sandstone outcrop.

Facilities
There are two *camp sites* with pit toilets, at Gurrandalng (15 km into the park) and Jarrnarm (28 km).

BUCHANAN HIGHWAY
The Buchanan Highway, named after legendary stockman, Nat Buchanan, is one of the Territory's loneliest stretches of road, but it's not without interest. It offers an alternative route into Western Australia, running roughly parallel to (and about 100 to 150 km south of) the Victoria Highway, connecting Dunmarra, 36 km south of Daly Waters on the Stuart Highway, with Halls Creek in

Nat Buchanan

Although Nathaniel Buchanan was not a great land-holder in the mould of Kidman or the Duracks, he was a great cattleman and drover, and was responsible for the settlement of huge areas of the outback.

Known as Old Bluey because of his shock of red hair, Buchanan led many drives through Queensland and the Northern Territory, including what was probably the largest cattle drive ever to be undertaken in Australia: the movement of 20,000 head from Aramac in Queensland to Glenco Station near Adelaide River in the Northern Territory.

In 1896, at the age of 70, Buchanan set off from Sturt Creek in northern Western Australia, trying to find a direct route across the Tanami Desert to Tennant Creek which was suitable for cattle, rather than having to take them much further north. Although the hoped-for route didn't eventuate, this was probably the first European crossing of the Tanami Desert.

Buchanan was accompanied on some of his drives by his son Gordon, who wrote about his experiences in the book *Packhorse & Waterhole*. ∎

Western Australia. Although you'll see very few vehicles on it, the road is in good condition and is mostly gravel; only the section from Kalkaringi to Top Springs is bitumen, as this forms part of the beef road which connects Wave Hill station with the Victoria Highway and Katherine.

From the Stuart Highway it's 180 km to Top Springs, a stretch of fairly monotonous road which can seem never ending. Only in the last 10 or 20 km before Top Springs does it go through some scenic undulating hills studded with termite mounds.

Top Springs

Top Springs is not a pretty place; it consists solely of a roadhouse and a road junction. The Top Springs themselves are nearby and good for a swim, and 15 km away is the remains of the original pub, which burnt down in the 1950s. The **Murranji Stock Route**, which connected Newcastle Waters with Wave Hill and was pioneered by Nat Buchanan (see aside), passed through Top Springs.

From Top Springs the bitumen **Delamere Road** heads north to join the Victoria Highway (164 km), or you can head southeast to Kalkaringi and WA, or travel north-west to Victoria River Downs and Timber Creek.

Places to Stay & Eat At the roadhouse, the *Wanda Inn* (☎ 8975 0767), there's a very lively bar, patronised largely by the local Aboriginal people. There's a grassy camping area ($8, $12 with power), swimming pool, three air-con motel units at $48/58, and pub rooms with common facilities at $35.

Victoria River Downs

The dirt road heading north-west from Top Springs takes you to the famous Victoria River Downs station (100 km). The road is generally in good condition and can easily be travelled by conventional vehicles in the Dry.

Victoria River Downs, known throughout the Top End as VRD, or the Big Run, is one of the largest stations in the area (over 12,000 sq km), and is the focal point of the area. It was one of the many large pastoral leases established in the 1880s and stocked with cattle brought in on the hoof from Queensland. Such is its stature that there's even been a book written about the place (*The Big Run* by Jock Makin).

The road passes right by the homestead area, which looks more like a small town than a station. Heli-Muster, a company specialising in helicopter mustering of cattle, also bases itself here. There are no tourist facilities, although the station does have a general store which the public are welcome to use (open weekdays 7 am to 5 pm, Saturday to 12.30 pm).

From VRD the road continues north to the Victoria Highway (140 km), passing through the spectacular **Jasper Gorge** (57 km, good camping) on the edge of the Gregory National Park. If you are heading for the

Vincent Lingiari & the Wave Hill Stockmen's Strike of 1966

Aboriginal stockmen played a large role in the early days of the pastoral industry in the Northern Territory. Because they were paid such paltry wages (which often never even materialised) a pastoralist could afford to employ many of them, and run his station at a much lower cost. White stockmen received regular and relatively high wages, were given decent food and accommodation, and were able to return to the station homestead every week. By contrast Aboriginal stockmen received poor food and accommodation, little or no money, and would often spend months in the bush with the cattle.

In the 1960s Vincent Langiari was a stockman on the huge Wave Hill station, owned by the British Vesteys company. His concern with the way Aboriginal workers were treated led to an appeal to the North Australian Workers' Union (NAWU), which had already applied to the federal court for equal wages for Aboriginal workers. The federal court approved the granting of equal wages in March 1966, but it was not to take effect until December 1968. The decision led Lingiari to ask the Wave Hill management direct for equal wages. The request was refused, and, on 23 August 1966, the Aboriginal stockmen walked off the station and camped in nearby Wattie Creek. They were soon joined by others, and before long only stations which gave their Aboriginal workers not only good conditions but also respect were provided with workers by Lingiari and the other Gurindji elders.

The Wattie Creek camp gained a lot of local support, from both White and Aboriginal people, and it soon developed into a sizeable community with housing and a degree of organisation. Having gained the right to be paid equally, Lingiari and the Gurindji people felt, perhaps for the first time since the arrival of the pastoralists, that they had some say in the way they were able to live. This victory led to the hope that perhaps they could achieve something even more important – title to their own land. To this end Lingiari travelled widely in the eastern states campaigning for land rights, and finally made some progress with the Whitlam government in Canberra. On 16 August 1975, Whitlam attended a ceremony at Wattie Creek which saw the handing over of 3200 sq km of land, now known as Daguragu.

Lingiari was awarded the Order of Australia Medal for service to the Aboriginal people, and died at Daguragu in 1988.

The well-known Australian songwriter and musician, Paul Kelly, has written a song about Lingiari and the stockman's strike called *From Little Things Big Things Grow* which is on his 1991 album *Comedy*. ∎

Gregory National Park and are travelling by 4WD vehicle, it's possible to enter the park via a rough track from Humbert River station, 30 km west of VRD. Before doing so, however, phone the Parks & Wildlife office in Timber Creek (☎ 8975 0888) and advise them of your plans.

Kalkaringi

From Top Springs the Buchanan Highway becomes bitumen and swings south-west on the 170-km stretch to Kalkaringi on the Victoria River. This small town exists basically to service the Aboriginal community of **Dagaragu**, eight km north. Dagaragu was formerly known as Wattie Creek and grew out of the Aboriginal stockmen's strike of 1966, which ultimately led to the granting of land to Aboriginal people (see aside).

For visitors the town offers a chance to refuel and refresh, and there's limited fishing and swimming opportunities in the river. The town is basically a 'dry' area, the only place with a liquor licence being the legendary *Frank's Bar & Grill* (see the following Places to Stay & Eat for details).

The gravel road west to Halls Creek in WA is generally good, although it gets badly corrugated at times when it hasn't seen the grader for a while, and can be treacherous, and even cut for (usually) short periods by creek crossings during the Wet.

Information Facilities in the town include a police station (☎ 8975 0790), service station (which is also the store, takeaway and caravan park, open 9 am to 6 pm weekdays, 3 to 6 pm weekends) and a medical centre staffed by a nursing sister.

Places to Stay & Eat The only accommodation is camping at the *Kalkaringi Service Station Caravan Park* (☎ 8975 0788), where there's plenty of grass and shade. Sites cost $7, or $12 with power.

Having come all this way you simply cannot leave without paying a visit to *Frank's Bar & Grill* out at the sports oval. This is the headquarters of the local cricket club (which is how it got its liquor licence) and is open from 4 pm. There are no walls, and the roof is only spinifex grass. The best day for atmosphere is Saturday when locals come in from hundreds of km around for a game.

Getting There & Away Airnorth (☎ toll-free 1800 627 474) have twice-weekly flights to Darwin ($314), Lajamanu ($80) and Katherine ($170).

South to Lajamanu & the Tanami Track The other possibility from Kalkaringi is to head south to Lajamanu (104 km) in the Tanami Desert, from where it's a further 232 km to the Tanami Track. Again, this track is generally in pretty good condition and a 4WD vehicle is probably not necessary, but check with the police in Kalkaringi before heading off. The road passes through some beautiful country, and about 10 km south of the Buchanan Highway the country changes from good cattle country (Mitchell grass plains with sparse tress) to much less hospitable spinifex country – the change is so sudden that it's almost as though a dividing line has been drawn between the two.

Lajamanu is an Aboriginal community, and while you don't need a permit to enter the town for fuel and supplies (10 am to noon and 3 to 5 pm weekdays, Saturday to noon only, Sunday closed; ☎ 8975 0896), there's nowhere to stay and no other facilities. There's also a police station (☎ 8975 0622).

Down the Track

From Mataranka the Stuart Highway continues its relentless progress south towards Alice Springs. It is on this section of the highway that the transition from the green of the Top End to the red ochre of central Australia is made.

Although there are long stretches on this road where there's not a great deal to see, there are enough distractions in between to make the journey pleasant. Don't fall into the trap of just trying to get it over and done with.

LARRIMAH
Larrimah (population 20) is a small settlement on the Stuart Highway, consisting of a roadhouse, a pub and the grandly named Green Park Tourist Complex. In its heyday it was the southern terminus of the North Australian Railway, although even then it wasn't much bigger than it is today.

The town is one of many along the highway which was important during WW II, and there are still reminders of that era around town today. There's also a great outback pub.

History

Late last century settlers established themselves at Birdum Creek, about five km from the town, and it was to here that the railway line ran. During WW II, however, the army established a base on the highway, which they named Larrimah ('meeting place'), largely because Birdum was subject to wet-season flooding. Nevertheless, at one stage the Birdum Hotel became the HQ for the American war effort in the Pacific.

In 1942 the RAAF (Royal Australian Air Force) started work on Gorrie Airfield, 10 km north of Larrimah. It became one of the largest in the Pacific, and nearly half a million pounds was spent by the American forces on the construction of the field and its facilities. At its peak, Gorrie was the base for 6500 military and personnel.

After WW II when the troops had gone home and the extensive army buildings sold off, Larrimah's population fell to less than 50, a level it has maintained ever since. The Birdum Hotel was dismantled and moved to its current location in Larrimah; the rest of the settlement was abandoned.

In 1976 the railway line closed as it had long since become uneconomical to run.

Things to See

It's worth having a look at the remaining military buildings and the airstrip at **Gorrie Airfield**, and the remains of the abandoned settlement of **Birdum**.

Places to Stay & Eat

If you just want a camp site without power, they are free at the *Wayside Inn* (☎ 8975 9931). For a powered site it's $5. They also have basic rooms with common facilities at $10 per person.

The *Green Park Tourist Complex* (☎ 8975 9937) is slightly more sophisticated and also has a swimming pool. Camping costs $3 per person, or $9 per person for a powered site.

The *Top of Town Shell Roadhouse* (☎ 8975 9932) has budget rooms with common facilities at $25 for a double, or with attached bath at $45.

Drop in to the *Wayside Inn* for a beer or a meal.

DALY WATERS

The historic little settlement of Daly Waters lies just four km off the Stuart Highway. With just a handful of houses it would be easy to pass over, but the pub here is an amazingly eccentric little place, and the nearby airfield was Australia's first international airport. This is one of the detours off the Stuart Highway which shouldn't be missed.

On the highway itself, four km south of the Daly Waters turn-off, is the Daly Waters Junction, where the Carpentaria Highway heads off due east the 234 km to Borroloola and the Gulf.

The Daly Waters Rodeo, held over two days in September, is the social event of the year, with a dance held at the pub on the Saturday evening.

History

It was on John McDouall Stuart's third attempt to cross the continent from south to north that he came upon the small creek here, which he named in honour of the then governor of South Australia. He also carved a large letter 'S' on a tree about a km from the pub (signposted).

In 1872 the Overland Telegraph Line came through, and a repeater station was built. An exploration party in the Kimberley led by Alexander Forrest was rescued by a party sent out from Daly Waters, after Forrest rode to the line and followed it to Daly Waters. A memorial cairn alongside the Stuart Highway about 50 km north of Daly Waters marks the approximate spot where Forrest found the line.

In the 1890s a pub sprang up, catering to the demand created by the drovers, who had started using Daly Waters as a camp on the overland stock route between Queensland and the Kimberley. The current building dates from the late 1920s, and from the outside at least looks now probably much like it looked then.

The next wave of activity to hit Daly Waters came from the air. The fledgling airline, Qantas, used Daly Waters as a refuelling stop on the Singapore leg of its Sydney-London run in the early 1930s. This led to the airstrip here being one of the major stops in northern Australia.

The RAAF also used Daly Waters as a refuelling stop for its bombers en route to Singapore, and in 1942 established a base here. It was in constant use throughout the war, and the recently restored hangar now belongs to the National Trust.

Things to See
The **Daly Waters Pub** is an attraction in itself. It has changed little since the 1920s, and inside has the most unusual array of mementos left by passing travellers – everything from bras to banknotes adorn the walls! The actual liquor licence has been used continuously since 1893, and so the pub lays claim to being the oldest in the Territory.

At the **Daly Waters Aerodrome** there's a historical display in the old hangar, and **Stuart's Tree** is also close by.

Places to Stay & Eat
The pub (☎ 8975 9927) has a *camp site*, with shade and grass. It costs $3 per person, $10 for a powered site. There are also some basic motel-type rooms at $25/35.

Meals at the pub are very good, and the $12 beef n' barra barbecue in the evening is very popular, and there's often live music in the dry season too. The menu on the wall inside is the product of a local wit – my favourite is the Dingo's Breakfast (A piss and a look around – no charge!).

Out on the highway there's the *Hi-Way Inn* (☎ 8975 9925), with camping, and motel rooms at $40/50.

DUNMARRA
Like so many other spots on the Stuart Highway, Dunmarra is these days little more than a roadhouse providing fuel and other services to travellers, and like other places on the highway it does have an interesting story behind it.

The settlement supposedly takes its name from the Overland Telegraph linesman, Dan

O'Mara, who disappeared in the area. Drover Noel Healey established a cattle station here in the 1930s, and found O'Mara's skeleton in the bush. The local Aboriginal peoples' attempts to say his name sounded like 'Dunmara', and that was the name Healey gave to his station.

In 1935 Healey opened up one of the first stores along the way, and when this was burnt down he built another, and the remains of this one are close to the current Shell roadhouse today. Across the road is a solitary Overland Telegraph Line pole.

Eight km north of town is the start of the **Buchanan Highway**, a beef road which runs right through to Halls Creek in Western Australia (see Victoria River District earlier in this chapter for details of that route).

About 35 km south of town is a **historic marker** to Sir Charles Todd, builder of the Overland Telegraph Line, and it commemorates the joining of the two ends of the line in August 1872.

Places to Stay
The *Dunmarra Wayside Inn* (☎ 8975 9922) has camping, as well as air-con motel rooms with attached bath and fridge, at $30/40. There's also a bar and restaurant, and takeaway food is available.

NEWCASTLE WATERS
Newcastle Waters is a former droving town which was right at the intersection of northern Australia's two most important stock routes – the Murranji and the Barkly. Today it is virtually a ghost town, the only permanent inhabitants being the families of employees from Newcastle Waters station. It is wildly atmospheric, and being three km off the Stuart Highway sees relatively few visitors. It's worth making the detour as the town is probably the best place in the Territory to get a feel for the hard life led by the early drovers.

History
The original inhabitants of this area are the Jingili Aboriginal people, and their name for it is Tjika. The European name comes once

again from John McDouall Stuart, who reached here during his expedition of 1861 and named the stretches of water after the Duke of Newcastle, secretary for the colonies.

The first pastoral activity was in the 1880s when the lease was taken up by A J Browne of Adelaide, who employed Alfred Giles (see Springvale Homestead near Katherine) to stock it. Cattle were brought overland from Queensland but the station did poorly and it was sold 20 years later for a pittance.

The Murranji stock route was pioneered by Nat Buchanan in 1886 to connect Newcastle Waters with the Victoria River. This way was 'only' 250-odd km, compared with the alternative route via Katherine, which was something like 600 km further. The only trouble was that there were long stretches without reliable water on the Murranji route (the name comes from a desert frog which is capable of living underground for extended periods without water).

The government recognised the need for permanent water along the stock routes, and to this end Newcastle Waters was made the depot for a bore-sinking team in 1917. Once the 13 bores along the Murranji were operational in 1924, the use of the route increased steadily.

The town site for Newcastle Waters was leased from the station by the government in 1930, and a store and pub were built, as was a telegraph repeater station in 1942.

The death knell for the town was the demise of the drover in the early 1960s due to the use of road transport for the moving of stock, and the fact that the Stuart Highway bypassed the town.

Today the old pub and store still stand on the town's one and only street. The latter has been restored by the National Trust and houses a small museum.

There are no facilities of any kind in the town, the nearest being at Dunmarra and Elliott.

Things to See
The **Junction Hotel** was built in 1932 out of scraps collected from abandoned windmills along the stock routes, and it became the town's focus. After weeks on the track thirsty drovers would get into Newcastle Waters and really cut loose. The beer was kept cool in wet straw, and it seems the barman would keep the limited supplies of cool beer for those who were sober; those who couldn't tell the difference were served it warm. The hotel's liquor licence was transferred to Elliott on the Stuart Highway, and the hotel itself became a station store and bottleshop until it eventually closed in the early 1970s.

The other notable building in town is **Jones Store**, also known as George Man Fong's house. It was built in the 1930s by Arnold Jones, who ran it until 1949, after which time it changed hands a couple of times until 1959 when it was acquired by George Man Fong, a saddler who worked on the premises until 1985. The building was restored in 1988 as part of a bicentennial project.

The first place you see on arrival in the town is the **Drovers' Memorial Park**, which commemorates the part played by the drovers in the opening up of the Territory. It was also part of the bicentennial project, and it was from here that the Last Great Cattle Drive headed off, also in 1988 as part of the bicentennial. For the drive, 1200 head of cattle, donated by pastoralists in the Territory, set off for Longreach in Queensland, 2000 km away to the south-east. They reached there almost four months later, and the cattle were auctioned off in a televised sale.

ELLIOTT

The one-street town of Elliott (population 420) owes its existence to Army Lieutenant 'Snow' Elliott, who established an army staging camp in the area in 1940. It was also helped in no small part by the demise of Newcastle Waters and the transfer of the liquor licence there to the Elliott Hotel in 1962.

Today it is a cattle service town, and is one of the cattle 'bath' centres where cattle coming from the north are given a chemical bath to kill any ticks so they don't infect herds to the south. The actual 'Tick Line' is the boundary of Banka Banka and Phillip Creek stations, about 250 km south of Elliott.

Lake Woods lies south-west of town. It measures around 420 sq km, and is the much reduced remains of a large freshwater basin. At its peak, about 23,000 years ago, it was 10 times as large. These days it is an important breeding ground for waterfowl and other birds. Note that the lake is on private property (Powell Creek station) and there is no public access.

If it's any help, Elliott is the half-way point between Alice Springs and Darwin.

Information

Facilities in the town include a roadhouse with a supermarket, a general store and post office, and a police station (☎ 8969 2010).

Places to Stay

There's the usual range of accommodation, although nothing stands out. The *Halfway Caravan Park* (☎ 8969 2025) is part of the Mobil roadhouse, and has powered sites for $10.

Much bigger is the *Midland Caravan Park* (☎ 8969 2037) which has camp sites at $10 ($15 with power), on-site vans at $35, and cabins with shared amenities for $40.

The *Elliott Hotel* (☎ 8969 2069) is good value with rooms with attached bath for $25/40.

RENNER SPRINGS

Renner Springs, an hour or so down the track from Elliott, is nothing more than a roadhouse/hotel by the highway. It's more interesting than it sounds, however, as the roadhouse is actually an old army hut which was removed after WW II from the army's staging camp at Banka Banka station to the south.

The actual Renner Springs lie just to the south of the roadhouse, but are hidden in an acacia thicket. These days the water for the roadhouse comes from a bore.

Renner Springs is generally accepted as being on the dividing line between the seasonally wet Top End and the dry Centre.

The often monotonous country which the highway passes through is relieved around here by the Ashburton Range, which parallels the road for some distance either side of Renner Springs.

Place to Stay

The only choice here is the *Renner Springs Hotel* (☎ 8964 4505), which has camping, and motel units are $35/45. The meals at the bar are quite acceptable.

ATTACK CREEK HISTORICAL RESERVE

About 90 km south of Renner Springs the highway crosses Attack Creek, and on the southern side is a memorial to John McDouall Stuart.

On Stuart's first attempt at a south-north crossing of the continent in 1860 he got as far as this creek before he was forced to return to Adelaide, partly due to being low on supplies. Stuart's version was that his party was attacked by hostile Warumungu Aboriginal men and that this forced the turn around. The attack certainly occurred, but it seems it was exaggerated by Stuart and that this was simply the last straw.

Although the attack did take place on Attack Creek, the monument here does not mark the actual spot; it's simply convenient for the highway.

About 10 km north of Attack Creek an old section of highway loops off the new for a few km, and passes a rock by the roadside in a cutting, which soldiers working on the road during WW II thought looked liked Britain's wartime prime minister, Winston Churchill. It's still there, complete with cigar in mouth (a large stick), but it's the most fanciful bit of nonsense I've ever come across; the soldiers must have had wild imaginations, or some excellent hallucinogenic drugs!

A grid about 10 km south of Attack Creek is the boundary fence between Banka Banka and Phillip Creek stations, and this is also the **Tick Line**, as a large sign points out (see Elliott earlier in this chapter for details).

Roughly midway between Attack Creek and Threeways to the south, and about four

THE BARKLY REGION

km east of the road, are the mudbrick ruins of **Phillip Creek Settlement**. The settlement was established after WW II as a settlement for Warumungu Aboriginal people from Tennant Creek whose land had been taken over by mining. It was closed in the mid-50s, and the people relocated to Ali Curung, a community about 150 km south of Tennant Creek which is today Aboriginal land.

THREEWAYS

Threeways, 537 km north of the Alice, 988 km south of Darwin and 643 km west of Mt Isa, is basically a bloody long way from anywhere, apart from Tennant Creek which is 26 km down the Track. This is a classic 'get stuck' point for hitchhikers, and a 'must stop' point for road trains.

On the Stuart Highway, on the north side of the junction, is a construction right by the side of the road that looks like a brick watertower. This is in fact the **Flynn Memorial**, commemorating the founder of the Royal Flying Doctor Service, the Reverend John Flynn. It's one of the least aesthetically pleasing monuments you're ever likely to see.

Place to Stay

There's stuff-all here other than the 24-hour *Threeways Roadhouse* (☎ 8962 2744), where if you're stuck you can camp ($4 per person, or $14 for a powered site), or lash out on a motel room at $42. There's a pool, bar, shop and a restaurant with OK meals for around $10.

TENNANT CREEK

Apart from Katherine, Tennant Creek (population 3550) is the only town of any size between Darwin and Alice Springs. It's 26 km south of Threeways, 511 km north of Alice Springs. A lot of travellers spend a night here and there are one or two attractions, mainly related to gold mining, to tempt you to stay a bit longer.

History

To the Warumungu people, Tennant Creek is Jurnkurakurr, the intersection of a number of dreaming tracks.

The European history of the town, as with so many places on the Track, starts with the expeditions of John McDouall Stuart. He passed through here in 1860 before turning back at Attack Creek some distance north. He named the creek, which is about 10 km north of town, after John Tennant, a prominent pastoralist from Port Lincoln in South Australia.

When the Overland Telegraph Line was put through in the 1870s a repeater station was set up at Tennant Creek.

The story goes that the town itself was established 10 km south of the repeater station because that was where a wagonload of beer broke down here in the early 1930s and rather than take the beer to the people, the people went to the beer and that's where the town has stayed. Although it spoils a good story, the truth is far more prosaic: the present site is close to the gold fields, the telegraph station area isn't.

The discovery of gold here in the 1930s led to minor gold rush and by WW II there was something in the vicinity of 100 small mines in operation.

Once the mining was under way the local Aboriginal people were in the way and so were moved to the Phillip Creek settlement on the Stuart Highway north of Tennant, where the mudbrick ruins are still visible.

The gold rush was shortlived, however, and the town might well have gone the way of a number of 'boom-and-bust' towns in the Territory, except that viable quantities of copper were found in the 1950s, and even today there are commercial gold mines in the area, the main one being Poseidon Gold's White Devil mine 42 km north-west of town.

Information

The helpful visitor centre (☎ 8962 3388) is in the transit centre in the main street (Paterson St). Tourist information is also broadcast on 88MHz FM.

Also on the main street you will find a couple of supermarkets, branches of the ANZ and Westpac banks, the police station

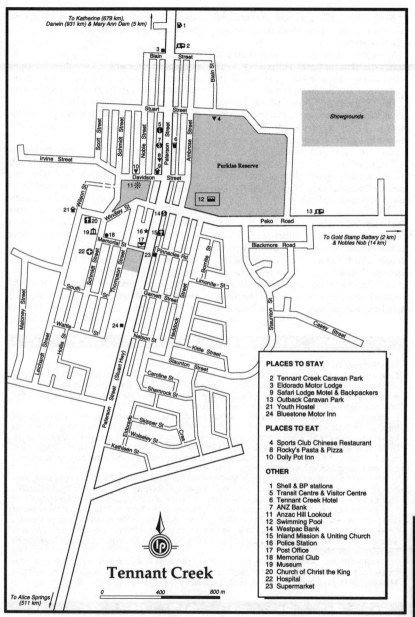

To Katherine (679 km),
Darwin (931 km) & Mary Ann Dam (5 km)

Showgrounds

Purkiss Reserve

Irvine Street

Davidson Street

Peko Road

To Gold Stamp Battery (2 km)
& Nobles Nob (14 km)

Blackmore Road

Casey Street

Kittle Street

Staunton Street

Caroline St

Shamrock St

Skipper St

Wolseley St

Kathleen St.

To Alice Springs
(511 km)

Tennant Creek

0   400   800 m

PLACES TO STAY

2 Tennant Creek Caravan Park
3 Eldorado Motor Lodge
9 Safari Lodge Motel & Backpackers
13 Outback Caravan Park
21 Youth Hostel
24 Bluestone Motor Inn

PLACES TO EAT

4 Sports Club Chinese Restaurant
8 Rocky's Pasta & Pizza
10 Dolly Pot Inn

OTHER

1 Shell & BP stations
5 Transit Centre & Visitor Centre
6 Tennant Creek Hotel
7 ANZ Bank
11 Anzac Hill Lookout
12 Swimming Pool
14 Westpac Bank
15 Inland Mission & Uniting Church
16 Police Station
17 Post Office
18 Memorial Club
19 Museum
20 Church of Christ the King
22 Hospital
23 Supermarket

THE BARKLY REGION

(☎ 8962 2606), the pub and a couple of takeaway joints, two roadhouses and a couple of motels.

A couple of blocks west on Schmidt St there's the Tennant Creek Hospital (☎ 8962 4399) and a small museum; and east of the road is the town swimming pool.

The Central Land Council (☎ 8962 2343) has an office on Paterson St, and the Department of Mines & Energy (☎ 8962 1288), also on Paterson St, is where you need to go if you want a permit for fossicking.

Anyinginyi Arts & Crafts is an interesting Aboriginal shop on Davidson St. Most of the pieces on sale are made locally and prices are lower than in Alice Springs.

Festivals & Events

Tennant Creek hosts a number of interesting annual events. As well as the usual **Tennant Creek Show** (July), there's the **Renner Springs Races** (not held in Renners Springs at all!; Easter weekend), the **Goldrush Folk Festival** (August) and the **Desert Harmony Arts Festival** (September). If you happen to

be in town for the show, you can witness the handbogging competition!

Things to See

For a good view of the town there's a small lookout on Anzac Hill, right next to the Safari backpackers on Davidson St, or about 2.5 km east of town along Peko Rd there's the **Bill Allen Lookout** with views over the town and the McDouall Ranges to the north.

In Town In town itself, the small **museum**, on Schmidt St opposite the Memorial Club, dates from 1942 when it was built as an army hospital. Up until 1978 it was used as an outpatients clinic for the hospital next door. These days it's owned by the National Trust, and has some interesting displays, including a re-creation of a miner's camp. It's open daily during the Dry from 3.30 to 5.30 pm ($2), but you can also get the key from the visitor centre at other times.

The corrugated-iron **Church of Christ the King** on Windley St was originally built in Pine Creek early this century, but was

---

The Sidney Williams Hut

Time and again visitors to the Territory who have an interest in history and architecture come across corrugated-iron buildings known as Sidney Williams Huts. These prefabricated buildings were supplied by Sidney Williams & Co, a Sydney-based company which was established in the 1920s by Sidney Williams, an architect and engineer.

Initially the company specialised in windmills, but from experience gained on his travels throughout remote parts of the country, Williams realised that there was the need for a building system that was cheap, easy to transport and simple to erect. The company developed the Comet Building, a system of interchangeable steel sections which bolted together so any configuration of walls, doors and windows could be achieved. The beauty of the steel frame was that it was not only stronger than local wood, but was also termite proof.

With the huge increase in activity in the Northern Territory during WW II, the defence forces bought and built large numbers of Sidney Williams huts all the way from Alice Springs to Darwin, as they were cheap and quick to assemble, and had none of the limitations of canvas tents.

In this way Sidney Williams huts went up in all corners of the Territory from the 1920s onwards and became very much a part of it – in 1935 the civic buildings in the new township of Tennant Creek were almost exclusively of Sidney Williams construction. Unfortunately the company was wound up in 1988 and all records destroyed, so it is not known just how many were shipped to the Northern Territory.

Because of their portable nature, many of these buildings have been moved, often to remote locations, but many still survive – the old Inland Mission building in Tennant Creek and the Totem Theatre buildings in Alice Springs were all supplied by Sidney Williams & Co. ■

trucked to Tennant Creek in 1935. The church has a National Trust classification.

On the main street just south of Peko St is another church building, this one the old **Australian Inland Mission** (Uniting Church). This corrugated-iron building was built in the 1930s by the Sydney company, Sidney Williams. (Many corrugated-iron buildings along the track are of Sidney Williams construction. See the aside for details.)

On the walls of the Central Land Council building in Paterson St is the **Jurnkurakurr Mural**, painted by the local Aboriginal people and depicting the dreamings from this area – among them the snake, crow, white cockatoo, budgerigar, fire and lightning.

Around Town East of town, about two km along Peko Rd, is the **Gold Stamp Battery**. It was built by the government after WW II to process ore for the individual miners. Today it is owned by the local tourism association, and they have turned the site into a museum. The 10-head battery still works, and they fire it up for visitors every day at 9 am and 5 pm during the winter ($8 adults, $16 family), but you are free to wander around at other times.

A further 12 km along Peko Rd brings you to **Nobles Nob Open Cut Mine**. The gold here was discovered in 1933 by one-eyed Jack Noble and his blind mate William Weaber. By the time it closed in 1985 it had yielded $65 million worth of gold, making it the richest mine in the country at that time. It was originally an underground mine but was converted to open-cut following a huge 1967 cave-in.

About five km north of town is the **Mary Ann Recreational Dam**, a good spot for a swim or a picnic. There's also a boat ramp (non-powered boats only). A bicycle track runs alongside the highway from Tennant Creek to the turn-off (three km) and then it's a further two km.

Twelve km north of town are the green-roofed stone buildings of the old **Telegraph Station**. This is one of only four of the original 11 stations remaining in the Territory (the others are at Barrow Creek, Alice Springs and Powell Creek). This station was the most northerly station to be provisioned from Adelaide, and the supplies were brought by camel from the railhead at Oodnadatta. The station's telegraph functions ceased in 1935 when a new office opened in the town itself, but it was in use up until 1950 as a linesman's residence, and then until 1985 as a station homestead. Today it is owned by the government and maintained by Parks & Wildlife, and it's well worth a wander around.

Just north of the Telegraph Station is a turn-off to the west to **The Pebbles**, a formation of granite boulders similar to the more well-known Devil's Marbles 100 km or so south of Tennant Creek. To the Aboriginal people the Pebbles area is known as Kundjarra, and is a women's dreaming sacred site. It's a great spot for late afternoon or early morning photos.

Organised Tours
An interesting diversion while in Tennant Creek is to take a morning Walala Bush Tucker Tour (☎ 8962 2358). These tours, which are led by local Aboriginal women, operate from March to November and delve into bush tucker and medicine. The cost is $25 ($15 for children) and the tour takes three hours; bookings need to be made a day or two in advance, and a minimum of four people is required.

Ten Ant Tours (☎ 8962 2358) in the transit centre offers tours around town.

Tours of the local Dot 6 Mine are operated each evening during winter at 7 pm ($12). For details ☎ 8962 2168.

Activities
If you're into fossicking, head for **Moonlight Rockhole** fossicking area, about 60 km west of town along the Warrego road. Note that a fossicking permit is required from the Department of Mines & Energy on the main street.

Places to Stay
Hostels There are a number of options here. The *Safari Lodge Motel* (☎ 8962 2207; fax

8962 3188) has a wing of backpacker rooms right next to the Anzac Hill lookout, across the road from its main building on Davidson St. A bed in these air-cooled rooms costs $10, and there are communal cooking facilities.

Another budget alternative is the *Tennant Creek Youth Hostel* (☎ 8962 2719), in a shady location on the corner of Leichhardt and Windley Sts. Beds in air-con twin rooms cost $12.

Camping & On-Site Vans The *Outback Caravan Park* (☎ 8962 2459) is one km east of town along Peko Rd. It has a swimming pool, tent sites at $12 a double ($15 with power) and on-site vans or cabins (some with air-con) for $25 to $47.50 double.

The other choice is the *Tennant Creek Caravan Park* (☎ 8962 2325) on Paterson St (Stuart Highway) on the northern edge of town. It has powered sites at $15, twin 'bunkhouse' rooms at $20 per person, and on-site cabins at $40.

Hotels & Motels Tennant Creek's motels aren't cheap. The *Safari Lodge Motel* (☎ 8962 2207) in the centre of town on Davidson St has singles/doubles for $62/72.

The *Goldfields Hotel Motel* (☎ 8962 2030), just around the corner on the highway, has singles/doubles for $55/65.

On the northern edge of town on the highway is the large *Eldorado Motor Lodge* (☎ 8962 2034), with units at $55. At the other end of town and also on the highway, the *Bluestone Motor Inn* (☎ 8962 2617) is the only place in this category with a swimming pool. Units range from $55 to $72.

Places to Eat
It comes as something of a surprise to find that one of the most highly regarded restaurants in the Territory is in the local squash centre. The *Dolly Pot Inn* (☎ 8962 2824) is open daily from 11 am to midnight and offers good-value meals such as steak and salad, and also features home-made waffles.

On the main street there's *Rocky's Pasta & Pizza* (☎ 8962 2049) with, yep, pizzas and pasta, and they also do deliveries. For takeaway snacks and ice cream there's *Mr Perry's Ice Creamery* near the post office on Paterson St, and the Transit Centre also does takeaways.

The Memorial Club on Schmidt St welcomes visitors and has good, straightforward counter meals at its *Memories Bistro*.

The *Bluestone Motor Inn* and the *Eldorado Motor Lodge* both have licensed restaurants, and there's a *Chinese restaurant* at the Sports Club on Stuart St.

Getting There & Around
Air Airnorth (☎ toll-free 1800 627 474) have flights to Alice Springs (daily except Sunday, $199), Darwin and Katherine (both daily except Saturday, $319 and $239 respectively).

Bus The long-distance buses all stop at the transit centre.

Car Rental If you want to do a bit of local exploring, the Outback Caravan Park is an agent for Hertz (☎ toll-free 1800 891 112), while Ten Ant Tours acts for Territory Rent-a-Car (☎ toll-free 1800 891 125).

Bicycle If you're feeling energetic and want to pedal yourself around, there's bike rental at the Safari Lodge Motel for $5 for a half day and $10 per day.

BONNEY WELL
On the western side of the highway 85 km south of Tennant Creek is Bonney Well, a well originally sunk by the pastoralist Alfred Giles (see Springvale Homestead in the Katherine section of the Darwin to Katherine chapter) in 1879. It was improved by the Telegraph Department five years later and again in 1892 as part of the upgrading of the North-South Stock Route.

The well was finally abandoned in 1936 and is now maintained by the National Trust.

DEVIL'S MARBLES CONSERVATION RESERVE
The famous granite boulders known as the Devil's Marbles are one of the more extraor-

dinary geological sights in the Territory. The 1800-hectare reserve lies in the Davenport Ranges, right beside the Stuart Highway, about 100 km south of Tennant Creek and 400 km north of Alice Springs. The Davenport Ranges are not the most spectacular on earth, but they are the oldest in that they have been continually exposed to the atmosphere for more than 1800 million years.

The huge boulders have been weathered into roughly spherical shapes, and are found strewn haphazardly throughout the reserve. In a number of places the boulders are stacked up in precarious piles, with some balanced at unlikely angles – it looks like a good shove could send them tumbling.

The boulders have come to be their present shape after millions of years of erosion along fault lines in the rock. The fault lines formed slabs roughly three to seven metres square, and these have been gradually rounded by the process of exfoliation (onion-peel weathering).

The whole process of how the boulders came to be is described in interpretive signs and diagrams found on the **self-guided walk** which does a 20-minute loop from the car park. This walk is well worth doing, and at one point you pass an amazing four-metre-high boulder which has been neatly split in half – the split is so neat it's as if a giant tomato has been sliced with a sharp knife.

Facilities

There are pit toilets at the car park, and during the peak months (July-August) an ice-cream van from nearby Wauchope often sets up during the day.

There's also a *camp site* around the eastern side of the boulders. Certainly the sight of the boulders early and late in the day is memorable, as is the remarkably hard ground of the camping area. Pit toilets, a shade shelter and fireplace are provided (BYO firewood).

WAUCHOPE

Pronounced '*war*-kup', this settlement is once again nothing more than a fuel stop by the highway. At least this one has some char-

acter, as the pub itself dates back to the late 1930s, the 'town' itself to the discovery of wolfram in the area in 1914. At its height around 50 miners were working on the small but rich field 12 km east of here. Many more worked larger fields at Hatches Creek, about 140 km to the east in the Davenport Ranges. After WW I the price of wolfram halved almost overnight, as the British no longer needed it in their war effort, and the Wauchope field became immediately unviable.

The price of wolfram revived in the late 1930s in the buildup to WW II, and it was at this time that the pub was established. During the war the wolfram fields were taken over by the Commonwealth government and the few miners remaining (most had joined the army) were paid wages to dig the ore, along with 500-odd Chinese quarrymen who the government had evacuated from islands in the Pacific. For a second time a war finished and the demand for wolfram fell dramatically. Before long the fields were deserted (the Chinese were transferred to Brisbane to work for the US army) and Wauchope became the stop on the highway that it is today. Out the front there's still some rusting equipment dating back to the days when there was much more activity. Sometimes the only thing moving these days seems to be the hotel's pet goat which patrols the car park hassling for scraps.

With a 4WD vehicle it's possible to visit the old wolframite field today. Ask at the pub for directions.

Places to Stay

The *Wauchope Hotel* (☎ 8964 1963) has grassed camp sites at $6 ($10 powered), or there are rooms at $25, up to $55 with attached shower and toilet. There's also an interesting bar full of the usual paraphernalia which outback pubs seem to accumulate, and there's decent meals in the restaurant.

WYCLIFFE WELL

Just 18 km south of Wauchope is Wycliffe Well, and close by there's a lake which attracts numerous birds.

The well referred to in the name dates

from 1872 and the Overland Telegraph Line, although the water quality was not all that flash. In the 1930s a bore was sunk to provide good water on the North-South Stock Route. During WW II a two-hectare army vegetable farm was established to supply the troops up the Track.

Wycliffe Well's most (and probably only) famous resident was one Doreen Crook (later Doreen Braitling). While still a young girl her family set up here around 1920, hauling water for cattle on the stock route, having had no luck at the wolfram field at Wauchope. She married pastoralist Bill Braitling, and they went on to establish Mount Doreen station on the Tanami Track north-west of Alice Springs. Doreen spent a great deal of time looking after the welfare of Aboriginal people on the station, and after her husband died she moved to Alice Springs and became involved with the preservation of historic buildings (it's largely thanks to her that the Stuart Town Gaol was not demolished in 1972). She eventually went on to form the National Trust of the Northern Territory, and was elected its first president.

These days the pub is probably most well known for the wide selection of beers available.

Places to Stay

At the *Wycliffe Well Hotel* (☎ 8964 1966) you can camp for $11 ($15 with power), stay in on-site cabins ($25 up to $48 with cooking facilities and attached bath), single/double pub rooms at $38/48, or in motel rooms with attached facilities for $58/73. Facilities at the pub include a pool, licensed restaurant and souvenir shop.

BARROW CREEK

Historic Barrow Creek, nestled by the highway at the foot of the Watt Range, has one of the more quirky outback pub-road-houses that you'll find along the Track, as well as a well-preserved telegraph station, and about 30 km to the north and one km east of the highway (signposted) are the ruins of a sizeable army staging camp from WW II.

Although the settlement itself is less than stunningly attractive, it's worth at least an hour or so to check out the telegraph station – and the bar, which is adorned with all manner of drawings, cartoons and a wall full of bank notes.

History

The area around what was to become Barrow Creek was the home of the Kaytetye Aboriginal people, and two trees near the black smith's shop at the telegraph station are registered sacred sites.

Once again, it is John McDouall Stuart who was the first European through the area, naming the creek after a South Australian journalist and politician, John Henry Barrow. The opening of the Overland Telegraph Line saw the establishment of a fort-like telegraph station in 1872.

In February 1874 the telegraph station, under stationmaster James Stapleton, was attacked by a group of Kaytetye Aboriginal men. Stapleton and a linesman were killed, and their graves are close to the station. The attack came as something of surprise as Stapleton had adopted a fairly enlightened (for the time) approach with the local Aboriginal population, and had provided food for those who were ill. The South Australian government authorised a punitive expedition which led to a two-month spree of killing which saw the deaths of at least 50 Aboriginal people.

Telegraphic operations at the station ceased in 1910, but it was in use as a depot up until 1980. The pub dates from the 1930s and has been providing travellers with refreshments ever since.

The WW II staging camp of New Barrow, the largest in the Territory, lies signposted about a km east of the highway, about 30 km north of Barrow Creek. Although it lies on Neutral Junction station, the owners don't mind if you wander in and look around the site, which these days really only consists of concrete foundations and various bits of scrap metal lying around. From 1942 to 1945 the station accommodated up to 1000 troops and equipment travelling up and down the Track. (As it is private property, please leave no trace of your visit, and leave gates how you found them.)

Places to Stay

At the *Barrow Creek Hotel* (☎ 8956 9753) there's camping ($7, $9 with power), although there's not much in the way of shade or grass, or on-site twin rooms (dongas) at $20, and hotel rooms at $20/35. A good, filling meal in the dining room will set you back about $10.

Barkly Tableland & The Gulf

To the east of the Stuart Highway lies the huge expanse of the Barkly Tableland and, beyond it, the Gulf region. It is primarily cattle country, characterised by arid grasslands of the tableland and open woodland country of the Gulf.

For the visitor the main attraction of the area is the fine fishing, especially in the waterways around Borroloola, close to the Gulf of Carpentaria, and on the Roper River on the southern edge of Arnhem Land. If fishing is not your bag then the pickings are pretty slim, although there is some fine scenery and camping by the Gulf at Wollogorang station near the Queensland border, on the sometimes rough gravel road which links Roper Bar with Borroloola, and there's a chance to get offshore to Barranyi National Park, which lies in the islands of the Sir Edward Pellew Group out from Borroloola. The area also has some colourful history attached to it.

Most of the area's visitors are simply passing through on the Barkly Highway, which connects the Stuart Highway with Mt Isa in Queensland. However, if you're not in a hurry it's well worth the diversion to visit this little-touristed corner of the Territory.

The Barkly Tableland, named after the Governor of Victoria in 1861, comprises a relatively featureless plain, with tussocky grasses being the dominant form of vegeta-

tion. Only in the few creek lines do many trees occur. The reason for this is the nature of the clay soil of the tableland. When wet, the soil becomes swampy and boggy; in dry conditions it shrinks and huge gaping cracks appear. As the soil shrinks any roots are torn as the gaps open up. On the positive side, the cracks are an important refuge for small native marsupials as snakes abound. The soil is productive even though it is not particularly rich as the underlying rock is so old that much of the nutrient has been leached out.

Geologically the Barkly Tableland is significant in that it is an area of extreme stability. For the last 500 million years or so the plain has changed little. Minor volcanic activity caused the area to be covered by a shallow sea, which then filled with sediment, forming the current underlying limestone rock. The area was then uniformly raised, and the current clay soils derive from the eroded limestone.

ROPER BAR

From just south of Mataranka on the Stuart Highway, the Roper Highway strikes out east for 175 km to Roper Bar, a popular fishing spot on the Roper River. It's also an access point into south-eastern Arnhem Land, or you can fuel up and continue south to Borroloola.

The 'bar' itself is a ford across the Roper River, the 'town' is a store/motel/caravan park with a population of less than a dozen. The road crosses the river here, then continues on for a further 30 km to the Aboriginal community at **Ngukurr**, which is off limits to visitors. In the early days, steam ships and large sailing vessels tied up at the bar to discharge cargo. The wreck of one of them, the *Young Australian*, lies about 25 km downstream.

Although it's on Aboriginal land, permits are not required for visits to the area.

History

This part of the country has played an important part in the opening up of the Top End, largely because the Roper River was used as the supply route for materials used in the construction of the northern section of the Overland Telegraph Line. Ludwig Leichhardt passed through here on his epic journey to Port Essington in 1845 and named the river after one of the members of his party. Roper Bar marks the navigable limit of the river.

In the 1870s Darcy Uhr, a Queensland overlander, took 400 bullocks from Charters Towers in Queensland to Darwin, for much of the way following the route which Leichhardt had taken through the Roper district. This was no mean feat as, apart from being virtually unknown to White people, the country en route was thickly timbered, poorly pastured and inhabited by thousands of hostile Aboriginal people. Nat 'Bluey' Buchanan drove 1200 cattle from Aramac in central Queensland to a station near Darwin via this route, and from this time on the hazardous track around the Gulf became the major stock route from Queensland to the Top End.

Places to Stay

The one and only choice here is at the *Roper River Store* (☎ 8975 4636), which caters mainly to tourist traffic and nearby Aboriginal communities. Its services include fuel sales, a store, clothing, fishing tackle, hardware items, motel-style accommodation and a caravan park. Overnight rates in the store's six air-con demountable units, each of which has shower facilities and sleeps four adults, are $35 a single plus $15 for each additional person. Sites in the grassed camping area, which is only about 100 metres from the river, cost $4 per person and an additional $4 for power if required (generator, limited hours).

Getting There & Away

From the Stuart Highway, all but the last 40 km are sealed, and even the gravel section is generally well maintained and poses few problems if you're sensible.

ROPER BAR TO BORROLOOLA

The road from Roper through to Borroloola is usually pretty good. It certainly does not require 4WD, but it's prudent to carry two spares as the shale can be sharp in places, especially if the grader has been over it recently.

The road presents good going through varied country – scrub, tall forest, open woodland, swamps, spectacular sandstone escarpments, stony hills and rivers.

About 70 km from Roper Bar you arrive at the old **St Vidgeon homestead** – a lonely ruin on a stony rise conjuring up stark images of battlers eking a scant living from the hostile bush. The station is owned by the Northern Territory government, and is set to become part of a 10,000-sq-km national park in the (hopefully) not-too-distant future. Close by is the superb **Lormaieum Lagoon**, a stone's throw from the homestead and only about a km from the Roper River. Fringed by paperbarks and covered by large water lilies, the lagoon has many birds and a peaceful atmosphere.

After crossing the Limmen Bight River, 178 km from Roper Bar, the countryside changes. For about 50 km southwards from here, the road runs up narrow valleys between rugged ridges, with some dramatic scenery along the way.

You pass the turn-off to **Nathan River homestead** 13 km from the Limmen Bight crossing. Nathan River, too, is set to be included in the same national park as St Vidgeons, as it contains some superb rock formations (known as the Lost City) which are said to rival the Bungle Bungles in WA. For the moment, it is off-limits, as it is the subject of an Aboriginal land claim.

Finally the track joins the bitumen Carpentaria Highway, 30 km from Borroloola. Of interest on this section are the metre-high termite mounds that rise like red fingers from the stones, showing that at least something other than flies can thrive in this hostile environment.

BORROLOOLA

Borroloola (population 800) is a small service-and-tourism town close to the Gulf of Carpentaria. It is connected to the outside world by bitumen roads leading to the Stuart and Barkly highways, and by scheduled daily air services to Darwin and Katherine.

History

Until 1885 there were no facilities at all between Burketown (then a busy little port) and the store at Roper Bar. It's true that there were a few widely scattered homesteads along the way, but these were little more than rough forts armed against Aboriginal attack. Then a racketeer by the name of John 'Black Jack' Reid brought his boat, the *Good Intent*, loaded with 'duty free' alcohol and supplies up the McArthur River to the Burketown Crossing, where he built a rough store, which became the Royal Hotel, and from this the settlement grew.

A year later, by which time traffic on the Gulf Track had greatly increased thanks to the Kimberley gold rush, the embryonic township had a population of up to 150 Whites – 'the scum of northern Australia', according to the government resident. It boasted four corrugated-iron stores (three of which doubled as pubs), a bakery, a Chinese market garden, police station and a dairy farm. A decade later, the gold rush and the great cattle drives were over and the White population had shrunk to six.

Borroloola probably would have died altogether were it not for its location on one of the Gulf's largest rivers; it survives today as a minor administrative centre and supply point for the region's cattle stations. After a century of obscurity, however, the town is set to boom again, with the on-going development of a giant silver, lead and zinc mine and the creation of a deep-water port on the Gulf.

Sprawled along two km of wide main street, Borroloola was blown away by Cyclone Kathy in 1984 and much of its old character was lost in the rebuilding.

Information

Although only small, Borroloola offers a wide range of government and business services and facilities. These include a medical centre (☎ 8975 8757), post office, police station (☎ 8975 8770), Parks & Wildlife office (☎ 8975 8792), aerodrome, mechani-cal repairs, car hire, tourist accommodation, supermarkets, butchery and marine suppliers. A number of businesses sell fishing tackle and bait, but there are no takeaway outlets for spirits and wine. An official 'passport' to the Gulf Capital costs $10 and gives you discounts on accommodation, fuel and meals at various outlets in Borroloola and elsewhere in the Top End.

The Commonwealth, Westpac and ANZ banks have agencies in town, and all three have EFTPOS facilities and take credit cards. The handiest is the Westpac agency at Gulf Mini Mart, which is open seven days a week.

Things to See

The town's colourful past is preserved mainly in the many interesting displays housed in the **old police station**, which dates from 1886 and is open from 10 am to noon Monday to Friday. (At other times the key is available from the Holiday Village.) Here you can learn about the Hermit of Borroloola and the Freshwater Admiral, two of the many colourful eccentrics spawned by the local lifestyle and the subject of a David Attenborough documentary in the 1960s. The town is much quieter these days, although bloody re-enactments of what it was like a century ago sometimes take place when the booze is flowing freely, such as on pension days.

Activities & Events

Borroloola attracts around 10,000 visitors annually, most of them coming for the fishing – the **Borroloola Fishing Classic** held in June each year draws a large number of enthusiasts. The McArthur River is tidal as far as the Burketown Crossing near town, and can be accessed by boat from formed ramps at Borroloola and King Ash Bay, about 40 km downstream. Fishers with large enough craft can venture out into the Gulf around the Sir Edward Pellew Group. Don't despair if you don't have a boat: you can catch a wide variety of fish, including barramundi and threadfin salmon, from various spots along the river's tidal section, between

Batten Point (near King Ash Bay) and the Burketown Crossing. Fishing safaris with a local guide are also available (see Organised Tours).

Other annual events include the inevitable rodeo (August) and the Borroloola Show (July).

Organised Tours

Croc Spot Tours (☎ 8975 8721), opposite the McArthur River Caravan Park, offers a choice of several boat tours, of which the nightly croc-spotting excursions are very popular – for $20 you cruise the river with a spotlight and discover why you should never go swimming there. They also run one-day river and reef fishing trips ($65 and $110 per person, respectively), as well as overnight safaris (by arrangement) out to the Sir Edward Pellew Group. Minimum numbers apply to all tours. Tackle and bait are provided if required.

Skyport (☎ 8975 8844) operates scenic flights (by arrangement) up the McArthur River and over the Sir Edward Pellew Group. The cost is $250 per hour for the plane, which carries a maximum of five passengers. Brolga Air (☎ 8975 8791) offers a similar service but is more expensive.

Places to Stay & Eat

The *Borroloola Inn* (☎ 8975 8766) has air-con rooms starting at $40 for a twin. Its bistro restaurant serves a range of sensibly priced and generous meals, including (of course) local barramundi. The pub's Sunday night barbecue is excellent value ($12 for all you can eat), and the swimming pool, which is surrounded by large mango trees, is arguably the nicest place in Borroloola.

Just down from the pub, the *Borroloola Holiday Village* (☎ 8975 8742) has air-con units with attached bath, cooking facilities, colour TV and telephone (from $92 for a twin room). There are four economy rooms sleeping just one person each ($50), while budget beds in the bunkhouse cost $30. The bunkhouse contains four rooms each sleeping five people, with shared kitchen and laundry. Excellent barbecue facilities with lawn and shade trees are scattered about the complex.

There is little shade at the *McArthur River Caravan Park* (☎ 8975 8734), also in the main street, where powered sites cost $13.50 per night (add $2.50 if you're using an air-conditioner). Unpowered sites cost $10 for two adults plus $2.50 per extra adult and $1.50 for each child aged under 12. Unfortunately, the park's on-site vans and cabins are rarely available because of the shortage of long-term accommodation in town. If you strike it lucky, the vans cost $30 for a double, the cabins $65.

There's good fishing from the river bank at King Ash Bay, where the *Borroloola Boat & Fishing Club* (☎ 8975 9861) has its headquarters. Bush camping is permitted nearby, and if you join the club (a life membership costs $50 and an annual membership $20) you can make use of its toilet, shower and bar facilities. The bar is open from 5 to 8 pm daily. Caravanning members can hook up to the club's electricity supply, provided they're prepared to help pay for the diesel.

Getting There & Away

Airnorth (☎ 8975 7885) has three flights a week to Darwin ($350) and Katherine ($220), and less frequently to Ngukurr ($135) and Numbulwar ($100) in Arnhem Land.

AROUND BORROLOOLA
Barranyi National Park

Offshore from the mouth of the McArthur River is the islands of Sir Edward Pellew Group. One of the islands, North Island, is owned by the Barranyi people and part of it is managed by Parks & Wildlife as the Barranyi National Park.

While there are no facilities in the park, it is possible to camp if you have all your own gear, and the waters around the park offer excellent fishing.

Contact Parks & Wildlife in Borroloola before heading out to the park.

CAPE CRAWFORD

Cape Crawford, on the Carpentaria Highway

113 km south-west of Borroloola and 234 km east of the Stuart Highway, consists solely of the roadhouse known as the Heartbreak Hotel. Despite its name, Cape Crawford is a long way from the coast.

Organised Tours
Tours in 4WD vehicles are operated from the roadhouse. These vary from two to eight hours' duration and take you to a variety of outstanding attractions, such as strange rock formations, cool ferneries and tumbling waterfalls, none of which are open to the general public. Travellers with money to burn can take a scenic flight by helicopter over the spectacular Lost City (see the Roper Bar to Borroloola section earlier in this chapter).

Places to Stay
The *Heartbreak Hotel* (☎ 8975 9928) has a pleasant camping area with grass and shade ($8, $14 powered), and air-con motel-style accommodation at $45/50 with communal facilities.

Other services available include fuel sales and takeaway meals, and there's also a licensed dining room with decent meals for around $10.

WOLLOGORANG
From Borroloola a good gravel road heads south-east to Wollogorang station, on the NT-Queensland border, 258 km away. This road is best traversed with a 4WD vehicle, but conventional vehicles with high ground clearance should have no difficulty. Highlights of this stretch include some fine river crossings (the Wearyan, Robinson and Calvert rivers), and 60 km beyond the Calvert River there's some dramatic scenery.

Wollogorang station itself covers over 7000 sq km, and it boasts a fully licensed roadhouse and an 80-km frontage of pristine sandy beaches on the Gulf of Carpentaria. The coast can only be reached by 4WD vehicle; a small fee is charged for access.

Organised Tours
Fishing, exploring and pig-shooting safaris operate from the roadhouse, with costs for fishing and exploring tours starting at $80 per person per day for six people. Hunting expeditions are more expensive.

Alternatively, for $40 and upwards per person per day, you use your own vehicle and equipment and just hire the guide. These costs do not include meals and accommodation.

Places to Stay
The *Wollogorang Roadhouse* (☎ 8975 9944; fax 8975 9854), open seven days a week, has a licensed restaurant offering good, wholesome country cooking at reasonable prices. There is also a snack menu (including steak sandwiches, which come highly recommended).

The roadhouse has six air-conditioned units, each sleeping three, at $50/65/71 a single/double/triple. Camp sites cost $5 per person with or without power. Fuel is also available, as is takeaway beer.

BRUNETTE DOWNS
Brunette Downs station, covering a shade over 12,000 sq km, is on the Tablelands Highway 140 km north of the Barkly Homestead Roadhouse. It is accessible by conventional vehicles with care.

The Tablelands Highway itself dates back to WW II, but pastoral activity goes back to late last century as the stock route from Queensland to the Top End was established and new pastoral leases were taken up. Initially it was sheep which were farmed, but it was soon found that cattle fared much better in the harsh climate.

This station would be no different from any other in the region if it wasn't for the **Brunette Downs Bush Races**, held in June each year. A cast of thousands flocks in from miles around and it's a lively four days. There is no charge for camping or to use the showers and toilets, and a professional caterer supplies meals (around $10) and keeps the beer flowing. The race track is around 20 km from the homestead.

THE BARKLY REGION

It's a great outback event and one well worth the detour if you happen to be in the area. You can find out exact dates from the station itself (☎ 8964 4522), but they offer nothing in the way of facilities for travellers.

CONNELL'S LAGOON CONSERVATION RESERVE

This lonely reserve is on the Barkly Stock Route, east of Brunette Downs station. Here 260 sq km of pancake-flat land has been set aside to preserve a typical tableland area of Mitchell grass tussock grassland.

The reserve was surveyed by the (then) Conservation Commission in 1982 so a benchmark for undisturbed grassland could be established. It may look pretty uninspiring, but there's a surprising range of botanical diversity – 189 plant species were found to exist in the area.

The namesake lagoon doesn't amount to much, and in fact only exists after good rains.

Mammals found here include the red kangaroo, the dingo, and the long-haired rat, which in the dry times lives in the huge cracks which appear in the shrinking clay soils.

There are no visitor facilities within the reserve, with the exception of an information bay on the southern side of the track.

DAVENPORT-MURCHISON NATIONAL PARK

This 1120-sq-km national park takes in the Davenport Ranges east of Wauchope. The ranges were the site of wolfram mines at **Hatches Creek** early this century, but the remains of these lie on the Anurrete Aboriginal land, which is surrounded on three sides by the park.

For visitors the only real attraction is the **Old Police Station Waterhole**, which can be reached by 4WD vehicle from the Stuart Highway from the north (170 km via the track to Kurundi and Epenarra stations, which leaves the Stuart Highway at Bonney Well, 90 km south of Tennant Creek) or from the south (also 170 km via the Murray Downs station track, which heads east off the Stuart Highway close to where it crosses Taylors Creek, about 40 km north of Barrow Creek).

As yet there are no facilities in the park itself, so keep in mind that you need to be completely self-sufficient. Fuel is available at Kurundi, Epenarra and Murray Downs (☎ 8964 1958).

HUGH FINLAY

HUGH FINLAY

Top: Boat cruises are an ideal way to get on to the water at Katherine Gorge
Bottom: A soak in the warm Mataranka thermal pool is a great way to wash out the dust
of the track

Top: In the absence of any rail link to the south, road trains are the freight carriers
Middle: Huge boulders perched precariously form an eerie landscape, Devil's Marbles
Bottom: Old cutting on the Old *Ghan* Line between Alice Springs and Finke. It is now a popular 4WD track

Alice Springs

• *Population: 22,000*

In its brief 125-year history, the Alice, as it's usually known, has gone from a simple telegraph station on the Overland Telegraph Line to a modern town. While it is the country's biggest and most isolated outback town, outwardly it has little of the frontier atmosphere which many people expect to find. With the tourist boom of the last decade, most of the old buildings have made way for modern shopping plazas, hotels and offices, and the new sprawling suburbs are as unappealing as those in any Australian city.

But while the appearance is modern, the underlying fact is that this is a fairly small rural town in a beautiful but harsh environment a bloody long way from anywhere. The realisation that the outback is only a stone's throw away, as are some of the country's most spectacular natural wonders, does give the town a unique atmosphere which is a major draw for tourists.

For many visitors the Alice is a place to relax and replenish supplies after a number of days on the road. It's tempting to rush off to the many surrounding attractions which beckon, but it's worth spending a few days to seek out the reminders of the pioneering days that existed not so long ago. A visit to places such as the Royal Flying Doctor Base, which provides a lifeline to people in remote areas, can help you to get a grasp on what the Alice means to the people of central Australia.

HISTORY

The Alice Springs area is the traditional home of the Arrernte Aboriginal people, and to them it is Mparntwe. For them the heart of the area is the junction of the Charles (Anthelke Ulpeye) and Todd (Lhere Mparntwe) rivers, just north of Anzac Hill. All the topographical features of the town were formed by the creative ancestral beings – known as the Yeperenye, Ntyarlke and Utnerrengatye caterpillars – as they crawled

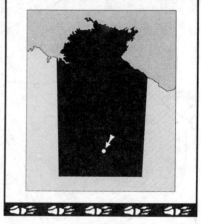

across the landscape from Emily Gap (Anthwerrke), in the MacDonnell Ranges south-east of town. Alice Springs today still has a sizeable Aboriginal community with strong links to the area.

The European history of Alice Springs begins with the Overland Telegraph Line in 1871. It was originally a staging point on the line, and a telegraph repeater station was built near a permanent water hole in the bed of the dry Todd River. The river was named after Charles Todd, Superintendent of Telegraphs back in Adelaide, and a spring near the water hole was named after Alice, his wife.

The taking up of pastoral leases in the Centre, combined with the rush of miners who flocked to the gold and 'ruby' fields to

ALICE SPRINGS

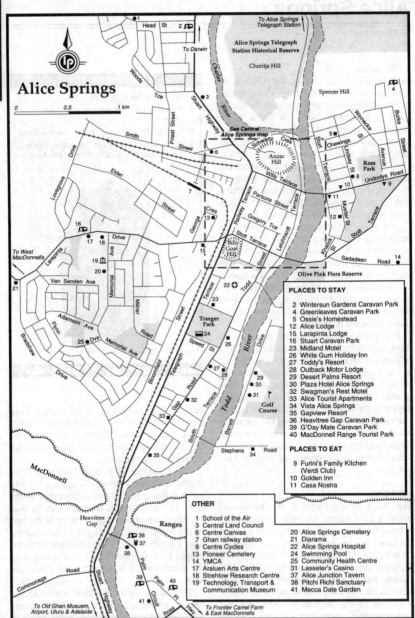

Alice Springs

0   0.5   1 km

See Central
Alice Springs map

To Darwin

To Alice Springs
Telegraph Station

Alice Springs Telegraph
Station Historical Reserve

Choritja Hill

Spencer Hill

Anzac
Hill

Ross
Park

Billy
Goat
Hill

To West
MacDonnells

Olive Pink Flora Reserve

Traeger
Park

River

Drive

Golf
Course

MacDonnell

Ranges

Heavitree
Gap

Stephens   Road

To Old Ghan Musuem,
Airport, Uluru & Adelaide

To Frontier Camel Farm
& East MacDonnells

PLACES TO STAY

2 Wintersun Gardens Caravan Park
4 Greenleaves Caravan Park
5 Ossie's Homestead
12 Alice Lodge
15 Larapinta Lodge
16 Stuart Caravan Park
23 Midland Motel
26 White Gum Holiday Inn
27 Toddy's Resort
28 Outback Motor Lodge
29 Desert Palms Resort
30 Plaza Hotel Alice Springs
32 Swagman's Rest Motel
33 Alice Tourist Apartments
34 Vista Alice Springs
35 Gapview Resort
36 Heavitree Gap Caravan Park
39 G'Day Mate Caravan Park
40 MacDonnell Range Tourist Park

PLACES TO EAT

9 Furini's Family Kitchen
    (Verdi Club)
10 Golden Inn
11 Casa Nostra

OTHER

1 School of the Air
3 Central Land Council
6 Centre Canvas
7 Ghan railway station
8 Centre Cycles
13 Pioneer Cemetery
14 YMCA
17 Araluen Arts Centre
18 Strehlow Research Centre
19 Technology, Transport &
    Communication Museum
20 Alice Springs Cemetery
21 Diarama
22 Alice Springs Hospital
24 Swimming Pool
25 Community Health Centre
31 Lasseter's Casino
37 Alice Junction Tavern
38 Pitchi Richi Sanctuary
41 Mecca Date Garden

the east, led to the establishment of Stuart in 1888, a few km south of the telegraph station, midway between it and Heavitree Gap in the MacDonnell Ranges. The expectation was that the town would grow quickly, especially as it was announced in 1890 that the railway line from the south was to extend all the way to Stuart.

Unfortunately the gold finds didn't amount to much, the rubies turned out to be worthless garnets and the railway took another 40 years to reach the town. The first pub, the Stuart Arms, was built in 1889, and within five years there was just three stores, one butcher and a handful of houses. Ten years later, the adventurous J J Murif, who was cycling across Australia from north to south, described the town as: 'Sleepy Hollow...all shade, silence and tranquillity'.

When the railway finally reached Stuart in 1929 the European population stood at about 30, but by the time the name was officially changed to Alice Springs in 1933, this had grown to around 400. This was partly due to the increased interest and prosperity generated by the railway, but also to the continuing expansion of the cattle industry. By the late 1930s the town had a hospital and a jail, and a population of around 1000.

WW II and the Japanese bombing raids over the Top End led to Alice Springs becoming a major military base and the administrative centre of the Northern Territory. It was the army's northern railhead, arsenal and troop reserve. The Darwin Overland Maintenance Force (DOMF) based in Alice Springs numbered around 8000 troops, and something like 200,000 troops passed through on their way to or from the Top End. Remarkably, many of the town's residents were actually classified as 'unessential' or 'undesirable' by the army area commander and were shipped south. It was during WW II that Alice Springs was connected to anywhere by a sealed road – the Track north to Darwin was bituminised to facilitate troop movements.

Following the activity of WW II, Alice Springs settled back into a period of slow but steady growth. The 1950s saw the begin-

nings of the Centre's vital tourism industry, which has played a lead role in the prosperity of the town ever since. The final boost to the Alice came with the sealing of the Stuart Highway from Port Augusta in 1987, and the Centre is now visited by almost half-a-million tourists each year.

CLIMATE

Summer days in Alice Springs can get very hot (up to 45°C) and even winter days are pretty warm. However, winter nights can freeze and a lot of people get caught off guard. In winter (June and July), five minutes after the sun goes down you can feel the heat disappear, and the average minimum nightly temperature is 4°C. Despite the Alice's dry climate and low annual rainfall, the occasional rains, which usually fall in summer, can be heavy and the Todd River may flood, as it did during the running of the 1993 and 1995 Henley-on-Todd Regatta resulting in the races being cancelled.

ORIENTATION

Alice Springs has one of the most dramatic locations of any inland town in the country. The MacDonnell Ranges form the southern boundary of the town, and the only access from the south is through the narrow Heavitree Gap (Ntaripe in Arrernte), named by OTL surveyor and discoverer of Alice Springs, William Mills, after his former school in Devon. The (usually dry) Todd River and the Stuart Highway both run roughly north-south through the town.

The centre of town is a conveniently compact area just five streets wide, bounded by the river on one side and the highway on the other. Anzac Hill forms the northern boundary to the central area while Stuart Terrace is the southern end. Many of the places to stay and virtually all of the places to eat are in this central rectangle.

Todd St is the main shopping street of the town; from Wills Terrace to Gregory Terrace it is a pedestrian mall. The bus centre is centrally located at the Melanka Lodge on

Todd St, one block south of the mall. The railway station is close to the centre, on the western side of the Stuart Highway in the town's light industrial area. The airport is 15 km south of town through the Gap and close to the Stuart Highway.

Larapinta Drive is the main road heading west, and a km or so west of the city there is a number of places worth visiting – the Araluen Arts Centre, Strehlow Research Centre, Aviation Museum and cemetery. To the east of the Todd River are most of the town's newer suburbs, and the more up-market accommodation and casino.

INFORMATION
Tourist Office

The Central Australian Tourism Industry Association (CATIA) office (☎ 8952 5199; fax 8953 0295) is on the corner of Hartley St and Gregory Terrace in the centre of town. The staff here are helpful and they have a range of brochures and maps. Parks & Wildlife also have a desk here. The office is open weekdays from 9 am to 6 pm, and on weekends from 10 am to 3 pm. This office issues permits to travel on the Mereenie Loop Rd in the Western MacDonnell Ranges.

The *Centralian Advocate* is Alice Springs'

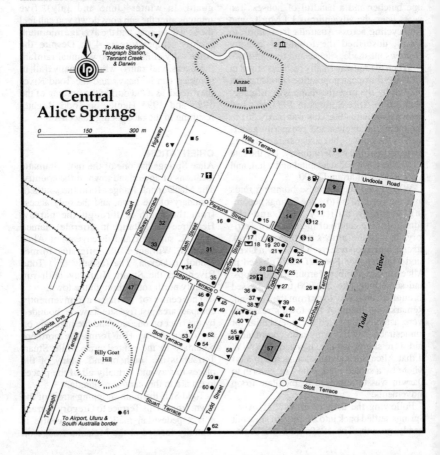

twice-weekly newspaper, and it's often a good source of info.

Post & Telecommunications

The main post office is on Hartley St, and there's a row of public phones outside.

Useful Organisations

Parks & Wildlife has a desk at the tourist office, with a comprehensive range of brochures on all the parks and reserves in the Centre. The main office (☎ 8951 8211) is just off the Stuart Highway at the Arid Zone Research Institute, about five km south of town.

The Department of Land, Planning & Environment office (☎ 8951 5344) on Gregory Terrace is a good source for maps, as is the Automobile Association of the Northern Territory (☎ 8953 1322), also on Gregory Terrace.

For fossicking permits and information, the Department of Mines & Energy (☎ 8951 5658) has its office in Minerals House on Hartley St, close to the tourist office.

The Alice Springs Library (☎ 8952 2303) is centrally located at the council offices on Todd St south of the mall.

Permits to visit Aboriginal land are issued by the Central Land Council (☎ 8951 6211; fax 8953 4345) at 31-33 Stuart Highway, north of the town centre.

The Alice Springs Peace Group (☎ 8952 2018) can tell you more about Pine Gap, the controversial US defence facility 20 km south of Alice Springs.

PLACES TO STAY

5	Desert Rose Inn
9	Todd Tavern
23	Pioneer YHA Hostel
26	Territory Motor Inn
59	Melanka's Backpackers Resort

PLACES TO EAT

1	Hungry Jacks
6	Red Rooster
11	Al Fresco
21	Ristorante Puccini
25	Flynn's on the Mall
27	Scotty's Tavern
34	Pizza Hut
37	Red Dog Cafe
38	La Cafeteriere
39	Cafe Mediterranean
40	Camel's Crossing Mexican Restaurant
44	La Casalinga
45	Uncles Tavern
49	Miss Daisy's
50	Eranova Cafeteria
51	Overlander Steakhouse
58	KFC

OTHER

2	RSL War Museum
3	Totem Theatre
4	Catholic Church
7	Anglican Church
8	Shell Service Station
10	Cinema

12	Westpac
13	ANZ Bank
14	Alice Plaza
15	Old Courthouse
16	Stuart Gaol
17	The Residency
18	Main Post Office
19	Commonwealth Bank
20	Ansett Airlines
22	Qantas
24	National Bank
28	Adelaide House
29	Flynn Church
30	Hartley St School
31	Yeperenye Centre
32	Coles 24-hr supermarket
33	Outdoor Territorian
35	Avis
36	Alice Springs Disposals
41	McCafferty's
42	Department of Land, Planning & Environment Offices
43	AANT & Arid Land Environment Centre
46	CATIA (Tourist Office)
47	K-Mart
48	Department of Mines & Energy
52	Panorama Guth
53	Hertz
54	Tuncks Store & Territory Rent a Car
55	Papunya Tula Artists
56	Bojangles
57	Library & Council Offices
60	Transit Centre & Thrifty Rent a Car
61	Royal Flying Doctor Service Base
62	Budget Rent a Car

Bookshops

There are a couple of good bookshops. The Aranta Gallery on Todd St just south of the mall is one, and there's a branch of Angus & Robertson in the Yeperenye Centre and Dymocks in the Alice Plaza.

The Arid Lands Environment Centre (☎ 8952 2497) on Gregory Terrace is a non-profit organisation which is full of info on both local and national environmental issues. It also sells a range of crafts and souvenirs.

Other Shops

Camping Gear There's a couple of choices here. Alice Springs Disposals (☎ 8952 5701) is a small shop with a surprisingly wide range of gear. It is in the small Reg Harris Lane, which runs off the southern end of the Todd St mall.

The Outdoor Territorian (☎ 8952 2848) is another possibility. The shop is in the large Coles complex on Gregory Terrace.

For locally made good quality swags, try Centre Canvas (☎ 8952 2453) on Smith St west of the centre.

Bicycle Sales & Repairs Centre Cycles (☎ 8953 2966) at 14 Lindsay St, across the river east of the centre, has a good range and also does short and long-term hire (see Getting Around later in this chapter for details).

Medical & Emergency Services

For medical problems and emergencies these are the agencies to contact:

Police
    For emergency police assistance ☎ 8951 8888 or 000.

Ambulance
    For ambulance service the number is ☎ 8952 2200, or simply ☎ 000.

Medical Treatment
    For emergency medical treatment phone the Alice Springs Hospital on ☎ 8951 7777.

Chemist
    For prescription services up until 8.30 pm there's the Alice Springs Amcal Chemist (☎ 8953 0089) in the Alice Plaza shopping centre.

Counselling
    Lifeline Crisis Line ☎ toll-free 1800 019 116.
    AIDS Council of Central Australia (☎ 8953 1118)
    Sexual Abuse Referral Centre (☎ 8951 5880)

Disabled Organisations
    For information on services for the disabled, contact the Disabled Services Bureau (☎ 8951 6722) at the Community Health Centre on Flynn Drive, south of the Araluen Arts Centre.

THINGS TO SEE

Anzac Hill

The best place to get an overview of the town is from Anzac Hill, at the northern end of Todd St. You can make the short, sharp ascent to the top on foot, or there's vehicle access from the western side. Aboriginal people call the hill Untyeyetweleye, the site of the Corkwood Dreaming, the story of a woman who lived alone on the hill. The Two Sisters ancestral beings (Arrweketye therre) are also associated with the hill.

From the top of the hill you have a fine view over modern Alice Springs and down to the MacDonnell Ranges that form a southern boundary to the town. At the western edge of the ranges is **Mt Gillen**, named after an explorer and naturalist. In Arrernte lore it is Alhekulyele, the nose of the wild dog creator where it lay down after an extended battle with an intruding dog from another area.

On the southern edge of the town centre you can see the small rise of **Billy Goat Hill** (Akeyulerre). Here the Two Sisters dreaming passed on their way north through the area. In the past water tanks were placed on top of the hill, but these have since been removed and the hill is now a registered sacred site.

Right at the foot of Anzac Hill on the north side is the **RSL War Museum**, which has an excellent collection of war memorabilia, and photos of Alice during WW II. This is also the RSL Club, so there's a bar and restaurant here too. It is open daily from 10 am.

Todd St Mall

Todd St is the main shopping street of the town and most of it is a pedestrian mall. Along this stretch there's an interesting array of sights, including a couple of historical buildings (see below), a proliferation of 'original' Aboriginal art galleries, pleasant outdoor cafes, a pub, and for real outback authenticity, a replica windmill. Of course there's also one of those useless signposts which tells you how many thousands of km you are from various places on the planet.

Historic Buildings

Although much of the town centre consists of modern buildings, there is still a surprising number of survivors from the old days.

Adelaide House – Flynn Church

Right in the centre of the Todd St mall is Adelaide House. Built in the 1920s as the Australian Inland Mission hospital, it was designed by the Reverend John Flynn and incorporated into its design was an air-cooling system which pushed cool air from the cellar up into the building. When a government hospital was opened in 1939, the building became a convalescent home for women. Today it houses the **John Flynn Memorial Museum**.

At the rear of the building stands a small stone hut, the former engine room for the hospital which also housed the radio where electrical engineer and inventor of the famous 'pedal radio', Alfred Traeger, and Flynn ran transmission tests of Traeger's new invention. It's open from 10 am to 4 pm Monday to Friday, and from 10 am to 12.30 pm on Saturday. Admission is $2.50 (children $1) and includes a cup of tea or coffee.

Flynn, who was the founding flying doctor, is also commemorated by the **John Flynn Memorial Church** next door.

Stuart Gaol

Hidden on Parsons St in the shadow of a modern building is the old jail, the oldest surviving building in Alice Springs. It was built in 1907-08, and had its first guests in 1909. Most of the early inmates were Aboriginal men, the most usual crime being the killing of cattle, with the usual sentence being not more than a few months. Prisoners with longer sentences were sent south to Port Augusta.

The building was used as a jail until a new one (now the Alice Springs Gaol) was built south of Billy Goat Hill in 1939. The police used the building first as a store and then as its unofficial club in the 1960s. Redevelop-

Alfred Traeger & the Pedal Radio

In the 1920s the severe isolation of outback stations was a major problem. Alfred Traeger, an electrical engineer and inventor from Adelaide, had for some years been playing around with radio transmitters, and was invited by Reverend John Flynn of the Inland Mission to come to the Centre and test out some radio equipment.

Outpost transmitters were set up at Hermannsburg and Arltunga, putting both these places in instant contact with the radio at the Inland Mission in the Alice. Realising that cumbersome equipment which relied on heavy copper-oxide batteries was impractical for use in the bush, Flynn employed Traeger to solve the problem, and he eventually came up with a radio set which used bicycle pedals to drive the generator.

Flynn commissioned Traeger to manufacture 10 similar sets, and these were installed in Queensland with a base at Cloncurry. Within a few years sets had been installed in numerous locations throughout the Territory, still using the Cloncurry base. The Alice Springs station officially started operation in April 1939.

Traeger's pedal sets revolutionised communications in the outback, and by the late 1930s voice communication (as against the previous Morse only) became the norm. Long after the pedal radios became obsolete, the two-way radios were often still referred to as 'the pedal'.

Traeger was awarded an OBE in 1944, and died in Adelaide in 1980. ∎

ment of the town centre in the 1970s threatened the building, but it was spared, largely thanks to the efforts of Doreen Brailing (see Wycliffe Well in The Barkly Region chapter). She managed to arouse enough public interest to save the building, and these days it is owned by the National Trust. It's open Tuesday and Thursday from 10 am to 12.30 pm, and on Saturday between 9.30 and noon.

Old Courthouse On the corner of Parsons and Hartley Sts, this building was constructed in 1928 as the office of the administrator of Central Australia (as the area was from 1927 to 1931). During the 1930s it was used as the local court, and it served this function up until 1980. These days it belongs to the NT Museums & Art Galleries, and it houses the fledgling **National Pioneer Women's Hall of Fame**. It is open from 10 am to 4 pm.

The Residency Across the road from the courthouse is the building which housed the Government Resident of Central Australia from 1927. It was in use as a government residence up until 1973, and it's now used for exhibits relating to the European history of Alice Springs. It is open from 9 am to 4 pm weekdays and 10 am to 4 pm on weekends.

Hartley St School Further along Hartley St, on the other side of the post office from the Residency, is the old Hartley St school. The core of the building was built in the late 1920s, but additions were made in the 1940s. By the 1950s there was more than 400 students at the school, and it was also the 'School of the Air' studio. The decision was finally taken to build a new school near Anzac Hill. The Hartley St School building was still used up until 1965, and since 1988 has been the home of the McDouall Stuart branch of the National Trust (☎ 8952 4516).

Tuncks Store On the corner of Hartley St and Stott Terrace is the verandahed Tuncks Store. It was built in 1939 and managed by Ralph Tuncks until it closed in 1979. The verandah overhanging the footpath was a common feature of early Alice Springs shops; this is the last to survive.

Pioneer Theatre Near the corner of Parsons St and Leichhardt Terrace, the old Pioneer Theatre is a former open-air, walk-in cinema dating from 1942. The cinema's owner, 'Snow' Kenna, opened a drive-in cinema in 1965 and this was the beginning of the end for the Pioneer Cinema; the coming of TV in 1972 was the real end. These days the cinema is a very comfortable YHA hostel.

Totem Theatre During WW II up to 8000 troops of the DOMF camped by what is now Anzac Oval, between Anzac Hill and the Todd River. All that remains of this once substantial camp are two Sidney Williams huts, which were part of the camps' first-aid post. They now serve as the Totem Theatre, the base for the Alice Springs Theatre Group for the last 30-odd years.

Museum of Central Australia
Upstairs in the Alice Plaza the Museum of Central Australia has a fascinating collection, including some superb natural-history displays. There's an interesting exhibition on meteors and meteorites (Henbury meteorites are on display). There are also exhibits on Aboriginal culture and displays of art of the Centre. Admission is $2 and it's open daily from 10 am to 5 pm.

Royal Flying Doctor Service Base
The RFDS base is close to the town centre in Stuart Terrace. It was established in 1939, largely with funds raised by the Women's Centenary Council of South Australia. The current studio building dates from 1979. The small museum here offers some interesting insights into the problems caused by isolation faced by many people in central Australia.

With most stations now having regular telephones, the RFDS radio-telephone service is not the vital link for most people which it once was. However, it still operates over-the-air routine medical clinics to isolated communities, with radio diagnosis by a doctor. It is also still the best way for vehicles travelling in remote areas to keep in touch.

The base (☎ 8952 1129) is open from 9 am to 4 pm Monday to Saturday, and from 1 to 4 pm on Sunday. Tours last half an hour and cost $2.50 (children 50c). There's also a small souvenir shop.

School of the Air

The School of the Air (☎ 8951 6800), which broadcasts school lessons to children living on remote outback stations, is on Head St, about a km north of the centre. This was the first school of its type in Australia, and it serves an area of 1.3 million sq km, reaching children on remote stations, roadhouses, Aboriginal communities and national parks. During school terms you can hear a live broadcast (depending on class schedules). The school is open from 8.30 am to 1 pm and 1.30 to 4.30 pm Monday to Friday, and admission is by donation ($2).

Technology, Transport & Communication Museum

Alice Springs has this interesting little museum housed in the former Connellan hangar on Memorial Ave, where the town's airport used to be in the early days. The museum includes a couple of poignant exhibits which pinpoint the dangers of outback aviation.

It's not all tragedy, however. There are exhibits on pioneer aviation in the Territory and, of course, the famous Royal Flying Doctor Service – that's Flynn's old plane out the front. The museum is open daily from 10 to 4 pm; admission is free.

Strehlow Research Centre

This centre (☎ 8951 8000), on Larapinta Dve close to the Technology Museum, commemorates the work of Professor Strehlow among the Arrernte people of the district (see the Hermannsburg Mission section in the James Ranges chapter). The main function of the building is to house the most comprehensive collection of Aboriginal spirit items in the country. These were entrusted to Strehlow for safekeeping by the Arrernte Aboriginal people years ago when they realised their traditional life was under threat. Because the items are so important, and cannot be viewed by an uninitiated male or *any* female, they are kept in a vault in the centre. There is, however, a very good display on the works of Strehlow, and on the Arrernte people.

The building itself is something of a feature too – it has the largest rammed-earth wall in the southern hemisphere. The centre is open daily from 10 am to 5 pm (no entry after 4.30 pm); entry is $4 ($2.50 children).

Araluen Arts Centre

The Araluen Arts Centre (☎ 8952 5022) on Larapinta Drive next to the Strehlow Centre has a small gallery of paintings by Albert Namatjira, members of the Arrernte community and Rex Batterbee, the European man who first introduced the young Namatjira to watercolour painting. The centre has another gallery which is used for temporary exhibitions and, as this is the town's performing arts centre, there's often other things happening too.

The stained-glass windows in the foyer are the centrepiece of the centre. The largest window features the Honey-Ant Dreaming (a popular central-Australian theme) and was designed by local artist Wenten Rubuntja. Other windows were designed by Aboriginal students at one of the local colleges.

The centre is open weekdays from 10 to 5 pm (4 pm on weekends). Entry to the Namatjira gallery is $2.

Alice Springs Cemetery

Adjacent to the aviation museum is this cemetery which contains a number of interesting graves. The most famous is that of Albert Namatjira – it's the sandstone one on the far side. This interesting headstone was erected in 1994, and features a terracotta tile mural of three of Namatjira's dreaming sites in the MacDonnell Ranges. The glazes forming the mural design were painted on by Namatjira's granddaughter, Elaine, and the other work was done by the other members of the Hermannsburg Potters.

Other graves in the cemetery include that of Harold Lasseter, who perished in 1931 while trying to rediscover the rich gold reef ('Lasseter's Reef) he found west of Ayers Rock 20 years earlier, and the anthropologist Olive Pink, who spent many years working with the Aboriginal people of the central deserts (see Olive Pink Flora Reserve later in this chapter).

Pioneer Cemetery

This is the original cemetery, and today it lies almost forgotten and rarely visited in the light-industrial area on the western side of the railway line on George Crescent. The gravestones here tell some of the story of the original settlers – including that of the young man who died of 'foul air'.

Panorama Guth

Panorama Guth (☎ 8952 2013), at 65 Hartley St in the town centre, is a huge, indoor, circular panorama which is viewed from an elevated, central observation point. It depicts almost all of the points of interest around the Centre with uncanny realism. Painted by a Dutch artist, Henk Guth, it measures about 60 metres in circumference. It's open daily except Sunday from 9 to 5 pm (Sunday 2 to 5 pm), and admission is $3 (children $1.50). Whether you think it's worth paying money to see a reproduction of what you may see for real is a different question!

Telegraph Station Historical Reserve

This 450-hectare reserve lies two km north of town by the Todd River, and it encloses the best preserved telegraph station of any of the original 12 which were built along the line in the 1870s.

Laying the telegraph line across the dry, harsh centre of Australia was no easy task, as the small museum at the old telegraph station shows. The original spring (which is in fact only a water hole), which the town is named

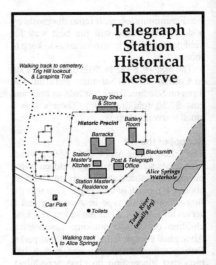

Telegraph Station Historical Reserve

Walking track to cemetery, Trig Hill lookout & Larapinta Trail

Buggy Shed & Store

Historic Precinct

Battery Room

Barracks

Station Master's Kitchen

Blacksmith

Post & Telegraph Office

Station Master's Residence

Alice Springs Waterhole

P Car Park

● Toilets

Todd River (usually dry)

Walking track to Alice Springs

after, is also here. The station was constructed of local stone and continued in operation until 1932. The barracks block (originally the telegraph office) was the first to be built, and dates from 1871, the buggy shed from 1874, the smith from 1876 and the telegraph office itself was built in the 1880s.

The station was also the original site of the settlement of Alice Springs until the town of Stuart was established to the south. As the post office (opened in 1878) was at Alice Springs there was much confusion over the names, and so when the post office moved to Stuart in 1932 the town's name was officially changed to Alice Springs.

After the post and telegraph functions were moved to Stuart in 1932, the buildings became an institution for Aboriginal and European children until the outbreak of WW II. The buildings were then used by the army to house Aboriginal conscripts, who were working on projects around town. They remained here until 1963 when they were moved to a new settlement south of Alice Springs, and the buildings became part of a historical reserve.

The buildings have been faithfully restored, and you get a good idea what life was like for the small community here, which consisted of the stationmaster and his family, four linesmen/telegraph operators, a cook, a blacksmith and a governess.

The station (☎ 8952 1013) is open daily from 8 am to 7 pm in winter, and until 9 pm in summer; entry is $2.50 ($1 for children). From April to October rangers give free guided tours several times daily, and a slide show three evenings a week; at other times you can use the informative self-guided brochure issued to all visitors.

The **Alice Springs** here are a great spot for a cooling dip, and the grassy picnic area by the station has barbecues, tables and some shady gum trees – a popular spot on weekends.

It's easy to walk or ride to the station from the Alice – just follow the path on the western (left hand) side of the riverbed; it takes about half an hour to ride. The main road out to the station is signposted to the right off the Stuart Highway about one km north of the centre of town. There's another pleasant circular walk from the station out by the old cemetery and Trig Hill. The station also marks the start of the **Larapinta Trail**, a trail for bushwalkers which heads out west through the MacDonnell Ranges (see the MacDonnell Ranges chapter for details).

Diarama

On the outskirts of town on Larapinta Drive, the diarama is open from 10 am to 5 pm daily. Admission to this rather quirky collection of three-dimensional illustrations of various Aboriginal legends is $2.50. Children love it.

Olive Pink Flora Reserve

Just across the Todd River from the centre, off Tuncks Rd, the 16-hectare Olive Pink Flora Reserve has a collection of shrubs and trees which are typical of the 200-km area around Alice Springs. This arid-zone botanic garden, named after a prominent central Australian anthropologist, is open from 10 am to 6 pm, and there's a rammed-earth visitor centre open between 10 am and 4 pm. There are some short walks in the reserve, including the climb to the top of Annie Meyer Hill in the Sadadeen Range, from where there's a fine view over the town.

The hill is known to the Arrernte as Tharrarltneme and is a registered sacred site. Looking to the south, in the middle distance is a small ridge running east-west; this is Ntyarlkarle Tyaneme, one of the first sites created by the caterpillar ancestors, and the name relates that this was where the caterpillars crossed the river.

Pitchi Richi Sanctuary

Just south of the Heavitree Gap causeway is Pitchi Richi ('gap in the range'), a miniature folk museum with a collection of sculptures by Victorian artist William Ricketts and an amazing range of various implements and other household items used by early pioneers. There's also billy tea and damper, an interesting and lively chat on Arrernte Aboriginal lore and traditions, and you can try your hand at boomerang throwing and that old Aboriginal skill, whip-cracking.

The sanctuary itself doesn't look too promising, but it's well worth a visit. It's open daily from 9 am to 2 pm; entry is $8 (children $5).

Mecca Date Garden

Just a little further along from Pitchi Richi on Palm Circuit is the Mecca Date Garden. Date palms were first introduced into central Australia by Afghan cameleers last century. Entry is free and, not surprisingly, there are dates and date products (such as muffins, scones, cakes and ice cream) for sale.

Frontier Camel Farm

A further five km along is the Frontier Camel Farm (☎ 8953 0444), where you have the chance to ride one of the beasts. These strange 'ships of the desert', guided by their Afghani masters, were the main form of transport before the railways were built. There's a museum with displays about camels, and a guided tour and camel ride is held daily at 10.30 am (and 2 pm April to October).

Also here is the **Arid Australian Reptile**

House, which has an excellent collection of snakes and lizards.

The farm is open daily from 9 am to 5 pm. The cost of the camel tour is $10 ($5 for children aged six to 12) including a visit to the reptile house. There are also extended camel trips from here (see Organised Tours later in this chapter).

The Old *Ghan* & Transport Hall of Fame

At the MacDonnell siding, off the Stuart Highway 10 km south of Alice Springs, a group of local railway enthusiasts have restored a collection of *Ghan* locomotives and carriages on a stretch of disused siding from the old narrow-gauge *Ghan* railway track. You can wander round the equipment, watch the restoration work and learn more about this extraordinary railway line at the information centre.

Also here is the Transport Hall of Fame, with a fine collection of old vehicles, including some very early road trains, and other transport memorabilia.

The area is open from 9 am to 5 pm daily and admission is $6 (children free), or $3 if you just want to visit one or other of the museums (☎ 8955 5047).

There are also trips on the old *Ghan* three days a week out to Mt Ertiva siding, nine km south of town. The trip starts at 10 am, takes 1½ hours and costs $18 (children $7), and this includes entry to both the museums. Morning tea is available in the dining car. MacDonnell siding is on the Alice Wanderer bus route (see Getting Around later in this chapter).

Chateau Hornsby

Alice Springs actually has a winery. Chateau Hornsby (☎ 8953 4800) is 15 km out of town, five km off the road, before you get to the airport turn-off. The wine they produce here (moselle, riesling-semillon and Shiraz) is not bad at all, although most of it gets sold to people intrigued at the novelty of a central Australian wine.

The pleasant restaurant here is open for lunchtime barbecues and in the evenings, and is a popular excursion from town. You can pedal out to Chateau Hornsby by bicycle – after tasting a little free wine the distance back seems much shorter. The easier option is to take the Alice Wanderer. The free Sunday afternoon jazz sessions are very popular, as is the Ted Egan show, which takes place from April to October (see the Entertainment section later in this chapter).

ACTIVITIES

Swimming

Most of the accommodation places have a pool, or else there's the council swimming centre on Speed St just south of the town centre. It's open from September to April, and the hours are 6 to 7.30 am, and 9 am to 6 pm weekdays, 10 am to 7.30 pm weekends, and entry is $2.25 ($0.90 children).

Cycling

Alice Springs is a flat town which lends itself to getting around by bicycle, and there are a number of marked bike tracks. For bike rentals try your accommodation, or Centre Cycles (see the Getting Around section later in this chapter for rates).

Golf

The Alice Springs Golf Club (☎ 8952 1921) is on Cromwell Dve east of the river.

Indoor Abseiling & Rockclimbing

At the YMCA (☎ 8952 5666), east of the river on Sadadeen Rd, there's the Rockratz indoor climbing gym, which features a 155-sq-metre climbing area with 14 routes ranging from grade eight to 28. Climbing costs $5.50, or $4 if you have your own equipment. Opening hours are 6 to 8 pm weeknights, noon to 2 pm Saturday and 2.30 to 4 pm Sunday (closed Tuesday).

ORGANISED TOURS

The tourist office can tell you about all sorts of organised tours from Alice Springs. There are the usual big-name operators and a host of small local operators. There are bus tours, 4WD tours, camel tours, even balloon tours.

Note that although many of the tours don't operate daily, there is at least one trip a day to one or more of the major attractions: Uluru-Kata Tjuta National Park (Ayers Rock & the Olgas), Kings Canyon, Palm Valley, both the Western and Eastern MacDonnell ranges, Simpson's Gap and Standley Chasm. Tours to less popular places, such as Rainbow Valley and Chambers Pillar, operate less frequently.

Most of the tours follow similar routes and you see much the same on them all, although the level of service and the degree of luxury will determine how much they cost. All the hostels can book tours, and they will also know exactly which company is offering the best deals.

Town Tours

Alice Wanderer Express Tours (☎ 8952 2111) can whiz you around five of the town's major sights in 2½ hours for $28 ($15 for children) including admission fees. The tours depart daily at 8.30 and 11.30 am, and you are collected from your accommodation.

Aboriginal Culture Tours

Rod Steinert (☎ 8955 5000; fax 8955 5111) operates a variety of tours, including the popular $65 ($42 for children aged three to 14) Dreamtime & Bushtucker Tour. It's a half-day trip in which you meet some Warlpiri Aboriginal people and learn a little about their traditional life. There are demonstrations of weapons and foods and samples of barbecued witchetty grubs. While this is basically a good tour, it does cater for the large bus groups and so can be impersonal. You can do the same tour with your own vehicle for $48 ($29).

Oak Valley Day Tours (☎ 8956 0959; fax 8956 0965) is an Aboriginal-owned and run organisation that makes day trips to Ewaninga and Rainbow Valley. These trips also go to Mpwellare and Oak Valley, both on the Hugh River Stock Route and both of cultural significance to the Aboriginal people. The cost is $110 ($90 for children aged four to 16) and this includes lunch, and morning and afternoon tea.

Visual Arts & Specialist Tours (VAST; ☎ /fax 8952 8233) is a small company that specialises in taking small groups to remote Aboriginal communities and rock-art sites which are otherwise inaccessible. The cost is $700 per group per day (one to nine people), including permits, camping equipment and meals.

Camel Rides

Camel treks are another central Australian attraction. You can have a short ride for a few dollars at the Frontier Camel Farm (☎ 8953 0444; fax 8955 5015), or take the longer Todd River Ramble, which is a one-hour ride along the bed of the Todd River ($35, $25 for children up to 15). There are also extended rides from $300 for a two-day trip.

Noel Fullerton's Camel Outback Safaris (☎ 8956 0925), based at Stuart Well 90 km south of Alice Springs, also operates camel tours.

Hot-Air Ballooning

Sunrise balloon trips are also popular and cost from $98 ($50 for children six to 16), which includes breakfast and the 30-minute flight. One-hour flights cost around $145 ($80), or you can just tag along as part of the chase crew for $35 ($25).

Operators include Outback Ballooning (☎ toll-free 1800 809 790; fax 8952 3869), Ballooning Downunder (☎ (089) 52 8816; fax 8952 3869) and Spinifex Ballooning (☎ toll-free 1800 677 893; fax 8952 2862), which operates from Chateau Hornsby.

Tours Further Afield

Sahara Tours (☎ 8953 0881; fax 8953 2414) offers very good daily camping trips to the Rock and elsewhere and these are popular with backpackers. It charges $200 for a two-day trip to the Rock and Olgas, or you can pay an extra $85 and spend an extra day taking in Kings Canyon – well worthwhile if you have the time.

Northern Territory Adventure Tours (☎ 8952 1474; fax 8952 3819) operates the popular Ayers Rock Plus, which has similar two/three-day tours for $195/285. It also offers a two-day trip to the Rock which includes Kings Canyon for $210, but this is cramming an awful lot into a very short time. AKT and Tracks are other cheaper operators.

4WD Tours Outback Flavour Tours (☎ 8955 0444) has evening tours to Rainbow Valley. These leave Alice Springs at 3.30 pm in winter and 4 pm in summer, and you are taken to Rainbow Valley for sunset and an evening meal. The cost is $49 per person.

Another operator is Outback Experience (☎ (089) 53 2666), which has day trips from Alice Springs to Chambers Pillar and Rainbow Valley for $95 per person ($85 for children under 16).

Austour (☎ toll-free 1800 335 009; fax (03) 9770-2773) does a good five-day loop from Alice Springs which heads off west to Mt Conner, Ipolera and Uluru, and then crosses the Stuart Highway returning to Alice Springs via Mount Dare and Old Andado. It's possible to tag along in your own vehicle, and the cost for this is $750 if you have your own camping gear, or $950 if you want budget accommodation and $1050 for slightly more expensive rooms.

Air Tours If your time is really limited you can take a one-day air safari to Uluru and back for around $330 ($245 children three to 12), which includes a tour around the Rock and entry fees. Contact Winjeel Airways (☎ toll-free 1800 064 141; fax 8953 2322).

Airnorth (☎ toll-free 1800 627 474; fax 8945 3559) also does a day air tour which includes climbing the Rock, a trip to the Olgas, buffet lunch and sunset viewing.

FESTIVALS & EVENTS
No Territory town would be complete without its list of eccentric festivals, and Alice Springs is no exception. Darwin has a race of boats made from beer cans; in Alice the boats have no bottom and the river has no water!

Heritage Week
Held in April, this is the week when the emphasis is on the town's European past. Re-enactments, displays and demonstrations of old skills are all held.

Alice Springs Cup Carnival
The autumn racing carnival takes place throughout April and May, the highlight being the Alice Springs Cup held on the holiday Monday in early May.

Camel Cup
This is one of the biggest events of the year, and is worth being around in early May just for the hell of it, as it's a great day out. It's held in Blatherskite Park, south of the Gap, and in addition to the camel races, there are sideshows, novelty events and lots of drinking.

Bangtail Muster
This is the Alice Springs answer to Melbourne's Moomba festival, with a parade of floats, also held on the Monday holiday in early May.

Alice Craft Acquisition
Held in May each year at the Araluen Arts Centre, this started out 20 years ago as the craft section of the local Alice Prize. Today it's a highly regarded national exhibition, where pieces are selected from entries to become additions to the Alice Crafts Acquisition Collection, part of which is displayed at the airport, the rest at the Araluen Centre.

Country Music Festival
While this isn't Tamworth, Territorians give this June festival a bash, and there's plenty of live music and foot-tappin' goin' on, buddy.

Finke Desert Race
This is a motorbike race held on the Queen's Birthday weekend in June. The race takes riders from Alice Springs south the 240 km to Finke along unmade roads, and the following day they race back again!

Alice Springs Show
The annual agricultural show, which is held in June, has the usual rides and attractions, as well as displays and events organised by local businesses.

Alice Springs Rodeo

Yep, Alice has one of these too and its held in August. All the usual events are featured including bareback riding, steer wrestling, calf roping and ladies barrel races.

Henley-on-Todd Regatta

This is the town's tilt at eccentricity when barefoot crews race bottomless boats down the dry sandy bed of the Todd River. It's a very colourful spectacle, and was recently moved from January to October as it was washed out twice in the space of five years. The last thing you need at a boat race is water for goodness sake!

Verdi Club Beerfest

This is held in early October, at the end of the regatta. It's held at the Verdi Club on Undoolya Rd and there are many frivolous activities including spit the dummy, tug of war, and stein-lifting competitions. Sample a wide range of Australian and imported beers, then fall over.

Corkwood Festival

This annual festival is held on the last Sunday in November. It's basically an arts and crafts festival, but there's also a good deal of music, other live entertainment and food. Craft stalls are the focus during the afternoon, while the evening is capped with a bush dance.

PLACES TO STAY

With tourism being the mainstay of the local economy, it comes as no surprise to find that Alice Springs has an excellent range of accommodation options.

Places to Stay – bottom end

Camping & Caravan Parks None of the Alice Springs caravan parks are really close to the centre, the closest probably being the Stuart on Larapinta Dve about three km west of the centre.

G'Day Mate Tourist Park (☎ 8952 9589), Palm Circuit, near the Mecca Date Garden and Pitchi Richi Sanctuary; camp sites ($14, $16 with power) and self-contained cabins which accommodate up to six people ($46 double, $7 each extra adult).

Greenleaves Tourist Park (☎ 8952 8645), three km north-east on Burke St; camp sites ($15, $17.50 with power) and four-bed on-site vans ($34, plus $8 each extra adult).

Heavitree Gap Caravan Park (☎ 8952 4866), Palm Circuit, three km south of town; camp sites ($12, $15 with power) and on-site vans ($37, plus $7 each extra adult).

MacDonnell Range Tourist Park (☎ 8952 6111), Palm Place, four km from town; camp sites ($13.50, $16.50 with power) and on-site cabins (from $30 to $60).

Stuart Caravan Park (☎ 8952 2547), three km west on Larapinta Drive; camp sites ($12, $15 with power), six-bed on-site vans ($37, $6) and four-bed cabins ($47, $7).

Wintersun Gardens Caravan Park (☎ 8952 4080), 3.5 km north on the Stuart Highway; camp sites ($12, $15.50 with power), six-bed on-site vans ($35 double, $6.30) and six-bed cabins ($41 to $49 double, $6.30).

Hostels There are plenty of hostels and guesthouses in Alice Springs. All the places catering to backpackers have the usual facilities and services – pool, courtesy bus, travel desk, bicycle hire, etc.

Right in the centre of town, on the corner of Leichhardt Terrace and Parsons St in the old Pioneer walk-in cinema, is the YHA *Pioneer Hostel* (☎ 8952 8855; fax 8952 4144). It has 62 beds in air-con dorms, and charges $12 in a four-share room, $14 for a twin. There's a swimming pool here, and bicycles for hire.

Also central is the very popular *Melanka's Backpackers Resort* (☎ toll-free 1800 815 066; fax 8952 4587) at 94 Todd St, just a couple of steps from the bus station. This is a huge place with a variety of air-con rooms, ranging from eight-bed dorms at $10 through to twin-shares at $15 per person. There are also singles/doubles for $40/45, or $55/65 with TV, fridge and attached bath. There's a cafeteria here, and the Waterhole Bar is one of the most popular travellers' drinking spots in the Alice.

Over the river and still just a short walk

from the centre, is the relaxed *Alice Lodge* (☎ 8953 1975) at 4 Mueller St. This is a small, quiet and friendly hostel with a garden and pool. Nightly rates are $12 in the dorm, $14 in a four-share room, $25 for a single and $16 per person in a double (prices include sheets; quilt hire is $1 with a $9 deposit). There's a small kitchen, and barbecue and laundry facilities.

Also on this side of the river, at 18 Warburton St, is *Ossie's Homestead* (☎ 8952 2308). A bed in the 12-bed dorm is $12, in a four-bed room $15, and a double is $35. There's a swimming pool and the usual facilities, as well as a pet kangaroo called Boomer.

Back on the other side of the river, at 41 Gap Rd, is *Toddy's Resort* (☎ toll-free 1800 806 240; fax 8952 1767). This complex has laundry facilities and a communal kitchen for those not in the self-contained units. There's a swimming pool, barbecue and small shop on the site. Prices are $10 for six-bed dorms with shared facilities, $12 with TV and bathroom, $34 for doubles, and $45 with bathroom. Cheap meals are available at $3 for breakfast and $6.50 for dinner, and there's also bike hire.

Places to Stay – middle

Hotels Right by the river, at 1 Todd Mall, is the *Todd Tavern* (☎ 8952 1255). This pub gets noisy when there are bands playing on weekends, but it's otherwise quite a reasonable place to stay. Room rates are $38 for singles/doubles (some with bath) including a light breakfast.

At the southern end of Gap Rd, just before you go through Heavitree Gap, is the *Gapview Resort Hotel* (☎ 8952 6611; fax 8952 8312). It's about one km from the centre, and charges from $58 to $74 for double room with bathroom, fridge and TV.

Apartments & Holiday Flats This is probably the category with the least choice. There's very few apartments and flats for rent; in most cases the best you can do is a motel-type room with limited cooking facil-

ities, which usually consists of an electric frypan and a microwave oven.

The *Alice Tourist Apartments* (☎ toll-free 1800 806 142; fax 8953 2950) is on Gap Rd. There's 24 one and two-room, self-contained, air-con apartments for $63 for a double, $95 for four and $105 for six people, about $10 less in summer. These places consist of a main room with sleeping, cooking and dining facilities, and the larger flats have a second room with two or four beds. There's a communal guest laundry and the obligatory swimming pool. This is a good option for families.

The *White Gum Holiday Inn* (☎ toll-free 1800 896 131; fax 8953 2092) at 17 Gap Rd, also has 24 rooms with separate kitchen at $78 for up to four people.

On Palm Circuit, south of the Gap, are the *Sienna Apartments* (☎ 8952 7655), where accommodation costs $55/65 in suites with attached bath, fridge and TV. Some units have cooking facilities, and these cost $65/75.

Another motel-type place with cooking facilities in the rooms is the *Outback Motor Lodge* (☎ toll-free 1800 896 133; fax 8953 2166) at 13 South Terrace. Rooms can sleep up to four people (one double and two single beds) and cost $75 for two and $95 for four people.

On Barrett Drive, next to the Plaza Hotel Alice Springs, the *Desert Palms Resort* (☎ toll-free 1800 678 037; fax 8953 4176) has spacious rooms, each with limited cooking facilities, at $68 for two, and $80 for two adults and two children. There's a large island swimming pool and nicely landscaped gardens.

Conveniently central is the *Larapinta Lodge* (☎ 8952 7255; fax 8952 7101), at 3 Larapinta Dve just over the railway line from the town centre. It has singles/doubles for $55/67, with communal kitchen and laundry, and the obligatory swimming pool.

Also close to the centre is the *Desert Rose Inn* (☎ toll-free 1800 896 116; fax 8952 3232) at 15 Railway Terrace. Rooms here have an electric frypan and microwave, and cost from $71/79.

Motels Alice Springs has a rash of motels, and prices range from around $50 to $100 for a double room. There are often lower prices and special deals during the hot summer months.

At 67 Gap Rd there's the *Swagman's Rest Motel* (☎ 8953 1333) with singles/doubles for $52/62. The units are self-contained and there's a swimming pool.

Close by, at 4 Traeger Ave, is the *Midland Motel* (☎ 8952 1588; fax 8952 8280) which charges from $50/55 for its rooms, and there's also a licensed restaurant.

On Leichhardt Terrace facing the Todd River is the *Territory Motor Inn* (☎ 1800 089 644; fax 8952 7829), with every available mod-con from $90. There's a licensed restaurant here and meals can be served in your unit.

Places to Stay – top end

The top-end accommodation is all on the eastern side of the river where there's more room to spread out.

At the top of the range there's the *Plaza Hotel Alice Springs* (☎ toll-free 1800 675 212; fax 8952 3822), on Barrett Dve, with rooms from $205 up to $400. The hotel is very well equipped, with facilities including heated pool, spa/sauna and tennis courts.

Almost next door is the *Lasseter's Hotel Casino* (☎ toll-free 1800 808 975; fax 8953 1680) with double rooms from $105.

Another top-end option is the *Alice Springs Pacific Resort* (☎ toll-free 1800 805 055; fax 8953 0995) at 34 Stott Terrace right by the Todd River, not far from the centre of town. Rooms here go for $140/150, and it includes such luxuries as a heated pool.

Lastly, there's the *Vista Alice Springs* (☎ toll-free 1800 810 664; fax 8952 1988), stuck in the middle of nowhere at the foot of the MacDonnell Ranges. The 140 units here go for $120 each.

Places to Stay – around Alice Springs

There are a couple of places to stay in the Alice area which offer an interesting alternative to staying in Alice Springs itself.

The *Ooraminna Bush Camp* (☎ 8953 0170; fax 8953 0171) is half-an-hour's drive south of town along the road to Maryvale station and Chambers Pillar. This is a tourism venture run by the owners of Maryvale station, and you can camp in a swag under the stars ($80 including dinner and breakfast). They also operate horse trail rides ($65 per day) and one-day camel safaris ($135). All prices include transfers from Alice Springs.

About 25 km north of Alice Springs is *Bond Springs Homestead* (☎ 8952 9888; fax 8953 0963), where there's one fully self-contained cabin which sleeps up to five people, and homestead rooms with en-suite bathrooms ($150 B&B, $180 full board).

PLACES TO EAT
Cafes, Snacks & Fast Food

There are numerous places for a sandwich or light snack along the Todd St mall. Many of them put tables and chairs outside – ideal for breakfast on a cool, sunny morning.

The *Jolly Swagman*, in Todd Plaza off the mall, is a pleasant place for sandwiches and light snacks. Also off the mall, but on the other side, *Joanne's Cafe* offers similar fare. *Le Cafeteriere* is at the southern end of the mall and is open for breakfast, burgers, sandwiches, etc. Right next door is the *Red Dog*, a very similar place with tables and umbrellas out on the footpath.

The big Alice Plaza has a lunchtime cafeteria-style eating place called *Fawlty's* with snacks, light meals, sandwiches and a salad bar. Also here is *Doctor Lunch*, which is good for pancakes and coffee. Across the mall, the Springs Plaza has *Golly it's Good*, with more sandwiches and snacks.

In the Yeperenye shopping centre on Hartley St there's the *Boomerang Coffee Shop,* the *Bakery*, another *Fawlty's* outlet and a big Woolworths supermarket.

The closest Alice Springs comes to a new-age restaurant is *Cafe Mediterranean*, in the small Fan Lane off the mall, opposite the Red Dog cafe. It has an excellent range of health-food dishes, and a very relaxed atmosphere. You can BYO and the front window is a good place to check out the notices for what's happening around town. Dishes here cost around $5 to $10.

The *Swingers Cafe* (☎ 8952 9291) on Gregory Terrace serves trendy items, such as foccaccia, and foreign treats like curry laksa. It's a good spot, despite the silly name.

Another popular place, especially on Friday evening, is *Uncles Tavern* on the corner of Gregory Terrace and Hartley St. Here you can have a beer or a cappuccino, as well as light meals and snacks.

Alice Springs also has its share of the well-known fast-food outlets such as *KFC, Hungry Jack's, Red Rooster* and *Pizza Hut* but, remarkably, no McDonald's.

Pub Meals

Far and away the most popular place is the *Caf* at the Todd Tavern. The food is tasty and cheap, and there are special nights when you can get a meal for $5 to $8.

Scotty's Tavern is a small bar in the mall, and it has substantial main courses, such as barra or steak, for $18, and other main courses range from $12 to $16.

Restaurants

Town Centre The *Eranova Cafeteria*, at 70 Todd St, is one of the busiest eating spots in town and it's a comfortable place, with a good selection of excellent food. It's open for breakfast, lunch and dinner from Monday to Saturday. Meals range from $7 to $15.

Round the corner at 105 Gregory Terrace, *La Casalinga* has been serving up pasta and pizza for many years; it's open from 5 pm to 1 am every night. Meals cost $10 to $15 and it has a bar. You can also get good pasta at the licensed *Al Fresco* at the northern end of the mall. It's open from 10 am daily.

Also in the centre is the licensed *Flynn's on the Mall*, opposite the John Flynn Memorial Museum. It's a popular place, with meals in the $13 to $17 range. Meats such as crocodile and kangaroo are featured here, and indeed at quite a few restaurants around town.

The *Ristorante Puccini* (☎ 8953 0935) is also on the mall and serves excellent home-made pasta and char-grilled fish, and have

Italian-inspired desserts such as marinated fruit with ricotta zabaglione. Expect to pay around $18 for a main course.

Miss Daisy's (☎ 8952 8977), at the Diplomat Motel on Hartley St, features a variety of exotic Territory flora and fauna on its menu, including emu steaks and desert plum sorbet.

Across the river from the centre, on the corner of Undoolya Rd and Sturt Terrace, the *Casa Nostra* (☎ 8952 6749) is another pizza-and-pasta specialist.

Of course the Alice has to have a steak-house, and you can try the *Overlander Steakhouse* (☎ 8952 2159) at 72 Hartley St. It features 'Territory food' such as beef, buffalo, kangaroo and camel – and the 'Drover's Blowout' ($32.50) is a carnivore's delight! It's quite popular, but not that cheap with other main courses in the $18 to $25 range.

Hidden away at the rear of Fan Lane off the mall is the *Camel's Crossing Mexican Restaurant* (☎ 8952 5522), which has a varied menu of both vegetarian and meat dishes. It's open nightly except Sunday, and a two-course meal will set you back about $25.

At the Bath St entrance to the Yeperenye Centre is the *Shanti* (☎ 8952 9115), a small Indian restaurant with beef, lamb, chicken, fish and vegetarian main courses for around $12. The dishes are mostly north Indian and are quite good value. You can BYO here, and it's open for lunch and dinner Monday to Saturday.

In the Verdi Club east of the centre there's *Furini's Family Kitchen* (☎ 8952 2113), which offers kebabs, pasta dishes and hot savoury crêpes; main courses are good value at around $7.50. The restaurant is open daily from 5 pm, and it does free home deliveries.

Chinese There are a number of Chinese restaurants around the Alice. The *Oriental Gourmet* (☎ 8953 088) is on Hartley St, near the corner of Stott Terrace.

Chopsticks (☎ 8952 3873), on Hartley St at the Yeperenye shopping centre, is said to be good, but it's only open in the evenings.

Also good is the bright-yellow *Golden Inn* (☎ 8952 6910) on Undoolya Rd, just over the bridge from the centre. Aside from the usual items you can sample some Malaysian and Szechuan dishes. It's open for lunch on weekdays and for dinner every day

Out of Town Out-of-town dining possibilities include a barbecue lunch or dinner at the *Chateau Hornsby* (☎ 8955 5133) winery south of town. At lunchtime main meals cost from $8.50 to $12, the dinner menu is more expensive at around $18. In the evenings you can also take in the Ted Egan Show, but you'll need to book in advance for this (see the Entertainment section later in this chapter).

Dining Tours

There are a few interesting alternatives which involve taking a ride out of town. One of these is *Dinner With the Old Ghan* tour at MacDonnell siding south of town. It operates twice weekly from April to October, and you travel by the old *Ghan* to a point south of town, where a campfire meal is provided; the cost of the tour is $69. The meal is actually provided by the *Camp Oven Kitchen* (☎ 8953 1411), and consists of soup and damper, and a roast, all cooked in 'camp ovens' – cast-iron pots which are buried in hot coals. It's also possible to have the meal without the train ride for $50 on Monday, Wednesday and Saturday evenings.

Take a Camel to Breakfast/Dinner is another popular dining option. This combines a one-hour camel ride with a meal at the Frontier Camel Farm (☎ 8953 0444). The cost for meals is $49 ($30 for children aged six to 12) for breakfast and $75 ($50) for dinner.

Tailormade Tours (☎ 8952 1731) and Alice Leisure Tours (☎ 8952 3357) both operate evening bush barbecues where you head out of town to a remote spot, throw a boomerang and tuck into a barbecue with all the trimmings. If you've never eaten food cooked on an open fire it may be worth the quite hefty price of $65 or $48 respectively, otherwise don't bother.

ENTERTAINMENT

Not much. At the Todd Tavern, by the river on the corner of Wills and Leichhardt terraces, the *Jam Session* has live bands on Monday night, sometimes featuring better known bands.

Bojangles is a restaurant and nightclub on Todd St, and the *Alice Junction Tavern* on Palm Circuit has a disco on Friday and Saturday nights.

The *Waterhole Bar*, at the Melanka on Todd St, is the place for a beer and to meet other travellers, and there's occasionally live bands as well. The bar upstairs in the Alice Plaza (formerly the Stuart Arms), should also by now have reopened.

Outback 'character' Ted Egan puts on a performance of tall tales and outback songs three nights a week at *Chateau Hornsby* ($15, or $33 with dinner).

If you want to watch the Australian gambling enthusiasm in a central Australian setting head for *Lasseter's Casino*, but dress up.

There are all sorts of events at the *Araluen Arts Centre* on Larapinta Drive, including temporary art exhibits, theatre and music performances and regular films. Bookings can be made at the Araluen booking office (☎ 8952 5022).

On Todd St there's a cinema centre which shows standard wide-release movies.

THINGS TO BUY

Alice Springs has a number of art galleries and craft centres. If you've got an interest in central Australian art or you're looking for a piece to buy, there's a couple of places where you can buy direct from the artists. The Papunya Tula Artists shop is on Todd St just south of the mall, or there's Jukurrpa Artists at 35 Gap Rd. Both of these places are owned and run by the art centres which produce the work.

The Central Australian Aboriginal Media Association (CAAMA) has a shop in the Yeperenye shopping centre on Hartley St and is another very good place, and prices are reasonable.

There are plenty of other, generally more

commercial outlets for Aboriginal art. Two of the better ones are Gallery Gondwana and the Original Aboriginal Dreamtime Gallery, both on the Todd St mall.

For top quality paintings and artefacts, including real boomerangs and dijeridus (the latter from the Top End, as traditionally they were never used in the Centre), check out the small VAST Gallery, in the Alice Springs Tour Professionals office on the corner of Gregory Terrace and Todd St.

GETTING THERE & AWAY
Air
You can fly to Alice Springs with Qantas Australian (☎ 13 1313) or Ansett (☎ 13 1300). The two companies face each other across Todd St at the Parson St intersection.

Both companies connect Alice Springs with Uluru ($179 one way), Cairns ($390), Darwin ($353), Adelaide ($372), Perth ($484), Sydney ($505) and Melbourne ($517). Ansett also flies to Broome ($329) in WA.

You can also fly direct to Uluru from Adelaide, Sydney, Perth and Cairns. So if you're planning to fly to the Centre and visit Uluru it would be more economical to fly straight to Uluru, then continue to Alice Springs, or vice versa. See the Getting There & Away and Getting Around chapters for more details.

On the regional routes, Airnorth (☎ toll-free 1800 627 474) has flights to Uluru (twice daily, $173), Darwin ($389), Katherine ($369) and Tennant Creek ($199, all daily except Saturday) and Kings Canyon (daily, $129).

Bus
Greyhound Pioneer (☎ 13 2030), at the Melanka Lodge on Todd St, has daily return services from Alice Springs to Uluru ($77), Darwin ($142) and Adelaide ($142). It takes about 20 hours from Alice Springs to Darwin (1481 km) or Alice Springs to Adelaide (1543 km). You can connect to other places at various points up and down the Track – Threeways for Mt Isa and the Queensland

coast, Katherine for Western Australia, Erldunda for Uluru, Port Augusta for Perth.

McCafferty's (☎ toll-free 13 1499), at 91 Gregory Terrace, also has daily departures to Adelaide ($135) and Darwin ($135), and also has connections to Uluru, Queensland and WA.

Both companies offer passes for visiting Uluru from Alice Springs. These are offered without accommodation but include park-entry fees and the climb. See the South to Uluru chapter for details.

Train
The *Ghan* between Adelaide and Alice Springs is a great way to enter or exit the Territory. There is a weekly service in each direction throughout the year, with a second service in operation from April to October.

Bookings must be made (☎ 13 2232), especially during the winter, and especially if you want to transport a vehicle. See the Getting There & Away chapter for full details.

Car
The basic thing to remember about getting to Alice Springs is that it's a long way from anywhere, although at least roads to the north and south are sealed. Coming in from Queensland it's 1180 km from Mt Isa to Alice Springs or 529 km from Threeways, where the Mt Isa road meets the Darwin to Alice Springs road. Darwin to Alice Springs is 1476 km. Even Uluru is over 400 km away.

Car Rental All the major hire companies have offices in Alice Springs, and Avis, Budget, Hertz and Territory Rent-a-Car also have counters at Alice Springs airport where cars can be picked up and dropped off.

Avis, Budget, Hertz and Territory all have 4WDs for hire. You're looking at around $95 per day for a Suzuki, including insurance and 100 km free per day. For a Toyota Land-cruiser or similar vehicle the price jumps to around $165 per day. Discounts apply for longer rentals (more than four to seven days, depending on the company).

Brits:Australia has campers and 4WDs for

hire, and with offices in all the major cities one-way rentals become an option. The cost is around $120 per day for unlimited km, including a collision damage waiver, but there is a seven-day minimum rental period.

Avis
  52 Hartley St (☎ toll-free 1800 225 533; fax 8953 0087)
Brits:Australia
  North Stuart Highway (☎ toll-free 1800 331 454; fax (03) 9416 2933)
Budget
  10 Gap Rd (☎ toll-free 1800 805 627; fax 8952 5308)
Hertz
  Corner Todd St & Wills Terrace (☎ toll-free 1800 891 112; fax 8952 3653)
Koala Camper Rentals
  North Stuart Highway (☎ toll-free 1800 998 029; fax 8952 9133)
Territory Rent-a-Car
  Corner Stott Terrace & Hartley St (☎ toll-free 1800 891 125; fax 8952 9797)
Thrifty
  94 Todd St (☎ 8952 2400; fax 8952 6560)

Hitching

Hitching to Alice is not the easiest trip in Australia since traffic is light. For those coming south from Darwin, Threeways (529 km north of Alice Springs) is a notorious bottleneck where hitchers can spend a long time. The notice boards in the various Alice Springs hostels are good places to look for lifts. See the Hitching section in the Getting Around chapter for general information about hitching.

GETTING AROUND

Although there is a limited public-bus system, Alice Springs is compact enough to get around on foot, and you can reach quite a few of the closer attractions by bicycle. If you want to go further afield you'll have to take a tour or rent a car.

To/From the Airport

The Alice Springs airport is 14 km south of the town, about $20 by taxi.

There is an airport shuttle bus service (☎ 8953 0310) which meets flights and takes passengers to all city accommodation and to the railway station. It costs $9.

Bus

Asbus Asbus buses leave from outside the Yeperenye shopping centre on Hartley St. The southern route (No 4) runs along Gap Rd to the southern outskirts of town – useful for Pitchi Richi, the Mecca Date Garden and the southern caravan parks. The western route (No 1) goes out along Larapinta Dve, for the Strehlow Centre, Araluen Arts Centre and the Transport & Technology Museum. Buses run approximately every 1½ hours from 7.45 am to 6 pm on weekdays and Saturday morning only. The fare for a short trip is $1.

Alice Wanderer The Alice Wanderer minibus does a loop around the major sights – Frontier Camel Farm, Mecca Date Garden, Pitchi Richi, Olive Pink Flora Reserve, the Old *Ghan*, Flying Doctor Base, Strehlow Centre, Anzac Hill, School of the Air and the telegraph station. You can get on and off wherever you like, and it runs every 70 minutes from around 9 am to 3 pm. The cost is $18 for a full day, and if you phone ahead (☎ 8952 2111), you can be picked up from your accommodation prior to the 9 am departure. The most convenient pick-up point is the Melanka Lodge.

Bicycle

Alice Springs has a number of bicycle tracks and a bike is a great way of getting around town and out to the closer attractions, particularly in winter. The best place to rent a bike is from the hostel you're staying at. Typical rates are $10 per day.

Centre Cycles (☎ 8953 2966), at 14 Lindsay Ave, east of the town centre has 15-speed mountain bikes for $12 per day, or if you want longer term it's $45 per week and $120 a month.

North of Alice Springs

While there's not a great deal to see directly north of Alice Springs itself, there are a couple of interesting stops you can make on the Stuart Highway on the way to Barrow Creek and beyond. There are also outback tracks which branch off the highway north-west across the Tanami Desert to Halls Creek in the Kimberley, and east to Camooweal and Mt Isa in Queensland. All these roads are traversable by conventional (2WD) vehicles with care, but it's not for inexperienced drivers and you should check locally for an update on road conditions before setting off. If there has been any rain recently you may need a 4WD vehicle.

Up the Track

The Stuart Highway heads north from Alice Springs, snaking through the low outliers of the MacDonnell Ranges before flattening out after about 20 km for the long haul north to Darwin.

Twenty km north of Alice Springs is the turn-off for the Tanami Track, a well-maintained gravel road connecting Alice with the Kimberley.

A further 11 km brings you to the marker for the Tropic of Capricorn, and another 19 km further on is the turn-off east of the Arltunga Tourist Drive, an alternative route to the historic town of Arltunga in the East MacDonnell Ranges. This gravel road is generally in good condition to Claraville station, 110 km east of the highway, but the 13-km stretch from there to Arltunga can be rough. Between The Garden and Claraville stations lie the Harts Range Gem Fields, but these are five km off the track and accessible by a 4WD vehicle only.

Leaving the Stuart Highway a further 20 km north is the Plenty Highway, which spears 742 km east across the northern fringes of the Simpson Desert to Boulia in

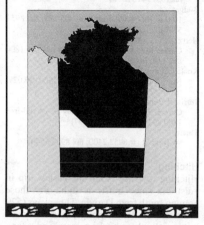

HIGHLIGHTS

- Take a 4WD across the remote Tanami Desert
- Join in an Aboriginal cultural festival at Yuendumu
- Fossick for gems at Harts Range gemfield

Western Queensland. The Sandover Highway leaves the Plenty highway after 27 km and heads north-east for 552 km to the Queensland border and then continues on to Camooweal.

NATIVE GAP CONSERVATION RESERVE

This is a rest stop on the Stuart Highway 110 km north of Alice Springs. It marks a gap in the Hann Range, and the first European reference to it is by William Wills, a surveyor on the central section of the Overland Telegraph Line in 1872. The Gap has great significance for the local Aboriginal people, who know it as Araulta Artwarcha, and is a registered sacred site as it contains sites related to a number of dreamings.

RYAN WELL HISTORIC RESERVE

After another 19 km the road crosses this small historic reserve, which preserves the ruins of a well and the remains of an early homestead.

The well was one of a number sunk in the late 1880s by a party led by Ned Ryan to provide water along the Overland Telegraph Line. The water was initially raised to the surface by bucket and windlass, but as the number of stock using the route increased and more water was needed, holding tanks were installed and these were filled by a larger bucket raised by a draught animal. While the head works of the well are all that remain today, it's still possible to make out the tank and trough foundations. Some restoration work is underway to get this well functioning again.

On the other side of the highway are the remains of **Glen Maggie Homestead**. This pastoral lease was taken up by Sam Nicker in 1914 and was named after his daughter, Margaret.

AILERON

The roadhouse of Aileron lies a few hundred metres off the highway, 138 km north of Alice Springs. It offers all the regular roadhouse facilities, and the homestead of Aileron station is right next door.

Places to Stay

The roadhouse (☎ 8956 9703) offers grassed camp sites ($10, $14 with power), and motel-style units at $50/60.

TI TREE

The small town of Ti Tree is 193 km north of Alice Springs. It is a service centre for the surrounding Aboriginal communities, such as Pmara Jutunta and Utopia, as well as for travellers on the Track.

The town, originally called Tea Tree Wells after the ti-tree lined water hole about 300 metres west of the roadhouse, started life as a European settlement on the Overland Telegraph Line. In 1971 the Anmatjera Aboriginal people won the lease of the Ti

Tree station, and this is now the settlement of Pmara Jutunta.

Facilities in the town include a medical centre (☎ 8956 9736) and police station (☎ 8956 9733).

Attached to the roadhouse is the Aakai Gallery, which is an outlet for art and crafts work, much of which is made locally. The prices for the unmounted dot paintings here are generally very competitive. The roadhouse also has a number of orphaned birds and animals in an enclosure outside, including a couple of wedge-tail eagles.

Places to Stay

The *Ti Tree Roadhouse* (☎ 8956 9741) offers camping ($8, $12 with power) and rooms at $45/55. There's also a decent restaurant and a bar and beer garden (no takeaway sales).

CENTRAL MOUNT STUART HISTORICAL RESERVE

This cairn beside the road 20 km north of Ti Tree commemorates Stuart's naming of Central Mt Stuart, a hill about 12 km to the north-west. Stuart thought he had reached the centre of Australia, and named the 'mountain' Central Mt Sturt, after his former expedition leader and friend, Charles Sturt. The name was later changed to honour Stuart himself.

From Central Mount Stuart the highway continues north for the 70-km stretch to Barrow Creek (see the Barkly Region chapter for details of Barrow Creek and points further north along the highway).

The Tanami Track

The Tanami Track cuts right through the heart of the Tanami Desert and some of Australia's least populated country. It connects Alice Springs in the Centre with the Kimberley's Halls Creek in the country's far north-west. Despite the remoteness, or perhaps because of it, the Tanami Track is becoming an increasingly popular route for those seeking to get off the beaten track, and it can save hundreds of km spent backtracking if you want to visit both the Top End and the Kimberley from Alice Springs. It's also possible to leave the Tanami Track at the Tanami Mine and head north for **Lajamanu** and **Kalkaringi** on the Buchanan Highway (see the Barkly Region chapter for details).

The Tanami Track is officially called the Tanami Road in the Territory and McGuires Track in Western Australia but it is universally known as the Tanami Track.

The 1000-km track has been much improved in recent years; it's possible to cover the track in a well-prepared 2WD vehicle. The Northern Territory section is wide and well graded, but between the WA/NT border and Halls Creek there are some sandy patches which require care – a high-clearance vehicle is advisable. After rain (rare), sections of the track can become impassable.

In the cooler months there is quite a bit of traffic – up to 40 vehicles a day pass through Rabbit Flat – so a breakdown need not be

Camels of the Outback

OK, which country has the only wild dromedary camels in the world? The answer is Australia, with an estimated 100,000 roaming the outback. The other 13 million, found mainly in north Africa, are domesticated.

The first camel was brought to Australia from the Canary Islands in 1840, but it was in 1860 that the first major group arrived, and these were imported especially for the ill-fated Bourke and Wills expedition. By the late 1860s camels were arriving in large numbers, many of them going to the stud set up by Thomas Elder (founder of the Beltana Pastoral Co which evolved to today's multinational Elders IXL) at Beltana in South Australia, established to meet the growing demand for these 'entirely new animals', as explorer Ernest Giles described them.

Other studs were set up in Western Australia, and for more than 50 years these provided high-class stock for domestic use. Imports from then British-India continued up until 1907, and in the years between 1860 and 1907 an estimated 12,000 camels were imported.

The Arabian camel (*Camelus dromedarius*), commonly thought of as the one-humped variety, was the most popular type as it was from hot desert areas and was particularly suited to the Australian climate. There were, however, several different varieties of camel and these were imported according to requirements – some were larger and more suited to heavy loads, others suitable for riding and light baggage and still others were suitable for riding and speed.

So-called 'Afghans' were also brought to Australia to handle the animals. Although these men came from various parts of west Asia (mainly from Peshawar in present-day Pakistan) they were all Afghans to the locals. They played a vital role in the development of central Australia, and the *Ghan* train was named after them. While the Afghans were generally treated well, they tended to live apart from the local population, often in so-called 'Ghan towns' on the edge of fledgling outback towns.

The camel strings were used both in exploration and to haul goods from the railheads in central Australia as the line gradually crawled further north. The poles on the Overland Telegraph Line were carted by camel, as were supplies and mail for Alice Springs, for sheep and cattle stations and remote missions, and for Aboriginal communities.

The biggest camel teams in use consisted of up to 70 camels with four Afghans, although strings of 40 camels were more common. In the desert they could travel up to 40 km a day, with each beast carrying between 300 and 600 kg. When Giles first used camels he travelled 354 km in eight days without watering his animals, while one 1891 expedition travelled over 800 km in a month.

By the 1920s motor vehicles had largely rendered the camel obsolete, although they continued to be used for exploration – the last major expedition to make use of them was Dr C T Madigan's 1939 crossing of the Simpson Desert. Gradually all the domesticated beasts were released and they formed the free-ranging herds which are found today.

In the last decade or so there has been a great resurgence of interest in the camel, the main cause for alarm if you are well prepared with food and water. In summer the heat can be extreme – days where the temperature hits 50°C are not uncommon – so think carefully before setting off at this time.

The Tanami Desert is the traditional homeland of the Walpiri Aboriginal people, and for much of its length the Tanami Track passes through Aboriginal land.

Permits are not required for travel on the Tanami Track, although if you want to venture more than 50 metres either side of the road, a permit is required. This does not apply to the settlement of Yuendumu, which lies two km off the road.

Although it is not compulsory to register with the police at either end of the Tanami Track, remember that travel in this area is no Sunday-school picnic and you should at least notify someone reliable of your travel plans.

History

The first European exploration of the Tanami Desert was undertaken by the surveyor and

---

emphasis being on recreational use. In central Australia there are three camel farms in the Alice Springs area.

Alice Springs is also home of the Camel Cup, an annual camel race. What started out as a race between two camels more than 20 years ago is now one of the major events in the Alice Springs calendar. As well as racing there is the unique sport of 'pocamelo' – camel polo.

Apart from being used for recreation, camels are exported live to countries as wide ranging as the USA, Taiwan and Saudi Arabia. Camel meat and other products are also becoming increasingly popular. There's an abattoir at Alice Springs, and 277 beasts were slaughtered in 1992. Camel milk keeps for six months without refrigeration or preservatives, and, unlike with dairy herds, even in dry areas supplementary feeding is not necessary to maintain milk supply and quality. The camel hides are also tanned in Alice Springs, and camel wool is an excellent insulator making it ideally suited for warm fabrics.

The camel has evolved over time to become an efficient desert dweller, indeed there is no animal of similar size which can survive in the arid places where camels range. The hump is the most obvious adaptation, but the camel has a number of other refinements which help it to survive. The metabolic rate is extremely low, mainly due to its 60 metres of intestines (humans have about seven metres), which allows it to extract nourishment out of little more than dry twigs. Digestion is aided by rumination, the process of regurgitating food for further chewing once indigestible substances, such as cellulose, have been destroyed by bacteria in the gut.

Camels also pass very little urine, with virtually all the moisture being reabsorbed into the body. Urine is also recycled by the kidneys and used to digest salty food and synthesise proteins. Other water-saving measures are the membrane in the nasal cavity which prevents moisture loss during exhalation, and the thick coat of hair which insulates the body and prevents sweating. When a human starts to dehydrate, the blood thickens rapidly and loses volume, reducing its ability to cool the body and stressing the heart. A 12% loss of body weight through dehydration is enough to kill a human. A camel can lose up to 40% of its body weight before it suffers unduly, mainly because it can use moisture from stores such as muscle tissue and digestive juices before taking it from the bloodstream.

The camel's hump is a fat store which can be drawn on in times of scarcity. It also helps in cooling the body as it helps shield the vital organs from the sun's heat and, because all the fat is concentrated in one place, heat is able to dissipate through the skin in other parts of the body.

Yet another feature of these remarkable animals is the ability to absorb heat during the day and dissipate it at night. Daytime body temperatures can rise as high as 41°C, while at night they can drop to 34°C – fluctuations which would kill a human.

Camels reach maturity at around seven years, although they can start to reproduce a couple of years before that. In good conditions females calve every two to three years up until the age of about 20. The mating season lasts from about August to November. Gestation ranges from 12½ to 14 months, depending on conditions. ■

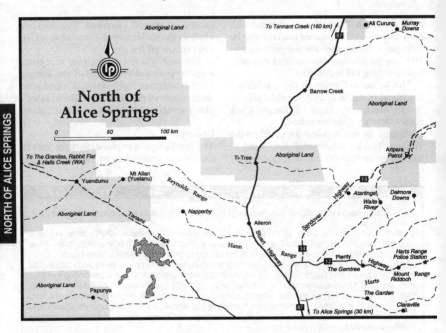

North of Alice Springs

explorer A C Gregory in 1855. His party headed south from the Victoria River to what is now Lajamanu, then headed west until they came to a dry watercourse near the present WA/NT border, which Gregory named Sturt Creek, after the explorer. He followed the creek south-west to a lake south-west of Balgo, which he humbly named after himself, before returning to his Victoria River base.

The first White crossing of the desert was probably in 1896 when the pioneering cattle driver Nat Buchanan crossed from Tennant Creek to Sturt Creek. Buchanan was responsible for some amazing cattle drives from Queensland, and he hoped to find a route suitable for stock so they didn't have to detour so far north. Although he crossed the desert without undue difficulty, no sources of permanent water were found and the hoped-for stock route never eventuated.

Allan Davidson was the first European to explore the Tanami Desert in any detail. In

1900 he set out looking for gold, and mapped, with amazing accuracy, likely-looking areas. Gold was discovered at a couple of sites in the Tanami and for a few brief years there was a flurry of activity as hopefuls came in search of a fortune. The extremely harsh conditions and small finds deterred all but the most determined, and there were never more than a couple of hundred miners in the Tanami. The biggest finds were at Tanami and The Granites, and after many years of inactivity, the latter was reopened in 1986 and is still being mined today; the Tanami Mine, however, closed in 1994.

Pastoral activity in the area has always been a precarious proposition, although some areas are quite suitable for grazing. Suplejack ('soo-pull-jack') Downs and Tanami Downs, respectively 60 km north and south-west of Rabbit Flat, are two which have survived. Suplejack is one of the few pieces of non-Aboriginal land in the Tanami

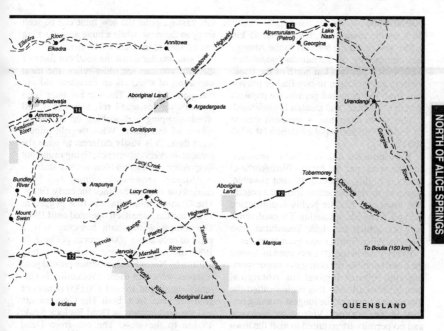

Desert, while Tanami Downs is owned by the Mangkururrta Aboriginal Land Trust.

During the 1920s Michael Terry, a geologist, led a number of expeditions across the northern half of Australia in vehicles as well as on camels, searching for minerals. During his 1928 expedition, when he used a couple of Morris six-wheel trucks on what were the first motorised trips through this part of the continent, he travelled from Broome, via Halls Creek (Old Halls Creek today) down to Tanami and then south-east to Alice Springs. His book, *Hidden Wealth and Hiding People*, recounts the adventures he and his men had and what life was like for the prospectors and Aboriginal people at this time.

TILMOUTH WELL
This roadhouse, on the banks of the (usually) dry Napperby Creek, is the first watering hole along the track 155 km after leaving the Stuart Highway. The somewhat daunting

sign at the junction of the Tanami Track and the Stuart Highway informs you that it's 703 km to the Western Australia border, the first 118 km of which are sealed.

Places to Stay
The modern *Tilmouth Well Roadhouse* (☎ 8956 8777) has a basic camp site for $5 per person, and dongas for $20. There's also a restaurant, and there's takeaway tucker as well. The roadhouse is open daily from 7 am to 9 pm.

MT ALLAN
This Aboriginal community, also called Yuelamu, lies 31 km north of the track at Mt Allan in the Ngalurbindi Hills. While there is no accommodation, you are allowed to enter without a permit to get food and fuel, and also to visit the Yuelamu Dreaming Art Gallery & Museum (☎ 8951 1520), which sells locally made arts and crafts (mainly acrylic paintings).

YUENDUMU

Back on the main track, it's another 45 km before you reach the turn-off to the Aboriginal community of Yuendumu (population 700), which lies two km north of the track. Visitors are welcome to buy fuel or provisions from the store, but permits are required to visit elsewhere, and alcohol is prohibited.

The town also has a medical centre (☎ 8956 4030) and a police station (☎ 8956 4004).

Yuendumu has a thriving art community, and the work put out by the Warlukurlangi artists is highly regarded. It's not possible, however, to visit the artists without a permit. The town also has the highly sophisticated Tanami Network, a satellite TV conference network which can link Yuendumu with Darwin, Alice Springs and even overseas.

Every year on the long weekend in August the town becomes the centre of a major sporting-and-cultural festival for Aboriginal people from all over this region called the Yuendumu Festival, the longest-running festival in the Territory. Visitors are welcome and no permits are required to visit the town over this weekend, although you will need your own camping gear.

Facilities

The *Yuendumu Store* (☎ 8956 4006) has fuel and a fairly well stocked supermarket. It's open on weekdays from 8 am to 5 pm, and on weekends from 2.30 to 4.30 pm.

The other option here is the *Yuendumu Mining Company* store (☎ 8956 4040). It is also well-stocked and has all types of fuel. Opening hours are from 9 am to 5 pm daily.

THE GRANITES GOLD MINE

Just before the new gold mine of The Granites, 256 km north-west of Yuendumu, a low rocky outcrop on the left of the road and a couple of **old ruins** can be seen. These are worth exploring as they are the original buildings dating back to the workings during the 1930s.

A rough vehicle track winds up to the top of the hill, about 500 metres from the road. It's best to leave the vehicle here and from this vantage point the new mine can be seen away to the west, while a huge new working can be seen at the base of the rise.

If you wander down the southern flank of the hill, you can see older relics, the most important of which is an excellent old ore stamper, or battery. The site has long been picked over for small relics, but it is still worth stopping and soaking up the atmosphere of this place. What the old miners went through is vastly different to what the present workers experience, flying in and out from Alice Springs on their weekly shift.

Although small-scale mining had been carried out in the area since the early 1900s, The Granites mine site was first pegged in 1927, and the mine itself operated until 1947. The returns were small, however, with a yield of only about 1000 ounces per year. In 1986 the mine reopened after exploratory drilling by North Flinders Mines proved gold reserves were still there. Production is currently running at around 170,000 ounces of gold per year, from both The Granites site and the area known as Dead Bullock Soak, 45 km to the west. The ore from Dead Bullock Soak is carted to The Granites site for treatment along a new bitumen road (definitely the only one for hundreds of km!) on huge four-trailer road trains, each carting well over 100 tonnes of ore. These monsters travel at great speed and require at least one km to stop. (There is no public access or facilities at the mine.)

RABBIT FLAT

It's just 48 km from The Granites to the most famous place in the Tanami, the Rabbit Flat Roadhouse, a km or so off to the north of the track. The roadhouse was established by Bruce Farrands and his French wife Jacqui in 1969 and has been serving travellers on the Tanami Track ever since. It's certainly not an attractive place – just a couple of breeze-block buildings and a few fuel tanks – but it's the social centre of the Tanami, not least because it's the only place for hundreds of km where Aboriginal people can buy a drink. On Friday and Saturday nights it can get pretty lively with all the workers in from the mines.

Places to Stay & Eat

The quirky *Rabbit Flat Roadhouse* (☎ 8956 8744) stocks fuel, basic provisions and beer, and there's a bar. It's also possible to camp here, and there's no charge for this. Be warned also that the roadhouse is only open from Friday to Monday, and that business is conducted on a cash-only basis.

RABBIT FLAT TO HALLS CREEK (WA)

From Rabbit Flat the track continues north-west for 44 km to the now-defunct **Tanami Mine**, which operated right up until 1994. There are no tourist services or public access to the mine site.

Just a km or so past the Tanami Mine, the **Lajamanu Road** heads off to the north (see the following section). After the turn-off, the Tanami Track swings due west for the 80-odd-km run to the Western Australia border and beyond. In the days of the area's minor gold rush, the track continued north-west, passing through Gordon Downs station and on to Halls Creek, but this route was abandoned once the rush was over. The route the current track takes between the Tanami Mine and **Billiluna Aboriginal Community** was established in the 1960s by Father McGuire from what was then the Balgo Aboriginal Mission.

It is 78 km from the roadhouse to the WA/NT border, and another 86 km will see you at the junction of the road to **Balgo Aboriginal Community**, nearly 40 km to the south.

From here it's 113 km to **Carranya Roadhouse** (☎ (091) 68 8927), along a stretch which is sandy in places and where low-clearance vehicles could get stuck. You can *sometimes* get fuel and limited supplies at Carranya, and this is also the turn-off to the **Wolfe Creek Meteorite Crater**, 20-odd km to the east. The crater is the second-largest of its type in the world. Known to the Aboriginal people as the place where some of their Dreamtime ancestors originated, early explorers and then the first aviators across

this vast desert region knew of it, long before its significance was recorded by geologists in 1947. It was first gazetted as a reserve in 1969.

Back on the main road, there is still another 111 km of dirt before the major T-intersection with Highway 1 and the bitumen. This is just 16 km south-west of Halls Creek and all the facilities of this small town.

LAJAMANU ROAD

The Lajamanu Road heads north off the Tanami Track at the Tanami Mine, although it's not even marked on many maps. It's generally kept in good condition, although it does get sandy towards Lajamanu, and there are numerous creek-bed crossings and the occasional washout. Even so, it is negotiable in dry conditions by a 2WD vehicle with care.

The road offers an interesting alternative to the Tanami Track and takes you through country which has very little tourist traffic. It passes through the Central Desert Aboriginal Land and the Lajamanu Aboriginal Land. A permit is not required to traverse the road, or to get fuel and supplies at Lajamanu.

From the Tanami Mine it's 231 km to **Lajamanu**, and the trip takes around four hours. The road goes through some very pretty countryside, especially around Suplejack Downs station, and is generally more interesting than the Tanami Track itself. See the Barkly Region chapter for details of Lajamanu and further north.

Plenty Highway

Leaving the Stuart Highway 70 km north of Alice Springs, the 742-km-long Plenty Highway spears across a semi-arid plain on the fringe of the Simpson Desert, terminating at Boulia in western Queensland. This is very remote country and isolation is almost guaranteed on the Plenty Highway – even in winter you can drive the entire route and see fewer than a dozen vehicles. Facilities are almost non-existent, there are none whatsoever in the final 456 km to Boulia, so you must be self-sufficient in everything and have a fuel range of at least 500 km.

The first 103 km from the Stuart Highway are sealed, but after that the road can be extremely rough and corrugated; large bulldust holes usually pose a hazard on the Queensland side, which is not so well maintained and is often more like a track than a road. Once past the bitumen, the highway is suitable for use only in dry weather and is definitely not recommended for caravans. Fuel is available at the Gem Tree Caravan Park (140 km from Alice Springs), Jervois homestead (356 km) and Boulia (812 km). The Atitjere Aboriginal Community (215 km from Alice Springs) sells diesel fuel and super only.

Before setting out on the road, check conditions with the Boulia Shire Office (☎ (077) 46 3188) or the Alice Springs police (☎ 8951 8888).

History

The disappearance of the German explorer Ludwig Leichhardt and his large, well-equipped party is one of Australia's great unsolved mysteries. Leichhardt vanished somewhere in the interior on his final expedition, in 1846, and it's possible that he crossed the area of the Plenty Highway while attempting to return to civilisation. The evidence that this actually happened is largely based on the discovery of marked trees in central Australia and far west Queensland.

In 1886 the surveyor David Lindsay, of Ruby Gap fame, found trees in the Harts Range that had been carved with Leichhardt's distinctive mark. Many years later, more trees bearing similar marks were discovered along the Georgina River on Glenormiston station. Also of interest is the fact that the bones of several unknown Europeans had been found by a water hole near Birdsville in the early 1870s, before the area was settled.

Henry Barclay was one of the next Europeans on the scene. In 1878, while engaged in carrying out a trigonometric survey from Alice Springs to the Queensland border, he was north-east of the Harts Range when he was faced with a critical water shortage. He dug into a sandy riverbed – this being the usual method of finding water in dry outback rivers – and found ample supplies of the precious fluid flowing beneath the surface. That is how the Plenty River got its name, and it's why the present beef road, which was first upgraded from a two-wheel track during the 1960s, is called the Plenty Highway.

THE GEMTREE

Seventy km from the Stuart Highway you come to the Gemtree caravan park, on the gum-lined banks of Gillen Creek. This is the only tourist facility of note on the Plenty Highway. Among its services it offers guests the chance to hire fossicking equipment and search for gems at the nearby **Mud Tank zircon field**. Advice on how to use the hired equipment is included in the price.

Alternatively, for a modest fee, you can take the park's accompanied trip to the zircon deposit (equipment provided) and get some practical experience with an expert. The top 80 cm of soil conceals zircons of various colours (including yellow, light brown, pink, purple and blue), ranging in size from small chips to large crystals. Provided they put their backs into it, even novices have an excellent chance of finding gem material with nothing more complicated than a shovel, a couple of small sieves and some water in a drum. There is usually a cut-down drum or two lying around that you can use, but don't count on it. If you find anything worth faceting, the caravan park's gem-cutter can turn your find into a beautiful stone ready to be set in gold or silver.

The zircon field and one or two of the garnet deposits can be reached by conventional vehicles (driven with care), provided it hasn't been raining. Don't forget that fossicking is illegal unless you hold a Northern Territory Miners Right which costs $20 and can be obtained at the Department of Mines & Energy office in Hartley Street, Alice Springs.

Place to Stay

The *Gemtree* caravan park (☎ 8956 9855) offers good shade, a kiosk, public telephone, fuel sales and a range of accommodation options. On-site caravans cost $37 for two people, while powered/unpowered sites cost $16/12 for two. Bush camping (with access to shower and toilet facilities) costs $6 per person. Games of paddymelon bowls, with tea and damper to follow, provide some light entertainment on Saturday night in the cooler months.

HARTS RANGE

The Harts Range starts at Ongeva Creek, and is one of Australia's premier fossicking areas. It yields a host of interesting gems and minerals, including mica, smoky and rose quartz, aquamarine, black and green tourmaline, sphene, garnet, sunstone, ruby, iolite and kyanite. Among the many magnificent stones found here is the world's largest known specimen of sphene. However, the area is extremely rugged and the best fossicking spots are quite hard to get to – high-clearance 4WD vehicles are required for most tracks. It's also essential to carry plenty of water at all times.

High ridges and mountains keep you company for the next 40 km to the **Harts Range police station** (☎ 8956 9772). The two police officers based here have the awesome task of preserving law and order over a sparsely populated area of 120,000 sq km. Apart from constant travel, they do everything from investigating murders to issuing driving licences. By all accounts they're kept busy controlling revellers during the annual Harts Range Races, which take place over the first weekend in August. This is a good weekend's entertainment, with a barbecue and bush dance on the Saturday night, but you need to get there early to find a camp site reasonably handy to the action.

Facilities

There's no accommodation in Harts Range, but the *Atitjere Community Store* (☎ 8956 9773) sells basic food requirements and cold drinks, as well as diesel and super. Aboriginal art and interesting gemstones from the nearby Harts Range are also on offer most of the time. The store is open between 9 am and 5 pm Monday to Friday and from 9 am to noon on Saturday.

In a medical emergency contact the Atitjere clinic (☎ 8956 9778).

JERVOIS

The road is wide and formed all the way from Harts Range to the border, but it can still be quite rough, depending on when it was last graded. The first 50 km is extremely scenic, with attractive tall woodlands of whitewood and weeping ironwood fronting the rugged Harts Range to the south. Later, mulga and gidgee become dominant and only flat-topped hills, scattered low ranges and occasional, beautiful gum-lined creeks break the monotony of the endless plain.

About 130 km east of Harts Range you reach Jervois station (☎ 8956 6307), where you can buy diesel, super and unleaded fuel during daylight hours. Shower and toilet facilities are also available. Camping isn't permitted at the homestead itself, but you can stop either at the turn-off, where there is a lay-by, or along the homestead access road between the highway and the first gate (about one km in). The many magnificent ghost gums growing along the nearby Marshall River make a beautiful setting for a bush camp.

For something different, you can inspect the huge rocket-proof shelter that was built at the homestead during the 1960s, when Blue Streak rockets were fired in this direction from Woomera in South Australia. Instead of huddling inside as they were supposed to, the stationfolk preferred to stand on top to watch the fireworks. Similar shelters were provided for all the stations in this area. It all seems to have been a waste of taxpayers' money, although a couple of rockets did come down near the highway.

JERVOIS TO BOULIA (QLD)

The highlight of this section is right beside the road, 50 km past the turn-off to Jervois homestead. Here a conical **termite mound** nearly five metres high and three metres thick towers above the surrounding sea of stunted mallees and spinifex – it's an extraordinary sight. The mound is the highest point around, and the white splashes on top tell you that it's a favourite perch for hawks. You pass similar termite mounds in the next 10 km but few of these rise above two metres.

At the Queensland border, the road changes its name and becomes known as the Donohue Highway. Crossing the border grid, you'll also usually notice a dramatic change in road conditions – the Boulia Shire does its best, but it only takes a few road trains to break the surface and form deep bulldust holes.

At 118 km from the border you come to the **Georgina River**, and other than the vast expanses of empty space, this waterway is the highlight on the Queensland section of the highway. The main channel features shady coolabahs, good camp sites and abundant bird life – you'll often see brolgas, emus and bustards as well as large flocks of budgies, cockatiels, galahs and corellas in the immediate area. The crossing is normally dry, but any flooding causes it to be closed until conditions improve, which can take many days.

Eight km from **Boulia** you meet the bitumen and joyous relief from the bulldust and corrugations. By the time most travellers reach this point, they're ready to kill for a cold beer in the pub. This isolated township has a good range of facilities, including a hospital, police station, post office, all-weather aerodrome, hotel, caravan park, two garages, a cafe and a handful of other shops.

Sandover Highway

Leaving the Plenty Highway 24 km east of the Stuart Highway, the Sandover Highway heads north-east across flat semi-desert for 552 km to terminate at Lake Nash homestead, near the Queensland border. Getting its name from the Sandover River, whose course it follows for about 250 km, this long,

wide ribbon of red dirt is an excellent short cut for adventurous travellers wishing to drive between central Australia and north-west Queensland. The highway offers a memorable experience in remote touring.

Road conditions depend to a great extent on the weather: prolonged rain creates bogs that can keep the highway closed for days. In the late 1980s the road was closed to all traffic for several months after exceptionally heavy rains caused long sections to be washed away. Although often rough, the road is normally suitable for conventional vehicles with high ground clearance and heavy-duty suspension.

Tourist facilities are non-existent along the road but you can buy fuel and supplies at the Arlpara Store (180 km from the Stuart Highway) and the Alpurrurulam Aboriginal Community (573 km from the Stuart Highway).

The best sources of current information on road conditions are the Arlpara Store at Utopia and the Alpurrurulam council office at Lake Nash (see that section later in this chapter). In the event of a medical emergency, you can obtain assistance at the Urapuntja Health Centre (☎ 8956 9875; to the north of the road, 21 km past the Arlpara Store), and at clinics at the Ampilatwatja (☎ 8956 9966) and Alpurrululam (☎ (077) 48-3111) Aboriginal communities.

History

For most of its distance the Sandover Highway crosses the traditional lands of the Alyawarra Aboriginal people, whose lives until recent times focussed on the relatively rich environment of the Sandover River. Europeans arrived in Alyawarra country in the 1880s, when Lake Nash and Argadargada stations, near the Queensland border, were established for sheep and cattle grazing.

The country to the south-west wasn't permanently settled by Europeans until 40 years later; Ooratippra was the last station to be taken up, being leased in the late 1940s. As elsewhere in the outback, the loss of food resources and the fouling of precious water supplies by cattle caused bloody conflicts

HUGH FINLAY

HUGH FINLAY

Top: The sandstone cliffs seem to glow in the setting sun – an awsome sight, Rainbow Valley
Bottom: A view of Alice Springs nestled behind the MacDonnell Ranges

HUGH FINLAY

HUGH FINLAY

HUGH FINLAY

Left: Mid-day sun briefly illuminates the depths of the narrow Standley Chasm
Top Right: Mural on Albert Namatjira's headstone depicts three of the artist's important dreaming sites
Bottom Right: The Lambert centre marks the geographical centre of the continent

between pastoralists and Aboriginal people. The Sandover Massacre of the 1920s resulted in the senseless deaths of about 100 Alyawarra, who were either shot or poisoned after committing the grievous crime of cattle-spearing.

Atartinga station, about 140 km north-east of Alice Springs, was taken up by R H (Bob) Purvis in 1920. Known as the Sandover Alligator because of his extraordinary appetite, R H was contracted by the government in the late 1920s to sink wells along the newly gazetted Sandover Stock Route, which was intended to link the stations of far western Queensland with the Alice Springs railhead. However, the water table's increasing depth caused the project to be abandoned near the halfway point. R H's last well, sited near present-day Ammaroo homestead, struck water at 80 metres, far too deep for the simple windlasses used in those days.

The stock route was continued from Ammaroo through to Lake Nash after the 1940s, when heavy drilling equipment became readily available in central Australia. This meant that bores could be sunk at regular intervals regardless of depth. Nevertheless, the Sandover Highway was, for the most part, little more than a bush track until the 1970s, when it was upgraded to a standard where it was just suitable for road trains.

UTOPIA

Turning off the Plenty Highway 26 km from the Stuart Highway, the Sandover crosses a vast, semi-arid plain virtually all the way to the Ammaroo turn-off. This is marginal cattle country – the average station en route has only about 25% useful grazing land. For example, Atartinga covers 2240 sq km but its 1200-head herd is concentrated on about 600 sq km. The spinifex areas along the highway carry billions of termites but only one cow to every 10 sq km.

At 127 km from the Plenty Highway you cross the western boundary of Utopia station. Purchased by the federal government in 1976 for local Aboriginal people, the station is home to about 700 Alyawarra people, who live in 20 small outstations scattered over an

area of 2500 sq km. These communities are governed by a council based at Arlparra, which you pass 27 km further on. The fence 23 km past Arlparra marks the boundary between Utopia and Ammaroo stations. Almost all the minor roads that turn off the highway between the two fences lead in to Aboriginal communities and are off-limits to the travelling public.

Facilities

The *Arlpara store* (☎ 8956 9910) mainly serves the Aboriginal communities of that area. It sells fuel and has a reasonably well-stocked mini-supermarket with all basic food requirements.

The women of Utopia are famous for their batik work, and you may be able to pick up some of their work here, although the outlets in Alice Springs are a safer bet. The store is open from 9 am to 5 pm Monday to Friday and from 9 am to noon on Saturday.

LAKE NASH

It's 317 km past Ammaroo that you see the glittering iron roofs of the **Alpurrurulam Aboriginal Community** come into view on the left and the end of the highway is just five minutes away, at Lake Nash homestead. The largest of the Sandover's stations, Lake Nash covers 13,000 sq km and carries, on average, a herd of 41,000 high-quality Santa Gertrudis beef cattle.

Everything about Lake Nash is big: it has the world's largest commercial herd of Santa Gertrudis, the property's bore runs are so long that the vehicles assigned to them travel a total of 96,000 km per year, and the average paddock covers several hundred sq km. The station's workforce of 28 is also huge by local standards.

The Sandover Highway ends at Lake Nash homestead, where you have a choice of three routes: north to Camooweal (183 km), east to Mount Isa (205 km) or south to Urandangi (172 km). All are minor dirt roads, and as they include black clay soil sections, they become impassable after rain. When dry, they are normally suitable for conventional vehicles in the hands of experienced outback motorists.

Caution must be exercised, as signposting is poor throughout and available maps seldom show the roads' true positions. If in doubt, the best approach is to fill up with fuel at Alpurrurulam and ask for directions and an update on road conditions – if the people at the store can't help, ask at the council office across the road.

Facilities

The *community store* sells fuel, all basic food requirements, minor hardware items and vehicle parts (including tyres). It's open from 8 to 11 am and 3 to 5 pm Monday to Friday and from 8 to 11 am on Saturday. Although visitors are welcome to use the commercial facilities, which are right at the entrance to Alpurrurulam, you should not proceed further into the community.

MacDonnell Ranges

The rugged MacDonnell Ranges form an imposing red barrier from east to west for 400 km across the vast central Australian plain, with Alice Springs situated conveniently in the middle.

The ranges consist of a series of long, steep-sided, parallel ridges that rise between 100 and 600 metres above the intervening valley floors. Scattered along the entire length are deep gorges carved by ancient rivers that flowed south into the Simpson Desert. Here also you find the four highest peaks west of the Great Dividing Range: Mt Zeil, the highest, is 1531 metres above sea level and 900 metres above the surrounding plain.

Although arid, the ranges are covered with a huge variety of plants, including many tall trees, with the majestic ghost gums as an outstanding feature. In hidden, moist places are relics of the rainforest flora that covered this region millions of years ago.

Wildlife enthusiasts will be delighted by the chance to observe some of the 167 species of birds, 85 species of reptiles, 23 species of native mammals, and 10 fish and five frog species; a number of the mammals are rare or endangered elsewhere in the arid zone.

Many of the most spectacular landscapes and most important biological areas are now included in national parks and reserves, most of which are readily accessible by conventional vehicle. The largest of these, the 2100-sq-km **West MacDonnell National Park**, stretches 160 km from the outskirts of Alice Springs. To the east, a string of generally small parks and reserves lies scattered through the ranges for nearly the same distance.

The ranges were explored a number of times by John McDouall Stuart on his various attempts to cross the continent from south to north, and he named the range after the South Australian governor, Sir Richard MacDonnell.

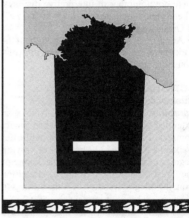

MACDONNELL RANGES

West MacDonnell National Park

The West MacDonnell National Park was only proclaimed in the early 1990s, and it encompasses a number of smaller reserves which previously existed at the major gorges and sites along the ranges. The park now continues unbroken along the range from the Stuart Highway just north of Alice Springs to Mt Zeil, 170 km to the west. There are a number of spectacular red gorges and several deep water holes along the way, with all but Standley Chasm located within the park. In dry conditions, all the main attractions along this route are accessible to conventional

259

vehicles. Spearing between high ridgelines, Larapinta Drive (the road west from Alice Springs), is sealed for the first 135 km, to the Finke River crossing near Glen Helen. From here the final 37 km past Redbank Gorge to the road between Haasts Bluff and Hermannsburg is rough dirt.

INFORMATION

The best place for park information is the visitor centre (☎ 8955 0310) at Simpsons Gap, 16 km west of Alice Springs, where there are a number of interpretive displays. There's another visitor centre (☎ 8956 7799) at Ormiston Gorge.

At the main sites of interest throughout the park there are generally excellent information signs and displays

ACTIVITIES
Bushwalking

Larapinta Trail The Larapinta Trail is an extended walking track which, when finally completed in the next few years, will offer walkers a 13-stage, 220-km trail of varying degrees of difficulty along the backbone of the West MacDonnell Ranges, stretching from the telegraph station in Alice Springs to

Mt Razorback, beyond Glen Helen. It will then be possible to choose anything from a two-day to a two-week trek, taking in a selection of the attractions in the West MacDonnells. At the time of writing, the following sections (with length, recommended walking time, and degree of difficulty) were open:

Section 1
  Alice Springs Telegraph Station to Simpsons Gap
  24 km; two days; Class B.
Section 2
  Simpsons Gap to Jay Creek
  23 km; two days; Class B.
Section 3
  Jay Creek to Standley Chasm
  14 km; eight hours; Class C.
Section 8
  Serpentine Gorge to Ochre Pits
  18 km; eight hours; Class B.
Section 10
  Ormiston Gorge to Glen Helen Gorge
  12.5 km; seven hours; Class B.
Section 12
  Out and back from Redbank Gorge to Mt Sonder
  16 km return; eight hours return; Class C.

Class B trail is defined as being wide, well

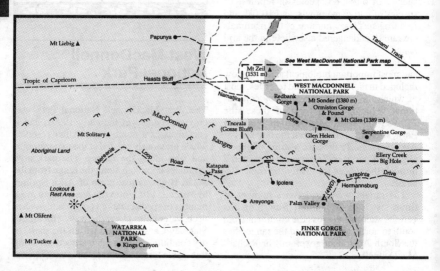

constructed and suitable for inexperienced walkers. Class C trail is narrow, steep and rough in places, suitable for experienced walkers.

Detailed trail notes and maps ($1 per section) are available from the Parks & Wildlife desk at the tourist office in Alice Springs, or contact the Parks & Wildlife office (☎ 8951 8211) for further details.

The problem lies in getting to the various trailheads, as there is no public transport out to this area.

Ochre Pits A three-hour return walk takes you to scenic **Inarlanga Pass** at the foot of the Heavitree Range. Although the track passes through uninspiring country, the gorge is interesting, as is the old Serpentine Chalet dam, an hour's walk to the east along the Larapinta Trail. For details, see the brochure on Section 8 of the Larapinta Trail. For more information on the Ochre Pits see that section later in this chapter.

Ormiston Gorge One of the best short walks in the MacDonnell Ranges is the three-hour loop from the information centre into remote Ormiston Pound and back through Ormiston Gorge. Do it first thing in the morning in an anticlockwise direction so you can enjoy a sunlit view of the big cliffs. Two other excellent but much longer cross-country excursions are mentioned in the *Walks of Ormiston Gorge & Pound* brochure – the walk up Ormiston Creek to Bowmans Gap takes at least one day while the **Mt Giles** route is a two-day affair. If you're an experienced bushwalker, do yourself a favour and spend a night on Mt Giles, as the dawn view across Ormiston Pound to Mt Sonder is sensational. Section 10 of the Larapinta Trail winds over rocky hills and along gum-lined creeks from Ormiston Gorge to Glen Helen, with fine views to Mt Sonder en route. For more information on Ormiston Gorge see that section later in this chapter.

Mt Sonder The full-day return walk along the ridgetop from Redbank Gorge to the summit of Mt Sonder will appeal to the well-equipped enthusiast. This is Section 12 of the Larapinta Trail, and while the trek itself is nothing to rave about (it's rather monotonous and seems never-ending), the view from Mt Sonder and the sense of achievement are ample reward. As on Mt

MACDONNELL RANGES

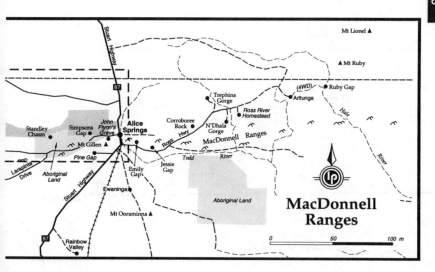

Giles, the atmosphere and panorama of time-less hills at sunrise makes it worth camping out on top.

Cycling

Simpsons Gap Cycle Track The 17-km sealed cycling path between Flynn's Grave on Larapinta Drive and Simpsons Gap wanders along timbered creekflats and over low rocky hills, with occasional kangaroos to keep you company. There are many bush picnic spots en route, and excellent views of **Mt Gillen**, **Rungutjirba Ridge** and the rugged **Alice Valley**. Flynn's Grave is seven km from the town centre, and you do this part along Larapinta Drive. For the best views (not to mention comfort), cycle out in the early morning and return in the afternoon. Carry plenty of drinking water in warm weather as there is none along the way.

Guided Walks & Talks

During the season (April to September), Parks & Wildlife rangers conduct a number of excellent activities in the park, and it's well worth making the effort to get along to any which may be on.

Nature Walks These are held at Simpsons Gap (four times weekly), Ormiston Gorge (Saturday and Sunday mornings) and the Ochre Pits (Wednesday and Sunday).

Slide Show Twice a week a slide show is held at 7 pm at the Ormiston Gorge visitor centre.

ORGANISED TOURS

One and two-day tours of the MacDonnell Ranges are very popular and there are numerous operators and styles to choose from – contact the tourist office in Alice Springs for details. Costs vary, but expect to pay around $75 for a day tour and $170 for a two-day camping safari. Camping safaris incorporating places such as Palm Valley and King's Canyon are also available. For instance, Alice Springs Holidays (☎ toll-free 1800 801 401; fax 8953 1327) offers a 2½-day tour which includes the Mereenie Loop Road, Gosse Bluff and Hermannsburg for $511. Better value perhaps, is the Ayers Rock Plus (☎ toll-free 1800 063 838; fax 8952 3819) five-day tour which costs $465 and also takes in Kings Canyon and Uluru.

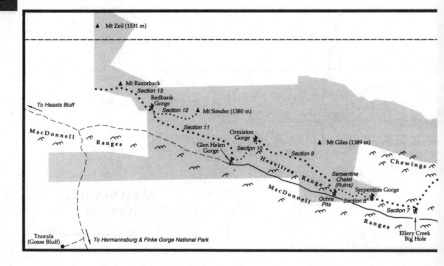

Sahara Outback Tours (☎ 8953 0881; fax 8953 2414) offers a similar trip for $485.

Discounts often apply during the off season, and it's also worth asking about standby rates.

For something entirely different, you can take a three-day camel safari through the wilds of the West MacDonnells between Redbank Gorge and Glen Helen with Frontier Camel Tours (☎ toll-free 1800 806 499; fax 8955 5015). This unique experience includes one night in a swag at the gum-studded Davenport River and one night at Glen Helen homestead. The cost is $405 per person.

DESERT WILDLIFE PARK & BOTANIC GARDENS

Heading west on Larapinta Drive you pass the site of this new desert flora-and-fauna park on the outskirts of Alice Springs. The park will offer something different in that it is neither simply a botanic garden nor a wildlife park; instead it will combine both, so that native animals will be seen in their native habitats. A number of desert ecosystems will be featured, with an emphasis on their traditional use by Aboriginal people.

Although still in the early stages of development, Stage 1, which includes a visitor centre and three major habitats – sand dunes/plains, woodland and riverine – was scheduled to open in May 1997. Stage 2 will feature the range, gorge and mulga habitats, as well as Mitchell grasslands and gibber plains.

FLYNN'S GRAVE

Seven km west of Alice Springs along Larapinta Dve, and just outside the eastern boundary of the West MacDonnell National Park, is the grave of Dr John Flynn, founder of the RFDS and the Australian Inland Mission. It's sited on a low rise with ghost gums and a Devil's Marble brought down the Track from Tennant Creek. From here there is a magnificent view of nearby **Mt Gillen**.

SIMPSONS GAP

Twenty-two km west of Alice Springs and seven km from Larapinta Dve is spectacular **Simpsons Gap**, where Roe Creek has exploited a fault in the quartzite Rungutjirpa Ridge and gouged a red gorge with towering cliffs. The area is popular with picnickers, and also has some good walks. Early

MACDONNELL RANGES

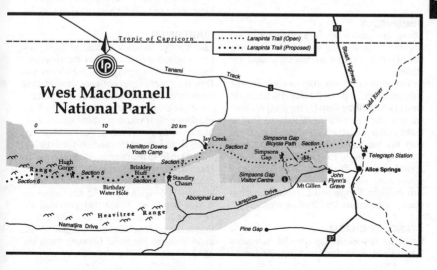

morning and late afternoon are the best times to see the black-flanked rock-wallabies that live among a jumble of huge boulders right in the gap. Birds spotted in the area include the uncommon peregrine falcon, the dusky grasswren and the rufous-crowned emu-wren.

Simpsons Gap is open between 8 am and 8 pm daily.

History

To the Arrernte people, Simpsons Gap is known as Rungutjirpa, the home of giant goanna ancestral beings.

During explorations which would eventually lead to the construction of the Overland Telegraph Line, Stuart advised that the line should cross the ranges at a place about 60 km west of here, but it was later deemed too rugged and an alternative sought. Consequently OTL surveyor, Gilbert McMinn, found the gap in the ranges in 1871, and described it as: 'one of the finest pieces of scenery I have met with for a long time...' It's not known who the gap was named after, although it appears on early survey maps as Simsons Gap.

Bushwalking

There are many opportunities for good walking here, and the short track up to the **Cassia Hill** lookout is recommended for starters.

You can also do day walks on the Larapinta Trail – peaceful **Bond Gap** (to the west) and **Wallaby Gap** (to the east) are both worthwhile – or take the Woodland Trail to **Rocky Gap**. This track continues on to Bond Gap via the Larapinta Trail, but it's hard walking through rough hills and won't appeal to many. The flatter wooded country south-east of Simpsons Gap, between **Rungutjirpa Ridge** and Larapinta Dve has plenty of potential for off-track walks.

STANDLEY CHASM

From the Simpsons Gap turn-off, you cross Aboriginal land for the next 29 km to Standley Chasm, which is owned and managed by the nearby community of **Iwupataka**, who know it as Ankerle. Its European name honours Ida Standley, who became the first school teacher in Alice Springs in 1914. The school for Aboriginal children was moved to Jay Creek (Iwupataka today) in 1925 and Mrs Standley became the first European woman to visit the chasm.

The narrow cleft of the chasm has smooth vertical walls and is famous for its midday light display – for a brief period around noon, reflected sunlight causes the rocks to glow red, and at this moment every camera for miles around seems to be focused here.

The 15-minute walk up the rocky gully from the refreshment kiosk to the chasm is crammed with moisture-loving plants such as river red gums, cycad palms and ferns, creating an unexpected lushness in this arid world of craggy bluffs. It's one of the best walks in the area but most visitors are in too much of a hurry to notice. For a real walking challenge with many rewards, you can return to Alice Springs along the Larapinta Trail (see that section earlier in this chapter).

Standley Chasm is open daily between 7.30 am and 6 pm and there's an entry fee of $3 per adult or $2 concession. There's a kiosk at the site selling basic food and drinks.

HUGH RIVER

Leaving the Standley Chasm turn-off, you pass through a scenic gap in the Heavitree Range before swinging right onto Namatjira Dve. (Larapinta Dve continues straight on to Hermannsburg and Palm Valley, and you can come back this way after exploring the West MacDonnells if you don't mind some travelling on some gravel roads. See the Mereenie Loop Road later in this section for details.)

Ten km from the intersection you cross the Hugh River, with its large river gums, before entering a steep-sided valley that takes you all the way to Glen Helen, 75 km further on. It was the Hugh River that provided the explorer John McDouall Stuart with a route through the MacDonnell Ranges on his expeditions to the north between 1860 and 1862.

ELLERY CREEK BIGHOLE

Ellery Creek Bighole, 87 km from Alice Springs, is a popular swimming hole in summer but, being shaded by the high cliffs of Ellery Gorge, is generally too cold for comfort most of the year.

The Ellery Creek was named by explorer Ernest Giles in 1872 after a Victorian astronomer. The 'bighole' is a local name used to distinguish the hole at the foot of the gorge from other smaller water holes along the creek. The Aboriginal name for the water hole is Udepata, and it was an important gathering point along a couple of dreaming trails which pass through the area.

The 20-minute **Dolomite Walk** is worth doing. An information shelter at the car park explains the area's fascinating geological history, which is exposed in the creek banks downstream from the water hole.

Facilities

There's a small, usually crowded camping area with wood-burning barbecues (no wood provided), tables, pit toilet and very limited shade within easy reach of the water hole. Fees (honesty box) are $1 per person and $3 per family.

SERPENTINE GORGE

A few km further along Namatjira Drive is the (often rough) gravel track which leads to the Serpentine Gorge car park. From here it's a one-km walk along the sandy creek bed to the main attraction, and this makes a pleasant introduction to the area. It's no accident that the car park is so far from the gorge – it limits the number of people who visit the gorge to those who are prepared to walk though the sand. The reason is that the gorge and its water holes contain some rare (for this area) plant species, such as the centralian flannel flower.

A water hole blocks access to the entrance of the narrow gorge, which snakes for over two km through the Heavitree Range. You can swim through (bloody cold!) the first section, and then walk up the rocky creek past large cycads to a second water-filled cleft. There is some stunning scenery here,

which can also be enjoyed from a lookout located a short scramble above the main entrance. Section 8 of the Larapinta Trail (see the section earlier in this chapter) starts at the car park and takes you via Counts Point Lookout to Serpentine Chalet dams and Inarlanga Pass, then on to the Ochre Pits.

SERPENTINE CHALET RUINS

Continuing on from Serpentine Gorge you soon arrive at the Serpentine Chalet turn-off. A rough track leads to the ruins of the old Serpentine Chalet. It seems an unlikely spot, but this was the site for an early 1960s tourism venture. Visitors would travel all day from Alice Springs to reach the chalet which was a haven of relative, but still basic, comfort in the harsh bush. Lack of water caused the chalet to close after only a couple of years and all that remains are the concrete foundations and floor slabs.

Facilities

Eleven bush camp sites scattered through the mulga and mallee along the track to and beyond the old Serpentine Chalet site have wood-burning fireplaces (collect your own wood) and a sense of isolation. These are ideal for winter camping but are too exposed in hot weather. The first five sites are accessible to conventional vehicles, the last six to 4WD vehicles only. No fees are charged.

MACDONNELL RANGES

The Magic of Ochre

The Ochre Pits are formed from layers of deposited silt which have been compressed, folded and buckled over millions of years. This results in vertical layers with different colours caused by different amounts of iron in each layer.

Ochre was an important commodity in local Aboriginal culture. It was used medicinally and was also a valuable trade item. Red ochre was mixed with grease and eucalyptus leaves to form a decongestant balm; and it was believed that white ochre had magical powers – it was mixed with water and then blown from the mouth, a practice which was said to cool the sun and calm the wind. Ochre was also used extensively for body decoration and in painting. ■

OCHRE PITS

The nearby Ochre Pits, with extensive parking and picnicking areas (free gas barbecues), has some interesting information signs relating to ochre and its importance to Aboriginal people. Except for a small deposit of yellow ochre, which is still used today, the material at this minor quarry site is of poor quality. Nevertheless, the swirls of red and yellow ochre in the walls of this little ravine make an attractive picture in the afternoon sun.

Bushwalking

A three-hour return walk takes you to scenic **Inarlanga Pass** at the foot of the Heavitree Range. Although the track passes through uninspiring country, the gorge is most interesting, as is the old Serpentine Chalet dam, an hour's walk to the east along the Larapinta Trail. For details, see the brochure on Section 8 of the Larapinta Trail.

ORMISTON GORGE

From the Ochre Pits it's a further 26 km to Ormiston Gorge, where soaring cliffs, tall gums, rich colours and a deep water hole combine to form some of the grandest scenery in the central ranges. Most visitors congregate at the gorge entrance, but for those who want to explore further afield there are several recommended walks that start and finish at the information centre.

Ormiston Gorge is a good spot for wildlife enthusiasts, thanks to the variety of habitats (mulga woodland, spinifex slopes, rock faces, large river gums and permanent water) that you find in close proximity to each other. Its also an ideal base for exploring the western half of the West MacDonnells.

The water hole itself is part of the Aboriginal emu dreaming and is a registered sacred site. Although the water is pretty cold year round, it is still a popular summer swimming spot.

The area is home to, among other marsupials, the rare long-tailed dunnart. This small marsupial was last recorded in the area late last century, until the chance discovery of a female trapped inside a discarded drink bottle in 1993. Subsequent trapping snared a male.

Facilities

This relatively up-market *camp site* almost in the shade of Ormiston Gorge features hot showers, toilets, picnic furniture and free gas barbecues, but there is no room for caravans. Fees are $4/10 per person/family. Water supplies become severely limited in drought times, when restrictions may apply.

GLEN HELEN GORGE & HOMESTEAD

Glen Helen Gorge, 135 km from Alice Springs, where there is another large water hole, has been carved through the Pacoota Range by the Finke River (lhere pirnte – pronounced 'lara pinta' – to the Arrernte) as its floodwaters rush south to the Simpson Desert; a major flood in 1988 backed up so high that it flooded the nearby tourist accommodation.

A 10-minute stroll takes you from the homestead/resort to the gorge entrance, but if you want to go further you'll have to either swim through the water hole or climb around it.

History

To the Arrernte people the gorge is known as Yapulpa, and is part of the Carpet Snake Dreaming. The area of the gorge is an Aboriginal sacred site as it is the home of the carpet snake.

In 1872 Ernest Giles was the first European to explore the area. The pastoral lease was first taken up by prominent pastoralists, Frederick Grant and Stokes, and the station (and gorge) was named after Grant's eldest daughter by their surveyor, Richard Warburton, in 1876.

In 1901 the station was bought by Fred Raggatt, and remnants from that time, such as the timber meathouse, still survive.

Stone buildings were built in 1940 by the new owner, Bryan Bowman, who also built the Glen Helen Chalets in 1955 as a tourist venture.

Facilities

A high red cliff provides a dramatic backdrop to the *Glen Helen Homestead* (☎ 8956 7489; fax 8956 7495), which is built on the site of the early homestead of Glen Helen station. One of the nice things about it is its comfortable lounge area, where you can drink bottomless cups of tea and coffee and enjoy the relaxed atmosphere.

The resort offers dorm-style accommodation ($10 per person), self-contained motel rooms ($80/92/120 a double/triple/family) and limited powered caravan sites. For meals there's a choice of takeaway, restaurant and bistro. Guided bushwalks, camel and horse rides, and helicopter scenic flights feature on the list of activities.

REDBANK GORGE

The bitumen ends at Glen Helen, and for the next 20 km to the Redbank Gorge turn-off you're on occasionally rough dirt with numerous sharp dips. As is the case anywhere, as soon as dirt roads are encountered, the number of vehicles drops dramatically as it seems most people are just not prepared to put their car over a dirt road. This is great for the few who don't mind the dirt roads as they have the places pretty much to themselves,

and this is certainly the case with the beautiful Redbank Gorge.

From the Redbank turn-off on Namatjira Drive it's five km to the Redbank car park, from which the final stage is a 20-minute walk up a rocky creek bed to the gorge. Redbank Gorge is extremely narrow, with polished, multi-hued walls that close over your head to block out the sky. You normally need an air mattress to get through, as its deep pools are freezing, but it's worth doing – the colours and cathedral atmosphere inside are terrific. Redbank Gorge is the starting point for the Larapinta Trail section to nearby Mt Sonder.

Facilities

There are two campsites at Redbank. The new *Woodland Camping Area* is on a creekflat with shady coolabahs and is very well set up. The sites are all spaced well apart so there is some degree of privacy and bushcamping atmosphere. Each site has a sand patch for a tent, fireplace (no wood provided), free gas barbecues and picnic tables, and there's a block with pit toilets. Fees are $1/3 per person/family, payable at the honesty box. An early morning stroll downstream beside the Davenport River, with the sun softly lighting the river gums, is a great way to start the day.

The ridgetop camp site is closer to the gorge and has excellent views of the ranges. It is, however, quite exposed and the ground is quite stony. Each site has a fireplace, and there's pit toilets here.

TNORALA (GOSSE BLUFF) CONSERVATION RESERVE

An alternative return route to Alice Springs once you reach Redbank Gorge is to continue west on Namatjira Dve for 17 km, then turn south over Tylers Pass on the sometimes rough dirt road to Hermannsburg and Larapinta Dve. En route you pass Gosse Bluff, the spectacular remnant of a huge crater that was blasted out when a comet plunged into the ground 130 million years ago. The power of such an impact is almost impossible to comprehend – the five-km diameter crater you see today was originally two km below the impact surface, and is just the very core of the original 20-km diameter crater. The best overall view is from the signposted lookout at Tylers Pass, a short distance to the north; in the early morning the light is stunning.

The crater was named by Ernest Giles in 1872 after Harry Gosse, a telegraphist at the Alice Springs telegraph station. In 1991 title was handed back to the traditional Aboriginal owners.

· The Aboriginal name for the crater is Tnorala, and in the local mythology it's a wooden dish belonging to some star ancestors that crashed down from the sky during the Dreamtime. The area is a registered sacred site, and is protected by a 4,700-hectare conservation reserve managed by the rangers at Ormiston Gorge. Although no permit is required to travel along this road, you do need a permit to enter the Tnorala Conservation Reserve, which lies about eight km off the main track. These permits are available from the tourist office in Alice Springs, and Glen Helen Homestead and the resort at Kings Canyon. The track goes right into the crater, where there is a car park, picnic facilities and information boards.

From Gosse Bluff you continue on to the historic mission station of **Hermannsburg** (see James Ranges chapter). Gosse Bluff is about 50 km from the Redbank Gorge turn-off, and it's about 60 km from the bluff to Hermannsburg. From Hermannsburg you can travel west and south along the recently opened **Mereenie Loop Road** to Kings Canyon, and from there on to Uluru without returning to Stuart Highway.

East MacDonnell Ranges

The East MacDonnells stretch in an unbroken line for about 100 km east of Alice Springs. The road from Alice Springs to Arltunga is extremely scenic for the most part, taking you through a jumble of high ridges and hills drained by gum-lined creeks. Along the way you pass several small parks and reserves where you can explore a variety of attractions such as rugged gorges, Aboriginal culture and abandoned mining areas. Despite the attractions of the area, it is a very poor second cousin to the much more popular West MacDonnells, and so the number of visitors here is far less, making it altogether more enjoyable.

The Ross Highway from Alice Springs is sealed for the 71 km to the Arltunga turn-off, where it changes to a good dirt road for the final nine km to Ross River Homestead. Arltunga is 32 km from the Ross Highway, and this unsealed road can be quite rough, as can the alternative return route via Claraville, Ambalindum and The Garden homesteads to the Stuart Highway (see North of Alice Springs chapter).

Access to John Hayes Rockhole (in Trephina Gorge Nature Park), N'Dhala Gorge and Ruby Gap is by 4WD vehicle only, but other main attractions east of Alice Springs are normally accessible to conventional vehicles.

EMILY & JESSIE GAPS NATURE PARK

Leaving the town centre you head south along the Stuart Highway through Heavitree Gap, then turn east after two km onto the Ross Highway. Parallelling a high quartzite ridge to the north, the road heads out through the South Alice tourist area, with its caravan parks and various attractions before, finally, you're in the bush.

Ten km from the Stuart Highway you arrive at **Emily Gap**, a beautiful spot with **Aboriginal rock paintings** and a deep water hole in the narrow gorge. Known to the Arrernte as Anthwerrke, this is one of the most important Aboriginal sites in the Alice Springs area as it was from here that the caterpillar ancestral beings of Mparntwe (Alice Springs) originated.

Jessie Gap, eight km further on, is equally scenic, and normally a much quieter place to enjoy nature.

Both sites are popular swimming holes and have picnic tables and fireplaces.

Bushwalking

For a minor challenge, the eight-km walk along the high, narrow ridgetop between these two gaps has much to recommend it. You get sweeping panoramas all the way and there's usually wildlife, such as euros, black-footed rock-wallabies and wedge-tailed eagles, to see. The idea is to get someone to drop you off at Emily Gap, then have them continue on to Jessie Gap to get the picnic ready. Allow at least 2½ hours for the walk, which isn't marked.

CORROBOREE ROCK CONSERVATION RESERVE

Past Jessie Gap you drive over eroded flats, the steep-sided Heavitree Range looming large on your left, before entering a valley between red ridges. Forty-three km from Alice Springs you arrive at Corroboree Rock, one of a number of unusual tan-coloured dolomite hills scattered over the valley floor. A small cave in this large dog-toothed outcrop was once used by local Aboriginal people as a storehouse for sacred objects. It is a registered sacred site and is listed on the National Estate. Despite the name, it is doubtful if the rock was ever used as a corroborree area, due to the lack of water in the vicinity.

Bushwalking

A short walking track leads from the car park to the 'windows' in the rock, and around the base.

TREPHINA GORGE NATURE PARK

About 60 km from Alice Springs you cross the sandy bed of **Benstead Creek**, with its lovely big gums. The thousands of young river gums that line the road germinated in the mid-1970s, when the Alice Springs region received unusually high rainfall. This delightful scenery, which is totally at odds with the common perception of central Australia, continues for the six km from the creek crossing to the Trephina Gorge turn-off.

Three km north of the Ross Highway, Trephina Gorge Nature Park offers some magnificent gorge, ridge and creek scenery, excellent walks, deep swimming holes, abundant wildlife and low-key camping areas. The main attractions are Trephina

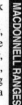

MACDONNELL RANGES

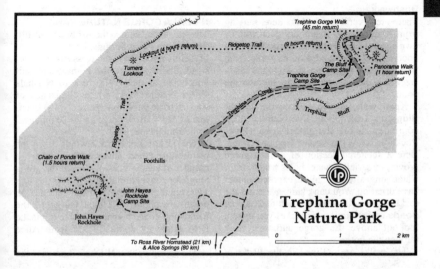

Trephina Gorge Walk
(45 min return)
Ridgetop Trail
(9 hours return)
Lookout (4 hours return)
Turners Lookout
The Bluff Camp Site
Panorama Walk
(1 hour return)
Trephina Gorge Camp Site
Trephina Creek
Trephina Bluff
Ridgetop Trail
Chain of Ponds Walk
(1.5 hours return)
Foothills
John Hayes Rockhole Camp Site
John Hayes Rockhole
To Ross River Homestead (21 km) & Alice Springs (80 km)

Trephina Gorge Nature Park

0   1   2 km

Gorge, **Trephina Bluff** and **John Hayes Rockhole**. The rockhole, a permanent water hole, is reached by a rough track that wanders for several km up the so-called **Valley of the Eagles** (you'll be lucky to see one) and is often closed to conventional vehicles.

The first Europeans to pass through the gorge were an advance survey party of the Overland Telegraph Line, led by John Ross, which came through here in 1870. The gorge contains a stand of huge river red gums, and many of these were logged in the 1950s to provide sleepers for the *Ghan* railway line. The area was excised from The Garden station in 1966 and gazetted as a park to protect both the gums and the gorge.

Trephina Gorge has a restful atmosphere and some grand scenery, making it a great spot to camp for a few days. It also boasts a colony of uncommon black-flanked rock-wallabies on the cliff above the water hole – wander down first thing in the morning and you'll usually spot them leaping nimbly about on the rock face. Plant life within the gorge area is also varied, and is home to a number of rare plants, including the Glory of the Centre Wedding Bush.

Bushwalking

There are several good walks here, ranging from 30 minutes to five hours, each with its own appeal. The **Trephina Gorge Walk** is a good walk along the edge of the gorge, from where the trail then drops down to the sandy creek bed and loops back to the starting point.

Keen walkers can follow the longer **Ridgetop Trail** (about five hours), which continues to the delightful John Hayes Rockhole, a few km west of Trephina Gorge. Here a sheltered section of a deep gorge provides a series of water holes which retain water long after the more exposed places have dried up. You can clamber around the rockholes or follow the 90-minute **Chain of Ponds** marked trail which takes you up to a lookout above the gorge and then back through the gorge.

The walks are outlined in the *Walks of Trephina Gorge Nature Park* published by Parks & Wildlife ($1).

Facilities

Small camp sites at Trephina Gorge, The Bluff and John Hayes Rockhole offer a variety of camping experiences, and all are cheap: $1/3 per person/family (payable into honesty boxes). You can collect firewood from a heap just before the first Trephina Creek crossing on the Trephina Gorge access road.

The *Trephina Gorge camp site* is in a timbered gully a short stroll from the main attraction, and has running water, pit toilets, fireplaces and picnic tables. It is suitable for caravans, unlike *The Bluff camp site*, which is only about five minutes' walk away. The Bluff has similar facilities, in addition to free gas barbecues, but a more spectacular creek bank setting under tall gums in front of a towering red ridge. *John Hayes Rockhole* has two basic sites beside a rocky creek just down from the water hole. The most obvious thing about this restricted area is its large population of ants.

If you need any emergency assistance, there is a ranger stationed in the park (☎ 8956 9765).

N'DHALA GORGE NATURE PARK

The sealed road ends at the Arltunga turn-off, 71 km from Alice Springs, leaving nine km of mainly good dirt to the Ross River homestead. Shortly before the homestead/resort you come to the 4WD track to N'Dhala Gorge Nature Park, where thousands of ancient **rock carvings** (petroglyphs) decorate a deep, narrow gorge about 20 minutes' walk from the car park.

The 11-km access track winds down the picturesque **Ross River valley**, where a number of sandy crossings make the going tough for conventional vehicles. As the sign says, towing is costly. You can continue on downstream past N'Dhala Gorge to the Ringwood Road, then head west to rejoin the Ross Highway about 30 km from Alice Springs.

The petroglyphs at N'Dhala (known to the

Arrernte people as Irlwentye) are of two major types: finely pecked, where a stone hammer has been used to strike a sharp chisel such as a bone or rock; and pounded, where a stone has been hit directly on the rock face. The carvings, which are generally not that easy to spot, are thought to have been made in the last 2000 years. Common designs featured in the carvings are circular and feather-like patterns, and these are thought to relate to the Caterpillar Dreaming.

Facilities

There is a *camp site* at the gorge entrance. Facilities are limited to fireplaces (collect your own wood), tables and a pit toilet; shade is limited. Camping fees are $1/3 per person/family, payable into the honesty box. The flies are friendly, too.

ROSS RIVER HOMESTEAD

Originally the headquarters for Loves Creek station, the Ross River homestead resort (☎ 8956 9711; fax 8956 9823) has a pretty setting under rocky hills beside the Ross River. It's much favoured by coach tours, but is an equally good place for independent visitors. It's a friendly sort of place and there's lots to do, including walks in the spectacular surrounding countryside, excursions to other attractions, short camel rides or safaris and horse riding. Or simply lazing around with a cold one.

A large camp site down on the river bank has unpowered sites ($5 per person), powered sites ($15 per site) and bunkhouse accommodation with linen supplied ($12 per person). Shade is limited, but there is a small, rustic-style bar in the camp site where you can enjoy a cold drink. The old homestead on the other side of the river has cosy timber cabins accommodating up to five people each. Rates are $107 (single or double) – add $25 per extra person over 14 years (anyone under is free). You can get generous buffet, carvery, bistro and barbecue meals, all at reasonable prices.

For something out of the ordinary, the resort puts on an overnighter with either horses or camels. This involves a two-hour ride to a bush camp site in the hills, where you enjoy a three-course campfire meal before unrolling the swag under the stars. In the morning you eat breakfast before returning to the resort. It's an expensive excursion, however, at $165 per adult and $115 for children.

Transfers are available from Alice Springs for $25 return ($15 children).

ARLTUNGA HISTORICAL RESERVE

Leaving the Ross Highway, the first 12 km of the Arltunga Road passes through scenic **Bitter Springs Gorge**, where red quartzite ridges tower high above dolomite hills. This was the route taken by the early diggers as they walked from Alice Springs to the goldfields at the turn of the century. The road can be quite rough at times and is impassable after heavy rain.

Located 103 km from Alice Springs, the Arltunga Historical Reserve features significant evidence of the gold-mining activity that took place in its arid hills between 1887 and 1913. The major attraction is a partially restored ghost town that contains the remains of a treatment plant and several stone buildings, including a police station and jail. Walking tracks take you past **old mines**, now complete with bat colonies, and one mine is open to visitors, so make sure to bring a torch.

The richest part of the goldfield was **White Range**, but showing remarkable short-sightedness, authorities allowed almost all the ruins and small mines that once dotted this high ridge to be destroyed during a recent short-lived open-cut mining operation. The White Range Mine operated for a few years in the late 1980s, and it was reopened in early 1996 as new technology made the area viable once more. Fortunately the mine is out of sight on the far side of the range, and the new operations are all underground.

Joseph Hele, who is credited with the discovery of gold at White Range, is buried in the nearby **cemetery**.

Arltunga is a fascinating place for anyone interested in history. To get some idea of

MACDONNELL RANGES

what life was like for the early diggers, call in to the visitor centre, which has interesting displays of old mining machinery and historic photographs.

Fossicking is not permitted at Arltunga, but there is a **fossicking reserve** in a gully just to the south where you may (with luck) find some gold. A permit is required, and you can obtain one from the Department of Mines & Energy in Alice Springs.

History

The rush to the so-called ruby fields a short distance to the east of here led to the chance discovery of alluvial gold at Paddy's Rockhole in 1887, and further exploration uncovered the reefs at White Range in 1897.

The field was not particularly rich, and the miners faced huge problems, especially against the extremes of weather and the lack of water. In 1898 the South Australian government constructed a 10-head gold-stamping battery and cyanide processing works at Arltunga, in itself a major logistical feat as all the equipment had to be brought by camel train from the railhead at Oodnadatta, 600 km to the south.

The increased facilities did little for the prosperity of the field, however, and even at its peak in the early 1900s there was never more than a few hundred miners working here; most of the time far less than 100. By 1916 the battery had treated 11,500 tons of rock, yielding around 15,000 ounces of gold.

In the 1930s an Aboriginal mission was established by the Catholic church in Alice Springs, and this was moved to Arltunga during WW II when the Alice became a military base. The Little Flower mission was moved to Santa Teresa, south-east of Alice Springs, in 1953.

Guided Walks & Talks

Rangers at the visitor centre (☎ 8956 9770) screen the interesting slide show on request, and on Sunday at 11 am they crank up the

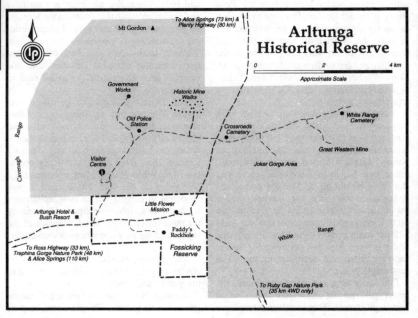

old Jenkins Battery behind the centre and crush some gold-bearing ore.

On Sunday at 2.30 pm they lead guided walks through one of the mines.

Bushwalking

Four interesting walks of under one hour give access to various old mining areas. One track leads to the MacDonnell Range Reef mine, where you can climb down steel ladders and explore about 50 metres of tunnels between two shafts. The adjoining walk to the nearby Golden Chance mine is also worth doing.

Facilities

Camping is not permitted within the historical reserve, but the nearby *Arltunga Hotel & Bush Resort* (☎ 8956 9797) promotes itself as 'the loneliest pub in the scrub' and is a good place to stay. There's camping at $5 and you can hire a swag for $6/8 single/double. There's also an on-site van for $35 (up to four people) and a couple of self-contained family rooms at $35. Meals, snacks and beer are also available.

RUBY GAP NATURE PARK

Leaving Arltunga you head east towards Atnarpa homestead. Turn left immediately before the gate at 11 km from the Claraville turn-off. The road now deteriorates and is restricted to 4WD vehicles thanks to its sandy creek crossings and sharp jump-ups.

Twenty-five km beyond the gate you arrive at the **Hale River**; follow the wheel ruts upstream (left) along the sandy bed for about six km to the turn-around point, which is through **Ruby Gap** and just short of rugged **Glen Annie Gorge**. If you're first on the scene after a flood, always check that the riverbed is firm before driving onto it, otherwise you may sink deep in sand.

The park's gorge-and-river scenery is some of the wildest and most attractive in central Australia, and being remote and hard to get to, it doesn't have the crowds that often destroy the atmosphere at more accessible places. The water holes at Glen Annie Gorge are usually deep enough for a cooling dip.

History

Ruby Gap was named after a frantic ruby rush in the late 1860s that crashed overnight when it was found that the rubies were worthless garnets. The man responsible for the rush was David Lindsay, an explorer and surveyor who came through this way while leading an expedition from Adelaide to Port Darwin. (It was also on this trip that he surveyed the first allotments for the new township of Stuart.) The word spread and before long more than 200 hopefuls had made the arduous trek from the railhead at Oodnadatta. It's easy to see how the prospectors got carried away because the surface of the river bed shimmers a deep-claret colour as the sun reflects off the millions of garnet specks. They faced incredible hardships here, not least of which were the lack of water and the fierce climate.

Bushwalking

There are no marked walks here, but for the enthusiast a climb around the craggy rim of Glen Annie Gorge features superb views of this beautiful spot. You can climb up on the southern side and return from the north along the sandy floor, or vice versa. The lonely grave of a ruby miner is located at the gorge's northern end.

Facilities

There are no facilities of any kind. Camping is allowed anywhere along the river, but you'll need to bring your own firewood and drinking water. The park is managed by the rangers at Arltunga (☎ 8956 9770), so check road conditions with them before heading out here.

MACDONNELL RANGES

James Ranges

The spectacular James Ranges form an east-west band south of the West MacDonnell Ranges. While they are relatively unknown in comparison to the MacDonnells, the ranges are still well visited as they contain a few of the Centre's best attractions: Hermannsburg, Palm Valley and Kings Canyon.

The Stuart Highway also cuts through the eastern edge of the ranges at Stuart's Well, and in this area there's the stunning sandstone formations of Rainbow Valley, and the diminutive Henbury Meteorite Craters.

Most people visit Hermannsburg and Palm Valley on a day-trip from Alice Springs, and King's Canyon on a separate trip which includes Uluru. You can save a lot of back-tracking, however, if you continue from Hermannsburg around the western end of the James Ranges on the gravel Mereenie Loop Road, an interesting option which brings you out at Kings Canyon.

LARAPINTA DRIVE
Taking the alternative road to the south from Standley Chasm in the West MacDonnells, Larapinta Drive crosses the Hugh River, and then Ellery Creek before reaching the turn-off for Wallace Rockhole, 17 km off the main road and 117 km from Alice Springs.

Wallace Rockhole
The Arrernte community of Wallace Rockhole offers **rock-art tours** (9.30 am and 1 pm, $6) and a chance to sample traditional bush tucker in season. Kangaroo tail cooked in the ground is a speciality. Wallace Rockhole has a pleasant camping area and caravan park ($6 per person, no power), and the general store sells ice and locally produced Aboriginal crafts. Ring the community office (☎ 8956 7415) for details of rates and activities.

Namatjira Monument
Back on Larapinta Drive, shortly before

HIGHLIGHTS

- Visit the historic Hermannsburg Mission, a vivid reminder of the early days in the Centre
- Walk through Palm Valley in Finke Gorge National Park
- View the spectacular Kings Canyon in Watarrka National Park
- Explore Rainbow Valley, one of the Centre's little known attractions

Hermannsburg, is the Namatjira Monument. Today the artistic skills of the central Australian Aboriginal people are widely known and appreciated. This certainly wasn't the case when the artist Albert Namatjira started to paint his central Australian landscapes in 1934.

HERMANNSBURG
Only eight km beyond the Namatjira monument you reach the Hermannsburg Aboriginal settlement (population 420), 125 km from Alice Springs.

Although the town is restricted Aboriginal land, permits are not required to visit the mission or store, or to travel through. Super-

Albert Namatjira (1902-59)

Probably Australia's most well-known Aboriginal artist, Albert Namatjira lived at the Hermannsburg Lutheran Mission west of Alice Springs and was introduced to the art of European-style watercolour painting by non-Aboriginal artist Rex Batterbee in the 1930s.

Namatjira successfully captured the essence of the Centre with paintings which were heavily influenced by European art. At the time his pictures were seen purely for what they appeared to be – renderings of picturesque landscapes. These days, however, it is thought he chose his subjects carefully, as they were Dreaming landscapes to which he had a great bond.

Namatjira supported many of his people with the income from his work, as was his obligation under tribal law. Because of his fame, he was allowed to buy alcohol at a time when this was otherwise illegal for Aboriginal people. In 1957 he was the first Aboriginal person to be granted Australian citizenship, but in 1958 he was jailed for six months for supplying alcohol to Aborigines. He died the following year, aged 57.

Although Namatjira died very disenchanted with White society, he did much to change the White's extremely negative views of Aboriginal people which prevailed at the time, and at the same time paved the way for the Papunya painting movement which emerged a decade after his death. ■

market shopping is available at the mission store near the historic precinct, and at the Ntaria Supermarket at the main entrance to town, and there's a service station next door.

Hermannsburg Mission

Shaded by tall river gums and date palms, and with a view over the Finke River's normally dry, shimmering bed, the old mission is a fascinating monument to the skill and dedication of the early Lutheran missionaries. The group of 11 low, white-washed stone buildings includes a church, a school and various houses and outbuildings. The buildings are probably as good an example of

traditional German farmhouse architecture as you'll find anywhere outside that country. They were fully restored with a federal government grant in 1988.

Admission costs $2.50 per adult and $1.50 per child and includes a guided tour of the art gallery, which provides an insight into the life and times of Albert Namatjira and contains examples of the work of 39 Hermannsburg artists, including three generations of the Namatjira family.

In 1876, fresh from the Hermannsburg Mission Institute in Germany, pastors A H Kempe and W F Schwarz left Adelaide bound for central Australia with a herd of

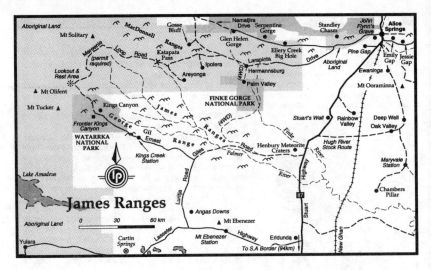

cattle and several thousand sheep. Eighteen months later they finally arrived at the new mission site, having been held up by drought at Dalhousie Springs for nearly a year. It was a nightmarish introduction to the harsh central Australian environment, but the pastors were committed to the task of bringing Christianity and 'civilisation' to the Aboriginal people.

Despite incredible hardships and difficulties, including strong opposition from White settlers to their attempts to protect Aboriginal people from genocide, the missionaries successfully established what became the first township in central Australia. However, problems with isolation, sickness and opposition from pastoralists soon led to the mission becoming rundown and neglected, and many of the Aboriginal residents drifted away.

This was all turned around with the arrival of Pastor Carl Strehlow in 1894. Within months the mission had been restored, and the buildings which constitute the core of the mission today were built. Strehlow was a tireless worker who learnt the Arrernte language, translated the New Testament into Arrernte and wrote a number of important

works on the Arrernte people. On the downside, however, he also had the touch of arrogance which typified missions at the time (dubbed 'muscular Christianity'), believing that the Aboriginal beliefs and customs were wrong.

At one time Hermannsburg had a population of 700 Western Arrernte people, a cattle herd of 5000 and various cottage industries, including a tannery. The mission was operated by the Synod of South Australia right up until 1982 when title was handed back to the Arrernte people under the Aboriginal Land Rights (NT) Act of 1976. Since that time most of its residents have left Hermannsburg and established small outstation communities on traditional clan territories. There are now 35 such outstations on the old mission lease. Although about 200 Aborigines still live at Hermannsburg, its main function is to provide support and resources for the outlying population.

One of Hermannsburg's most famous resident was Professor T G H (Ted) Strehlow, youngest child of Carl Strehlow. He was born on the mission and spent more than 40 years studying the Arrernte people. His books about them, like *Aranda Traditions*

(1947), *Australian Aboriginal Anthropology* (1970) and *Songs of Central Australia* (1971), are still widely read. The Arrernte people entrusted him with many items of huge spiritual and symbolic importance when they realised their traditional lifestyle was under threat. These items are now held in a vault in the Strehlow Research Centre in Alice Springs.

The best place to start a visit to the historic precinct is the *Kata-Anga Tea Room* (☎ 8956 7402) in the old missionary house. Open seven days a week from 9 am to 4 pm, the tea room has a marvellous atmosphere in which, for a very reasonable price, you can relax with a light lunch, or a bottomless cup of tea or coffee and a large slice of delicious home-baked cake – the apple strudel is highly recommended. If you're making a special trip out from Alice Springs in the summer months, call first to check that they'll be open.

The tea room sells a good range of traditional and watercolour paintings, artefacts and pottery, all items being the work of local Aboriginal people. The quality is generally very good, and the prices reasonable. The staff here also issue permits for travel on the Mereenie Loop Road (see that section later in this chapter).

FINKE GORGE NATIONAL PARK
From Hermannsburg the trail follows the Finke River south to the Finke Gorge National Park, only 12 km further on.

Famous for its rare palms, Finke Gorge National Park is one of central Australia's premier wilderness areas. The landscape is spectacular and colourful. The main gorge features high red cliffs, stately river gums, cool water holes, plenty of clean white sand and clumps of tall palms. Combine this tremendous natural beauty with the area's fascinating history and you have an excursion that's packed with interest.

For thousands of years, the Finke River formed part of an Aboriginal trade route that crossed Australia, bringing goods such as sacred red ochre from the south and pearl shell from the north to the central Australian tribes. Far from being desert, the area around Hermannsburg had an abundance of animals and food plants. It was a major refuge for the Western Arrernte people in times of drought, thanks to its permanent water, which came from soaks dug in the Finke River bed. An upside-down river (like all others in central Australia), the Finke flows beneath its dry bed most of the time. As it becomes saline during drought, the Western Arrernte call it *Lhere pirnte* (hence Larapinta), which means salty river. It was their comprehensive knowledge of its freshwater soaks that enabled them to survive in the harshest droughts.

Access into the park is restricted to 4WD vehicles, but there are plenty of tour operators who do day-trips here from Alice Springs.

History
The explorer Ernest Giles arrived on the scene in 1872, when he travelled up the Finke on his first attempt to cross from the Overland Telegraph Line to the west coast. To his amazement he found tall palms growing in the river, which had been named 12 years earlier by John McDouall Stuart, and went into raptures over the beauty of the scenery that he saw there.

Occasional visits were made to the area by various people from the Hermannsburg mission, but it has only been since the 1960s that tourism has really developed.

Palm Valley
Leaving the Finke at its junction with Palm Creek, you head west past the old ranger station (the houses were flooded in 1988 and are now abandoned), and a km further on arrive at the Kalarranga car park. En route there's a small information bay that gives you an introduction to the area and to some of the walks you can do (see Activities). Kalarranga, more usually known as the **Amphitheatre**, is a semi-circle of striking ochre-coloured sandstone formations sculpted by a now-extinct meander of Palm Creek. Be there in early morning or late afternoon for the best views.

Continuing on from the Amphitheatre, the track becomes extremely rough and rocky for the final three km to Palm Valley. Along the way you pass the camping ground and picnic area before arriving at **Cycad Gorge**, where a chocolate-coloured cliff towers over a clump of tall, slender palms. The gorge is named for the large number of shaggy cycads found growing on and below the cliff face. Lending a tropical atmosphere to their barren setting, the palms and cycads are leftovers from much wetter times in central Australia. They only survive here because of a reliable supply of moisture within the surrounding sandstone.

Just past Cycad Gorge you come to Palm Valley itself, with the first oasis of palms just a stone's throw away. The valley is actually a narrow gorge that in places is literally choked with lush oases of waving **Red Cabbage Palms** up to 25 metres high. Found nowhere else in the world, the species (*Livistona mariae*) grows within an area of 60 sq km and is over 800 km from its nearest relatives. To the Arrernte people the palms are associated with the Fire Dreaming. There are only 3000 mature palms in the wild, so the rangers ask that you resist the temptation to enter the palm groves – the tiny seedlings are hard to see and are easily trampled underfoot. This is probably why there are hardly any young ones near the Palm Valley car park.

The gorge is a botanist's paradise, as it is home to over 400 plant species, which is almost one-fifth of all those found in the Centre, and around 10% of them are either rare or have a restricted distribution.

Finke Gorge

If you are travelling by 4WD vehicle there's a track which traverses the full length of the picturesque Finke Gorge, much of the time along the bed of the (usually) dry Finke River. It's a rough but worthwhile trip, and the camp sites at Boggy Hole, about 2½ hours from Hermannsburg, make an excellent overnight stop, although if you are in a hurry you can get from Palm Valley all the way to Kings Canyon (Watarrka National Park) in less than eight hours via this route. This is a great trip, but it's also serious 4WD territory and you need to be suitably prepared. See Lonely Planet's *Outback Australia* for full details.

Bushwalking

There are three walking tracks in the Palm Valley area, all of them suitable for family use. The most popular is the five-km **Mpulungkinya Track** which loops through Palm Valley and back over the top to the car park. It offers excellent views down the gorge and shows you how the availability of water determines plant life in the area.

A second five-km track, the **Mpaara Track**, starts and finishes at the Kalarranga car park and takes in the Finke River, Palm Bend and the rugged Amphitheatre. It leads you in the footsteps of a mythological hero from the Aboriginal Dreamtime, whose adventures are explained by signs along the way. The third track, a relatively short one, takes you up to **Kalarranga Lookout** on a sandstone knob; the view over the Amphitheatre is striking.

Facilities

A small camp site beside Palm Creek has shady trees, hot showers and gas barbecues, as well as numerous friendly birds that are always on the lookout for a free feed. You have to keep your food under cover, but otherwise it's a very pleasant place in a scenic setting of red sandstone ridges and the spectacular Amphitheatre is just a few minutes' walk away. Overnight charges are $4 per adult or $10 per family, paid into the honesty box; day-trippers have free use of the nearby picnic area and its shade shelters, flush toilets and gas barbecues. Dead timber cannot be collected past the park entry sign in the Finke River, so if you want a fire, be sure to collect firewood in advance.

IPOLERA

Continuing west from Hermannsburg along the road to Areyonga, there's a turn-off to the Arrernte Aboriginal community of Ipolera. Here it's usually possible to stay with the

Malbunka family who offer excellent two-hour cultural tours. Male and female visitors are taken on separate tours to help preserve and maintain the unique laws which apply to the two sexes. The tours take place from February to November on Monday, Wednesday and Friday at 10 am and cost $25. There's also basic camping at $5 per person.

Permits are not required to visit Ipolera, but bookings for either camping or the tours are obligatory (☎ 8956 7466); alcohol is prohibited. The turn-off for Ipolera is 45 km west of Hermannsburg, and it's then 13 km along a dirt road.

MEREENIE LOOP ROAD

From the Ipolera turn-off you can continue west to the Areyonga turn-off (no visitors), and then take the recently opened Mereenie Loop Road, which loops around the western edge of the James Ranges to Kings Canyon. This dirt road offers an excellent alternative to the Ernest Giles Road as a way of reaching Kings Canyon.

The Mereenie Loop Road was opened in June 1994. You need a permit from the Central Land Council to travel along it, as it passes through Aboriginal land. The permit includes the informative *Mereenie Tour Pass* booklet, which provides details about the local Aboriginal culture and has a route map. Permits are issued on the spot by the tourist office in Alice Springs, at Glen Helen Homestead, the Kata-Anga Tea Rooms at Hermannsburg, and the Frontier Kings Canyon resort at Watarrka National Park.

The countryside is interesting and varied, although hardly breathtaking, the highlight perhaps being the classic outback road sign which you pass on the southern part of the track – a rusty old 44-gallon drum sits by the side of the road on the approach to a sharp bend, and it carries a warning to slow down: 'lift um foot'. If you are travelling towards Kings Canyon, you reach the sign after the danger, and so the message reads: 'puttum back down'!

The road is generally in reasonable condition, and it takes around four hours to travel the 204 km from Hermannsburg to Kings

Canyon. It is quite OK for conventional vehicles to travel on this road, although it can become corrugated if the grader hasn't been through for a while. If you're towing a caravan it's probably best to give it a miss, although people do take vans through here.

STUART'S WELL

Stuart's Well is a stop on the Stuart Highway 90 km south of Alice Springs, where the highway passes through a gap in the James Ranges. The main attraction here is the **Camel Outback Safaris** operation (☎ 8956 0925; fax 8956 0909), owned and run by central Australia's 'camel king', Noel Fullerton. It's a good opportunity to take a short camel ride ($2 around the yard, $10 for half an hour, $20 one hour, $55 half day and $80 for a full day). Extended safaris of seven to 14 days into places like nearby Rainbow Valley or Palm Valley also operate on a regular basis. The rate for these is around $100 per person per day.

Places to Stay

Next door to the camel farm is *Jim's Place* (☎ 8956 0808; fax 8956 0809), run by another central Australian identity, Jim Cotterill. There's camping ($10, $15 powered) with grass and shade, $24 for a dorm bed in demountables, and there are self-contained cabins at $45/60. The store here stocks a few basic provisions, and the restaurant dishes up hearty meals and good takeaways, and serves beer (no takeaways). On the wall is an interesting collection of photos, particularly of the old Wallara Ranch on the Ernest Giles Road.

RAINBOW VALLEY CONSERVATION RESERVE

Rainbow Valley is one of the more extraordinary sights in central Australia, and thanks largely to Parks & Wildlife it sees relatively few visitors. The scenic sandstone bluffs and cliffs on the eastern edge of the James Ranges seem to glow at sunset when the bands of different coloured sandstone are highlighted. Although colourfully named, the crumbling sandstone cliffs at Rainbow

Valley are various shades of cream and red. If you're lucky enough to visit when there's water in the claypans, you can get some stunning photos.

The park is not as instantly attractive as some of the more spectacular sights in central Australia, but it has a charm which certainly repays any time spent here. Because it doesn't get overrun with visitors, it's a great place to spend a couple of days – wander and scramble in the James Ranges, admire the views and soak up the timeless atmosphere of the Centre.

From the far end of the parking area at the foot of the bluff, there's a walking track which takes you to an excellent vantage point on the edge of the cliff; it's a 20-minute scramble up loose sand. From here the views are superb – spinifex sand plains to the north, and desert oaks and more hills to the south. The reserve is important to the southern Arrernte people, and the large rock massif known as Ewerre in the south of the reserve is a registered sacred site.

The sandstone rocks here were laid down about 300 million years ago, and weathering and leaching has led to a concentration of red iron oxides in the upper layers; lower down the stone is bleached almost white. The sandstone here is extremely soft and brittle, and is very easily damaged, so visitors are asked to tread lightly.

The reserve lies 22 km east of the Stuart Highway along a well-used but unsignposted track 14 km north of Stuart's Well by a cattle grid. It's no accident that there's no sign on the highway; Parks & Wildlife are well aware that this is a very fragile area and hordes of visitors could do major damage in a short time. A sign at the start of the track warns that access is by 4WD vehicle only, mainly due to a couple of deep sandy patches which could bog conventional vehicles. The track also crosses a claypan just before you reach the cliff, but it's prudent to take the track which skirts the claypan if there's been recent rain.

Organised Tours

A number of companies do 4WD trips to Rainbow Valley, usually combined with visits to Chambers Pillar. Companies to contact include the Aboriginal-owned and run Oak Valley Tours (☎ 8956 0959; fax 8956 0965), Centralian Luxury Touring (☎ 8989 7441; fax 8955 5401) and The Outback Experience (☎ 8953 2666; fax 8953 2313).

Extended camel safaris from Camel Outback Safaris (☎ 8956 0925) at Stuart's Well also visit Rainbow Valley.

Facilities

There's a sandy *camp site* right at the foot of the bluff. It's a little exposed with little shade and no water, but the location is superb and is perfectly positioned for prime sunset viewing – sitting here with a cooling ale watching the show (especially if a full moon is rising) is something not to be missed. The camp site has a couple of fireplaces, and pit toilets. Payment is $1/3 per person/family into the honesty box. Firewood must be brought in with you; collect it on the way in from the highway.

Parks & Wildlife do have plans to upgrade the facilities and move the camp site some distance away from the cliff. This certainly will be the best thing from a conservation viewpoint, although it will dilute the experience somewhat for campers.

OAK VALLEY

It's worth calling in at this small Aboriginal community if you happen to be passing. It's on the Hugh River Stock Route, a good track which connects the Stuart Highway with the old *Ghan* line and Maryvale station.

The community operates day tours out of Alice Springs, but there's also a 2½-hour guided tour which operates from Oak Valley. The tour takes in local rock-art and fossil sites and delves into bush tucker, and costs $15 ($7 children seven to 14). There's also horse riding ($20 per hour) and an art & craft shop.

If you want to stop there for the night there's a *camp site* (with on-site swags!) with hot showers, shade shelters and barbecues (firewood supplied). For more details ☎ 8956 0959.

HENBURY METEORITE CRATERS CONSERVATION RESERVE

About 40 km south of Stuart's Well the gravel **Ernest Giles Road** heads off west the 200 km to Kings Canyon. The first 97 km is a notoriously rough stretch with many narrow, winding sections through the dunes. After this the track joins the Luritja Road from the Lasseter Highway (and Uluru) and is bitumen the rest of the way to Kings Canyon.

Eleven km west of the Stuart Highway is a deeply corrugated side road which leads the five km to the Henbury Meteorite Craters, where a cluster of small craters dots an exposed, stony plain. The 12 craters were formed several thousand years ago when a meteorite broke up on entering the earth's atmosphere and hit the ground. The largest crater is 180 metres wide and 15 metres deep; it was formed by a piece of rock about the size of a 44-gallon drum.

The reserve is worth a quick stop if you want to stretch the legs or have a deep interest in this sort of thing. Otherwise you can drive on by without feeling as though you have missed something which is worth seeing .

Facilities

There's a *camp site* here, but it is extremely exposed and the ground is very hard and stony – on a cold, windy day it's pretty grim; on a hot, windy day it's worse. There are fireplaces (but barely a tree in sight) and pit toilets.

WATARRKA NATIONAL PARK

In the western half of the George Gill Range, an outlier of the James Ranges, is Watarrka National Park, which includes one of the most spectacular sights in central Australia – the 100-metre high sheer walls of **Kings Canyon**.

The name Watarrka comes from the Luritja Aboriginal word for the umbrella bush (*Acacia ligulata*) and it also refers to the Kings Canyon district. The park offers spectacular walking and photographic opportunities, and there's a range of accommodation options nearby.

The gorge itself is barely one km long, yet within it is a number of different habitats, and

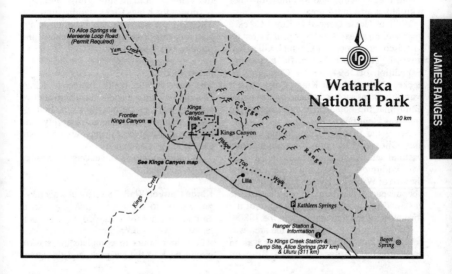

over 600 plant species have been recorded in the park, giving it the highest plant diversity of any place in Australia's arid zone. At the head of the gorge is the spring-fed **Garden of Eden**, where a moist micro-climate supports a variety of plants. The narrow, rocky bed of Kings Creek along the floor of the canyon is covered with tall ghost gums and an unusual bonsai variety. Also seen along the valley walls is the MacDonnell Ranges cycad (*Macrozamia macdonnellii*), a bushy palm which appears only in the range country of central Australia.

The gorge is surrounded by a sandstone plateau which is covered in many places by small, weathered sandstone domes.

History

The Luritja Aboriginal people have lived in this area for at least 20,000 years and there is a number of registered sacred sites within the park. There are also three communities of Aboriginal people living within the park.

In 1872 Ernest Giles was the first European through this area, and he named the George Gill Range after his brother-in-law, who also helped fund the private expedition. Giles also named Kings Creek after his friend Fielder King, and a number of other natural features in the area.

William Gosse camped at Kings Creek a year later on an exploratory trip, and went on to 'discover' Ayers Rock, which Giles had missed. The Horn Scientific Exploring Expedition of 1894, led by Charles Winnecke, also camped at Kings Creek, and it was only thanks to finds made by this expedition that the botanical importance of the area was identified.

Being the first European to explore the area, Giles had first option on applying for a pastoral lease, and this he did in 1874. It covered almost 1000 sq miles and included the area of Watarrka. By 1885 Giles' land had become part of the Tempe Downs lease to the east, and it was run from there up until the formation of the national park in the 1980s.

The first tourism venture in the area was set up by Jack Cotterill in 1960. It was an accommodation place at Yowa Bore on Angus Downs station. It became known as Wallara Ranch, and was operated by Jack's son, Jim (see Stuart's Well earlier in this chapter), right up until 1990. With a change of ownership, name and buildings it continued to operate until 1992. (It is still marked on some maps, either as Wallara or Stockyard Homestead). Jack Cotterill built the road from Wallara to Kings Canyon, and a small cairn and plaque at Kings Canyon commemorates the huge effort he put into developing the tourist trade in this area.

In the early 1960s Ansett graded an airstrip near Kings Creek and started a service between Kings Canyon, Alice Springs and Uluru.

Information

There's a ranger station and visitor centre (☎ 8956 7460) 22 km east of the canyon close to the park entrance.

In case of medical emergencies, there is a solar radiophone at the canyon car park, and a comprehensive first-aid kit up on the plateau on the northern side of the canyon.

Ranger Talks

On Thursday and Saturday evenings at 7.30 the rangers hold a slide show and chat session at the Kings Creek station camp site. They do the same at the Frontier Kings Canyon resort camp site on Friday and Sunday evenings.

Bushwalking

The only way to really appreciate Kings Canyon is to get out and walk. There are two walking trails at the canyon itself, both of which require a fair degree of agility, and another at Kathleen Springs, about 12 km east of Kings Canyon.

In addition there's the excellent two-day Ridge-Top Walk.

Kings Canyon Walk The canyon walk takes you up on to the plateau and then skirts around the rim off the canyon. It's an excellent walk which offers some stunning views. Allow four hours to complete the six-km circuit back to the car park, and this gives you enough time to make the short detour to the **Garden of Eden** on the northern edge of the canyon. The trail is clearly marked with flashes on metal posts along the way. This walk is very popular, so it's a good idea to get a jump on the mobs and start out really early. The light is also excellent at this time.

Kings Creek Walk This is a much shorter walk (more of a scramble really) along the rocky bed of Kings Creek. While you do get some good views of the canyon walls through the ghost gums, it's not a patch on those from the canyon rim. Allow an hour to do the return walk.

Kathleen Springs This 2.5-km wheelchair accessible path leads to a beautiful rock pool at the base of the range.

Ridge-Top Walk This is a marked 28-km walking trail which, as the name suggests, follows the ridge from Kings Canyon to Kathleen Springs. If you don't want to do the whole two days, it's possible to do a day walk as there is also access from Lilla, which is about half-way along the trail. Although there are water holes in the area, these cannot be relied upon so you need to be fully self-sufficient in both food and water. There's a designated camp site along the ridge above Lilla, and small campfires are permitted here. Check in with the rangers at the visitor centre and get a bushwalking permit before setting off.

Organised Tours
Kurkara Tours (☎ 8956 7865; fax 8956 7843) is an Aboriginal-owned and run tour company which has a variety of trips from the Frontier Kings Canyon resort:

Guided Canyon Walk This four-hour trip departs at 7 am daily and an Aboriginal guide takes you on the canyon-rim walk. The cost is $17 ($8.50 for children under 15).

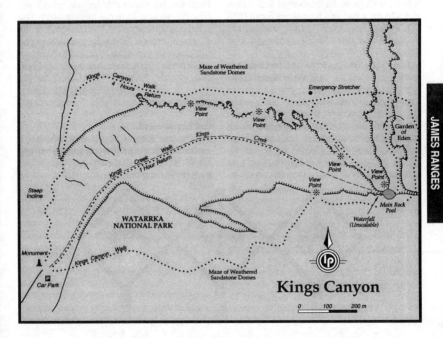

Kings Canyon

JAMES RANGES

Mungartji (Sunset) Tour This is an introduction to Aboriginal culture combined with sunset views of the canyon. The tour departs at 5 pm (6 pm in summer) takes 1½ hours and costs $20 ($10).

Willy Wagtail Tour This is a 2½-hour tour which takes in cave paintings and an introduction to Luritja traditions. It departs at 2 pm and the cost is $30 ($15).

Scenic Flights The constant intrusive buzzing of planes and helicopters overhead are the bane of the bushwalker, but give an excellent view of the canyon. Enquire at the Frontier Kings Canyon.

Places to Stay & Eat
Accommodation within the park is confined to the *Frontier Kings Canyon* (☎ toll-free 1800 891 101; fax 8956 7410), a resort which has up-market motel rooms with private facilities at $182 for a twin room. Rooms with share facilities cost $65 a twin and $24 for a bed in a four-share room ($88 to take the whole room). Family rooms have a double and three single beds, and cost $105.

For meals you have the choice of an à la carte restaurant or cafe-style meals. The latter are good value at $10 for a choice of three main courses with salads and sweets. The complex includes a souvenir shop with limited, and expensive, food supplies, which also sells fuel from 7 am to 7 pm seven days a week.

The *Frontier Resort camp site* won't be everyone's cup of tea, as the idea seems to be to get as many into a given space as possible. It's also overpriced, at $11/9 per person with/without power, although there is plenty of grass and shade, and also a swimming pool. For something friendlier, cheaper and more akin to a bush experience, try *Kings Creek Station* (☎ 8956 7474), on Ernest Giles Rd just outside the national park's eastern boundary and about 35 km from the canyon. The very pleasant camp site is set among large desert oaks and costs start at $6 per person. Fuel, ice and limited stores are available seven days a week at the shop.

Getting There & Away
Air Airnorth (☎ toll-free 1800 627 474) has daily flights to Kings Canyon from Alice Springs ($129) and Uluru ($79).

Road There are a number of choices when it comes to travelling to or from Kings Canyon. The most interesting option from Alice Springs is via the West MacDonnells, Hermannsburg and the Mereenie Loop Road (see that section earlier in this chapter). You can then continue on to Uluru and back to the Stuart Highway at Erldunda, from where you can head north to Alice Springs (200 km), or south to the South Australian border (94 km) and beyond. This round-trip circuit from the Alice is about 1200 km, only 300 km of which is gravel.

Getting Around
The Frontier Kings Canyon resort operates a shuttle bus between the resort and the canyon for $9.50 return ($5 for children under 15). Enquire at reception.

South to Uluru

The very southern section of the Territory consists largely of sweeping spinifex-grass sand plains, and these support large stands of desert oaks and mulga trees. Many people would regard this semi-arid region as desert, but in fact it is relatively fertile country which is a blaze of colour after spring rains when dozens of varieties of wildflowers bloom. To the east the tracks fade into the vastness of the Simpson Desert, while to the west lies the equally formidable Gibson Desert in WA.

The Stuart Highway spears due south right through the centre of this region, and you would probably not spare it a passing thought except for one thing, it is in this area that you find Australia's most readily identifiable icon – Uluru (Ayers Rock). 'The Rock' lies some 250 km west of the highway along a fine bitumen road.

To the east of the highway there are some excellent diversions you can make into the fringes of the Simpson Desert. It was along here that the Overland Telegraph Line and the old *Ghan* railway line ran, and it's still possible to follow the latter along its route from the Alice to the small town of Finke, about 150 km east of the highway.

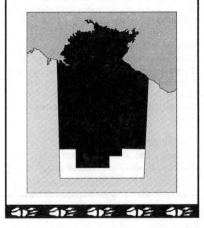

ERLDUNDA

Erldunda is a modern roadhouse-and-motel complex on the Stuart Highway 200 km south of Alice Springs, at the point where the Lasseter Highway branches off 244 km west to Uluru. It's a very popular rest-and-refuelling stop, but the fuel prices are among the highest along the 2700-odd-km length of the Stuart Highway between Port Augusta and Darwin.

In addition to accommodation, there's a licensed restaurant/bistro, takeaway-food section, souvenir shop, grocery store and vehicle spare-parts section.

Places to Stay

The *Desert Oaks Resort* (☎ 8956 0984; fax 8956 0942) has shaded and grassy camp sites for $12 ($16 with power), and there's a shaded swimming pool and tennis court. The air-con bunkhouse section consists of interconnected dongas with four-bed rooms and communal facilities, where single/double accommodation costs $26/36, plus $9 for each extra adult.

The motel rooms all have en-suite facilities, fridge and TV, and cost $61/72.

KULGERA

Depending on which way you're heading, the scruffy settlement of Kulgera will be your first or last taste of the Territory. It is on the Stuart Highway 20 km north of the South

Australian border, and from here the gravel road known as the Goyder Stock Route heads off east for the 147 km trip to Finke.

The pub/roadhouse and police station (☎ 8956 0974) here service the outlying Pitjantjatjara Aboriginal community and pastoral leases.

Places to Stay
The basic *Kulgera Caravan Park* (☎ 8956 0973) has sites at $6, $10 with power. At the *Kulgera Roadhouse* (☎ 8956 0973) there are 10 air-con units with fridge and en-suite facilities for $38. The roadhouse also has a shop, bar and dining room, and does painfully slow takeaways.

NORTH SIMPSON DESERT
Some distance to the east of the Stuart Highway lies the Simpson Desert, but even without a 4WD vehicle excursions into this area are possible, and with a little effort you can travel to the geographical centre of Australia.

The Old *Ghan* Line
Following the 'old south road' which runs close to the old *Ghan* railway line, it's only 35 km from Alice Springs to **Ewaninga**, with its prehistoric Aboriginal rock carvings. The carvings found here and at N'Dhala Gorge are thought to have been made by Aboriginal people who lived here before those currently in the Centre.

Chambers Pillar, an eerie sandstone pillar, is carved with the names and visit dates of early explorers – and, unfortunately, the work of some much less worthy modern-day graffiti artists. To the Aboriginal people of the area Chambers Pillar is the remains of Itirkawara, a gecko ancestor of great strength. It's 160 km from Alice Springs and a 4WD vehicle is required for the last 44 km from the turn-off at Maryvale station. There's a basic *camp site* but you need to bring water and firewood.

Finke
Back on the main track south, you eventually arrive at Finke, a small Apatula Aboriginal settlement 230 km south of Alice Springs. This is another town which owes its existence to the railway line. It started life as a railway siding and gradually grew to have a European population of about 60. With the opening of the new *Ghan* line further west in

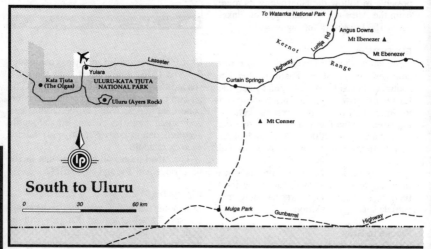

South to Uluru

1982, administration of the town was taken over by the Apatula Aboriginal community. The community store here is also an outlet for the local artists, who make crafts such as carved wooden animals, bowls, traditional weapons and seed necklaces. Be aware that this is Aboriginal land – alcohol and the taking of pictures are prohibited.

Finke is linked to the Stuart Highway, 147 km to the west, by the well-maintained dirt road sometimes known as the Goyder Stock Route. It's a fairly uninteresting stretch of road, although the Lambert Centre (see the following section), just off the road, is an interesting curiosity.

From Finke there are some exciting possibilities – east to New Crown station, and then south to Oodnadatta (passable with a robust conventional vehicle), or further east to Old Andado station then south to Dalhousie Mound Springs in the Witjira National Park. This is definitely 4WD territory; for full details of travel in this area, see the Lonely Planet *Outback Australia* book.

Facilities The basic *community store* (☎ 8956 0968), sells fuel on weekdays from 8 am to noon and 1 to 4 pm, and on Saturday

from 8 am to noon. If you want fuel outside these hours there's a $10 surcharge.

Lambert Centre

Just 21 km west of Finke along the Kulgera road, and 13 km north of the road along a sandy, signposted track, stands a five-metre-high replica of the flagpole, complete with Australian flag, found on top of Parliament House in Canberra. The reason? This point has been determined as Australia's geographical centre! For those of you who like precision, the continent's centre is at latitude 25°36'36.4"S and longitude 134°21'17.3"E, and was named after Bruce Lambert, a surveyor and first head of the National Mapping Council. In addition to the flagpole there's a visitors' book which makes interesting reading. It seems some people get all emotional on reaching this point and blabber on with some of the most parochial and rabidly nationalistic crap you're ever likely to come across!

The 13-km section of track off the road seems to wind and twist all over the place, and in a straight line you're probably no more than a couple of km off the road! Maybe this is to make you think you've just

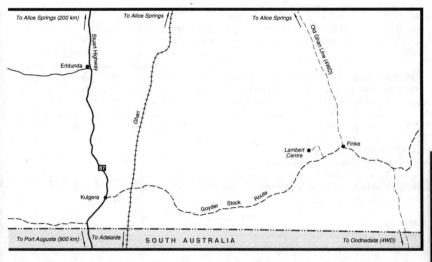

completed a gruelling desert trip to reach this point. In actual fact even though the track is sandy in patches you could probably make it in a 2WD vehicle with care.

LASSETER HIGHWAY

The bitumen Lasseter Highway connects the Stuart Highway with Uluru-Kata Tjuta National Park, 244 km to the west. It is a wide, well-engineered road which only takes a couple of hours to travel, a far cry from the old days when a journey to Uluru was a major expedition.

The highway passes through very pretty sand-plain country, which is dotted with stands of desert oak.

Mt Ebenezer

Mt Ebenezer is an Aboriginal-owned station on the Lasseter Highway, 56 km west of the Stuart Highway in the shadow of the Basedow Range and Mt Ebenezer to the north. The roadhouse itself dates back to the 1950s and the original part is built from hand-sawn desert-oak logs, which gives it a good deal more atmosphere than most places of this kind.

As well as the usual services, the roadhouse is the art-and-craft outlet for the local Imanpa Aboriginal community, and prices here are very competitive. Chances are you'll be approached by freelancers to buy souvenirs the minute you step out of your vehicle.

Facilities The *Mt Ebenezer Roadhouse* (☎ 8956 2904) has eight self-contained, air-con motel-style units at $40/46. Camping is also available at $8, or $12 with power, although it's not a particularly attractive site.

Luritja Road

Just over 50 km beyond Mt Ebenezer is the Luritja Road turn-off. This recently sealed 68-km road links Uluru with the Ernest Giles Road and Kings Canyon.

Mt Conner

From the Luritja Road the Lasseter Highway swings towards the south, and it's along this stretch that you get the first glimpses of Mt Conner, the large mesa (table-top mountain) which looms 350 metres high out of the desert, about 20 km away to the south of the road. On first sighting many people mistake this for Ayers Rock, but a closer look reveals it bears no resemblance. There's a rest area on the highway 26 km beyond the Luritja Road turn-off which is a good vantage point to take in the scene.

Mt Conner was 'discovered' by explorer William Gosse in 1873, who named it after M L Conner, a prominent South Australian member of parliament. It has great significance for the local Aboriginal people, who know it as Artula, the home of the ice-men.

The mountain lies on Curtin Springs Station and there is no public access.

Curtin Springs

The Curtin Springs homestead roadhouse is a further 26 km from the rest area, and it's a very lively little spot, not least because the bar is very popular among the local Aboriginal community. The station was named after the nearby springs, which were in turn named after the prime minister at the time, John Curtin. The original buildings date from around the 1950s, with many additions of varying vintages.

Facilities In addition to the bar, the *roadhouse* (☎ 8956 2906; fax 8956 2934) has fuel, a store with limited supplies and takeway food and a swimming pool (guests only). Camping is free, unless you want power, and there's double rooms in demountables with common facilities for $42, or so-called 'deluxe' double rooms for $65 with attached bath. Good meals are available for $14.

Uluru-Kata Tjuta National Park

Top: Kata Tjuta (The Olgas) reflects the brilliant red of the desert sunset
Bottom: Ranger-guided walks around the base of Uluru (Ayers Rock) are an excellent
way to learn more about the park

Central

In the arid centre of Australia life is most conspicuous in shaded gorges and along dry river courses where river red gums, home to colourful and noisy parrots, are able to tap deep reserves of water. On this ancient, eroded landscape, sparse vegetation and red sandy soils are infrequently and temporarily transformed by rain into a carpet of wildflowers. Tell-tale tracks in the sand lead to clumps of spinifex grass and burrows. Small marsupials and mice are mostly nocturnal; the rare and endangered bilby was once common to much of Australia but is now only found in the deserts of

galah

sulphur-crested cockatoo

desert oak

spinifex

dingo

red kangaroo

bilby

thorny devil

Desert

central Australia. A few of the lizards, such as the thorny devil, will venture out into the heat of the day for a feed of ants. Among the scattered mulga and desert oak, mobs of kangaroos, the males brick-red and over two metres tall, seek shelter from the sun; but seemingly impervious to the heat, emus, with an insulating double layer of feathers, continue the search for seeds and fruit. In the evenings rock-wallabies emerge from rocky outcrops to browse on nearby vegetation. Most animals breed in the cooler winter – their eggs and young attracting the attention of dingoes, eagles and perenties.

cabbage palm

ghost gum

cycad

wedge-tailed eagle

black-footed rock-wallaby

emu

perentie

Sturt's desert pea

death adder

HUGH FINLAY

HUGH FINLAY

Top: Sheer walls tower over 100 meters above the rocky valley floor at Kings Canyon
Bottom: Outback roads can be lonely. Border marker on the track near New Crown Station

Uluru-Kata Tjuta National Park

For most visitors to Australia a visit to Uluru (Ayers Rock) is a must, and it is undoubtedly in the ranks of the world's best natural attractions. The national park is one of eleven places in Australia included on the UN World Heritage list. Not surprisingly it's also on the Register of the National Estate.

The entire area is of deep cultural significance to the local Pitjantjatjara and Yankuntjatjara Aboriginal people (who refer to themselves as Anangu). To them the Rock is known as Uluru and the Olgas as Kata Tjuta, the name given to Ayers Rock and the national park which surrounds it.

There are plenty of walks and other activities happening around Uluru, Kata Tjuta and the township of Yulara, and it is not at all difficult to spend several days here. Unfortunately most group tours here are so rushed it's ridiculous with a quick afternoon rock climb, photos at sunset, a morning at the Olgas next day and then off – 24 hours in total if you're lucky.

HISTORY
Aboriginal Heritage

Archaeological evidence suggests that Aboriginal people have inhabited this part of Australia for at least 10,000 years. According to Aboriginal law laid down during the creation period (*tjukurpa* 'chook-oor-pa'), all landscape features were made by ancestral beings, and the Anangu today are the descendants of the ancestral beings and are the custodians of the ancestral lands. The most important ancestors in the Uluru area are the Mala (rufous hare wallabies), the Kuniya (woma pythons) and the Liru (poisonous snakes), and evidence of their activities is seen in features of the rock.

According to Anangu legend, Uluru was built by two boys who played in the mud after rain in the tjukurpa, and is at the centre of a number of 'Dreaming tracks' which crisscross central Australia.

The Anangu officially own the national park, although it is leased to the Australian Nature Conservation Agency (ANCA), the Commonwealth government's national parks body, on a 99-year lease. The traditional owners receive an annual rental of $150,000 plus 25% of the park-entrance

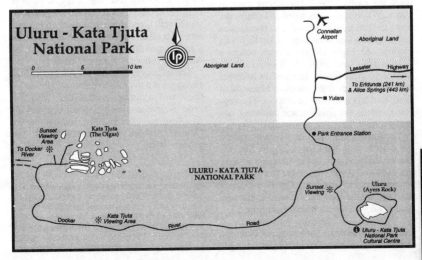

Uluru - Kata Tjuta National Park

0   5   10 km

Connellan Airport

Aboriginal Land

Lasseter Highway

To Erldunda (241 km) & Alice Springs (443 km)

Yulara

Park Entrance Station

Aboriginal Land

Sunset Viewing Area

Kata Tjuta (The Olgas)

To Docker River

ULURU - KATA TJUTA NATIONAL PARK

Sunset Viewing

Uluru (Ayers Rock)

Kata Tjuta Viewing Area

Docker   River   Road

Uluru - Kata Tjuta National Park Cultural Centre

SOUTH TO ULURU

fees. Decisions related to the park are made by the 10 members of the Board of Management, six of whom are nominated by the traditional owners.

Mala Tjukurpa The Mala wallabies travelled from the Yuendumu area to Uluru for ceremonies (*inma*). The men climbed to the top of Uluru to plant a ceremonial pole, while the women collected and prepared food at Taputji, a small isolated rock on the northeastern side.

During the ceremonies, the Mala were invited by the Wintalka (mulga-seed) men to attend dance ceremonies away to the west. Being already committed to their own celebrations, the Mala refused, and the angered Wintalka created a nasty, dingo-like creature (Kurpany) which snuck up on the women's dancing ceremonies at Tjukatjapi on the northern side of the Rock. The frightened women fled right into the middle of the men's secret ceremony, ruining it and in the confusion a Mala man was killed and eaten by the Kurpany. The remaining Mala fled south towards the Musgrave Ranges.

Kuniya & Liru Tjukurpa The tjukurpa tells of how the Kuniya (woma python) came from the east to hatch her young ones at Uluru. While she was camped at Taputji, she was attacked by a group of Liru (poisonous snakes), who had been angered by Kuniya's nephew. At Mutitjulu she comes across a Liru warrior, and performs a ritual dance, mustering great forces. In an effort to dispel this terrifying force she picks up a handful of sand, and lets it fall to the ground. The vegetation where the sand fell was poisoned, and today remain unusable to Anangu.

The force within her remains strong and a great battle with the Liru is fought. She hits him on the head, attempting to inflict a 'sorry cut', but overcome with anger she hits him a second time, killing him. The two wounds received by the Liru can be seen as the vertical cracks on the rock near Mutitjulu.

Lungkata Tjukurpa The Lungkata Tjukurpa is the story of how Lungkata (blue-tongue lizard man) found an emu, which had been wounded by other hunters, at the base of the rock. He finished it off and started to cook it. The original hunters, two bell-bird brothers, found Lungkata and asked him if he had seen their emu. He lied, saying he hadn't seen it, but the hunters sussed him out and chased him around the base of the rock. While being pursued Lungkata dropped pieces of emu meat, and these are seen as the fractured slabs of sandstone just west of Mutitjulu, and at Kalaya Tjunta (emu thigh) on the southeastern side of Uluru, where a spur of rock is seen as the emu's thigh.

European History

The first European to venture into the area was Ernest Giles in 1872 on his attempted crossing from the Overland Telegraph Line to the west of the continent. His party had travelled west from Kings Canyon, and sighted Kata Tjuta, which he named Mt Ferdinand after his financier, the noted botanist Baron von Mueller. However, von Mueller later changed the name to Mt Olga, after Queen Olga of Wurttemburg. Giles tried to reach Kata Tjuta in the hope of finding water around its base, but was repeatedly thwarted by the large salt lake which lay in front of him. He named it Lake Mueller, again after von Mueller, and described it as 'an infernal lake of mud and brine'. Baron von Mueller also renamed this one, calling it instead Lake Amadeus, after the King of Spain.

The following year a party led by William Gosse set out to cross to the west. Hot on his heels was a disappointed Giles, who was keen to have another go. Gosse reached the area first, and after sighting and naming Mt Conner, sighted a hill to the west. His account states:

The hill, as I approached, presented a most peculiar appearance, the upper portion being covered with holes or caves. When I got clear of the sandhills, and was only two miles distant, and the hill, for the first time, coming fairly into view, what was my astonishment to find it was one immense rock rising abruptly from the plain. ... I have named this Ayers Rock, after Sir Henry Ayers the premier of South Australia.

The early explorers were followed by pastoralists, missionaries, doggers and various miscellaneous adventurers who travelled through the area. Among these was Harold Lasseter, who insisted he had found a fabulously rich gold reef in the Petermann Ranges to the west in 1901, and died a lonely death in the same ranges in 1931 trying to rediscover it.

As European activity in the area increased, so did the contact and conflict between the two cultures. With the combined effects of stock grazing and drought, the Anangu found their hunting and gathering options becoming increasingly scarce, which in turn led to a dependence on the White economy.

In the 1920s the three governments of Western Australia, South Australia and the Northern Territory set aside a reserve (the Great Central Aboriginal Reserve) for Aboriginal people. In the era of assimilation, reserves were, according to the *NT Annual Report of 1938*, seen as '... refuges or sanctuaries of a temporary nature. The Aboriginal may here continue his normal existence until the time is ripe for his further development'. 'Development' here refers to the assimilation aim of providing Aboriginal people with skills and knowledge which would enable them to fit into White society. The policy failed across the country, and the Anangu shunned this and other reserves, preferring instead to maintain traditional practices.

The early 1950s saw interest develop in tourism in the area. By 1950 a road had been pushed through from the east, and as early as 1951 the fledgling Connellan Airways applied for permission to build an airstrip near Uluru. In order to facilitate this, the area of Uluru and Kata Tjuta was excised from the reserve in 1958 for use as a national park. Soon after motel leases were granted and the airstrip constructed.

The first official ranger at the Ayers Rock & Mt Olga National Park, and Keeper of Ayers Rock, was Bill Harney, a famous Territorian who spent many years working with Aboriginal people and contributed greatly towards White understanding of them.

With the revoking of pastoral subsidies in 1964, which up until that time had compensated pastoralists for food and supplies distributed to passing Aboriginal people, many Anangu were forced off the stations and gravitated to Uluru. As they could no longer sustain themselves completely by traditional ways, and needed money to participate in the White economy, they were able to earn some cash by selling artefacts to tourists.

The 1970s saw the construction of the new Yulara Resort some distance from the rock, as the original facilities were too close to the rock and were having a negative impact on the environment. The Commonwealth government held the leases for providing accommodation within the park, and allowed these to run until 1983 when Yulara opened. Many of the old facilities, close to the northern side of the rock, were bulldozed, while some are still used by the Mutitjulu Aboriginal community.

Increased tourism activity over the years led to Aboriginal anxiety about the desecration of important sites by tourists. The federal government was approached for assistance, and by 1973 Aboriginal people had become involved with the management of the park. Although title to many parcels of land in the Territory had been handed back to Aboriginal people under the Aboriginal Land Rights (NT) Act of 1976, this act did not apply here as national parks were excluded from the legislation.

It was not until 1979 that traditional ownership of Uluru-Kata Tjuta was recognised by the government, and then in 1983, following renewed calls from traditional owners for title to the land, the Hawke government announced that freehold title to the national park would be granted and the park leased back to the ANCA for a period of 99 years. The transfer of ownership took place on 26 October 1985.

Since then the park has become one of the most popular in Australia. In 1995 nearly 500,000 people visited Uluru.

GEOLOGY

Uluru itself is 3.6 km long by 2.4 km wide,

stands 348 metres above the surrounding dunes and measures 9.4 km around the base. It is made up of a type of coarse-grained sandstone known as arkose, which was formed from sediment from eroded granite mountains. Kata Tjuta, on the other hand, is a conglomerate of granite and basalt gravel glued together by mud and sand.

The sedimentary beds which make up the two formations were laid down over a period of about 600 million years, in a shallow sea in what geologists know as the Amadeus Basin. Various periods of uplift caused the beds to be buckled, folded and lifted above sea level, and those which form Uluru were turned so that they are almost vertical, while at Kata Tjuta they were tilted about 20°. For the last 300 million years or so the processes of erosion have worn away the surface rocks, leaving what we see today.

The sculptured shapes seen on the surface of Uluru today are the effects of wind, water and sand erosion. At Kata Tjuta the massive upheavals led to the rock being fractured, and erosion along the fracture lines has formed the distinctive valleys and gorges.

CLIMATE

Uluru is in the centre of the arid zone which covers 70% of the Australian continent. Here the average yearly rainfall is around 220 mm per year. Although rainfall varies greatly from year to year, the most likely time for rain and thunderstorms is during the Top End wet season, from November to March, when the tail of tropical depressions often move over the centre of Australia, bringing widespread rainfall. Droughts are not uncommon, and a year or two may go by without any rainfall; the longest drought on record ended in 1965 and lasted for more than six years. Not surprisingly, humidity is low throughout the year.

Many people are surprised at how cold it gets at Uluru in winter. Daytime temperatures in winter can be pleasant, but if there's cloud and a cold wind around it can be bitter. Clear nights often see the temperature plunge to well below freezing; it dropped to -5°C early one morning when I was camping here!

In summer the temperatures soar, peaking during February and March when it gets as hot as 45°C. Normally it's a mere 30 to 35°C. Climbing the Rock is prohibited between 10 am and 4 pm on days when the temperature is forecast to reach 38°C or above.

FLORA & FAUNA
Flora

The dominant flora of the red sand plains of central Australia are plants which have adapted to the harsh, dry climate – mainly spinifex grasses, mulga bushes and desert oak trees. These plants remain virtually dormant during times of drought, and shoot into action after good rains.

The mulga has heavy, hard wood and so was used by Anangu for firewood, and for making implements such as boomerangs and digging sticks. Stands of desert oaks are usually found in areas of deep sand. The rough, corky bark protects and insulates the trunk, giving it a level of fire protection.

Common eucalypts found in the area include the centralian bloodwood, the river red gum and the blue mallee.

Except in the times of severe drought, numerous grevilleas and fuchsias thrive in the sand dunes.

As is the case in the Top End, Aboriginal people in central Australia used fire to manage the land. Controlled burns encourage regrowth and limit the amount of accumulated vegetation. Large fires burn too hot over a large area and can be very destructive. These days the park managers are trying to re-create the 'mosaic' pattern of small burns which was in existence before European settlement.

Fauna

Although this arid country around Uluru doesn't look very encouraging, it is home to a wide variety of animals and birds – the fact that most of the *tjukurpa* sites within the park are animal related is evidence of that. There are 19 species of native mammals found within the park and another six introduced species.

The most common native mammals include red kangaroos, euros, dingoes and marsupial rodents such as dunnarts and marsupial moles. The moles have become specialised desert dwellers – they are completely blind, and use their short, strong limbs to burrow through the loose sand, feeding on insect larvae and small reptiles.

The introduced animals are the same ones which are found in large areas of Australia – foxes, cats, rabbits, camels and dogs. As elsewhere, foxes and cats especially prey on native wildlife, while rabbits also compete for food and habitat.

While you may not see many animals in the park, bird sightings are common, with everything from large eagles down to small wrens seen in a variety of habitats. A checklist of birds found within the park is available from the visitor centre.

ORIENTATION

The 1326-sq-km Uluru-Kata Tjuta National Park takes in the area of Uluru (Ayers Rock) and Kata Tjuta (the Olgas). Yulara is the modern town which has been built to service the almost half-a-million tourists who visit the area each year. The township lies outside the northern boundary of the national park, and is 17 km from the Rock; the Olgas lie 48 km to the west. All roads within the park are bitumen and are open all year round.

INFORMATION

The Uluru-Kata Tjuta National Park Cultural Centre (☎ 8956 3138) is inside the national park, just one km before the Rock on the road from Yulara. This excellent facility was only opened late in 1995, and is open from 7 am to 5.30 pm in winter (to 6 pm in summer). It's worth putting aside at least one hour, preferably more, to have a good look around the cultural centre before visiting Uluru itself.

There are two main display areas, both with multi-lingual information: the Tjukurpa display features Anangu art and tjukurpa; while the Nintiringkupai display focuses on the history and management of the national park.

The centre also houses the Aboriginal-owned Maruku Art & Crafts shop (8 am to 5.30 pm), and there's the opportunity to see artists at work and dancers performing. It's about the cheapest place in the Centre to buy souvenirs (carvings, etc) and you're buying direct from the artists. There's also the Aboriginal-run Ininti Store, which sells snacks, books, videos and other souvenirs, and a picnic area with free gas barbecues, and the Anangu Tours desk (☎ 8956 2123), where you can book Aboriginal-led tours around Uluru.

There's also a visitor centre at Yulara. This one is open daily from 8 am to 9 pm and is also a good source of information (see the Yulara section later in this chapter).

The park is open daily from half an hour before sunrise to sunset.

Entry Fees

Entry to the national park costs $10 (free for children under 16), and this is good for a five-day visit. Entry permits can be bought from the visitor centre at Yulara, or from the park entry gate on the road between Yulara and Uluru.

ULURU

The world-famous Uluru towers above the pancake-flat surrounding scrub. It's believed that two-thirds of the Rock lies beneath the sand. Its colour changes as the setting sun turns it a series of deeper and darker reds before it fades into grey and a performance in reverse, with fewer spectators, is performed at dawn each day.

Uluru Walks

There are a number of walking trails around Uluru, and on a number of them park rangers lead informative tours which delve into a particular aspect of the area. On some of the walks there are tours operated by Anangu Tours.

Note that there are several Aboriginal sacred sites around the base of Uluru. They're clearly fenced off and signposted

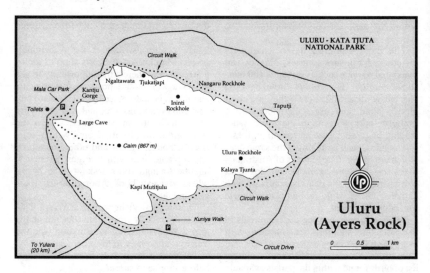

and to enter these areas is a grave offence, not just for non-Aboriginal people but for 'ineligible' Aboriginal people as well.

Full details of the Mala and Mutitjulu walks (see below) are given in the self-guided walks brochure available from either of the visitor centres for $1.

Circuit Walk It takes around three hours to make the walk around the base of Uluru, looking at the caves and paintings on the way. This is a good way to explore Uluru without the mobs as most people are in too much of a rush to do this walk and you'll often have the path pretty much to yourself.

Pick up a brochure for the self-guided walk around the base.

Mala Walk This walk starts from the base of the climbing point and takes about 1½ hours at a very leisurely pace. The tjukurpa of the Mala is of great importance to the Anangu. You can do this walk on your own, or there are guided walks daily at 10.30 am from the car park (no booking necessary).

Liru Walk The Liru Walk starts from the cultural centre and gives an insight into the

way the local Anangu people made use of the various shrubs and bush materials found in the area. It is a two-hour guided walk with Anangu Tours, and it only operates on Tuesday, Thursday, Saturday and Sunday at 9.30 am (8.30 am October to March); the cost is $49 ($36 for children) and bookings are essential (☎ 8956 2123).

Kuniya Walk Mutitjulu is a permanent water hole on the southern side of Uluru. The tjukurpa tells of the clash between two ancestral snakes, Kuniya and Liru. The water hole is just a short walk from the car park on the southern side, and you can either do the walk yourself, or go with Anangu Tours (daily, two hours, 3 pm, 4 pm in summer, $49, children for $36, bookings essential), where you'll learn more about the Kuniya tjukurpa, and also about food and medicine plants found here.

Climbing Uluru
Those climbing Uluru should take care – in the last 30 years 28 people have met their maker doing so, usually by having a heart attack, but some by taking a fatal tumble. Avoid climbing in the heat of the day during

Climbing Uluru

It's important to note that it goes against Aboriginal spiritual beliefs to climb Uluru, and Anangu would prefer you didn't. The reasons for this are that the route taken by visitors is associated closely with the Mala Tjukurpa (see the History section earlier in this chapter), and also that Anangu feel responsible for all people on the rock, and are greatly saddened when a visitor to their land is injured or dies on the rock. Interestingly, although the number of visitors to Uluru has risen steadily over the years, the number of people actually climbing the rock is declining, while sales of the ideologically sound 'I Didn't Climb Ayers Rock' T-shirts are on the rise. ■

the hot season. There is an emergency phone at the car park at the base of the climb, and another at the top of the chain, about halfway up the climbing route. The climb is actually closed between 10 am and 4 pm on days when the forecast temperature is more than 38°C.

The climb itself is 1.6 km and takes about two hours up and back with a good rest at the top. The first part of the walk is by far the steepest and most arduous, and there's a chain to hold on to. It's often extremely windy at the top, even when it isn't at the base, so make sure hats are well tied on. In winter it can also be quite cold.

Facilities

About half-way between Yulara and Uluru there's a **sunset viewing area** with plenty of car parking space. This place is amazingly busy at sunset and it's hardly a quiet and peaceful experience. The alternative is to park by the side of the road somewhere nearby and climb a dune close by – the view may not be quite as good but you can escape the crowds.

There is little in the way of facilities at the rock itself. There is a small toilet block at the climb car park, but this is just a small facility using composting methods and is easily

overloaded. It's better to use those at the cultural centre if possible.

KATA TJUTA (THE OLGAS)

Kata Tjuta, a collection of smaller, more rounded rocks, stands 30-odd km to the west of Uluru. Though less well known, the monoliths are equally impressive and, indeed, many people find them more captivating. The tallest rock, Mt Olga, at 546 metres, is nearly 200 metres higher than Uluru.

Meaning 'many heads', Kata Tjuta is of great significance to Anangu and is associated with a number of tjukurpa stories. However, as these relate to secret ceremonies involving the education and initiation of men, they are only revealed to men involved in these rituals and are not for general consumption.

A lonely sign at the western end of the access road points out that there is a hell of a lot of nothing if you travel west – although, suitably equipped, you can travel all the way to Kalgoorlie and on to Perth in Western Australia. It's 200 km to Docker River, an Aboriginal settlement on the road west, and about 1500 km all the way to Kalgoorlie. Permits are required for travel on this road. See the Lonely Planet *Outback Australia* book for full details of travel in this remote area of Australia.

Kata Tjuta Walks

There are two marked walking trails at Kata Tjuta, neither of them are highly used compared with those at Uluru.

Valley of the Winds The Valley of the Winds walk takes around three hours and winds through the gorges giving excellent views of the domes. Although well constructed, the track can be rough in places and you'll need sturdy footwear, in addition to drinking water and a hat.

Olga Gorge (Tatintjawiya) There is a short signposted track into the pretty Olga Gorge from the car park. The return trip takes

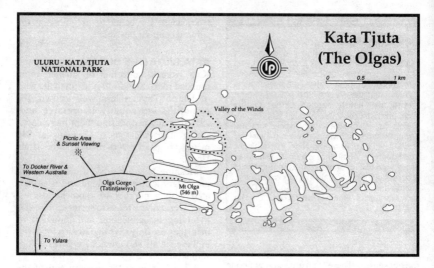

around an hour to complete and, again, offers good views.

Facilities
The car park, complete with toilet block, shade shelters and picnic tables, is close to the western edge of the Olgas. There's also a solar-powered radio here for use in an emergency.

A short distance to the west, on the main access road, is a **sunset viewing area**. It's worth organising your activities so you can be out here at sunset as the views are often stunning as the rocks change through varying shades in the mellow evening light.

Along the road between Yulara and Kata Tjuta there's a marked **dune viewing area**. From the car park here it's 15 minutes along a boardwalk through the dunes to a viewing platform which gives sweeping views over the surrounding dune country, with Kata Tjuta in the background. Interpretive signs here outline the features of the complex dune environment.

ORGANISED TOURS
From Yulara
Only three companies (AAT-Kings, Uluru

Experience and the Aboriginal-owned Anangu Tours) operate tours out of Yulara itself. If you arrive here from anywhere other than Alice Springs without a tour booked then you're pretty much limited to these three.

Uluru Experience Uluru Experience (☎ toll-free 1800 803 174) offers a number of possibilities. The five-hour Uluru Walk includes the base walk and breakfast for $64 ($49 for children aged six to 15), Spirit of Uluru is a four-hour vehicle-based tour around the base of the rock, also for $64 ($49), while the Olgas & Dunes Tour includes the walk into Olga Gorge and the sunset at the Olgas for $49 ($36). The Uluru Experience pass lets you choose any two of the three tours above, and includes champagne and sunset at the rock for $102 ($78), and also gives you a discount on the Night Sky Show (see the following Yulara section for details).

AAT-Kings AAT-Kings (☎ 8956 2171) has a Rock Pass which includes guided base tour, sunset, climb, sunrise and Kata Tjuta (Olga Gorge only) tours for $122 ($87 for children under 15). The pass is valid for three days, and includes the $10 national park entry fee. All these activities are also available in various combinations on a one-off basis: base tour ($33/22 adults/children), sunrise tour ($31/22), climb ($31/22), sunset ($20/16), base and sunset ($44/36), sunrise and climb ($51/33), climb and base ($56/36), sunrise and base ($51/33), sunrise, climb and base ($69/56), Olgas and Uluru sunset ($54/41). These prices do not include the park entry fee.

AAT-Kings also offers a couple of options which include a barbecue meal, and these can be good fun. The Uluru Sunrise & Breakfast Tour costs $56 ($44 for children), or you can combine it with the base tour for $72 ($61). On the Olgas Sunset & Dinner Tour you can do the three-hour Valley of the Winds walk, then enjoy a very relaxing barbecue with the sunset on the Olgas for $80 ($63).

Anangu Tours Anangu Tours (☎ 8956 2123) is a new tour company owned and operated by Anangu from the Mutitjulu community. The tour desk is at the cultural centre inside the park, but they also arrange transfers from Yulara to the cultural centre and Uluru.

The Anangu tours are led by two Anangu guides and one interpreter, and they offer a wonderful chance to meet and talk with Anangu.

Two of the three tours currently offered are walks in the Uluru vicinity (see Uluru Walks earlier in this chapter for details), while the third, the **Lungkata Tour**, is a 1½-hour cultural tour where visitors sit in a traditional shade shelter (*wiltja*) and listen to some Anangu storytelling. The cost for the Lungkata Tour is $44 ($33 for children six to 15) and it operates on Monday, Wednesday and Friday at 10.30 am (9.30 am in summer), and bookings are essential for all tours as there is a limit of 25 people.

If you book a tour, transfers on the shuttle cost $13 return, and you can return to Yulara at any time on either the Anangu Tours or AAT-Kings bus.

From Alice Springs
All-inclusive tours to Uluru by private operators start at about $285 for a three-day camping trip which includes Kings Canyon. Companies such as Sahara Tours (☎ 8953 0881) and Northern Territory Adventure Tours (☎ toll-free 1800 063 838) are popular with the budget conscious.

You have to shop around a bit because the tours run on different days and you may not want to wait for a particular one. Other things to check for include the time it gets to the Rock and Kata Tjuta, and whether the return is done early or late in the day. Prices can vary with the season and demand, and sometimes there may be cheaper 'stand-by' fares available. Bus-pass travellers should note that the bus services to the Rock are often heavily booked so if your schedule is tight it's best to plan ahead.

Tours which include accommodation other than camping are generally much more expensive, starting at around $257 for two days.

Another option is the passes offered by Greyhound Pioneer and McCaffertys. These are good value as they give you return transport to Yulara, the base tour, climb, Olgas and sunrise and sunset tours, and include the park entry fee. See the Getting There & Away section for more details.

YULARA
Yulara (population 930), the service village for the national park, has effectively turned one of the world's least hospitable regions into an easy and comfortable place to visit. Lying just outside the national park, 20 km from Uluru and 53 km from Kata Tjuta, the complex, which is administered by the Northern Territory government's Ayers Rock Corporation, makes an excellent and surprisingly democratic base for exploring the area's renowned attractions. Opened in 1984, the village was specifically designed to blend in with the local environment and is a very low-rise affair. It is nestled in between the dunes and so is remarkably unobtrusive. Yulara supplies the only accommodation,

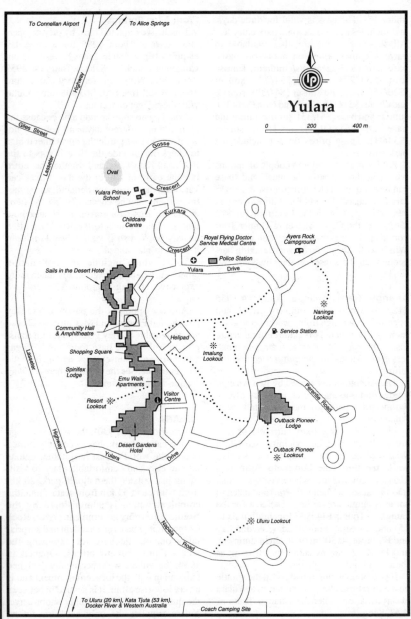

food outlets and other services available in the region.

By the 1970s it was clear that planning was required for the development of the area. Between 1931 and 1946 only 22 people were known to have climbed Uluru. In 1969 about 23,000 people visited the area. Ten years later the figure was 65,000 and now the annual visitor figures are approaching the 500,000 mark!

It was intended when Yulara was built that the ugly cluster of motels, restaurants and other commercial enterprises at the eastern base of Uluru would be demolished, leaving the prime attraction pleasingly alone in its age-old setting. Some of the original buildings are still there because they were turned over to the local Aboriginal people; they are not so obvious now because all access to Uluru is from the west and the Aboriginal community is off limits to the public.

Orientation

In the spacious village area, where everything is within a 15-minute walk, there is a visitors centre, four hotels, apartments, a backpacker lodge, two camp sites, a bank, post office, petrol station, newsagency, numerous restaurants, a Royal Flying Doctor Service medical centre, supermarket, craft gallery, pub (of course) and a police station.

There are a number of walking tracks connecting various places in the village, and also lookouts on the top of strategic dunes.

Information

The visitor centre (☎ 8956 2240) is open from 8 am to 9 pm daily and contains good displays on the geography, flora and fauna, and history of the region. You can also buy park entry permits here, and book tours with the only three operators licensed to run tours from Yulara (all other local tours originate in Alice Springs). Information is also available at the Cultural Centre inside the park, near the Rock itself.

The recently revamped shopping square complex includes a supermarket (open daily from 8.30 am to 9 pm), newsagency, bakery, ice-cream parlour, post office and travel agency. You can get colour film processed at Territory Colour's same-day service. The only bank at Yulara is ANZ, and it has an ATM machine. For $2 you can also use the electronic funds transfer (EFTPOS) facility in the pub and at the Mobil service station to withdraw up to $100 with most credit and bank cards.

There's a childcare centre in the village for children aged between three months and eight years, which operates from 8 am to 5.30 pm daily. The cost is $16.50 for half a day or $27.50 for a full day. Bookings can be made on ☎ 8956 2097.

Also within the village is a Royal Flying Doctor Service medical centre (☎ 8956 2286), which is open from 9 am to noon and 2 to 5 pm weekdays, and from 10 to 11 am on weekends, and a police station (☎ 8956 2166) which is probably the only pink police station in the country!

The service station sells all types of fuel, and is open daily from 7 am to 9 pm.

Guided Walks & Talks

There are a number of activities in the village.

Uluru – Heart of Australia Slide Show This one-hour slide show and talk gives you a useful introduction to all aspects of the Uluru-Kata Tjuta National Park. It takes place at 1 pm daily in the auditorium behind

Alcohol Warning

Please be aware that alcohol (grog) is a problem amongst the local Mutitjulu Aboriginal people living near Uluru. It is a 'dry' community and, at the request of the Mutitjulu leaders, the liquor outlets have agreed not to sell it to Aboriginal people. For this reason you may be approached in the car park at the shopping centre by Aboriginal people who want you to buy alcohol on their behalf. The community leaders appeal to you not to do so. ∎

the visitor centre. It's free and you don't need to book.

Garden Walk This is a guided tour through the native garden of the Sails in the Desert Hotel. It takes place on weekdays at 7.30 am and is led by the hotel's resident gardener. This tour is also free and there's no need to book; it starts from the hotel lobby.

Night Sky Show Each evening there's the Night Sky Show, an informative look into Anangu and Greek astrological legends, and viewing of the startlingly clear outback night sky through telescopes and binoculars. Trips in English are at 8.30 and 10.15 pm, and bookings are required (☎ toll-free 1800 803 174). The cost is $20 ($11 for children aged six to 16) and you are picked up from your accommodation.

Cocktails at Sunset From the vantage point of a high dune within the village you can watch the sunset, sip champagne and munch 'outback canapés'. It's all very civilised, and very expensive too, at $28 ($14 for children under 15).

Scenic Flights
While the enjoyment of those on the ground may be diminished by the constant buzz of light aircraft and helicopters overhead, for those actually up there it's an unforgettable, and very popular, trip. Two companies operate the trips and they collect you from wherever you're staying. Bookings are essential, preferably one day in advance.

Rockayer (☎ 8956 2345) charges $60 ($45 for children aged three to 14) for a 30-minute plane flight over the Rock and Kata Tjuta, while a 30-minute helicopter flight is $150. For a 15-minute helicopter flight over the Rock it's $75.

The other operator is Jayrow (☎ 8956 2077), which charges $75 for the 15-minute Uluru helicopter flight, and $145 for the 30-minute Uluru and Kata Tjuta helicopter flight.

There are no child concessions on any of the helicopter flights, which make it an expensive proposition for families.

Places to Stay
Yulara has something for every budget, from a camp site up to a five-star hotel. With the rise in visitor numbers over the last few years, it is advisable to book all accommodation, including dorm beds at the Outback Pioneer Lodge and tent or van sites at the camp site, especially during school holiday periods.

Camping The *Ayers Rock Campground* (☎ 8956 2055) costs $18 for two people on an unpowered site, or $24 with power. There are six-berth on-site vans for $60 for up to four adults, and $9 for each additional adult. Most of the camp sites have beautifully manicured patches of green grass, while the spaces for vans and caravans are gravel. The camp site is set amongst native gardens, and there's quite a bit of shade. There's also a swimming pool and the reception kiosk sells basic food supplies.

Dormitory & Cheaper Accommodation
For backpackers the place to head for is the well-equipped *Outback Pioneer Lodge* (☎ 8956 2170; fax 8956 2320), on the far side of the village from the shopping centre, about a 10-minute walk by a path across the dunes. Accommodation here consists of beds in 20-bed dorms for $20 for the first night, dropping to $12 on subsequent nights. There's excellent communal cooking facilities, and baggage storage lockers are available for $1. There are also cabin-type rooms with either two bunk beds or a double bed and one bunk, costing $80 for two, and $20 for each extra person up to four people, including bedding. The rooms have fridges and tea/coffee-making facilities, but bathrooms are communal. All buildings are air-conditioned in summer and heated in winter and there's a swimming pool. Out the back is a good lookout point for sunset views of Uluru.

Part of the same complex is known as the

Outback Pioneer Hotel and this has expensive units with bathroom for $169.

Next up is the *Spinifex Lodge* (☎ 8956 2131; fax 8956 2163) near the visitor centre. It has 68 one-bedroom units which accommodate from two to four people at a cost of $85 for a double. These are quite good value, the main drawback being that the cooking facilities are pretty limited.

Apartments Probably the best deal at Yulara is offered by the *Emu Walk Apartments* (☎ 8956 2100; fax 8956 2156). There are one and two-bedroom flats which accommodate four and six people respectively. They have a lounge room with TV, a fully equipped kitchen and there's a communal laundry. They are also very central, being right between the visitor centre and the shopping square. The cost is $206 for the small apartments and $256 for the larger ones.

Top-End Hotels The two remaining options are both top-end hotels. The *Desert Gardens Hotel* (☎ 8956 2100; fax 8956 2156) has 100 rooms with TV, phone, minibar and room service, and these cost $226 for a double. The hotel has a pool and a restaurant.

At the top of the range is the *Sails in the Desert Hotel* (☎ 8956 2200; fax 8956 2018), which has all the facilities you'd expect in a top-class hotel, including in-house movies, 24-hour room service, spa and tennis court. Rooms start at $292 for a double.

Places to Eat

The range of eating options is equally varied. At the shopping centre the *Yulara Take-Away* does pretty reasonable fast food which you can take back to eat wherever you are staying, or you can eat at the tables in the shopping area. It's open daily from 7.30 am to 9.30 pm. Also in the shopping centre is a *bakery* (open 9 am to 7 pm daily) and an *ice-cream parlour* (11 am to 5 pm daily).

The *Outback Pioneer Lodge* also has a couple of choices. The kiosk here offers light meals and snacks and is open from early in the morning until early evening. One of the best deals at Yulara is the 'Self-Cook

Barbecue' which takes place here every night. For around $12 you get meat (beef, chicken, sausages, hamburger or fish) which you then barbecue yourself, and there's a range of salads which you can help yourself to. There's also a cheaper vegetarian dish offered, or you can just have the salads. It's a popular place to eat, probably made more so by the fact that 'exotic' meats such as kangaroo, buffalo and crocodile are often available, and there's often live entertainment. For more conventional dining the hotel also has the *Bough House*, which is open daily from 6 am.

The *Outback Barbecue* at the Tavern in the shopping square is yet another option. In the *Tavern* itself you can get good-value buffet meals for around $15.

The Desert Gardens Hotel has the *Rock View* restaurant for casual dining and the more formal *White Gums*, which is open only in the evening. Main courses here are in the $20 to $25 range.

Finally there's the Sails in the Desert Hotel which has the *Rock Pool* outdoor restaurant, the *Desert Rose Brasserie*, which features buffet meals, and the more sophisticated *Kunia Room* for up-market dining.

Entertainment

Each evening at the *Amphitheatre* there's live entertainment. The resident band is Indiginy, and they play an interesting range of music on a variety of instruments, the focus being on the dijeridu, and there's some fun audience participation too. The charge is $5.

The *Tavern* has a disco or live bands on Wednesday and Saturday nights, and these go until 2 am.

Or if you are really bored you could see a movie at the *Auditorium*. Recent releases are screened from Friday to Sunday and cost $5 ($3 for children). For listings see the noticeboard outside the visitor centre.

GETTING THERE & AWAY
Air

Connellan Airport is about five km from Yulara. You can fly directly to Uluru from various major centres as well as from Alice Springs, which remains the popular starting point for Uluru. Ansett has at least three flights daily for the 45-minute, $179 hop from Alice to the Rock; Qantas has one.

The numerous flights direct to Uluru can be money-savers. If, for example, you were intending to fly to the Centre from Adelaide, it makes a lot more sense to go Adelaide-Uluru-Alice Springs rather than go to Adelaide-Alice Springs-Uluru-Alice Springs. You can fly direct between Uluru and Perth ($464), Adelaide ($523), Cairns ($468), Melbourne ($567), Sydney ($505) and Darwin ($490) with Qantas or Ansett, and to Coober Pedy ($206) with the weekly Kendell Airlines flight (Saturday).

Airnorth (☎ toll-free 1800 627 474) has daily direct flights between Uluru and Alice Springs ($173) and Kings Canyon ($79).

Day trips to Uluru by air from Alice Springs cost from about $330.

Bus

Apart from hitching, the cheapest way to get to the Rock is to take a bus or tour. Greyhound Pioneer and McCaffertys both have daily services between Alice Springs and Uluru. The 441-km trip takes about 6½ hours.

The fare for one-way travel with McCaffertys is $70 from Alice Springs to Yulara, and $60 from Erldunda on the Stuart Highway; with Greyhound Pioneer it's $77.

Passes If you don't already have a pass, McCaffertys has its Rock Pass. This is valid for three days and includes return transport from Alice Springs, and then at the Rock itself you join all the AAT-Kings tours: Kata Tjuta & Sunset Tour, Uluru Climb, Uluru Sunrise & Uluru Sunset. The pass includes the park entry fee and costs $199. The only condition is that you must stay for two nights, and this is at your own expense.

With Greyhound Pioneer you can either take a two-day accommodated package from Alice Springs (Ayers Rock Experience), which includes the company's own morning Ayers Rock Climb & Base Tour and the

afternoon Olgas & Sunset Tour. The price depends on the level of accommodation you want; in the dorms at the Outback Pioneer it's $170, at the Sails in the Desert it's $291.

If you already have a Greyhound Pioneer pass which gets you to Yulara, you can opt to do the two half-day tours for $50 (normally $38 each).

There are also direct services between Adelaide and Uluru, although this actually means connecting with another bus at Erldunda, the turn-off from the Stuart Highway. Adelaide to Uluru takes about 22 hours for the 1720-km trip and costs $183 ($102 if you can book 15 days in advance).

Car Rental

If you haven't got your own vehicle, renting a car in Alice Springs to go down to Uluru and back can be expensive. You're looking at $70 to $100 a day for a car from the big operators, and this only includes 100 km a day, each extra km costing 25c. Thrifty and Territory Rent-a-Car in Alice Springs both have deals which include 300 free km per day, and this is a much more realistic option. On one of these deals if you spent three days and covered 1000 km (the bare minimum) you'd be up for around $400, including insurance and petrol costs. Still, between four people that's cheaper than taking a bus there and back.

The road from Alice to Yulara is sealed and there are regular food and petrol stops along the way. Yulara is 441 km from Alice, 241 km west of Erldunda on the Stuart Highway, and the whole journey takes about six to seven hours.

Avis, Budget, Territory and Hertz are all represented at Yulara.

GETTING AROUND
To/From the Airport

A free shuttle bus operated by AAT-Kings meets all flights and drops at all accommodation points around the resort. Otherwise you can take a taxi, which costs around $5 one way.

Around Yulara

The village sprawls a bit, but it's not too large to get around on foot, and there's a free shuttle bus which runs between all accommodation points every 15 minutes from 10.30 am to 2.30 pm and from 6.30 pm to 12.30 am daily. Walking trails lead across the dunes to little lookouts overlooking the village and surrounding terrain.

Around the National Park

Several options are available if you want to go from the Yulara resort to Uluru or Kata Tjuta in the national park. AAT-Kings and Anangu Tours offer transport from Yulara to the Rock for $12 ($24 return). The Anangu Tours buses run hourly from 7 to 10 am, and from 3 to 7 pm, the AAT-Kings buses from 10 am to 3 pm from Yulara; the return trips are on the half-hour from 7.30 am to 7.30 pm. You can only buy one-way tickets, which means you can return to Yulara at any time with either operator. The ticket price includes a stop at the Cultural Centre, and you can then take a later bus to Uluru at no extra charge. Obviously the fare does not include the park entry fee.

There are taxis at Yulara which operate on a multiple-hire basis. Costs include Yulara to Uluru and return for $20 per person, to Kata Tjuta and return $35, sunset $15, sunrise or sunset and climb $20, or to the airport $5. The operator is Sunworth (☎ 8956 2152).

Hertz (☎ 8956 2244) and Avis (☎ 8956 2266) both have desks at the airport, and Territory Rent-a-Car (☎ 8956 203) is at the Outback Pioneer Hotel.

South to Port Augusta

From the border, 20 km south of Kulgera, there's lots of very little to see as you head south the 900-odd km to Port Augusta. The only town of any size is Coober Pedy, about 400 km from the border.

MARLA

It's 156 km south from the border to the small settlement of Marla, where the *Ghan* railway line crosses the Stuart Highway.

The opal fields of **Mintabie**, 35 km to the west, are worth a visit, although you need to get a permit from the Marla police station.

Places to Stay & Eat

The *Marla Travellers Rest Hotel* (☎ 8670 7001) has camp sites at $10, or with power at $15. There are also on-site cabins with shared facilities at $14/28. The hotel section has motel-style units at $59/65.

COOBER PEDY

Coober Pedy (population 2520) is one of the best known outback towns. The name is Aboriginal and means 'white fellow's hole in the ground', which aptly describes the place, as a large proportion of the population live in dugouts to shelter from daytime summer temperatures that can soar to over 50°C and from cold winter nights. Apart from the dugouts, there are over 250,000 mine shafts in the area.

Coober Pedy is in an extremely inhospitable area and the town reflects this; even in the middle of winter it looks dried out and dusty with piles of junk everywhere. This is no attractive little settlement, in fact it's hardly surprising that much of *Mad Max III* was filmed here – the town looks like the end of the world!

The town has a very mixed population, 53 nationalities are represented here, and also has a reputation for being pretty volatile. Since 1987 the police station has been bombed twice, the courthouse once, the most successful restaurant (The Acropolis) was demolished in a blast and hundreds of thousands of dollars worth of mining equipment has gone the same way. While it is perfectly safe for the visitor, it is wise for lone females not to wander around unaccompanied late at night, or accept invitations from unknown men to visit mines or opal collections.

Information

The tourist office (☎ 8672 5298) is in the council offices, opposite the Opal Inn as you enter the town. It is open weekdays and sometimes weekends. The Underground Bookshop is very good for information on the local area and the outback in general. They also sell second-hand books.

Buses leave from the new service station opposite the council offices.

Dugout Homes

Many of the early dugout homes were simply worked-out mines but now they're often cut specifically as residences. Several homes are open to visitors – all you have to do is create an eccentric enough abode and you can charge admission.

Other Attractions

Coober Pedy has a number of other attractions worth a look. The most dominant of these is the **Big Winch**, which is a lookout over the town and an extensive display of cut and uncut opal.

The **Old Timers Mine** is an old mine and underground home which is well worth the $3 entry fee.

The **Umoona Mine & Museum** is right in the centre of town and opal was still being pulled out of here until mining within the town limits was banned some years ago. Informative tours of the mine ($2) are given twice daily.

A couple of km out of town to the north is the **Underground Potteries** which has some nice pottery for sale. A couple of km further on is **Crocodile Harry's** ($2), an interesting dugout home which has featured in a number of documentaries and movies, including *Mad Max III*, *Ground Zero* and *Stark*. Harry is an interesting character who spent 13 years in far north Queensland and the Northern Territory hunting crocodiles. His wrecked cars out the front of his dugout make novel vegetable beds.

Opal Mining

The town survives from opals which were first discovered in 1911. Keen fossickers can have a go themselves after acquiring a prospecting permit from the Mines Department in Adelaide. Fossicking through the outcasts is known as noodling. There are literally

hundreds of mines around Coober Pedy but there are no big operators. When somebody makes a find, dozens of others head off to the same area.

Of the many migrant groups represented in Coober Pedy, Greeks, Yugoslavs and Italians are the largest, but the gem buyers are mainly from Hong Kong. They stay in the Opal Inn and when one heads back to base another Hong Konger takes the room over.

Organised Tours

There are several tours, most taking three hours and costing around $15, which cover the sights and take you into an opal mine, underground home and a working opal field. Joe's Tours (book at the Budget Motel) include Crocodile Harry's.

On Monday and Thursday you can travel with the mail truck along 600 km of dirt roads as it does the trip round Coober Pedy, Oodnadatta and William Creek. There's a backpackers' special price of $49, or the standard fare including lunch is $59. This is a great way to get off the beaten track. You can stay at Oodnadatta or William Creek and return to Coober Pedy on the next mail truck (☎ toll-free 1800 802 074, or contact the Underground Bookshop).

Places to Stay

Camping There are two caravan parks in town itself and another further out. The *Oasis Caravan Park* (☎ 8672 5169) is good and has tent sites (hard gravel) and on-site vans. They also show an informative video on the town and opal mining in general each evening.

The *Stuart Range Caravan Park* (☎ 8672 5179) has less shade and is also less central. Even further out (about five km along the William Creek road), *Rudy's Camel Mine* (☎ 8672 5614) costs $4 per person.

Hostels The *Backpacker's Inn* at Radeka's Dugout Motel (☎ 8672 5223) offers underground dormitories at $10.

Tom's Backpackers (☎ 8672 5333) on the main street opposite the Desert Cave Motel is the most popular and has underground

accommodation at $10 for 24 hours, or above-ground rooms for $8.

The *Bedrock* is another place popular with travellers, and the *Opal Cave* also has backpacker accommodation.

Hotels & Motels There are a number of hotels and motels, some underground, some with big air-conditioners. Listed here are some of the cheaper places. The *Umoona Opal Mine* (☎ 8672 5288) on Hutchison St has singles/doubles for $15/25. Bathrooms are communal but there are kitchen facilities. The *Budget Motel* (☎ 8672 5163) has rooms from $16/26 or from $40 with bathrooms. The *Opal Inn Hotel/Motel* (☎ 8672 5054) has pub rooms for $25/35, or motel rooms for $65/70. *Radeka's Dugout Motel* (☎ 8672 5223) costs from $55/65.

Places to Eat
The *Last Resort Cafe*, next to the Underground Bookshop, does a good line in drinks and desserts as well as meals, including breakfast and is easily the best place in town. Unfortunately it's open only during the day.

Sergio's has Italian food, including spaghetti from $6, and the servings are enormous.

There are a couple of Greek places, the *Taverna* and *Traces*, and these are both popular in the evenings, and Traces stays open until 4 am. There are also a couple of pizza places, and the *Opal Inn* does counter meals. The *Miners' Store*, next to the post office, is the best of the supermarkets.

The *Underground Dugout Restaurant* is indeed underground and has a few interesting menu items, including kangaroo fillets. It's not all that cheap, however, and the service can be brusque.

Entertainment
Playing pool at the Oasis Inn seems to be the main form of entertainment in town.

Getting There & Away
Air Kendell Airlines (☎ 8233 3322) fly from Adelaide to Coober Pedy most days of the week ($238), and from Coober Pedy to Uluru (Ayers Rock) once a week. The Desert Cave Motel handles reservations.

Bus It's 413 km from Coober Pedy to Kulgera, just across the border into the Northern Territory, and from there it's another 280 km to Alice Springs. Greyhound Pioneer buses pass through on the Adelaide-Alice Springs route. It's about $68 from Adelaide and $70 from Alice Springs.

AROUND COOBER PEDY
Breakaways
Breakaway Reserve is an area of low hills about 30 km from Coober Pedy, which have 'broken away' from the Stuart Range. You can drive to the lookout in a conventional vehicle and see the natural formation known as the **Castle**, which featured in *Mad Max III*.

With a 4WD vehicle you can make a 65-km loop from Coober Pedy, following the Dog Proof Fence back to the road from Coober Pedy to Oodnadatta. The Underground Bookshop in Coober Pedy has a leaflet and 'mud map'.

COOBER PEDY TO PORT AUGUSTA
From Coober Pedy the highway continues along its inexorable way south 251 km to **Glendambo**, a roadhouse and refuelling stop, before it swings east for the 115-km run to the scruffy little settlement of **Pimba**, along the way passing the usually dry salt lakes of Island Lagoon and Lake Hart. Pimba itself sits on a virtually treeless plateau and, despite its accessibility, is one of the most desolate places imaginable.

Woomera
During the '50s and '60s Woomera (population 1600) was used to launch experimental British rockets and conduct tests in an abortive European project to send a satellite into orbit. The Woomera Prohibited Area occupies a vast stretch of land in the centre of the state. The town of Woomera, in the southeast corner of the Prohibited Area, is now an 'open town' but it is just a shadow of its former self. These days its main role is as a

service town for the mostly American personnel working at the so-called Joint Facility at Nurrungar, a short distance south of Woomera near Island Lagoon. At the town's peak about 5000 people lived here.

A small **heritage centre** in the centre of town has various local oddments and a collection of old aircraft and missiles. The museum tells you something about the missile testing in the past but little about what goes on today. The centre is open from 9.45 am to 5 pm daily from March to November, and is closed over the summer.

Places to Stay & Eat The *Woomera Travellers' Village* (☎ 8673 7800), near the entrance to the town, has backpackers' accommodation for $12 a bed, tent sites for $5 per person (although the ground is like concrete) and on-site vans from $25 a double. There's also a very basic kiosk here.

The only alternative is the *Eldo Hotel* (☎ 8673 7867) in town on Kotana Ave. It has singles/doubles for $32.50/45 ('Eldo' is the acronym for the European Launcher Development Organisation).

The small shopping centre has a snack bar with the usual takeaway fare; for something better you'll have to try the restaurant in the *Eldo Hotel*. It serves reasonable but unexciting pub-type meals for around $8 a main course. The Eldo also has poker machines for those who feel like a flutter.

Getting There & Away Kendell Airlines (☎ 8233 3322) fly from Adelaide to Woomera most days of the week for $131.

Woomera is seven km off the Stuart Highway from Pimba, 175 km north of Port Augusta. Stateliner and the long-distance bus lines pass through Woomera daily. It's about $40 to Adelaide, and $120 to Alice Springs.

PORT AUGUSTA

Matthew Flinders was the first European to set foot in the area, but the town was not established until 1854. Today, this busy port city (population 14,500) is the gateway to the outback region of South Australia. It's also a major crossroads for travellers.

From here, roads head west across the Nullarbor to Western Australia, north to Alice Springs and Darwin in the Northern Territory, south to Adelaide and east to Broken Hill and Sydney in New South Wales. The main railway line between the east and west coasts and the Adelaide to Alice Springs route both pass through Port Augusta.

There are tours of the **School of the Air**, at the southern end of Commercial Rd, at 10 am and 2 pm on weekdays (entry by donation). The School of the Air may be relocating – check at the Wadlata Outback Centre.

Other attractions include the **Curdnatta Art & Pottery Gallery**, in Port Augusta's first railway station, and the **Homestead Park Pioneer Museum**, Elsie St, open daily from 10 am to 5 pm ($2.50). Pick up a brochure from the Wadlata Outback Centre detailing a heritage walk around the town.

Information
The Wadlata Outback Centre (☎ 8642 4511), at 41 Flinders Terrace, is the tourist information centre; it also has an interpretive centre ($6), with exhibits tracing the Aboriginal and European history of the outback. The centre is open weekdays from 9 am to 5.30 pm and weekends from 10 am to 4 pm.

Places to Stay
Port Augusta Backpackers (☎ 8641 1063), at 17 Trent Rd, is a friendly place with beds for $12. You can arrange Flinders Ranges tours here. The hostel is just off Highway No 1, and if you let the bus drivers know, they'll let you off near the hostel.

The *Flinders Hotel* (☎ 8642 2522), at 39 Commercial Rd, has backpacker accommodation for $12, pub-style rooms for $38/48 and single/double motel-style rooms for $44/55. The *Fauna Caravan Park* (☎ 8642 2974) has for $12, on-site vans for $28 and cabins for $45. They also have a bunkhouse for backpackers ($10) with an adjacent campers' kitchen.

Getting There & Away

Air Augusta Airways (☎ 8642 3100) flies to Adelaide on weekdays for $98. On Saturday you can take the mail plane to Boulia in outback Queensland, stopping in Birdsville and Innamincka on the way, for $325.

Bus The bus station (☎ 8642 5055) is at 23 Mackay St. Stateliner runs to Adelaide ($26.10), Coober Pedy ($56.70), Wilpena Pound ($22.90), Whyalla ($10.50), Port Lincoln ($37), Ceduna ($48.60) and other places on the Eyre Peninsula. Greyhound Pioneer travels to Perth ($180) and Alice Springs ($134).

Train By train Sydney is 32 hours away and a standard economy ticket costs $133. An economy/1st-class sleeper is $227/345. It takes 33 hours to Perth; an economy seat is $170; an economy/1st-class sleeper is $337/556.50 It's four hours to Adelaide ($28). In Port Augusta phone ☎ (086) 41 8111 for enquiries and bookings.

Index

TEXT

Map references are in **bold** type.

PLANET TALK

Lonely Planet's FREE quarterly newsletter

We love hearing from you and think you'd like to hear from us.

When...is the right time to see reindeer in Finland?
Where...can you hear the best palm-wine music in Ghana?
How...do you get from Asunción to Areguá by steam train?
What...is the best way to see India?

For the answer to these and many other questions read PLANET TALK.

Every issue is packed with up-to-date travel news and advice including:

* a letter from Lonely Planet co-founders Tony and Maureen Wheeler
* go behind the scenes on the road with a Lonely Planet author
* feature article on an important and topical travel issue
* a selection of recent letters from travellers
* details on forthcoming Lonely Planet promotions
* complete list of Lonely Planet products

To join our mailing list contact any Lonely Planet office.

Also available: Lonely Planet T-shirts. 100% heavyweight cotton.

LONELY PLANET ONLINE

Get the latest travel information before you leave or while you're on the road

Whether you've just begun planning your next trip, or you're chasing down specific info on currency regulations or visa requirements, check out the Lonely Planet World Wide Web site for up-to-the-minute travel information.

As well as travel profiles of your favourite destinations (including interactive maps and full-colour photos), you'll find current reports from our army of researchers and other travellers, updates on health and visas, travel advisories, and the ecological and political issues you need to be aware of as you travel.

There's an online travellers' forum (the Thorn Tree) where you can share your experiences of life on the road, meet travel companions and ask other travellers for their recommendations and advice. We also have plenty of links to other Web sites useful to independent travellers.

With tens of thousands of visitors a month, the Lonely Planet Web site is one of the most popular on the Internet and has won a number of awards including GNN's Best of the Net travel award.

http://www.lonelyplanet.com

LONELY PLANET PRODUCTS

Lonely Planet is known worldwide for publishing practical, reliable and no-nonsense travel information in our guides and on our web site. The Lonely Planet list covers just about every accessible part of the world. Currently there are eight series: *travel guides*, *shoestring guides*, *walking guides*, *city guides*, *phrasebooks*, *audio packs*, *travel atlases* and *Journeys* – a unique collection of travellers' tales.

EUROPE

Austria • Baltic States & Kaliningrad • Baltic States phrasebook • Britain • Central Europe on a shoestring • Central Europe phrasebook • Czech & Slovak Republics • Denmark • Dublin city guide • Eastern Europe on a shoestring • Eastern Europe phrasebook • Finland • France • Greece • Greek phrasebook • Hungary • Iceland, Greenland & the Faroe Islands • Ireland • Italy • Mediterranean Europe on a shoestring • Mediterranean Europe phrasebook • Paris city guide • Poland • Prague city guide • Russia, Ukraine & Belarus • Russian phrasebook • Scandinavian & Baltic Europe on a shoestring • Scandinavian Europe phrasebook • Slovenia • St Petersburg city guide • Switzerland • Trekking in Greece • Trekking in Spain • Ukranian phrasebook • Vienna city guide • Walking in Switzerland • Western Europe on a shoestring • Western Europe phrasebook

NORTH AMERICA

Alaska • Backpacking in Alaska • Baja California • California & Nevada • Canada • Hawaii • Honolulu city guide • Los Angeles city guide • Mexico • New England • Pacific Northwest USA • Rocky Mountain States • San Francisco city guide • Southwest USA • USA phrasebook

CENTRAL AMERICA & THE CARIBBEAN

Central America on a shoestring • Costa Rica • Eastern Caribbean • Guatemala, Belize & Yucatán: La Ruta Maya • Jamaica

SOUTH AMERICA

Argentina, Uruguay & Paraguay • Bolivia • Brazil • Brazilian phrasebook • Buenos Aires city guide • Chile & Easter Island • Colombia • Ecuador & the Galápagos Islands • Latin American Spanish phrasebook • Peru • Quechua phrasebook • Rio de Janeiro city guide • South America on a shoestring • Trekking in the Patagonian Andes • Venezuela

ALSO AVAILABLE:

Travel with Children • Traveller's Tales

AFRICA

Arabic (Moroccan) phrasebook • Africa on a shoestring • Cape Town city guide • Central Africa • East Africa • Egypt & the Sudan • Ethiopian (Amharic) phrasebook • Kenya • Morocco • North Africa • South Africa, Lesotho & Swaziland • Swahili phrasebook • Trekking in East Africa • West Africa • Zimbabwe, Botswana & Namibia • Zimbabwe, Botswana & Namibia travel atlas

MAIL ORDER

Lonely Planet products are distributed worldwide. They are also available by mail order from Lonely Planet, so if you have difficulty finding a title please write to us. North American and South American residents should write to Embarcadero West, 155 Filbert St, Suite 251, Oakland CA 94607, USA; European and African residents should write to 10 Barley Mow Passage, Chiswick, London W4 4PH; and residents of other countries to PO Box 617, Hawthorn, Victoria 3122, Australia.

NORTH-EAST ASIA

Beijing city guide • Cantonese phrasebook • China • Hong Kong, Macau & Canton • Hong Kong city guide • Japan • Japanese phrasebook • Japanese audio pack • Korea • Korean phrasebook • Mandarin phrasebook • Mongolia • Mongolian phrasebook • North-East Asia on a shoestring • Seoul city guide • Taiwan • Tibet • Tibet phrasebook • Tokyo city guide

MIDDLE EAST & CENTRAL ASIA

Arab Gulf States • Arabic (Egyptian) phrasebook • Central Asia • Iran • Israel • Jordan & Syria • Middle East • Turkey • Turkish phrasebook • Trekking in Turkey • Yemen

Travel Literature: The Gates of Damascus

ISLANDS OF THE INDIAN OCEAN

Madagascar & Comoros • Maldives & Islands of the East Indian Ocean • Mauritius, Réunion & Seychelles

INDIAN SUBCONTINENT

Bengali phrasebook • Bangladesh • Delhi city guide • Hindi/Urdu phrasebook • India • India & Bangladesh travel atlas • Indian Himalaya • Karakoram Highway • Nepal • Nepali phrasebook • Pakistan • Sri Lanka • Sri Lanka phrasebook • Trekking in the Indian Himalaya • Trekking in the Nepal Himalaya

SOUTH-EAST ASIA

Bali & Lombok • Bangkok city guide • Burmese phrasebook • Cambodia • Ho Chi Minh city guide • Indonesia • Indonesian phrasebook • Indonesian audio pack • Jakarta city guide • Java • Laos • Lao phrasebook • Malaysia, Singapore & Brunei • Myanmar (Burma) • Philippines • Pilipino phrasebook • Singapore city guide • South-East Asia on a shoestring • Thailand • Thailand travel atlas • Thai phrasebook • Thai audio pack • Thai Hill Tribes phrasebook • Vietnam • Vietnamese phrasebook • Vietnam travel atlas

AUSTRALIA & THE PACIFIC

Australia • Australian phrasebook • Bushwalking in Australia • Bushwalking in Papua New Guinea • Fiji • Fijian phrasebook • Islands of Australia's Great Barrier Reef • Melbourne city guide • Micronesia • New Caledonia • New South Wales & the ACT • New Zealand • Northern Territory • Outback Australia • Papua New Guinea • Papua New Guinea phrasebook • Queensland • Rarotonga & the Cook Islands • Samoa • Solomon Islands • South Australia • Sydney city guide • Tahiti & French Polynesia • Tasmania • Tonga • Tramping in New Zealand • Vanuatu • Victoria • Western Australia

Travel Literature: Islands in the Clouds • Sean & David's Long Drive

THE LONELY PLANET STORY

Lonely Planet published its first book in 1973 in response to the numerous 'How did you do it?' questions Maureen and Tony Wheeler were asked after driving, bussing, hitching, sailing and railing their way from England to Australia.

Written at a kitchen table and hand collated, trimmed and stapled, *Across Asia on the Cheap* became an instant local bestseller, inspiring thoughts of another book.

Eighteen months in South-East Asia resulted in their second guide, *South-East Asia on a shoestring*, which they put together in a backstreet Chinese hotel in Singapore in 1975. The 'yellow bible', as it quickly became known to backpackers around the world, soon became *the* guide to the region. It has sold well over half a million copies and is now in its 8th edition, still retaining its familiar yellow cover.

Today there are over 180 titles, including travel guides, walking guides, language kits & phrasebooks, travel atlases and travel literature. The company is one of the largest travel publishers in the world. Although Lonely Planet initially specialised in guides to Asia, we now cover most regions of the world, including the Pacific, North America, South America, Africa, the Middle East and Europe.

The emphasis continues to be on travel for independent travellers. Tony and Maureen still travel for several months of each year and play an active part in the writing, updating and quality control of Lonely Planet's guides.

They have been joined by over 70 authors and 170 staff at our offices in Melbourne (Australia), Oakland (USA), London (UK) and Paris (France). Travellers themselves also make a valuable contribution to the guides through the feedback we receive in thousands of letters each year.

The people at Lonely Planet strongly believe that travellers can make a positive contribution to the countries they visit, both through their appreciation of the countries' culture, wildlife and natural features, and through the money they spend. In addition, the company makes a direct contribution to the countries and regions it covers. Since 1986 a percentage of the income from each book has been donated to ventures such as famine relief in Africa; aid projects in India; agricultural projects in Central America; Greenpeace's efforts to halt French nuclear testing in the Pacific; and Amnesty International.

'I hope we send the people out with the right attitude about travel. You realise when you travel that there are so many different perspectives about the world, so we hope these books will make people more interested in what they see. These are guidebooks, but you can't really guide people. All you can do is point them in the right direction.'
– Tony Wheeler

---

lonely planet

LONELY PLANET PUBLICATIONS

Australia
PO Box 617, Hawthorn 3122, Victoria
tel: (03) 9819 1877 fax: (03) 9819 6459
e-mail: talk2us@lonelyplanet.com.au

USA
Embarcadero West, 155 Filbert St, Suite 251,
Oakland, CA 94607
tel: (510) 893 8555 TOLL FREE: 800 275-8555
fax: (510) 893 8563
e-mail: info@lonelyplanet.com

UK
10 Barley Mow Passage, Chiswick,
London W4 4PH
tel: (0181) 742 3161 fax: (0181) 742 2772
e-mail: 100413.3551@compuserve.com

France:
71 bis rue du Cardinal Lemoine, 75005 Paris
tel: 1 44 32 06 20 fax: 1 46 34 72 55
e-mail: 100560.415@compuserve.com

World Wide Web: http://www.lonelyplanet.com

PLANET TALK

Lonely Planet's FREE quarterly newsletter

We love hearing from you and think you'd like to hear from us.

When...is the right time to see reindeer in Finland?
Where...can you hear the best palm-wine music in Ghana?
How...do you get from Asunción to Areguá by steam train?
What...is the best way to see India?

For the answer to these and many other questions read PLANET TALK.

Every issue is packed with up-to-date travel news and advice including:

* a letter from Lonely Planet co-founders Tony and Maureen Wheeler
* go behind the scenes on the road with a Lonely Planet author
* feature article on an important and topical travel issue
* a selection of recent letters from travellers
* details on forthcoming Lonely Planet promotions
* complete list of Lonely Planet products

To join our mailing list contact any Lonely Planet office.

Also available: Lonely Planet T-shirts. 100% heavyweight cotton.

LONELY PLANET ONLINE

Get the latest travel information before you leave or while you're on the road

Whether you've just begun planning your next trip, or you're chasing down specific info on currency regulations or visa requirements, check out the Lonely Planet World Wide Web site for up-to-the-minute travel information.

As well as travel profiles of your favourite destinations (including interactive maps and full-colour photos), you'll find current reports from our army of researchers and other travellers, updates on health and visas, travel advisories, and the ecological and political issues you need to be aware of as you travel.

There's an online travellers' forum (the Thorn Tree) where you can share your experiences of life on the road, meet travel companions and ask other travellers for their recommendations and advice. We also have plenty of links to other Web sites useful to independent travellers.

With tens of thousands of visitors a month, the Lonely Planet Web site is one of the most popular on the Internet and has won a number of awards including GNN's Best of the Net travel award.

http://www.lonelyplanet.com

LONELY PLANET PRODUCTS

Lonely Planet is known worldwide for publishing practical, reliable and no-nonsense travel information in our guides and on our web site. The Lonely Planet list covers just about every accessible part of the world. Currently there are eight series: *travel guides*, *shoestring guides*, *walking guides*, *city guides*, *phrasebooks*, *audio packs*, *travel atlases* and *Journeys* – a unique collection of travellers' tales.

EUROPE

Austria • Baltic States & Kaliningrad • Baltic States phrasebook • Britain • Central Europe on a shoestring • Central Europe phrasebook • Czech & Slovak Republics • Denmark • Dublin city guide • Eastern Europe on a shoestring • Eastern Europe phrasebook • Finland • France • Greece • Greek phrasebook • Hungary • Iceland, Greenland & the Faroe Islands • Ireland • Italy • Mediterranean Europe on a shoestring • Mediterranean Europe phrasebook • Paris city guide • Poland • Prague city guide • Russia, Ukraine & Belarus • Russian phrasebook • Scandinavian & Baltic Europe on a shoestring • Scandinavian Europe phrasebook • Slovenia • St Petersburg city guide • Switzerland • Trekking in Greece • Trekking in Spain • Ukranian phrasebook • Vienna city guide • Walking in Switzerland • Western Europe on a shoestring • Western Europe phrasebook

NORTH AMERICA

Alaska • Backpacking in Alaska • Baja California• California & Nevada • Canada • Hawaii • Honolulu city guide • Los Angeles city guide • Mexico • New England • Pacific Northwest USA • Rocky Mountain States • San Francisco city guide • Southwest USA • USA phrasebook

CENTRAL AMERICA & THE CARIBBEAN

Central America on a shoestring • Costa Rica • Eastern Caribbean • Guatemala, Belize & Yucatán: La Ruta Maya • Jamaica

SOUTH AMERICA

Argentina, Uruguay & Paraguay • Bolivia • Brazil • Brazilian phrasebook • Buenos Aires city guide • Chile & Easter Island • Colombia • Ecuador & the Galápagos Islands • Latin American Spanish phrasebook • Peru • Quechua phrasebook • Rio de Janeiro city guide • South America on a shoestring • Trekking in the Patagonian Andes • Venezuela

ALSO AVAILABLE:

Travel with Children • Traveller's Tales

AFRICA

Arabic (Moroccan) phrasebook • Africa on a shoestring • Cape Town city guide • Central Africa • East Africa • Egypt & the Sudan • Ethiopian (Amharic) phrasebook • Kenya • Morocco • North Africa • South Africa, Lesotho & Swaziland • Swahili phrasebook • Trekking in East Africa • West Africa • Zimbabwe, Botswana & Namibia • Zimbabwe, Botswana & Namibia travel atlas

MAIL ORDER

Lonely Planet products are distributed worldwide. They are also available by mail order from Lonely Planet, so if you have difficulty finding a title please write to us. North American and South American residents should write to Embarcadero West, 155 Filbert St, Suite 251, Oakland CA 94607, USA; European and African residents should write to 10 Barley Mow Passage, Chiswick, London W4 4PH; and residents of other countries to PO Box 617, Hawthorn, Victoria 3122, Australia.

NORTH-EAST ASIA

Beijing city guide • Cantonese phrasebook • China • Hong Kong, Macau & Canton • Hong Kong city guide • Japan • Japanese phrasebook • Japanese audio pack • Korea • Korean phrasebook • Mandarin phrasebook • Mongolia • Mongolian phrasebook • North-East Asia on a shoestring • Seoul city guide • Taiwan • Tibet • Tibet phrasebook • Tokyo city guide

INDIAN SUBCONTINENT

Bengali phrasebook • Bangladesh • Delhi city guide • Hindi/Urdu phrasebook • India • India & Bangladesh travel atlas• Indian Himalaya• Karakoram Highway • Nepal • Nepali phrasebook • Pakistan • Sri Lanka • Sri Lanka phrasebook • Trekking in the Indian Himalaya • Trekking in the Nepal Himalaya

SOUTH-EAST ASIA

Bali & Lombok • Bangkok city guide • Burmese phrasebook • Cambodia • Ho Chi Minh city guide • Indonesia • Indonesian phrasebook • Indonesian audio pack • Jakarta city guide • Java • Laos • Lao phrasebook • Malaysia, Singapore & Brunei • Myanmar (Burma) • Philippines • Pilipino phrasebook • Singapore city guide • South-East Asia on a shoestring • Thailand • Thailand travel atlas • Thai phrasebook • Thai audio pack • Thai Hill Tribes phrasebook • Vietnam • Vietnamese phrasebook • Vietnam travel atlas

MIDDLE EAST & CENTRAL ASIA

Arab Gulf States • Arabic (Egyptian) phrasebook • Central Asia • Iran • Israel • Jordan & Syria • Middle East • Turkey • Turkish phrasebook • Trekking in Turkey • Yemen

Travel Literature: The Gates of Damascus

ISLANDS OF THE INDIAN OCEAN

Madagascar & Comoros • Maldives & Islands of the East Indian Ocean • Mauritius, Réunion & Seychelles

AUSTRALIA & THE PACIFIC

Australia • Australian phrasebook • Bushwalking in Australia• Bushwalking in Papua New Guinea • Fiji • Fijian phrasebook • Islands of Australia's Great Barrier Reef • Melbourne city guide • Micronesia • New Caledonia • New South Wales & the ACT • New Zealand • Northern Territory• Outback Australia • Papua New Guinea • Papua New Guinea phrasebook • Queensland • Rarotonga & the Cook Islands • Samoa • Solomon Islands • South Australia • Sydney city guide • Tahiti & French Polynesia • Tasmania • Tonga • Tramping in New Zealand • Vanuatu • Victoria • Western Australia

Travel Literature: Islands in the Clouds • Sean & David's Long Drive

THE LONELY PLANET STORY

Lonely Planet published its first book in 1973 in response to the numerous 'How did you do it?' questions Maureen and Tony Wheeler were asked after driving, bussing, hitching, sailing and railing their way from England to Australia.

Written at a kitchen table and hand collated, trimmed and stapled, *Across Asia on the Cheap* became an instant local bestseller, inspiring thoughts of another book.

Eighteen months in South-East Asia resulted in their second guide, *South-East Asia on a shoestring*, which they put together in a backstreet Chinese hotel in Singapore in 1975. The 'yellow bible', as it quickly became known to backpackers around the world, soon became *the* guide to the region. It has sold well over half a million copies and is now in its 8th edition, still retaining its familiar yellow cover.

Today there are over 180 titles, including travel guides, walking guides, language kits & phrasebooks, travel atlases and travel literature. The company is one of the largest travel publishers in the world. Although Lonely Planet initially specialised in guides to Asia, we now cover most regions of the world, including the Pacific, North America, South America, Africa, the Middle East and Europe.

The emphasis continues to be on travel for independent travellers. Tony and Maureen still travel for several months of each year and play an active part in the writing, updating and quality control of Lonely Planet's guides.

They have been joined by over 70 authors and 170 staff at our offices in Melbourne (Australia), Oakland (USA), London (UK) and Paris (France). Travellers themselves also make a valuable contribution to the guides through the feedback we receive in thousands of letters each year.

The people at Lonely Planet strongly believe that travellers can make a positive contribution to the countries they visit, both through their appreciation of the countries' culture, wildlife and natural features, and through the money they spend. In addition, the company makes a direct contribution to the countries and regions it covers. Since 1986 a percentage of the income from each book has been donated to ventures such as famine relief in Africa; aid projects in India; agricultural projects in Central America; Greenpeace's efforts to halt French nuclear testing in the Pacific; and Amnesty International.

'I hope we send the people out with the right attitude about travel. You realise when you travel that there are so many different perspectives about the world, so we hope these books will make people more interested in what they see. These are guidebooks, but you can't really guide people. All you can do is point them in the right direction.'
– Tony Wheeler

LONELY PLANET PUBLICATIONS

Australia
PO Box 617, Hawthorn 3122, Victoria
tel: (03) 9819 1877 fax: (03) 9819 6459
e-mail: talk2us@lonelyplanet.com.au

USA
Embarcadero West, 155 Filbert St, Suite 251,
Oakland, CA 94607
tel: (510) 893 8555 TOLL FREE: 800 275-8555
fax: (510) 893 8563
e-mail: info@lonelyplanet.com

UK
10 Barley Mow Passage, Chiswick,
London W4 4PH
tel: (0181) 742 3161 fax: (0181) 742 2772
e-mail: 100413.3551@compuserve.com

France:
71 bis rue du Cardinal Lemoine, 75005 Paris
tel: 1 44 32 06 20 fax: 1 46 34 72 55
e-mail: 100560.415@compuserve.com

World Wide Web: http://www.lonelyplanet.com